# EDGAR ALLAN POE:
# AN ANNOTATED BIBLIOGRAPHY
# OF BOOKS AND ARTICLES
# IN ENGLISH
# 1827-1973

Esther F. Hyneman

G. K. HALL & CO., 70 LINCOLN STREET, BOSTON, MASS. 1974

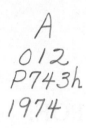

RESEARCH BIBLIOGRAPHIES IN AMERICAN LITERATURE NO. 2

*This publication is printed on permanent/durable acid-free paper.*

**Library of Congress Cataloging in Publication Data**

Hyneman, Esther F
  Edgar Allan Poe:  an annotated bibliography of
books and articles in English, 1827-1973.

  (Research bibliographies in American literature,
no. 2)
  1.  Poe, Edgar Allan, 1809-1849--Bibliography.
Z8699.H94      016.818'3'09        74-16359
ISBN 0-8161-1104-9

# Preface

My intention in this bibliography is to organize the chaotic mass of Poe criticism into a serviceable tool for the scholar/critic of Poe and to bring generally unknown or previously inaccessible material to his attention. Although the bibliography cannot be regarded as complete -- that is, as containing every book or article in which Poe has been mentioned since the 1820s -- it should contain all major criticism written about Poe in English and a good deal of what is minor.

The material is first organized into broad chronological categories: Section A: 1827-1850, Section B: 1851-1899, Section D: 1900-1973. There are a handful of exceptions to this rule, when the subject of a book or article seemed to predominate over the date of publication. An article on the Poe canon written in the nineteenth century, for example, is listed in subsection CA: The Poe Canon instead of Section B. To avoid confusion about this, and also to assist scholars who wish to study the chronological development of Poe's reputation, a complete Chronological Index is provided at the end. An Index of Authors is also provided.

Section C, which covers the twentieth century, is organized according to subject, except for subsection CJ, which comprises a list of full-length books about Poe. For obvious reasons, they do not always lend themselves to subject indexing. Books or articles which belong in two or more categories are cross-referenced at the end of each section.

I have followed the *PMLA Style Sheet (Revised Edition)* and used abbreviations in the *PMLA Annual Bibliography* "Master List" except where I created abbreviations of my own for titles of Poe's works and for periodicals no longer in print.

The annotations are based on my reading of the books and articles listed. When the original material was not available, I omitted annotations altogether or I relied on references to it in other articles, books and bibliographies. The most helpful sources in this situation were the annotated bibliographies in *Poe Newsletter* and

# PREFACE

*American Literary Scholarship.* The annotations are usually summaries of the central point of an article or descriptions of the
main topics of a book. When books defied a simple summary, I
relied on the author's statement of purpose, if he wrote one, or
on his conclusions.

# Contents

# CONTENTS

# Introduction

As the notices and reviews in Section A of this bibliography
show, Poe's work received considerable attention during his lifetime;
and despite his beleaguered position in the literary world, most of
that attention was favorable. As Killis Campbell pointed out (CQ4),
Poe's tales and literary reviews were the object of wider critical
interest than the poetry, which, except for "The Raven," seems to
have been slighted. It was customary for literary reviews to be reprinted in newspapers around the country, and the fact that Poe received notices in such farflung papers as the *Brownsville Observer*
(Pennsylvania), the *Charleston Courier,* the *Cincinnati Mirror,* the
*Natchez Christian Herald,* the *St. Louis Commercial Bulletin* and
*Daily Reveille,* and an obscure Albany, New York, journal indicate
that his reputation--or his notoriety--extended far beyond the cities
in which he lived and worked. The fact that he probably wrote some
of these reviews himself does not detract from his wide literary
reputation, nor do the minority of negative reviews, since many of
them were sensational enough to have actually attracted a large
audience to his work. One wonders, for example, how many readers
were drawn to Poe by Charles Dana's assertion that his imagination
was diseased (A115).

Students of Poe know that the picture changed quite radically
after his death. Although a handful of critics treated Poe objec-
tively (William H. Browne's essay [B80] on *Eureka* is an example of
such treatment), the majority of articles about him written between
1850 and 1899, as Alice Chandler has noted (B260), are in one way or
another a response to the infamous Griswold obituary (A138). This
means that negative criticisms of his work were not objective literary assessments but moralistic sanctions against his life. Both
Poe's work and life were characterized as morally weak, morbid,
sensually depraved, malignant, dishonest, alcoholic, drug-ridden,
shallow, wasted, and insane: Poe "is somehow out of relation with
his race" (B71); Poe's failure "is originally due to a deficient interest in morals" (B72). Upon refusing to review Poe's work, William
Cullen Bryant wrote that "his difficulty arises from the personal
character of Edgar Allan Poe of which I have in my time heard too
much to be able to join in paying especial honor to his memory" (B82).
Even admirers of Poe were not entirely free of the moral prejudices

of their time and reveal their ambivalence when they claim to admire his talent despite his personal depravity.

These critics, however, ought not to be swept into obscurity, for they are historically interesting to us today as specimens of a deeply moralistic age, a counterpoint to today's alienated, existentially-oriented critics. We mistakenly charge them with misunderstanding Poe; actually they understood him well and deplored in him what later critics have valued. They found in his work verification of Griswold's slanders and were repelled by an overall sense of his morbidness, alienation and literary eccentricities, just as they were repelled by similar qualities in the novels of Melville, who lived a life of moral rectitude.

Criticism of Poe in the first quarter of the twentieth century (Section C) advanced considerably, probably as a result of Woodberry's biography (B253) and the Stedman-Woodberry edition of Poe's works (B221). I notice, for example, a growing interest in establishing the definitive Poe canon, and although some biographical articles are still marred by an interest in the lurid, the purpose of most of them is to establish Poe's biography on firm, factual ground. Major studies to emerge from this period are James Harrison's *The Life and Letters of Edgar Allan Poe* (1903, CJ34), Arthur Ransome's *A Critical Study: Edgar Allan Poe* (1912, CJ63), D. H. Lawrence's *Classic American Literature* (1922, CK196), Margaret Alterton's *Origins of Poe's Critical Theories* (1925, CJ3), and William Carlos William's *In the American Grain* (1925, CK376). Predictably, the nineteenth-century fascination with Poe's moral life crystalized into an interest in his religious themes and affiliations, and criticism leaped in four years from Augustus H. Strong's denial that Poe was an athiest (1916, CP10) to C. Alphonso Smith's startling conclusion that he was a fundamentalist (1920, CP8).

Of more than five hundred essays in English published in the twentieth century on individual works of Poe, only about two dozen were written between 1900 and 1925, and most of these are source studies. Rather than focusing on individual works, critics endeavored to characterize and evaluate the entire canon, with the result that Poe emerges from this attention as an epicurean, a sensationalist, a Romantic, and a decadent. Critics both affirm and deny that his characters are alienated from ordinary human experience and morality, that Poe is a typically American writer, that he contributed to the short story genre. The criticism is marred by a confusion between author and persona in the poetry and by a failure to define point-of-view in the tales.

The amount and quality of critical attention devoted to Poe during the next thirty-five years (1925-1960)--several hundreds of articles and an average of a book a year appeared--elevated him to the rank of a major American writer. Hervey Allen's biography *Israfel: the Life and Times of Edgar Allan Poe* (1925, CJ1) was super-

# INTRODUCTION

seded in 1941 by Arthur Hobson Quinn's *Edgar Allan Poe* (CJ60), which remains the definitive biography. Specific areas of study developed: the psychological approach initiated by Joseph Wood Krutch (1926, CJ41) and advanced by Oscar Cargill (1941, CK67) and Marie Bonaparte (1949, CJ9); the Romantic approach of Edmund Wilson (1926, CK377), C. M. Bowra (1949, CK36), R. P. Adams (1952, CK13), and Edward Davidson (1957, CJ23); considerations of Poe as an American writer of American themes, by Edward Hungerford (1930, CJ168), Constance Rourke (1931, CK298), H. M. McLuhan (1944, CK235), Malcolm Cowley (1945, CK85), Jay B. Hubbell (1954, CK162 and 1960, CK163), and Howard Mumford Jones (1955, CK179); and interest in Poe's poetry and style, by Gay Wilson Allen (1935, CN1), Yvor Winters (1937, CK382), Horace Gregory (1943, CK414), T. S. Eliot (1949, CK109), and Richard Wilbur (1959, CK372).

At the same time critics began to focus on individual works: Floyd Stovall on "Al Aaraaf" (1929, CL5); Darrel Abel on "Berenice" (1955, CL47); Abel (1949, CL146), Maurice Beebe (1956, CL148), and Leo Spitzer (1952, CL190) on "The Fall of the House of Usher"; and James Gargano (1960, CL54) on "The Black Cat." The penetrating and often controversial studies of this period established Poe as a highly sophisticated artist of the irrational and demonic impulses in life, a conception which contrary points of view like the closely reasoned argument of Joseph Ridgely and Iola Haverstick (CL359) failed to undermine. The argument of Allan Tate (CK340) that Poe had "a distant if impressive insight into the disintegration of modern personality" stimulated critics to consider Poe's heroes as precursors of modern man, who like them is psychically disoriented, both attracted to and repelled by the manifestations of his spiritual disorders.

Many Poe critics of the last fifteen years have added indispensible information to our knowledge of Poe. Sidney Moss's study *Poe's Literary Battles* (1963, CJ50) and Robert Jacob's *Poe, Journalist and Critic* (1969, CJ138) have permanently erased our lingering misconceptions about Poe's career, and Gary Thompson's analysis of Poe as an ironist and Richard Wilbur's studies of allegory in Poe have opened new avenues of approach to Poe's work.

Despite these advances, however, Poe's criticism during this period is disappointing. Stuart Levine was right to complain, in "Scholarly Strategy: the Poe Case" (CQ10), that critics of Poe fail to build on the information and insights of their predecessors. Levine strikes at a major deficiency in Poe criticism and summons an impressive body of evidence to prove his point. Levine doesn't mention other problems which persist in recent Poe criticism, however: the nit-picking and haggling over problems which have no solutions (whether Poe died in a diabetic coma, a suggestion made to John S. Hill in 1972 by a doctor over dinner, CC91); endless source studies in which guesswork plays a greater role than scholarship; and articles which have no point at all: "This paper will attempt to prove that, in spite of the spartan regime, Poe had both time and opportunity for intellectual pursuits other than curriculum-related studies while he was at West Point" (CC150). Another serious problem is sheer repetitiousness, a tendency of critics to rehash old issues--Poe as Romantic, the unity in Poe's themes, *Eureka* as the philosophical foundation of Poe's work, Poe as a typically American writer--without contributing new insights.

In the introductory essay to the first issue of the *Poe Newsletter*, J. Albert Robbins wrote of his frustration in seeing "such quantities of scholarship add up to so little" (CQ16). In fact, the extraordinary abstruseness of much Poe criticism of the last few years threatens to add up to too much. The status of Poe's work does not depend upon the ponderousness of interpretations. Quite the contrary. The real test of its value is whether it will survive the critical weight it now bears.

ESTHER F. HYNEMAN

Brooklyn Center
Long Island University

# Key to Abbreviations

Periodicals

| | |
|---|---|
| ABC | American Book Collector |
| ABUV | Alumni Bulletin of the University of Virginia |
| AC | American Collector |
| Acad | Academy |
| AH | American Heritage |
| AI | American Imago |
| AL | American Literature |
| AM | American Mercury |
| AN&Q | American Notes and Queries |
| AppJ | Appleton's Journal |
| AQ | American Quarterly |
| AQRM | American Quarterly Register and Magazine |
| Arist | Aristidean |
| ArQ | Arizona Quarterly |
| AS | American Speech |
| Ath | Athenaeum |
| Atl | Atlantic Monthly |
| ATQ | American Transcendental Quarterly |
| AWM | Alexander's Weekly Messenger |
| AWR | American Whig Review |
| | |
| BB | Bulletin of Bibliography |
| BJ | Broadway Journal |
| Bkm | Bookman |
| Bl | Blackwood's |
| BL | Book-Lover |
| BNM | Book News Monthly |
| BNYPL | Bulletin of the New York Public Library |
| BPLQ | Boston Public Library Quarterly |
| BQR | British Quarterly Review |
| BSM | Baltimore Saturday Museum |
| BSUF | Ball State University Forum |
| BSV | Baltimore Saturday Visitor |
| BuR | Bucknell Review |
| BUSE | Boston University Studies in English |

| | |
|---|---|
| CE | College English |
| CEA Critic | College English Association Critic |
| ChEJ | Chamber's Edinburgh Journal |
| Cen | Century |
| CER | Catholic Education Review |
| Chaut | Chautauquan |
| ChiR | Chicago Review |
| CJ | Classical Journal |
| CL | Comparative Literature |
| CLAJ | College Language Association Journal (Morgan State College) |
| CLGM | Columbian Lady's and Gentleman's Magazine |
| CLS | Comparative Literature Studies |
| CO | Current Opinion |
| Cpn | Colophon |
| Cr | Critic |
| CSM | Christian Science Monitor |
| CUQ | Columbia University Quarterly |
| CurLit | Current Literature |
| CW | Classical Weekly |
| | |
| DAR | Daughters of the American Revolution |
| DUJ | Durham University Journal |
| DUM | Dublin University Magazine |
| | |
| Ecl | Eclectic |
| EIC | Essays in Criticism |
| EJ | English Journal |
| ELH | English Literary History |
| ELN | English Language Notes |
| ER | Edinburgh Review |
| ESQ | Emerson Society Quarterly |
| EUQ | Emory University Quarterly |
| Expl | Explicator |
| | |
| FQR | Foreign Quarterly Review |
| FortnR | Fortnightly Review |
| | |
| GaR | Georgia Review |
| GLB | Godey's Lady's Book |
| GM | Gentleman's Magazine |
| Gr | Graham's |
| | |
| HJ | Home Journal |
| HLQ | Huntington Library Quarterly |
| HNMM | Harper's New Monthly Magazine |
| HudR | Hudson Review |
| HW | Harper's Weekly |
| | |
| IM | International Monthly |
| IMLA | Illustrated Magazine of Literature and Art |

# Key to Abbreviations

| | |
|---|---|
| Ind | Independent |
| IQR | Irish Quarterly Review |
| IR | International Review |
| IUB | Indiana University Bookman |
| | |
| JA | Jahrbuch für Amerikastudien |
| JEGP | Journal of English and Germanic Philology |
| JHAM | Johns Hopkins Alumni Magazine |
| JHI | Journal of the History of Ideas |
| JQ | Journalism Quarterly |
| | |
| Kn | Knickerbocker |
| KR | Kenyon Review |
| | |
| LCUT | Library Chronicle of the University of Texas |
| LG | Literary Gazette (London) |
| LHUS | Literary History of the United States |
| Lipp | Lippincott's |
| LLA | Littell's Living Age |
| LQR | London Quarterly Review |
| LW | Literary World |
| | |
| MAMP | Muse Anthology of Modern Poetry |
| MAH | Magazine of American History |
| MHM | Michigan Historical Magazine |
| MinnR | Minnesota Review |
| MissQ | Mississippi Quarterly |
| MLN | Modern Language Notes |
| MLQ | Modern Language Quarterly |
| MLR | Modern Language Review |
| MP | Modern Philology |
| MyHM | Maryland Historical Magazine |
| | |
| NAR | North American Review |
| NBR | North British Review |
| NC | Nineteenth Century |
| NCF | Nineteenth-Century Fiction |
| NCR | North Carolina Review |
| NEM | New England Magazine |
| NEMLA | Northeast Modern Language Association |
| NEQ | New England Quarterly |
| NI | National Intelligencer |
| NMQR | New Mexico Quarterly Review |
| N&Q | Notes and Queries |
| NQM | New Quarterly Magazine |
| NR | New Republic |
| NSN | New Statesman and Nation |
| NY | New Yorker |
| NYFQ | New York Folklore Quarterly |
| NYHSQB | New York Historical Society Quarterly Bulletin |

# KEY TO ABBREVIATIONS

| | |
|---|---|
| PAAS | Proceedings of the American Antiquarian Society |
| PBSA | Papers of the Bibliographical Society of America |
| Person | The Personalist |
| PL | Poet-Lore |
| PMHB | Pennsylvania Magazine of History and Biography |
| PMLA | Publications of the Modern Language Association |
| PN | Poe Newsletter |
| PNJHS | Proceedings of the New Jersey Historical Society |
| PQ | Philological Quarterly |
| PR | Partisan Review |
| PrS | Prairie Schooner |
| PSC | Philadelphia Saturday Courier |
| PSM | Philadelphia Saturday Museum |
| PSt | Poe Studies |
| PSMo | Popular Science Monthly |
| PULC | Princeton University Library Chronicle |
| Put | Putnam's |
| PW | Publishers Weekly |
| | |
| QJCA | Quarterly Journal of Current Acquisitions (Library of Congress) |
| QRL | Quarterly Review of Literature |
| | |
| RLC | Revue de Littérature Comparée |
| RLV | Revue des Langues Vivantes (Bruxelles) |
| RR | Romantic Review |
| | |
| SAB | South Atlantic Bulletin |
| SAQ | South Atlantic Quarterly |
| SatR | Saturday Review |
| SB:BSUV | Studies in Bibliography: Papers of the Bibliographical Society of the University of Virginia |
| Scrib | Scribner's |
| SLG | Southern Literary Gazette |
| SLJ | Southern Literary Journal |
| SLM | Southern Literary Messenger |
| SM-NEM | Southern Monthly-New Eclectic Magazine |
| SP | Studies in Philology |
| SQR | Southern Quarterly Review |
| SR | Sewanee Review |
| SRL | Saturday Review of Literature |
| SSF | Studies in Short Fiction |
| SUM | Sartain's Union Magazine |
| SWR | Southwest Review |
| | |
| TB | Temple Bar |
| TBSAS | Transactions of the Bronx Society of Arts and Sciences |
| TLS | Times Literary Supplement |
| TSE | Tulane Studies in English |
| TSL | Tennessee Studies in Literature |
| TSLL | Texas Studies in Literature and Language |

# KEY TO ABBREVIATIONS

| | |
|---|---|
| UCPMP | University of California Publications in Modern Philology |
| UKCR | University of Kansas City Review |
| UMPLL | University of Michigan Publications in Literature and Language |
| UR | University Review (Kansas City, Missouri) |
| USCLB | University of Southern California Library Bulletin |
| USG | United States Gazette |
| USMDR | United States Magazine and Democratic Review |
| USRLG | United States Review and Literary Gazette |
| UTQ | University of Toronto Quarterly |
| UTSE | University of Texas Studies in English |
| | |
| VMHB | Virginia Magazine of History and Biography |
| VQR | Virginia Quarterly Review |
| | |
| WHR | Western Humanities Review |
| WMQ | William and Mary Quarterly |
| WWN | Walt Whitman Newsletter |
| WWR | Walt Whitman Review |
| | |
| YBLG | Yankee and Boston Literary Gazette |
| YFS | Yale French Studies |
| YR | Yale Review |
| YULG | Yale University Library Gazette |
| YLM | Yale Literary Magazine |

## Works

| | |
|---|---|
| "ATMP" | Al Aaraaf, Tamerlane and Minor Poems |
| "Cask" | The Cask of Amontillado |
| "City" | The City in the Sea |
| "DL'O" | Duc de L'Omelette |
| "Descent" | A Descent into the Maelstrom |
| "Devil" | The Devil was in It |
| "Facts" | Facts in the Case of M. Valdemar |
| "FHU" | Fall of the House of Usher |
| "Hans Pfaall" | The Unparallelled Adventure of One Hans Pfaall |
| "Happiest Day" | The Happiest Day, The Happiest Hour |
| "Masque" | The Masque of the Red Death |
| "MSFB" | Manuscript Found in a Bottle |
| "Murders" | Murders in the Rue Morgue |
| "NAGP" | The Narrative of Arthur Gordon Pym |
| "PP" | The Pit and the Pendulum |
| "ROP" | The Raven and Other Poems |
| "Some Words" | Some Words with a Mummy |
| "Tarr and Fether" | The System of Dr. Tarr and Professor Fether |
| "TGA" | Tales of the Grotesque and Arabesque |
| "Three Sundays" | When Three Sundays Fall in a Week |
| "To One" | To One in Paradise |
| "TOP" | Tamerlane and Other Poems |
| "TTH" | The Tell-Tale Heart |
| "WW" | William Wilson |

*A: 1827-1850*

A1  ANON. *Baltimore Clipper* (Oct. 9, 1849), 2.
        Brief obituary.

A2  _____. *Baltimore Gazette*. Reprinted in Appendix of TGA.
        Favorable review of "The Tale of Jerusalem."

A3  _____. *Baltimore Patriot*. Reprinted in SLM, II (Apr. 1836),
        342.
            Favorable reviews of "Epimanes" and "To Helen." The
        former is one of Poe's "queerities," in which "he feigns
        the enactment of a real scene of the times before your
        eyes."

A4  _____. *Baltimore Sun* (Oct. 8, 1849), 2.
            Brief obituary of Poe. "This announcement coming so
        sudden [sic] and unexpected, will cause poignant regret
        among all who admire genius, and have sympathy for the
        frailties too often attending it."

A5  _____. "'The Bells'," SuM. V (Dec. 1849), 386-7.
            The magazine had received three versions of the poem,
        which "illustrate the gradual development of an idea in the
        mind of a man of original genius."

A6  _____. Bl, LXII (Nov. 1847), 582-7.
            Lukewarm review of Poe's tales, focusing on his analyt-
        ical style and attention to detail. The critic concludes
        that the stories lack taste; he has no desire to read them
        again although he does not regret having read them once.

A7  _____. *Boston Courier*. Reprinted in Appendix of ROP.
        Brief but favorable remark about Poe's tales.

A8  _____. BJ. Reprinted from the *Sunday Times and Messenger* (Oct.
        26, 1845).
            Favorable review of Poe's disastrous recital in Boston
        with an indictment of the inhospitable audience.

*A: 1827-1850*

A9 \_\_\_\_\_. *Brother Jonathan,* I (Apr. 9, 1842), 409.
Criticism of Poe's severity as a critic of Gr.

A10 \_\_\_\_\_. *Brownsville Observer* (Pennsylvania). Reprinted in
Appendix of TGA.
Favorable review of the tales.

A11 \_\_\_\_\_. *Charleston Courier.* Reprinted in SLM, II (Jan. 1836),
138; and in Appendix of TGA.
Brief but favorable mention of Poe as contributor to SLM,
describing him as "equally ripe in graphic humor and various
lore."

A12 \_\_\_\_\_. *Charlottesville Jeffersonian.* Reprinted in SLM, II
(Jan. 1836), 136.
Favorable review of "MSFB." "Its wild impossibilities
are pictured to the imagination with all the detail of
circumstances, which truth and the fearful reality might be
supposed to present. Whilst we do not agree to the just-
ness of the praise which has been bestowed upon some of Mr.
Poe's pieces, we concur in the general commendation which
he has received as a writer of great originality, and one
who promises well."

A13 \_\_\_\_\_. *Cincinnati Mirror.* Reprinted in SLM, II (Apr. 1836),
343.
Commends the literary notices of the SLM, while pitying
the "luckless wights who feel the savage skill with which
the editor uses his tomahawk and scalping knife."

A14 \_\_\_\_\_. "Critical Notices." *Biblical Repository,* I, Third
Series (1845), 776.
Describes Poe's tales as "extravagant" and "hurtful."

A15 \_\_\_\_\_. CLGM, IV (Sept. 1845), 144.
Believes Poe's *Tales* to be "worthy of a place in the
best selected library."

A16 \_\_\_\_\_. "Curious Alleged Plagiarism by the Late Edgar Allan
Poe," LW, XII (Feb. 5, 1893), 102-3. Reprinted from the
*London Spectator.*

A17 \_\_\_\_\_. *Fraser's.* Reprinted in Ecl, XX (Aug. 1850), 567-9.
Poe's poetry, which compares unfavorably with Tennyson's,
is artificial and mechanical and relies too heavily on the
refrain.

*A: 1827–1850*

A18 _____. *Freeman* (Pennsylvania), ns. VI (Oct. 11, 1849), 3.
Brief obituary of Poe.

A19 _____. Gr, XXVII (Sept. 1845), 143.
The 1845 *Tales* are "among the most original and characteristic compositions in American letters." Poe leads the
reader "through the whole framework of crime and perversity,
and [enables] the intellect to comprehend their laws and
relations."

A20 _____. *Brother Jonathan*, I (Oct. 8, 1842), 158.
Disapproves of Poe's negative criticism of Dawes'
poetry.

A21 _____. HJ (Feb. 1848).
Mentioned in Quinn as containing a brief description of
Poe's genius and unequalled originality.

A22 _____. LG (London), no. 1490 (1845), 528.
Brief notice of *Tales*.

A23 _____. LW (New York):(Feb. 12, 1848), 30.
Very favorable review of Poe's lecture.

A24 _____. LW (New York), III (Jul. 29, 1848), 502.
Describes *Eureka* as unintelligible and smacking of the
"cuttle-fish."

A25 _____. LW (New York), V (Oct. 13, 1849), 319.
Enthusiastic mention of Griswold's "Ludwig" notice in the
*Tribune*. Describes Poe as "a strange combination of good
and evil, of strength and weakness. He had originality, the
fastidiousness, the delicacy, the invention for achievement
in the higher walks of literature; but he lacked the common
heart of humanity, on which success must always be based."

A26 _____. LW (New York), V (Nov. 24, 1849), 443.
Brief note on an article about Poe in SLM (Nov. 1849).

A27 _____. *Lynchburg Virginian*, XIV (Dec. 10, 1835), 3. Reprinted
in SLM, II (Jan. 1836), 139.
Rejects *Politian*. Poe wasted his talents on "trifles."

A28 _____. McMakin's *Model American Courier*, XIX (Oct. 13, 1849),
2.
Brief obituary.

*A: 1827-1850*

A29    \_\_\_\_\_. "A Mirror for Authors," *Holden's Magazine*, III (Jan. 1849), 22.
>> Doggerel about Poe beginning:
>>> With tomahawk upraised for deadly blow,
>>> Behold our literary Mohawk, Poe!
>>> Sworn tyrant he o'er all who sin in verse -
>>> His own the standard, damns he all that's worse....

A30    \_\_\_\_\_. *Natchez Christian Herald*. Reprinted in SLM, II (Apr. 1836), 344.
>> Praise of Poe's early efforts as a critic for SLM.

A31    \_\_\_\_\_. *New Haven Courier*. Reprinted in Appendix of 1845 *Tales*.
>> "These Tales by Mr. Poe will be hailed as a rare treat by all lovers of the exciting and the marvelous. Full of more than German mysticism, grotesque, strange, improbable, but intensely interesting, they will be remembered when better things are forgotten."

A32    \_\_\_\_\_. *New World*, IV (Jun. 4, 1842), 367.
>> Judges Poe "one of the best writers in the English language now living."

A33    \_\_\_\_\_. *New York Courier and Enquirer*. Reprinted in SLM, II (Jan. 1836), 135.
>> Criticizes Poe for his harsh treatment of *Norman Leslie*.

A34    \_\_\_\_\_. NY. Reprinted in SLM, II (Jan. 1836), 140.
>> Very favorable review of Poe's critical articles in SLM.

A35    \_\_\_\_\_. *New York Evangelist* (Nov. 27, 1845).
>> Generally favorable review of ROP, attributing to Poe great originality and skill in versification.

A36    \_\_\_\_\_. *New York Evening Post* (Feb. 1848).
>> Favorable criticism of Poe's lectures.

A37    \_\_\_\_\_. *New York Evening Star*. Reprinted in SLM, II (Apr. 1836), 348.
>> Favorable reference to Poe as critic with the SLM.

A38    \_\_\_\_\_. *New York Journal of Commerce* (Oct. 9, 1849).
>> "Few men were his equals." He was envied and admired as a writer, but "early disappointments" and dashed hopes embittered him until "he wandered over the world in search of a substitute."

A39    \_\_\_\_\_. *New York Mirror*, XIII (Apr. 9, 1836), 324-5.
>> Satire which names Poe "Bulldog, the critic."

# Edgar Allan Poe: An Annotated Bibliography

*A: 1827-1850*

A40 \_\_\_\_\_. *New York Mirror*, XVI (Aug. 11, 1838), 55.
Condemns NAGP for "gross improbabilities and preter-
natural adventures" while conceding Poe's "fine mastery
over language, and powers of description rarely excelled."

A41 \_\_\_\_\_. *New York Mirror,* XVII (Dec. 21, 1839), 207.
Brief review calling TGA "one of the most extraordinary
and original works of the day." The reviewer compares
"Ligeia" with the minor prose pieces of Bulwer and heartily
recommends the book to the public.

A42 \_\_\_\_\_. *New York Mirror* (Mar. 8, 1845), 347.
Favorable review of Poe's lecture on poetry in America.

A43 \_\_\_\_\_. *New York Morning Express* (Dec. 15, 1846), 2.
Suggestion that the publishers contribute to a fund to
assist Poe and Virginia.

A44 \_\_\_\_\_. *New York Spirit of the Times.* Reprinted in SLM, II
(Jan. 1836), 138.
Compliments Poe's articles in SLM.

A45 \_\_\_\_\_. *New York Tribune* (Feb. 4, 1848).
Compliments Poe on lecture on poetry in America.

A46 \_\_\_\_\_. *New York Weekly Messenger.* Reprinted in SLM, II (Jul.
1836), 524.
Objection to Poe's treatment of *Norman Leslie.*

A47 \_\_\_\_\_. *New York Weekly Mirror* (Jul. 5, 1845), 2.
Favorable review of 1845 *Tales,* commenting on the book's
"subtle ingenuity," originality and power.

A48 \_\_\_\_\_. *Norfolk Herald.* Reprinted in SLM, II (Jan. 1836), 135.
Favorable mention of "MSFB" and of Poe's reputation.
Reminds readers that the author of "Lunar Hoax" is indebted
to "Hans Pfaall."

A49 \_\_\_\_\_. *Norfolk Herald.* Reprinted in SLM, II (Apr. 1836), 343.
Favorable mention of "Epimanes" and "To Helen."

A50 \_\_\_\_\_. NAR, XXV (Oct. 1827), 471.
Mentions publication of TOP.

A51 \_\_\_\_\_. NAR, LXIII (Oct. 1846), 359.
Describes 1845 *Tales* as "belonging to the forcible-
feeble and the shallow-profound school...poor enough materials for an American Library."

*A: 1827-1850*

A52    \_\_\_\_. *Pennsylvania*, XXXIII (Oct. 9, 1849), 2.
Reprints brief obituary from *Baltimore Sun*.

A53    \_\_\_\_. *Pennsylvania*. Reprinted in <u>SLM</u>, II (Jan. 1836), 135.
Poe's criticism is the answer to the "dull monotony of praise which rolls smooth in the wake of every new book."

A54    \_\_\_\_. *Petersburg Constellation*. Reprinted in <u>SLM</u>, II (Jan. 1836), 140.
Praises Poe's review of *Normal Leslie*.

A55    \_\_\_\_. *Petersburg Constellation*. Reprinted in <u>SLM</u>, II (Apr. 1836), 346.
Favorable mention of "DL'O."

A56    \_\_\_\_. *Philadelphia Casket*, VI (May 1831), 239-40.
Mentions publication of 1831 *Poems*.

A57    \_\_\_\_. *Philadelphia Easton Star* (Jan. 5, 1847).
Requests aid for Poe.

A58    \_\_\_\_. *Philadelphia Inquirer*. Reprinted in Appendix of 1845 *Tales*.
"Mr. Poe's tales are written with much power, while all possess deep interest."

A59    \_\_\_\_. *Philadelphia Public Ledger*, XXVIII (Oct. 9, 1849), 2.
Reprints brief obituary from *Baltimore Sun*.

A60    \_\_\_\_. <u>PSC</u> (Jul. 25, 1846).
Brief mention of the enormous popularity of "The Raven" in England and America.

A61    \_\_\_\_. "Poe, Longfellow and Peter Pindus," <u>LW</u> (New York), VII (Sept. 28, 1850), 247.
Concerning the plagiarism controversy over Poe's "The Haunted Palace" and Longfellow's "The Beleaguered City."

A62    \_\_\_\_. "Poe's Last Poem," <u>SUM</u>, VI (Jan. 1850), 99.
On the publication of "The Bells."

A63    \_\_\_\_. "Poe's Obituary," <u>AQRM</u>, III (Dec. 1849), 493.
"He was a poet of singular originality and power - of rare genius, great scholarship, and a caustic and severe critic....At about 38 years of age, he terminated a life of those trials to which genius is too often subject."

# Edgar Allan Poe: An Annotated Bibliography

*A: 1827-1850*

A64     \_\_\_\_\_. "Poe's Obituary," Washington *National Era*, III (Nov. 1849), 175.
    Summary of article from *Cleveland True Democrat* which claims that since Poe's talent is undisciplined by a "high principle," he has nothing to offer society.

A65     \_\_\_\_\_. *Poet's Magazine* (1842). Reprinted by T. O. Mabbott, "An Undesirable Reaction to Poe, in 1842," *N&Q*, CXCIV (Mar. 19, 1949), 123.
    Criticizes Griswold for including Poe in *Poets and Poetry of America* and describes Poe as "the cynical critic, the hunter up of small things, journeyman editor of periodicals, and Apollo's man of all work."

A66     \_\_\_\_\_. "'The Raven'," *AWR*, I (Feb. 1845), 143.
    Preface to an early printing of "The Raven," calling the poem "one of the most felicitous specimens of unique rhyming which has for some time met our eye."

A67     \_\_\_\_\_. *Richmond Compiler*. Reprinted in Appendix of *TGA*.
    Brief note on Poe as caricaturist and satirist.

A68     \_\_\_\_\_. *Richmond Enquirer* (Oct. 12, 1849).
    Editorial in praise of "The Raven" and Poe's lectures.

A69     \_\_\_\_\_. *Richmond Whig* (Oct. 9, 1849).
    Brief obituary.

A70     \_\_\_\_\_. *St. Louis Commercial Bulletin*. Reprinted by Dr. J. Snodgrass, *BSM* (Sept. 1839).
    "...there are few writers in this country - take Neal, Irving and Willis away and we would say none - who can compete successfully, in many respects, with Poe. With an acuteness of observation, a vigorous and effective style, and an independence that defies control, he unites a fervid fancy and a most beautiful enthusiasm. His is a high destiny."

A71     \_\_\_\_\_. *SUM*, VI (Apr. 1850), 311-12.
    Review of the Griswold Edition of Poe's works claims that "to whatever he did publish, he gave the full force of his...extraordinary and highly original genius."

A72     \_\_\_\_\_. *Saturday Evening Post* (Sept. 21, 1850).
    Defense of Poe against Griswold's *Memoir*. Quinn attributes this article to Henry Peterson.

*A: 1827-1850*

A73     \_\_\_\_\_. *Saturday Evening Post* (1846). Mentioned in George Eveleth's letter to Poe (Jan. 19, 1847).
      The article accuses Poe of plagiarizing the *Conchologist's First Book* and publicizes his illness and poverty.

A74     \_\_\_\_\_. *Saturday Gazette*. Reprinted in *Oquawka* (Illinois) *Spectator* (Nov. 7, 1849).
      Believes that Poe produced no great works and that his reputation will decline.

A75     \_\_\_\_\_. <u>SLM</u>, I (Mar. 1835), 387.
      Review of "Berenice." "Whilst there is too much German horror in his subject, there can be but one opinion as to the force and elegance of his style."

A76     \_\_\_\_\_. <u>SLM</u>, I (Apr. 1835), 460.
      Review of "Morella." The critic laments Poe's attraction to German mysticism while praising his powers of imagination and command of language.

A77     \_\_\_\_\_. <u>SLM</u>, I (May 1835), 531.
      Praises the accuracy of the satirical picture in "Lionizing."

A78     \_\_\_\_\_. <u>SLM</u>, I (Jun. 1835), 533.
      "Hans Pfaall" deals with an imaginary experience in such detail that the reader accepts the story as plausible.

A79     \_\_\_\_\_. <u>SLM</u>, I (Aug. 1835), 716.
      Reprint of the Kennedy, Latrobe, Miller letter awarding the <u>BSV</u> contest prize to Poe for "MSFB."

A80     \_\_\_\_\_. <u>SLM</u>, II (Dec. 1835), 1. Reprinted in Appendix of <u>TGA</u>.
      Poe has a "uniquely original vein of imagination, and of humorous, delicate satire."

A81     \_\_\_\_\_. <u>SLM</u>, V (Oct. 1839), 708.
      Believes that Poe is "too much attached to gloomy German mysticism, to be a useful and effective writer, without a total divorce from that sombre school." "FHU," for example, "leaves on the mind a painful and horrible impression, without any redeeming admonition to the heart."

A82     \_\_\_\_\_. <u>SLM</u>, VI (Jan. 1840), 126.
      Despite Poe's genius and imagination, he will not produce anything worthwhile. A dark cloud hangs over all his work, eclipsing his bold, fertile talent.

# Edgar Allan Poe: An Annotated Bibliography

## A: 1827-1850

A83 _____."Southern Literary Messenger," BJ, I (Mar. 22, 1845), 183.
Brief mention of the success of the SLM under Poe's editorship.

A84 _____. SQR, I (Jan. 1842), 30.
Brief mention of the success of SLM under Poe's editorship.

A85 _____. *Talisman and Odd Fellow's Magazine,* I (Sept. 1846), 105.
Calls Poe "the tomahawk man" and "the Comanche of literature."

A86 _____. USRLG, II (Aug. 1827), 399.
Mentions the publication of TOP.

A87 _____. USRLG. Reprinted in Appendix of 1845 *Tales.*
"Mr. Poe's singular and powerful style of prose writing is a charm which ought to be enjoyed more than once."

A88 _____. *United States Telegraph* (Washington City), X (Dec. 5, 1835), 1262. Reprinted in SLM, II (Jan. 1836), 136.
Negative review of *Politian* which claims that Poe has a "defect of ear alone, which can only be corrected by more study than the thing is worth."

A89 _____. *Weekly Universe* (Feb. 12, 1848).
Favorable report of Poe's lecture.

A90 _____. "What is a National Literature Worth?" New York IMLA, III (Feb. 1847), 93.
Chastises the public for not responding to appeals for aid for Poe and Virginia.

A91 A.S.P. "Fugitive Poetry of America," SQR, XIV (Jul. 1848), 115-9.
Discussion of the unusual musicality of "The Raven," its rhyme scheme and alliteration, concluding that the poem is sound without sense. "It would seem that the raven is only a turkey-buzzard, after all."

A92 BRIGGS, CHARLES F. BJ, I (Feb. 8, 1845), 93.
"The Raven" is "a piece of verse which the best of our poets would hardly wish to disown."

A93 _____. *Holden's,* LV (Dec. 1849), 765-6.
Deplores the tendency of critics to hide Poe's faults and calls for an unbiased analysis of his character. Briggs

*A: 1827-1850*

also suggests that Poe was "an intellectual machine without a balance wheel," and that his poetry is mechanical.

A94  BURTON, WILLIAM E. <u>GM</u>, III (Sept. 1838), 210-11.
Unfavorable review of NAGP. Considers the book an attempt to "humbug" the public, an insult to the readers, and even beneath critical contempt. "We regret to find Mr. Poe's name in connection with such a mass of ignorance and affrontery."

A95  CALVERT, GEORGE M. *Baltimore American*. Reprinted in <u>SLM</u>, II (Apr. 1836), 347.
Favorable review of "DL'O."

A96  CARTER, ROBERT. *Boston Notion* (Apr. 29, 1843).
Abridged version of Hirst article in <u>PSM</u>. *See* A146.

A97  CHANDLER, J. R. <u>USG</u> (Jan. 8, 1844).
Favorable review of Poe's lecture, "Poets and Poetry of America."

A98  _____. <u>USG</u>. Reprinted in Appendix of <u>TGA</u>.
Favorable review of "FHU."

A99  CHIVERS, THOMAS HOLLY. "The Valley of Diamonds," Georgia *Citizen* (Jul. 12, 1850); and "Caelicola," *Peterson's Magazine*, XVII (Feb. 1850), 102.
Chivers' first charge that Poe plagiarized "The Raven" from his poetry.

A100  CLARK, LEWIS GAYLORD. <u>Kn</u>, XII (Aug. 18, 1838), 167.
Blast at Poe's novel, calling it "loose and slip-shod," graceless, defective, and gory. Clark apparently believed that Pym was a real person, but questioned "the gentleman's word, who should affirm...that he <u>believed</u> the various adventures and hairbreadth scapes therein recorded."

A101  _____. <u>Kn</u>, XIV (Dec. 1839), 564.
Clark promises to review <u>TGA</u>, but never does.

A102  _____. <u>Kn</u>, XV (Apr. 1840), 75.
Brief notice of "The Journal of Julius Rodman," which Clark recognizes as Poe's.

A103  _____. <u>Kn</u>, XXV (Mar. 1845), 282.
"The very best thing in its [AWR] pages is a unique, singularly imaginative, and most musical effusion, entitled 'The Raven'."

*A: 1827-1850*

A104   _____. Kn, XXV (Apr. 1845), 386.
     Retraction of his favorable review of "The Raven".
*See* A103.

A105   _____. Kn, XXVII (Jan. 1846), 69-72.
     Unfavorable and vicious review of ROP. Poe has an "apti-
tude for rhyme" but no ideas, and his poetry is childish.
"If we were disposed to retort upon Mr. Poe for the exceedingly gross and false statements which, upon an imaginary
slight, he made in his paper respecting this *Magazine,* we
could ask for no greater favor than to be allowed to criti-
cize his volume of poems. Surely no author is so much indebted to the forebearance of the critics as Mr. Poe, and
no person connected with the press in this country is entitled to less mercy or consideration. His criticisms, so
called, are generally a tissue of coarse personal abuse or
personal adulation."

A106   _____. Kn, XXVII (May 1846), 461.
     Personal attack on Poe, "at present in a state of health
which renders him not completely accountable for all his
peculiarities."

A107   _____. Kn, XXVIII (Jul. 1846), 94.
     Describes certain of the Wiley and Putnam Library of
American books, which included the 1845 *Tales,* as "so
little noteworthy as to demand no remark."

A108   _____. Kn, XXVIII (Oct. 1846).
     Brutal attack on Poe's character.

A109   _____. Kn, XXVIII (Nov. 1846), 452.
     Brief note on the NAR review of Poe's *Tales. See* A51.

A110   _____. Kn, XXXI (Jan. 1848), 68-71.
     Summary of unfavorable review of Poe's *Tales* in B1.

A111   _____. Kn, XXXV (Feb. 1850), 163-4.
     Post mortem look at Poe, which combines moral displeasure
with aesthetic approval. "Certain it is that the most
careful student of his works will search in them vainly for
elevated and generous sentiments. But very few of our
American authors have possessed more of the creative energy
or the constructive faculty; and the remarkable ingenuity,
compactness, and simplicity with which he wrought out the
gloomy forms of his imagination; the distinctness and com-
pleteness and force of his metaphysical analysis and illustrations; and the...artist-like finish of his productions,

## A: 1827-1850

may secure for them an enduring and not unenviable fame."
Clark also accuses Poe of plagiarizing some of his tales
from Hoffmann and Longfellow and of writing negative criticism out of vindictiveness.

A112 _____. Kn, XXXVI (Oct. 1850), 370-2.
Unfavorable review of Griswold's edition of Poe's works,
Vol. III. Repeats charges of plagiarism and denies that
Poe's criticism presents "any considerable claim to the
regard of the public."

A113 COLTON, GEORGE. "Poe's Tales," AWR, II (Sept. 1845), 306-9.
Favorable review of the Wiley and Putnam edition of
Poe's *Tales* , which "displays the most undisputable marks
of intellectual power and keenness; and an individuality
of mind and disposition, of peculiar intensity....No one
can read them without obtaining some metaphysical knowledge
as well as having his curiosity stimulated and his sympa-
thies awakened."

A114 COOKE, PHILIP PENDLETON. "Edgar Allan Poe, his Literary
Merits Considered," SLM, XIV (Jan. 1848), 34-38. Reprinted
in CJ16.
Very favorable review attributing to Poe DeFoe's "peculiar talent for filling up his pictures with minute life-
like touches--for giving an air of remarkable naturalness
and truth to whatever he paints." Cooke also finds "the
fires of a great poet...seething under those analytical and
narrative powers in which no living writer equals him."

A115 DANA, CHARLES A. "Tales," *Brook Farm Harbinger*, I (Jul. 12,
1845), 73-4.
Review of Poe's *Tales,* which concentrates on Poe's
"intense order" of genius and excess of nervous agitation.
Dana concludes that the *Tales* are "clumsily contrived, un-
natural, and every way in bad taste." The power in them is
diseased.

A116 DANIEL, JOHN M. "Eulogium," SLM, XVI (Mar. 1850), 172-87.
Diatribe against Griswold, Willis, and Lowell for their
eclectic introductions to Griswold's edition of the works.
Daniel, who approved of Poe as a critic, believed the *Tales*
to be unrealistic. Ingram wrongly attributes this review
to Griswold (Ecl, LXXXIII [Aug. 1874], 210).

A117 DOW, J. E. *Index* (Alexandria D.C.), I (Sept. 25, 1841), 3.
Poe is "the severest critic, the best writer, and the
most unassuming little fellow in the United States."

# Edgar Allan Poe: An Annotated Bibliography

*A: 1827-1850*

A118 _____. *Index*, I (Nov. 2, 1841), 3.
Favorable review of Poe's "Autographs."

A119 DU SOLLE, JOHN S. *Philadelphia Spirit of the Times* (Jan. 8, 1847).
"If Mr. Poe had not been gifted with considerable gall, he would have been devoured long ago by the host of enemies his genius has created."

A120 DUYCKINCK, EVERET A. LW (New York), VI (Jan. 26, 1850), 81.
Reprinted in CJ16.
Post-mortem on Poe which suggests that he was removed from reality. "Briefly, he was...a man of ideas. He lived entirely apart from the solidities and realities of life: was an abstraction; thought, wrote, and dealt solely in abstractions."

A121 _____. LW (New York), VII (Sept. 21, 1850), 228.
Garbled review of the *Literati* with an accusation that Griswold presented only those articles that would make Poe look biased and vicious. Griswold may yet learn "that he has lent himself to an enterprise where no honor can be acquired, and where, for the momentary gratification of his own personal feelings, he has wrought a lasting hurt to whatever of character his principal had left behind him."

A122 DWIGHT, JOHN S. *Brook Farm Harbinger*, I (Dec. 6, 1845), 410-11.
Witty and incisive review of the Wiley and Putnam edition of ROP. Poe's hostile criticism is evidence of his paranoia; his poetry, although beautiful, powerful, and original, is unreal and unsubstantial. It seems "to stand shivering, begging admission to our hearts in vain because [it] looks not as if [it] came from the heart." Poe has "more of the art than the soul of poetry."

A123 ENGLISH, THOMAS DUNN. "Our Bookshelves, #8," Arist, I (Nov. 1845), 399-403.
Indictment of Poe and his audience for the confusion at the Boston Lyceum lecture and a review of ROP. Although English praises the mechanics of "The Raven," he is un-enthusiastic about the other poems in the book, calling "Al Aaraaf" "peurile, and so deeply transcendental that no one can tell what it is all about." Poe is "the first poet of his school," but he is also the only member.

A124 _____. "Poe's Tales," Arist, I (Oct. 1845), 316-19.
Highly favorable review of Poe's *Tales*, attributing to

him a "clear and forcible style" and the ability to arouse complete trust in his readers. "...he has produced works of the most notable character, and elevated the mere 'tale,' in this country, over the larger 'novel'...."

A125 _____. "Poe's Tales,' ll <u>Arist</u>, I (Sept. 1845), 238.
In a review which Mary Phillips believes Poe wrote, English claims that the tales are "unapproachable by any other writer."

A126 FORSTER, JOHN. "Review of Griswold's *Poets and Poetry of America,* <u>FQR</u>, XXXII (Jan. 1844), 159-76.
Suggests that Poe imitates Tennyson and that some passages in his poems "have a spirituality in them, usually denied to imitators; who rarely possess the property recently discovered in the mocking-birds--a solitary note of their own."

A127 FROST, PROFESSOR. <u>AWM</u> (1839).
In a letter to Dr. Snodgrass (Dec. 19, 1839), Poe claims that a favorable review of <u>TGA</u> appeared in this magazine.

A128 FULLER, MARGARET. *New York Daily Tribune,* V (Nov. 26, 1845).
Unfavorable mention of <u>ROP</u> which agrees with Poe that there is "nothing in this volume of much value to the public or very creditable to myself," and suggests that Poe probably has talent for better things.

A129 _____. "Poe's Tales," *New York Daily Tribune* (Jul. 11, 1845).
Reprinted in CJ16.
Poe's tales penetrate "into the causes of things which leads to original but creditable results." Poe achieves vigorous narrative and meaningful, though fantastic effects. "The degree of skill shown in the management of revolting or terrible circumstances makes the pieces that have such subjects more interesting than the others. Even the failures are those of an intellect of strong fiber and well-chosen aim."

A130 GRAHAM, GEORGE R. "The Late Edgar Allan Poe," <u>Gr</u>, XXXVI (Mar. 1850), 224-6.
Defense of Poe against the "Ludwig" obituary. Graham discusses Poe's commitment to literature, his integrity, and his devotion to his family and imputes his failure to achieve popularity to the narrowness of most readers and to the strangeness of the tales. "Let the moralist who stands upon tufted carpet...pause before he lets the anathema, trembling upon his lips, fall upon a man like Poe!

who, wandering from publisher to publisher...finds no mar-
ket for his brain--with despair at heart, misery ahead for
himself and his loved ones, and gaunt famine dogging at his
heels, thus sinks by the wayside, before the demon that
watches his steps and whispers. OBLIVION."

A131  GREELEY, HORACE. NY, I (Dec. 12, 1835).
      Unenthusiastic notice of *Politian*.

A132  _____. *New York Tribune*, IV (Feb. 3, 1845).
      "The Raven" would have "enriched Blackwood's."

A133  _____. *New York Tribune*, IV (Mar. 1, 1845).
      Review of Poe's lecture "Poetry in America" criticizes
      Poe for exaggerated harshness toward American critics,
      denies Poe's charges that critics puff the works of their
      friends, and objects to his treatment of Longfellow.

A134  GRISWOLD, RUFUS WHITE. *New England Weekly Gazette* (Hartford).
      Mentioned in Poe's letter to George W. Eveleth (Dec. 15,
      1846).
      The critic, often confused with Rufus Wilmot Griswold,
      complains about inconsistencies in "The Raven."

A135  GRISWOLD, RUFUS WILMOT. "Edgar Allan Poe," IM, I (Oct. 1850),
      325-44. Reprinted in *Tait's*, ns. XXII (1852), 33; Ecl,
      XXVI (May 1852), 115-19; LLA, XXXIII (May 1852), 422-24.
      Article modeled on the Ludwig obituary: "...the closest
      investigation...will only lead us to wonder and regret that
      so much intellectual power may coexist with so much moral
      weakness....His character...was steeped at once in depravity
      and poetry."

A136  _____. "The Intellectual History, Condition, and Prospects of
      the Country," NI (Aug. 30, 1845), 2.
      Favorable review of *Tales* suggests that Poe explores
      mental pathology with the skill and artistry of Brockden
      Brown and that his tales are unique in American literature.

A137  _____. "Memoir," *The Works of the Late Edgar Allan Poe*, I, New
      York: 1850-1856.
      More vituperative than the "Ludwig" obituary.

A138  _____. (Ludwig) *New York Tribune*, IX (Oct. 9, 1849), 2. Re-
      printed in CJ16.
      The slanderous obituary which describes Poe as roaming
      the streets drunk and half-mad.

A: *1827-1850*

A139 _____. "Preface," *The Works of the Late Edgar Allan Poe,* III
New York: 1850-1856.
Defense of his Memoir which includes forged letters describing his relations with Poe and condemns Graham for his
"tenderness for the poor author."

A140 _____. *The Prose Writers of America.* Philadelphia: Carey and
Hart, 1847.
Incorrect biographical information joined with an excellent summary of Poe's talent as a writer of short stories.
Repeating his previous remarks about Poe's interest in
mental pathology, Griswold expresses regret that certain
events in Poe's life prevented him from succeeding as a
great poet.

A141 HALE, SARAH JOSEPHA. "Literary Notices," *Ladies Magazine,* III
(Jan. 1830), 47.
Review of Poe's early poems, describing them as in part
"exceedingly boyish, feeble and altogether deficient in the
common characteristics of poetry," and also reminiscent of
the work of Shelley.

A142 HERVEY, THOMAS K. "*The Raven and Other Poems,*" Ath. Reprinted
in LLA, IX (Apr. 18, 1846), 106-7.
Accused Poe of imitating "the worst of our London
Schools," the one which complicates the simple and reduces
what is profound to inanity. "The best advice we can give
to Mr. Poe is to be simple and natural: --and, above all,
to strike his harp amid the grand novelties which his own
country presents."

A143 HEWITT, JOHN HILL. *Baltimore Minerva and Emerald* (1830).
Contemptuous review of ATMP, calling the poems "a pile
of Brick Bats." *See* A197.

A144 HIRST, HENRY B. *McMakin's Model American Courier,* XIX (Oct.
20, 1849), 2.
Defense of Poe against Griswold: "He [Poe] was a man of
great and original genius, but the sublime 'afflatus' which
lifted him above his fellows, made him a shining mark for
the covert as well as open attacks of literary rivals...."
Poe was an impoverished poet, suffering for his art, while
men of lesser talents "were winning gold from the Magazines of the day."

A145 _____. PSC (Oct. 20, 1840).
Claims that Poe was "unrivalled as a tale-writer."

# EDGAR ALLAN POE: AN ANNOTATED BIBLIOGRAPHY

*A: 1827-1850*

A146 _____. PSM (Feb. 25 and Mar. 4, 1843).
Erroneous biography and very favorable review of Poe
work believed by most critics to have been written by P
himself. Announces plans for *The Stylus*.

A147 HOLDEN, E. PSC. Reprinted in Appendix of TGA.
Brief comments on Poe's originality, richness of des
tion, and popularity.

A148 HOPKINS, E. A. *New York Express* (1848).
Discussion of Poe's lecture on *Eureka*.

A149 HUNT, J. *National Archives* (March 13, 1845).
Accuses Poe of being recklessly critical of other
writers. Poe responded in BJ (Mar. 8, 1845), 147-50.

A150 JERDAN, WILLIAM. *"The Raven and Other Poems,"* LG, no. 1
(Mar. 14, 1846), 237-8.
Suggests that Poe study his model, Elizabeth Barre
more closely than he has done. "...there is not so m
method in his *furor* as could be desired by readers no
flamed and carried away by his vague thoughts and dic

A151 KENNEDY, JOHN PENDLETON. BSV (Oct. 12, 1833).
Notice that Poe won first prize in the contest, pr
nouncing his tales to be "eminently distinguished by
vigorous, and poetical imagination, a rich style, a
invention, and varied and curious learning," and "ve
creditable to the rising literature of our country."

*See also* CC151.

A152 KETTELL, SAMUEL. *Specimens of American Literature* (Bos
III (1829), 405.
First public mention of Poe's publication TOP.

A153 LABREE, LAWRENCE. New York IMLA, I (Oct. 11, 1845), 6
Discusses Poe's defense of Lowell against charge

A154 _____."*The Raven and Other Poems*," New York IMLA, I (Ja
192.
Describes the volume as "creditable to American
ature."

A155 LAMSON, A. "American and English Criticism of Edgar *
Poe," *Chronicle Examiner*, XXXVI (1844), 390.

A156 LONGFELLOW, HENRY WADSWORTH. "The Late Edgar Allen P
XV (Nov. 1849), 696.
Excerpt from a letter about Poe: "I never knew

17

A: *1827-1850*

personally, but have always entertained a high appreciation
of his powers as a prose writer and a poet. His prose is
remarkably vigorous, direct and yet affluent; and his verse
has a particular charm of melody, an atmosphere of true
poetry about it, which is very winning. The harshness of
his criticism, I have never attributed to anything but the
irritation of a sensitive nature, chafed by some indefinite
sense of wrong."

A157  LOWELL, JAMES RUSSELL. "Edgar Allan Poe," <u>Gr</u>, XXVI (Feb.
1845), 49-53. Reprinted in *The Function of the Poet*. Ed.
by Albert Mordell, Boston: Houghton Mifflin Co., 1920,
153-54; and CJ16.
   Very favorable analysis of Poe as critic, poet, and
writer of short stories. Poe is "the most discriminating,
philosophical, and fearless critic upon imaginative works
who has written in America." Lowell admires Poe's balance
of imaginative and analytical powers, his portraits of
monomaniacal personalities, his talent for achieving verisimilitude.

A158  MORRIS, GEORGE P. "Literary Notices," *New York Mirror*, VIII
(May 7, 1831), 349-50.
   Admires the mechanical facility but deplores the lack of
content and unintelligibility of the 1831 *Poems*.

A159  NEAL, JOHN. "Edgar Allan Poe," *Portland Daily Advertiser*
(Apr. 23, 1850).
   "I believe...that he was by nature, of a just and generous temper, thwarted, baffled, and self-harrassed by his
own wilfullness to the most unbecoming drudgery." Woodberry
describes this article as "rambling and vituperative."

A160  _____. <u>YBLG</u>, III (Sept. 1829), 168. Reprinted in CJ16.
   One of the earliest reviews of Poe's poetry, describing
it as promising nonsense.

A161  _____. <u>YBLG</u>, III (Dec. 1829), 295-8.
   Very flattering review of <u>ATMP</u>, urging Poe to pursue the
career of poet by keeping his mind and soul pure.

A162  NOAH, MAJOR MORDECAI M. *Richmond Whig and Public Advertiser*,
VII (Dec. 15, 1835), 1.
   Negative review of *Politian*.

A163  OTIS, J. F. <u>NI</u>. Reprinted in <u>SLM</u>, II (Apr. 1836), 346; and in
Appendix of <u>TGA</u>.
   Comments on originality and power of "DL'O" and other
stories by Poe.

A164    OUTIS. "Plagiarism," *New York Mirror*, I (Mar. 8, 1845), 346-7.
Letter to editor Willis condemns Poe for charging Long-fellow with plagiarism.

A165    PATTERSON, E. H. N. *Oquawka Spectator*, Illinois (Oct. 24, 1849),
Brief obituary of Poe by editor who had planned a pub-lishing venture with him.

A166    _____. *Oquawka Spectator*, Illinois (Nov. 7, 1849).
Defense of Poe against obituary in *Saturday Gazette*. *See* A74.

A167    PAULDING, J. K. *Richmond Whig*. Reprinted in SLM, II (Jan. 1836), 138; and in Appendix of TGA.
Poe is "decidedly the best of all our young writers."

A168    PECK, G. W. "The Works of Edgar Allan Poe," AWR, XI (Mar. 1850), 301-15.
Peck dwells on Poe's emotional instability and denies the absence of morality or sentimentality in the tales. His work was "wrung from a soul that suffered and strove; from a fancy that was driven out from the sunny palaces of youth and hope...." He concludes, however, that although Poe's work has a powerful effect on the reader at first reading, "it is with a sort of misgiving that we may out-grow or become indifferent to him hereafter."

A169    POWELL, THOMAS. "Edgar Allan Poe," *Living Authors of America*. New York: Stringer and Townsend, 1850, 108-35.
Americans, who are intellectually dependent on England, will eventually recognize Poe's great talent.

A170    RICHMOND, HJ (Mar. 16, 1850).
Defense of Poe against Daniel's essay in SLM. Admits that Poe's life was filled with "shadows," but denounces Daniel's "cruel misrepresentations." *See* A116.

A171    RIPLEY, GEORGE. *New York Tribune* (Jan. 19, 1850). Reprinted in LLA, XXV (Apr. 1850), 77-8.
Obituary with the theme of wasted genius. Poe was "a man of extraordinary boldness and originality of intellect, with a power of sharp and subtle analysis that has seldom been surpassed, and an imagination singularly prolific both in creations of beauty and terror." But the writings fail to appeal to "universal principles of taste" because Poe "had no earnestness of convictions, no faith in human excellence, no devotion to a higher purpose—not even the desire to produce a consummate work of art...."

*A: 1827-1850*

A172   SAVAGE, JOHN.  <u>USMDR</u>, XXVII (Dec. 1850), 542-4; XXVIII (Jan.
         and Feb. 1851), 66-9, 162-72.
              Lengthy discussion of Poe's writing influenced by Gris-
         wold.

A173   SIMMS, WILLIAM GILMORE.  *Southern Patriot* (Nov. 10, 1845).
              Defense of Poe's Boston Lyceum lecture.  His pure imagin-
         ation renders his work "intensely spiritual for the ordinary
         reader," and his poetry is "too original, too fanciful, too
         speculative" for the public.

A174   _____. *Southern Patriot* (Mar. 2, 1846).
              Discusses the "music of his verse, the vagueness of the
         delineation, [its] mystical character."  Some of his stories
         are "the most remarkable specimens of the power of intensi-
         fying a conception of pure romance, to the exclusion of all
         the ordinary agents of fiction, which have been written."

A175   _____. *Southern and Western*, II (Dec. 1845), 426.
              Poe is a "writer of rare imaginative excellence, great
         intensity of mood, and a singularly mathematical directness
         of purpose...nothing more original has ever been given to
         the American readers" than his stories.

A176   SNODGRASS, DR. J. E.  *Baltimore Post*.  Reprinted in Appendix
         of <u>TGA</u>.
              Mentions Poe's ability to create harmony between his
         characters and their environment and maintains that Poe has
         written "some of the most popular tales of American origin."

A177   _____. <u>BSV</u> (Apr. 2, 1842).
              Describes Poe as "provokingly hypercritical at times."

A178   _____. <u>BSV</u> (Feb. 2, 1844).
              Favorable mention of Poe's lecture at the Odd Fellow's
         Hall (Jan. 31, 1844).

A179   TALLEY, SUSAN ARCHER.  *Richmond Republican* (Oct. 15, 1849).
              Pretends to defend Poe against Griswold but actually
         adds fuel to the fire: "He never felt the impulse and
         desire of good within him, even while yielding to evil,
         and it was to him a constant source of remorse."

A180   TASISTRO, LOUIS F.  "A Notice of Poe's Tales," *New York
         Mirror*, XVII (Dec. 28, 1839), 215.  Reprinted in CJ16.
              Very favorable notice of Poe's *Tales*, in which the
         critic finds "fine poetic feeling, much brightness of
         fancy, and excellent taste, a ready eye for the picturesque,

much quickness of observation, and great truth of sentiment and character."

A181 THOMPSON, JOHN REUBEN. "The Late Edgar Allan Poe," SLM, XV (Nov. 1849), 694-6.
Reviews Poe's early years as a critic with the SLM and discusses his reputation in England and France, his origininality, "rhetorical propriety" and power of analysis. Concludes that Poe's tales are gloomy and lack the human element.

A182 TUPPER, MARTIN FARQUAR. "American Romance," LG, no. 1515 (Jan. 31, 1846), 101-2. Reprinted in LLA, IX (May 23, 1846), 381-4; and in CJ 16.
"Fresh fields and pastures now are obviously the likeliest places wherein to look for inventive genius and original power; accordingly, we are not surprised to hear that the author of this remarkable volume is an American. His work has come to our shore recommended by success upon his own; and that such success is no more than it deserves we will undertake to demonstrate to our readers...."

A183 WILMER, LAMBERT A. BSV, II (Aug. 4, 1832), 3.
"...for originality, richness of imagery and purity of the style, few American authors in our opinion have produced any thing superior."

A184 _____. "Edgar Allan Poe and his Calumniators," *Our Press Gang: A Complete Exposition of the Corruptions and Crimes of the American Newspapers.* Philadelphia: J. T. Lloyd, 1859.
Reprint of Wilmer's earlier vindication of Poe. "I do not know that this vindication was copied by a single paper; whereas the whole press of the country seemed desirous of giving circulation and authenticity to the slanders." Describes Poe as morally and intellectually superior to Griswold.

A185 WILLIS, NATHANIEL PARKER. "Editor's Table," *American Monthly Magazine,* I (Nov. 1829), 587.
Unsympathetic remarks about ATMP.

A186 _____. HJ (Dec. 26, 1846).
Answers slanders against Poe published in *Saturday Evening Post* and *New York Express* with the explanation that he suffered moments of insanity during which he lost control of himself.

# Edgar Allan Poe: An Annotated Bibliography

A: *1827-1850*

A187 _____. HJ (Jan. 1, 1848).
Describes "Ulalume" as an "exquisitely piquant and skillful exercise of rarity and niceness of language." At Poe's suggestion, Willis pretended not to know who wrote the poem.

A188 _____. HJ (Oct. 13, 1849).
Brief notice of Poe's death.

A189 _____. HJ (Oct. 20, 1849). Reprinted in CJ16.
Defense of Poe against Ludwig obituary. Describes him as "a quiet, patient, industrious, and most gentlemanly person, commanding the utmost respect and good feeling by his unvarying deportment and ability."

A190 _____. "Poe's Last Poem," HJ (Oct. 27, 1849).
Favorable notice of "The Bells," which describes its "rhythmical harmony" as perfect.

A191 _____. "'The Raven'," LLA, VI (Jul. 26, 1845), 185.
Reprint of Introduction to "The Raven," originally published in *New York Mirror:* "In our opinion it is the most effective single example of fugitive poetry ever to be published in this country; and unsurpassed in English poetry and subtle conception, masterly ingenuity of versification, and consistent sustaining of imaginative lift. It is one of those 'dainties bred in a book' which we feed on. It will stick in the memory of everybody who reads it."

[The following articles, although written after 1900, concern reviews of Poe's poetry written between 1827 and 1851.]

A192 CHURCH, RANDOLPH. "'Al Aaraaf' and the Unknown Critic," *Virginia Cavalcade,* V (Summer 1955).
Review of ATMP from unidentified contemporary Baltimore newspaper.

A193 MABBOTT, T. O. "An Unfavorable Reaction to Poe in 1842," N&Q, CXCIV (Mar. 19, 1949), 122-3.
Reprint of an unfavorable review of Poe's poetry from an obscure Albany journal. *See* A65.

A194 MOSS, SIDNEY P. "Poe and the *St. Louis Daily Reveille,* PN, I (Oct. 1968), 18-21.
A record of notices of Poe in the *St. Louis Daily Reveille* from Jun. 11, 1845 to Jul. 15, 1847.

*A: 1827-1850*

A195 POLLIN, BURTON R. "An 1839 Review of Poe's *Tales* in Willis'
    *The Corsair*," PN, V (Dec. 1972), 56.
        Review of Poe's *Tales* in *Corsair*, XLI (Dec. 21, 1839),
    653.

A196 _____. "Poe and the *Boston Notion*," ELN, VIII (1970), 23-8.
        Review of criticisms of Poe in the Boston periodical.

A197 STARRETT, VINCENT. "A Mystery Uncovered: The Lost *Minerva*
    Review of 'Al Aaraaf'," SRL, XXVI (May 1, 1943), 4-5.
        Reprint of John Hill Hewitt's review of "Al Aaraaf."

A198 TANSELLE, G. THOMAS. "Poe and Vandenhoff Once More," AN&Q,
    I (Mar. 1963), 101-2.
        Notes reference to Poe in *New York Weekly News*, 1845 and
    1846, and also a review of "The Raven" in *Weekly News*, Apr.
    19, 1845.

*See also* CC18, CC38, CC39, CC138, CC196, CQ4.

B:   1851-1900

B1   ANON. "'Annabel Lee'," SLM, XX (Feb. 1854), 124.
          Publishes the poem from the manuscript received five days
     before Poe died.

B2   _____. Ath, 2752 (Jul. 24, 1880), 107-9.
          Favorable review of Ingram's *Edgar Allan Poe: His Life,
     Letters and Opinions*.

B3   _____. "'The Bells'," Cr, XX (Feb. 13, 1892), 102.
          Report on an auction of the manuscript.

B4   _____. "A Bibliography of Edgar Allan Poe," LW (Boston), XIII
     (Dec. 16, 1882), 457.
          Brief list of Poe's publications and translations of his
     work into French, German, Spanish, Italian, and Greek from
     1850 through 1870.

B5   _____. "Biography of Edgar Allan Poe," *Tait's*, ns. XIX, 231-4
     (Apr. 1852).   Reprinted in Ecl, XXVI (May 1852), 115-19.
          Considers the poetry and tales remarkable, but laments
     that "so much intellectual power may co-exist with so much
     moral weakness."   If Poe had written more poetry like "The
     Raven," he would have been "in the foremost ranks of modern
     poetry"--although "to allow any literary excellence to our
     American brethren is considered a tolerably good proof of
     a low standard of taste."

B6   _____. Bkm, VII (May 1898), 257.
          Brief note on Poe in a review of Bierce's stories:
     "...with the single exception of Poe, no American writer
     has ever written any short stories that can compare with
     these."

B7   _____. *Canadian Journal of Industry, Science and Art*, ns. II
     (Mar. 1857), 103-9.

B8   _____. Chaut, XXX (1899), 453.
          Regarding a rumor that Poe removed Virginia's bones from

*B: 1851-1900*

her coffin and that "in Baltimore fragments of the coffin in which Poe was buried are held as priceless relics."

B9     \_\_\_\_\_. "A Commentary on Poe's 'Raven'," <u>Cr</u>, VII (Dec. 26, 1885), 302.
        Review of Ingram's Edition of "The Raven."

B10     \_\_\_\_\_. *Concerning the Removal of the Poe Cottage*. Poe Memorial Association. New York, 1896.

B11     \_\_\_\_\_. "Daguerreotype of Poe," <u>SLM</u>, XVII (Apr. 1851), 253.

B12     \_\_\_\_\_. *Dedication Exercises of the Actor's Monument to Edgar Allan Poe*. New York: Metropolitan Museum of Art (May 4, 1885).
        Contributions by A. S. Sullivan, Edwin Booth, John Gilbert, G. E. Montgomery, Gen. L. P. de Cesnola, William R. Alger.

B13     \_\_\_\_\_. <u>Ecl</u>, XXXI (Feb. 1854), 263-72. Original in *Hogg's Instructor*.
        "His poetry runs over with spiritual beauty, even when dealing with gloom and guilt; but his history from earliest boyhood down to his premature death in a tavern, is all be-mired with the coarsest sensualism, and was not wanting in displays of the meanest malignity, envy, and positive dis-honesty."

B14     \_\_\_\_\_. "Edgar Allan Poe," <u>Acad</u>, LVII (Aug. 5, 1899), 137.
        Poe was "a moral and temperamental invalid. He had that fatal wish to possess beauty without the earth in which it is rooted."

B15     \_\_\_\_\_. "Edgar Allan Poe," <u>ER</u>, CVII (Apr. 1858), 419-42. Re-printed in <u>LLA</u>, LVII (Jun. 12, 1858), 803-16; and <u>Ecl</u>, XLIX, 338ff.
        Review of Griswold's edition. "Edgar Allan Poe was in-contestibly one of the most worthless persons of whom we have any record in the world of letters." Hopefully, the stories of his profligate habits will fade away and the high points of his career, such as his review of *Barnaby Rudge*, will receive the attention they deserve.

B16     \_\_\_\_\_. "Edgar Allan Poe," *Eliza Cook's Journal*, VII, (May 15, 1852), 45-8.

B17     \_\_\_\_\_. "Edgar Allan Poe in France," <u>Put</u>, II (Dec. 1853), 686-7.
        Brief discussion of the French interest in Poe with quota-tions from M. Th. Bernard's article in *Athenaeum Francais*.

*B: 1851-1900*

B18 _____. "Edgar Allan Poe," *Leisure Hour,* III (1854), 427-9.
Biography which describes Poe as "covered with debt and
infamy."

B19 _____. "Edgar Allan Poe," *Once a Week,* XXV (Nov. 4 and 18,
1871), 404-410, 447-450.
Biography of Poe and brief discussion of the Griswold
and Willis Memoirs.

B20 _____. "Edgar Poe and his Biographers," TB, LXVIII (Aug. 1883),
535-6.
Attacks Ingram's biography.

B21 _____. "Edgar Poe and New York," SatR, LI (Jan. 29, 1881),
139-40.
General remarks on Poe occasioned by an announcement
that New York City would erect a monument in his honor.

B22 _____. HJ (Dec. 4, 1852), 3.
Note on Tennyson's familiarity with Poe. Reprinted in
ESQ, LIX (Spring 1970), 31.

B23 _____. HNMM, LXI (Oct. 1880), 787-8.
Compares Poe with Willis and reviews Ingram's biography.

B24 _____. *Hogg's Instructor,* ns. X (1853), 616-22, 634-38.
"The Gold Beetle" was influenced by an incident in
Dumas' *Monte Cristo.*

B25 _____. "Lang on Poe, Cr, XXI (Jul. 2, 1892), 7.
Reference to Lang's remark about exorbitant auction
prices for TOP in the *London Daily News.*

B26 _____. "The Life and Poetry of Edgar Poe," ChEJ, XIX
(Feb. 23, 1853), 137-40. Reprinted in LLA, XXXVII, Second
Series I (Apr. 1853), 157-61.
Considers Poe "a writer of more than ordinary power...
[who has] evinced far more originality than any of his
contemporaries." After a rather dramatic biography, which
alludes to the depravity of Poe's life, the critic discusses the autobiographical strain in his poetry and concludes that Poe was "unquestionably the most original
imaginative writer America has yet produced."

B27 _____. LW, XII (Feb. 5, 1853), 102-3.
Regarding a note in *The Spectator* that "To One" was
plagiarized from a poem by Tennyson.

B: 1851-1900

B28 ____. LQR, II (1854), 453-9.
Review of 1852 and 1853 London editions of Poe's poetry
and tales. Poe is a "pure" artist with exquisite perception of the essentials of art, whose "exclusively aesthetic
bent" made him insensible to human interests. His poetry,
"not meant for universal approbation...is a sacrifice upon
the altar of taste"--especially in "utilitarian America."

B29 ____. "Memorial to Poe at the University of Virginia," Cr, XXX
ns. XXVII (May 29, 1897), 378.
Whether or not a memorial to Poe should be erected in
the Rotunda Library.

B30 ____. Nation, XX (Mar. 25, 1875), 208-9.
Criticizes Ingram for whitewashing Poe's character.

B31 ____. "A New Edition of Poe," Cr, V (Jul. 5, 1884), 10-11.
Original in Pall Mall Gazette.
Ingram's edition of Poe's works has benefited Poe
studies.

B32 ____. "The New Edition of Poe," Cr, XXVI (May 4, 1895),
323-4.
Vague and general review.

B33 ____. "The New and the Old Edgar Poe," Cr, VI (Jan. 31,
1885), 50-1.
"There is no face--certainly no story--in all literature more tragical, more uneven. The thirst for drink
meandering like a line of fire from one end of Poe's career
to the other; the bitter temper involving itself in a
thousand contradictions toward friend and foe; the all-
swallowing egotism that burnt its perpetual taper day and
night before the shrine of Self; the envy, hatred, and
malice, and all uncharitableness of a vindictive career,--
all these come out page by page...."

B34 ____. "The New Poe," Atl, LXXVII (April 1896), 551-4.
Review of the Stedman-Woodberry Edition of Poe's works
describes Poe as a product of his time, deeply affected by
"the new enthusiasm for the individual," which appealed to
him on a psychological level. "...the human mind became,
in his estimation, a treasure-house of undreamed-of possibilities, which was but the poets' version of the value of
the individual...." Coleridge's humanizing of nature was a
great influence on Poe as were Gottfried August Bürger,
Madam de Staël and The Lyrical Ballads.

*B: 1851-1900*

B35 ____. "New School of Poetry," *Literary Union* (Syracuse, 1851 or 1852).

According to Chivers (*Waverly,* VII, Jul. 30, 1853) this article quotes Willis' claim that Poe originated a new school of poetry which is in revolt against the "dull pedantry of antiquated prosodists."

B36 ____. *New York Herald* (Oct. 25, 1880), 8.

Poe is a "clever but not an eminent writer, who ranks among the Maginns, and Mangams, and Savages of literature, gifted but unfortunate men, whom we pity but cannot respect, and whose ill-starred lives are a melancholy moral to genius." His work is narrow, tricky, shallow but clever.

B37 ____. *New York Times* (Oct. 24, 1880), 10.

Brief review of Ingram and Stoddard memoirs.

B38 ____. "Plagiarist or 'Precursor'?" *Dial,* XXVII (Nov. 16, 1899), 367.

Review of Benton's *In the Poe Circle* deplores Benton's confusion over the Poe-Chivers controversy. *See* B75.

B39 ____. "The Poe Memorial," Cr, VI (May 9, 1885), 223.

Concerning the unveiling of the actor's monument to Poe at the Metropolitan Museum.

B40 ____. "Poems of Poe," DUM, XLII (Jul. 1853), 88-96.

Review of Hanney's edition of Poe's poetry. The poems are characterized by "spotless purity of thought, and an ethereal spirituality of fancy." Also discusses the melody of the verse and similarities between Poe and James Clarance Mangan.

B41 ____. "Poe as a Poet," LW (Boston), XIII (1882), 96.

B42 ____. "Poe's Affectation of Learning," Cr, I (Mar. 26, 1881), 80.

Negligible.

B43 ____. "Poe's Connection with Graham's," Cr, XX, ns. XVII (Apr. 16, 1892), 228.

Letter from Edgar Allan Poe to Daniel Bryan of Alexandria, D.C. (Jul. 6, 1842) regarding his connection with Gr.

B44 ____. "Poe's Cottage," Cr, V (Jul. 19, 1884), 31.

Concerning the sale of Poe's cottage to P. J. Keary.

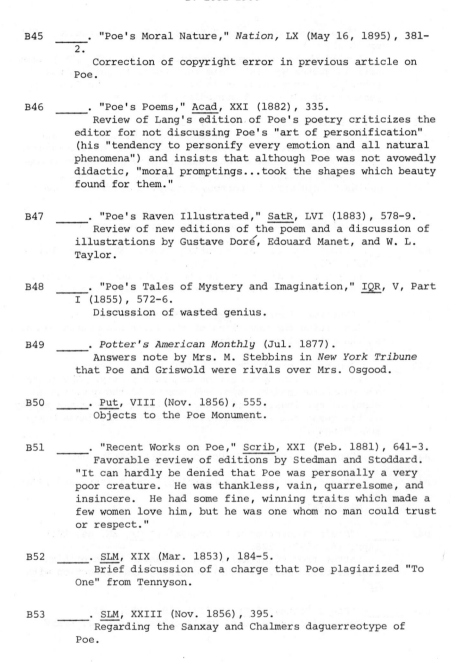

B45 _____. "Poe's Moral Nature," *Nation,* LX (May 16, 1895), 381-2.
   Correction of copyright error in previous article on Poe.

B46 _____. "Poe's Poems," Acad, XXI (1882), 335.
   Review of Lang's edition of Poe's poetry criticizes the editor for not discussing Poe's "art of personification" (his "tendency to personify every emotion and all natural phenomena") and insists that although Poe was not avowedly didactic, "moral promptings...took the shapes which beauty found for them."

B47 _____. "Poe's Raven Illustrated," SatR, LVI (1883), 578-9.
   Review of new editions of the poem and a discussion of illustrations by Gustave Doré, Edouard Manet, and W. L. Taylor.

B48 _____. "Poe's Tales of Mystery and Imagination," IQR, V, Part I (1855), 572-6.
   Discussion of wasted genius.

B49 _____. *Potter's American Monthly* (Jul. 1877).
   Answers note by Mrs. M. Stebbins in *New York Tribune* that Poe and Griswold were rivals over Mrs. Osgood.

B50 _____. Put, VIII (Nov. 1856), 555.
   Objects to the Poe Monument.

B51 _____. "Recent Works on Poe," Scrib, XXI (Feb. 1881), 641-3.
   Favorable review of editions by Stedman and Stoddard. "It can hardly be denied that Poe was personally a very poor creature. He was thankless, vain, quarrelsome, and insincere. He had some fine, winning traits which made a few women love him, but he was one whom no man could trust or respect."

B52 _____. SLM, XIX (Mar. 1853), 184-5.
   Brief discussion of a charge that Poe plagiarized "To One" from Tennyson.

B53 _____. SLM, XXIII (Nov. 1856), 395.
   Regarding the Sanxay and Chalmers daguerreotype of Poe.

*B: 1851-1900*

B54     ____. "Review of Works of Edgar Allan Poe," *Southern Magazine* (Jun. and Jul. 1875).

B55     ____. "'Tamerlane'," <u>Cr</u>, XXVI (May 4, 1895), 330-1. Concerning an auction of the book for $2,500.

B56     ____. "Tamerlane and Other Poems," <u>Cr</u>, V (May 10, 1884), 222. Brief history of the book's publication.

B57     ____. <u>ABUV</u>, VI (Nov. 1899), 65-74. Description of ceremonies at unveiling of Poe's bust.

B58     ____. "Unpublished Correspondence by Edgar Allan Poe," <u>AppJ</u>, XIX (May 1878), 421-9. Letters from Poe to Virginia (Jun. 12, 1846); to Mrs. Shew (Jan. 29, 1847 ; May, 1848; Jun. 1849);to Mrs. Osgood (Nov. 16, 1848; Nov. 23, 1848; Jan. 1849; Feb. 19, 1849; Mar. 23, 1849; Jun. 16, 1849).

B59     ____. "Woodberry's Poe," <u>Atl</u>, LV (May 1885), 705-7. Favorable review of Woodberry's biography deplores the artificiality of Poe's poetry and criticism.

B60     ____. "The Works of Edgar Allan Poe," *Nation,* LX (May 2, 1895), 349-50. Review of Stedman-Woodberry edition considers Woodberry's Memoir needlessly harsh. Concludes with familiar remarks about Poe's troubled life.

B61     ____. "The Works of the Late Edgar Allan Poe," <u>Gr</u>, XLVIII (May 1856), 466. Believes that <u>NAGP</u> illustrates Poe's "love of mischief and intellectual frolic, which formed so prominent an element of Poe's brilliant and ingenious mind."

B62     ____. "The Works of Poe," <u>LW</u> (Boston), XV (Nov. 29, 1884), 417. Brief review of Stoddard's edition of Poe's works.

B63     ____. "The Works of Poe," <u>USMDR</u>, XXXVII (1856), 334.

B64     ____. "Writings of Poe," <u>NAR</u>, LXXXIII (Oct. 1856), 427-55. Review of Griswold's edition suggests that Poe's poetry is deficient because it excludes moral and spiritual themes. As a critic, Poe often overlooked the "animating principle" of a work while he hunted down an "awkward expression, or...ill-chosen word." The themes of his stories generally involve monomania and madness, and

*B: 1851-1900*

"the anomalies and deformities of humanity." Unfortunately
he never "applied his energies to any one noble purpose."

B65   ADAMS, WILLIAM H. D. *Wrecked Lives or Men Who Have Failed.*
New York: Pott, Young & Co., 1880.

B66   ANGIER, MINNA.   "Three-Quarters of the Nineteenth Century,"
*Dial*, XXVII (Nov. 16, 1899), 359-62.
Review of John Sartain's *Reminiscences of a Very Old Man*
describes the association between Poe and Sartain.

B67   ARGUS.   "New Light on Poe," Cr, XIX (1891), 254.
Disagrees with article in *American Catholic Quarterly
Review* (Nov. 1891).

B68   ATHERTON, GERTRUDE.   "Bierce Overlooks Poe," *Cosmopolitan*, X
(Jan. 1891), 271.
Bierce's stories are superior to Poe's in "reserve and
cynical brutality, subtle structure and construction and
power."

B69   AUSTIN, HENRY.   "Poe Coming to his Kingdom," *Dial*, XXVII (Nov.
1, 1899), 307-8.
Review of ceremony in Poe's honor at the University of
Virginia.   The old animosity toward Poe has disappeared,
and there is "almost absolute unanimity of opinion as to
his literary merits...in the literary world."

B70   _____.   "Poe's Last Poem,'Lilitha'," *Southern Bivouac*, IV
(Apr. 1886), 655.

B71   BAIRD, W. "Edgar Allan Poe," SM-NEM, XV (Aug. 1874), 190-203.
Generally sympathetic article which emphasizes Poe's
loneliness and inhumanity.   "He is somehow out of relation
with his race. He can not view things from the ordinary
human standpoint, and hence the great difficulty of judging
him by ordinary rules."   The author is happy to see that
his reputation is improving and that he is no longer a
victim of the "narrow and vindictive Boston clique."

B72   BARROWS, A. C. "Why is Poe Rejected in America?" *Dial*, XXVI
(Feb. 1, 1899), 109-110.
Answer to Moore.   Poe's characters are completely unrealistic and lack motivation.   His failure to understand
human nature "is originally due to a deficient interest in
morals...a severe criticism on a man's artistic quality"

*B: 1851-1900*

because morality in art is not a problem of didacticism but "a demand for moral motive as the impelling power of human action." *See* B180 and B181.

B73    BATES, KATHERINE LEE. *American Literature*. New York: Mac-millan, 1897.
        Romantic biography.

B74    BENSON, E. "Poe and Nathaniel Hawthorne," *Galaxy*, VI (Dec. 1868), 742-8.
        Reviews the relationship between Poe, Chivers and Baudelaire. Unsympathetic to Poe.

B75    BENTON, JOEL. *In the Poe Circle*. New York: M. F. Mansfield and A. Wessells, 1899.
        Reviews the relationship between Poe and Chivers and Baudelaire. Unsympathetic to Poe.

B76    _____. "Was Poe a Plagiarist?" *Forum*, XXIII (May 1897), 363-72.
        Discussion of Chivers' charges of plagiarism. Poe created fine poetry out of Chivers' ideas.

B77    BOYD, ANDREW K. H. "Edgar Allan Poe," *Fraser's*, LV, 684. Reprinted in LLA, LIV (Jul. 1857), 150-64; and in *The Critical Essays of A Country Parson*. London, 1867.
        Error-ridden biography, interrupted by a lecture on alcoholism. Despite his wretched life, Poe produced excellent poetry and short stories. "Principle he seems to have had none. Decision of character was entirely lacking. His envy of those more favored by fortune than himself amounted to raging ferocity. He starved his wife and broke her heart."

B78    BRIGGS, CHARLES F. "The Personality of Poe," Ind, XXIX (Dec. 13, 1877), 1-2.
        Briggs concedes that "as a literary artist [Poe] is entitled to rank among the greatest of American writers, if not of contemporary writers in the English language." On the other hand, Poe was treacherous, insincere, insensitive to moral obligations, disloyal and aimless.

B79    BROWNE, IRVING. "Concerning the New Poe," Cr, XXVI, ns. XXIII (Jan. 26, 1895), 66.
        Brief note on Poe's corrupt life and the Stone-Kimball edition of his work.

B80  BROWNE, WILLIAM H.  "Poe's *Eureka* and Recent Science Specu-
     lation," SM-NEM, V (Aug. 1869), 190-9.
          Compares theories in *Eureka* with contemporary scientific
     theories advanced in W. R. Grove's *On the Correlation of
     Physical Forces* (1865); Faraday's *Some Thoughts on the
     Conversion of Force*; Dr. Winslow's *Force and Nature* (1869);
     and Hirn's *Consequences philosophiques et metaphysiques de
     la Thermodynamique* (1868).  Concludes that "at every point
     we meet the ideas of Poe, arising independently in the minds
     of thinkers furnished with all the lights of later dis-
     coveries."

B81  _____.  "The Works of Edgar Allan Poe," SM-NEM, XVI (Jun. 1875),
     640-50.
          Favorable review of Ingram's edition.  Agrees that Poe
     was "proud, sensitive, and sometimes unreasonable," that
     he was an alcoholic and a victim of occasional insanity,
     but there was nothing truly disgraceful in his life.

B82  BRYANT, WILLIAM CULLEN.  *Baltimore Sun* (Jan. 17, 1909).
          Reprints Bryant's refusal to write a favorable notice
     about Poe (letter to Miss Sara Sigourney Rice, Nov. 6,
     1865).  "My difficulty arises from the personal character
     of Edgar A. Poe of which I have in my time heard too
     much to be able to join in paying especial honor to his
     memory.  Persons younger than myself who have heard less
     of the conduct to which I refer may take a different view
     of the matter, and certainly I do not intend to censure
     them for doing so.  I think...that there should be some
     decided element of goodness in the character of those to
     whom a public monument directs the attention of the world."

B83  BURR, C. CHAUNCEY.  "The Character of Edgar Allan Poe," NC, V
     (Feb. 1852), 19-33.
          Very favorable account of Poe as an affectionate son and
     solicitous husband, with some letters to Mrs. Clemm as
     proof.

B84  BURROUGHS, JOHN.  "Mr. Gosse's Puzzle over Poe," *Dial*, XV
     (Oct. 16, 1893), 214-20.  Reply to B121.
          Attributes the American rejection of Poe to the in-
     humanity and artificiality of his poetry and his failure
     to capture even "one flash of the universal mind."  Little
     wonder that he is dismissed in favor of the New England
     poets, who have "helped enrich and ennoble human life; the
     world is fairer, life is sweeter, because they lived and
     sang; character, heroism, truth, courage, devotion, count

for more since Emerson and Longfellow and Whitman and Lowell were inspired by these themes."

B85 CHIVERS, THOMAS HOLLY. "Letters from the North," *Georgia Citizen* (Oct. 1851).

Second charge that Poe plagiarized from Chivers' "To Allegra Florence in Heaven" and "Lament on the Death of My Mother."

B86 _____. "Poe's Plagiarism," *Waverly*, VII (Jul. 30, Aug. 13, Aug. 20, Sept. 10, Oct. 1, Oct. 8, 1853), 73, 105, 120, 168-9, 216, 233.

Under various pseudonyms (such as "Felix Forresti" and "Fiat Justitia") Chivers charges Poe with plagiarizing from his poetry. Several letters to the magazine defend Poe. *See* B76.

B87 CODY, SHERWIN. *Four Famous American Writers*. New York: Werner School Books, 1899.

B88 COLE, SAMUEL V. "Stedman and Poe Again," Cr, VII (Nov. 28, 1885), 257.

Continues the argument about "The slender body of [Poe's] poetical remains." *See* B221 and B231.

B89 COOKE, JOHN E. *Poe as a Literary Critic*. Edited with introduction by N. Bryllion Fagin. Baltimore: Johns Hopkins Press, 1946.

Cooke's essay, rejected by SUM and GLB, pictures Poe as a greedy, envious man, out to destroy other writers. "He did not confine himself to this high ground of letters, but descended into the valley to busy himself with...petty spites and rivalries...."

B90 CURTIS, GEORGE. HW, IV (Mar. 17, 1860), 163.

Very favorable review of Whitman's *Edgar Allan Poe and his Critics,* with a prayer that when we die, "some hand as firm and gentle as this may pull away the briers to plant rosemary where we lie." *See* B246.

B91 CURTIS, WILLIAM O. "Edgar Allan Poe," *American Catholic Quarterly Review*, XVI (Oct. 1891), 818-33.

After a romanticized and melancholy biography, Curtis describes "The Raven" as "a masterpiece of seriogrotesque poetry: the protesque element being introduced with the most consummate artistic judgement in such a manner as not to clash with the spirit of profound melancholy which pervades the poem...."

*B: 1851-1900*

B92    CURWEN, HENRY.  "Edgar Allan Poe," *Sorrow and Song*.  London:
       H. S. King, 1875, 93-169.
           Inaccurate biography.

B93    CUTLER, S. P.  "Poe's *Eureka* Reconsidered," SM-NEM, V (Nov.
       1869), 533-8.
           "Scientific" disagreement with Poe's theories in *Eureka*.

B94    DALBY, JOHN WATSON.  "Edgar Allan Poe, A Vindication," *St.
       James*, XXXVI (Aug. 1876), 473-87.  Reply by Ingram, XXXVII
       (1876), 331.
           Biographical notice.

B95    DAVIDSON, I. W.  "Edgar Allan Poe," *Russell's*, II (Nov. 1857),
       161-73.
           Lengthy, somewhat hysterical essay in which tentative
       psychological insights into Poe's work are obscured by the
       critic's phrenological approach: "The central region of his
       brain was markedly deficient, although the occipital was
       full.  The basilar region, again, was powerful, but the
       coronal feeble....His heroes are monstrous reflections
       his own heart in its despair, not its peace."

B96    DIDIER, EUGENE.  "An Early Poem by Edgar Allan Poe," Scrib,
       X (Sept. 1875), 608.
           Reprint of the manuscript of "Alone."

B97    _____.  "Poe--Real and Reputed," GLB, CXXVIII (Apr. 1894),
       452-55.
           "...Poe was a most refined and cultured gentleman, whose
       friends were the purest and loveliest ladies in the land--
       a man whose society was sought by all who admired genius
       and pitied the misfortune that often attends it."  Didier
       repudiates Griswold, Gilfillan and Boyd.

B98    _____.  "Poe's Female Friends," Chaut, XV (Sept. 1892), 723-9.
           Discussion of Poe's relations with Mrs. Allan, Helen
       Stannard, Virginia ("He was seldom away from home for an
       hour, unless his darling Virginia or Mrs. Clemm was with
       him.") and Mrs. Whitman ("The woman he most passionately
       loved").

B99    _____.  "Portraits of Edgar Allan Poe," LW (Boston), XVI (Mar.
       7, 1885), 81-3.
           Discusses daguerreotypes and photographs of Poe--
       especially their treatment of his forehead.

B100   _____.  "Recent Biographies of Edgar Allan Poe," IR, X (1881),
       26-36.
           Reviews biographies of Poe by Gill and Ingram.

# Edgar Allan Poe: An Annotated Bibliography

*B: 1851-1900*

B101 DIMMOCK, THOMAS. "Notes on Poe," Cen, L, ns. XXVIII (June 1895), 315-16.
Discussion of a daguerreotype of Poe with brief reminiscence by John R. Thompson.

B102 DUGDALE, JENNIE B. "The Grave of Edgar Allan Poe," PL, XI (Oct. 1899), 583-8.

B103 DUYCKINCK, EVERET A. *Cyclopaedia of American Literature*. II, Philadelphia: Wm. Rutter and Co., 1856.
Poe's stories "are expressions of the disappointment and despair of the soul, alienated from happy human relations," and grew out of "pain, suffering, and...[a] prodigal expense of human nature, of broken hopes, and bitter experiences...."

B104 ELLIS, T. H. "Edgar Allan Poe," *Richmond Standard* (May 1889).

B105 ENGLISH, THOMAS DUNN. "Reminiscences," Ind, XLVIII (Oct. 15, 22, 29; Nov. 5, 1896), 1-2, 3-4, 4, 4-5.
Personal defense against attacks by Woodberry and Ingram and brief discussions of Poe's last days with the BJ, his association with Burton and Graham, his drunkenness, and his indiscretions with women.

B106 FAIRFIELD, FRANCIS. "A Madman of Letters," Scrib, X (Oct. 1875), 690-99.
Discusses the possibility that Poe had inherited "cerebral epilepsy...sudden attacks of the maniacal type, without contemporaneous convulsions...." and that many of his later tales are "based upon the hallucinations incident to that malady...." "FHU," for example, traces symptoms and delusions concomitant to epilepsy and could not have been written by someone who did not suffer from the disease.

B107 FIELD, EUGENE, ed. *Some Letters of Edgar Allan Poe to E. H. N. Patterson of Oquawka, Illinois*. Chicago: The Caxton Club, 1898.

B108 FISHER, MARY. *A General Survey of American Literature*. Chicago: A. C. McClurg, 1899, 231-60.
Objective though superficial essay which regards him as a victim of an inherited morbidity that led to revolt and emotionalism.

B109 FLESHER, HELEN G. "Literary Workers of the Pacific Coast," *Munsey's*, XV (Apr. 1896), 100.
Note suggesting similarities between Ambrose Bierce and Poe.

*B: 1851-1900*

B110 FLETCHER, J. B. "Poe, Hawthorne and Morality," *Harvard Monthly*, III (Feb. 1887), 176-81.
     Compares the writers in terms of their "extensive use of the weird and horrible." Applying to their work the theory that "the repulsive which makes for right conduct is alone permissable in literature," he concludes that Poe's work is inferior to Hawthorne's because it lacks intellectual and spiritual content, moral purpose and human sympathy.

B111 FOWLER, LORENZO. *Illustrated Phrenological Almanac for 1851.* New York: 24-25.
     Includes a study of Poe.

B112 _____. *Lectures.* London, 1862.
     Poe "was wanting in Firmness, Self-Esteem, Continuity, and in the basilar brain and vital power."

B113 FRUIT, JOHN PHELPS. *The Mind and Art of Poe's Poetry.* New York: A. S. Barnes, 1899.
     The theme of Poe's poetry is the luxury of sorrow.

B114 GIBSON, THOMAS W. "Poe at West Point," <u>HNMM</u>, XXXV (Oct. and Nov. 1867), 754-6.
     Recalls that Poe impressed most cadets favorably.

B115 GILBERT, FRANK. *American Literature.* Chicago: Fairbanks, Palmer and Co., 1882.
     Brief and uninformative.

B116 GILFILLAN, GEORGE. <u>Cr</u>. Reprinted in <u>LLA</u>, XLI, Fifth Series V, (Apr. 1854), 166-71; <u>SLM</u>, XX (Apr. 1854), 249-53; and *A Third Gallery of Portraits.* New York: 1855, 325-38.
     Among worthless poets, Poe "was probably <u>the</u> most worthless and wicked....His heart was as rotten as his conduct was infamous." The <u>SLM</u> deleted the biographical portion of the slanderous essay, charging that it was needlessly unjust but admitting that "little, unhappily, can be said in defense of the dead poet." In the critical section, Gilfillan implies that Poe broke Virginia's heart, "that he might write *Annabel Lee* and *The Raven*," finds similarities between his work and that of Coleridge and Brown and admires his power of analysis.

B117 GILL, WILLIAM F. "Edgar Allan Poe After Fifty Years," *Arena*, XXII (Oct. 9, 1899), 526-9.
     Brief discussion of Griswold's charge that Poe was an alcoholic and a reprint of Poe's letter to Snodgrass about his drinking problems.

*B: 1851-1900*

B118 _____. "Edgar Allan Poe and his Biographer: Rufus W. Griswold," *Lotos Leaves*. New York: R. Worthington, 1882, 279-306.
Indictment of Griswold which exposes his errors.

B119 _____. *The Life of Edgar Allan Poe*. London: Chatto and Windus, 1878.
Overwhelmingly biased in Poe's favor.

B120 _____. "Some New Facts about Edgar Allan Poe," *Laurel Leaves*. Boston: William F. Gill, 1876, 359-88.
The facts are no longer new.

B121 GOSSE, EDMOND. <u>Cr</u>, III (1893). Reprinted in *Questions at Issue*. New York, 1893, 88-90.
Concerns the "extraordinary and sinister" omission of Poe's work from a list of Ten Best American Books, "While every year sheds more luster on the genius of Poe among the most weighty critical authorities of England, of France, of Germany, of Italy, in his own country prejudice is still... rampant....it makes one wonder what is the standard of American style." *See* reply in B84.

B122 GOSTWICK, J. W. *Handbook of American Literature*. London, 1856.
Questions Griswold's fairness.

B123 GOVE-NICHOLS, MARY. "Reminiscences of Edgar Poe," *Sixpenny Magazine*, XX (Feb. 1863). Reprinted in Woodberry's *Life of Poe*.
Brief discussion of several meetings between Poe and the author.

B124 GRAHAM, GEORGE R. "The Genius and Characteristics of the Late Edgar Allan Poe," <u>Gr</u>, XLIV (Feb. 1854), 216-25.
Defense of Poe against Griswold's party. Readers should not confuse Poe's life, admittedly "a piteous, a deplorable, a shocking spectacle," with his art. Among other virtues, his work reveals "earnestness of manner, an intensity of conviction," which moves the reader, "management of the supernatural never attained or approached by any other writer," and an articulateness "which we shall seek in vain in any other American, if not English writer."

B125 GRISWOLD, HATTY. "Edgar Allan Poe," *Home Life of Great Authors*. Chicago: A. C. McClurg, 1887, 312-22.
No new information.

*B: 1851-1900*

B126 GRISWOLD, RUFUS WILMOT. *Poets and Poetry of America.*
Eleventh Edition. Philadelphia: A. Hart, 1852.
Brief, objective biography, with some errors, followed
by an evaluation of Poe's poetry. "In poetry, as in prose,
he is most successful in the metaphysical treatment of the
passions. His poems are constructed with wonderful ingenuity and finished with consummate art. They illustrate a
morbid sensitiveness of feeling, a shadowy and gloomy
imagination...."

B127 HALE, EDWARD EVERETT. "Mr. John Burroughs on Poe," *Dial*, XV
(Nov. 1893), 254.
Rejects Burroughs' thesis that thought is more important
than form in art, but argues that Poe's opposite theory is
equally unhealthy for literature. *See* B84.

B128 HARRINGTON, H. F. "Not to be Apotheosized," Cr, VII (Oct. 3,
1885), 157-8.
Any attempt to vindicate Poe of charges of immorality,
especially those by Minto in *The Encyclopedia Britannica,*
is an example of the American tendency "to make the culture
of the intellect paramount to the activity of the moral
sense."

B129 HART, JOHN S. *A Manual of American Literature.* Philadelphia:
Eldredge and Brother, 1872.
Poe's drunkenness interfered with his creative abilities.

B130 HAWTHORNE, JULIAN and LEONARD LEMMON. *American Literature: a
Textbook For the Use of Schools and Colleges.* Boston:
D. C. Heath, 1891, 58-62.
Brief biography for young students describes Poe as a
weak and vain man "neither more nor less than insane,
though, of course, such insanity was entirely consistent
with right-mindedness in matters removed from the sphere
...of his daily existence." His style was artificial and
without taste, and his stories cross the line from the
"legitimately horrible" to the revolting.

B131 HAWTHORNE, JULIAN. "My Adventures with Edgar Allan Poe,"
Lipp, XLVIII (1891), 240-6.
Imaginary meeting with Poe.

B132 HERVEY, JOHN L. "Is Poe Rejected in America?" *Dial*, XXVI
(Feb. 1, 1899), 73.
Reply to Moore essay. The recent editions of Poe's
work, the widespread teaching of "The Raven," and the
attraction of elocutionists to "The Bells" are evidence

that Poe is not ignored in America. "If the acceptance of
Poe is in any way doubtful, it is not because of the antique
Poe legends...but because of the apotheosis of the 'grotesque and arabesque,' miasmas of the pit and the charnel
house, the ghastly light of the baleful planets from which
the work of Poe--the name of Poe--may never be dissociated
....it would be strange indeed if Poe the man were ever to
escape from the atmosphere of Poe the artist." *See* B180
and B181.

B133 HIGGINSON, THOMAS WENTWORTH. "Edgar Allan Poe," *Short Stories
of American Authors*. Boston: Lee and Shepard, 1879; originally published in LW (1879). Reprinted in CJ16.
   Brief comparison of Poe with Hawthorne mentions the low
moral tone of Poe's work and his vacilating critical judgment. "No one ever did more than Poe to lower the tone of
literary criticism in this country...." As a short story
writer he penetrated "the artistic indifference of the
French mind," but his work is disfigured by inequalities
and imitations.

B134 _____. "Recent Works on Edgar Allan Poe," *Nation,* XXXI (Nov.
18, 1880), 360-1.
   Uncomplimentary review of the Ingram biography with
praise for the Stedman biography and Stoddard's edition of
Poe's works.

B135 _____. "Woodberry's Life of Poe," *Nation,* XL (Feb. 19, 1885),
157-8.
   Objects to mixing criticism with biography and feels
that Woodberry overemphasized Poe's role as a critic.

B136 HOPKINS, FRED M. "Poe's Fordham Cottage," *American* Bkm, II
(Aug. 1895), 14.
   Concerning the purchase of the cottage by the Shake-
speare Society of New York.

B137 HOWE, MARK A DeWOLFE. "Edgar Allan Poe," Bkm, V (May 1897),
205-16.
   A glance at "the conspicuous events of his ill-
controlled life."

B138 HUNT, LEIGH. NBR, XVII (Aug. 1852), 222-4.
   Essay on Longfellow, Read, Poe and Bryant, "the very
best blossoms out of the garden...of American verse."
America has exceeded England in producing "respectable
versifiers," but her poets are "deficient in the 'faculty
divine,' which shews us thoughts, and feelings, and facts

from a totally new point of view...." They have produced only "repetitions--which are not necessarily imitations-- of first rate original poetry."

B139 HUNTER, WILLIAM E. "Poe and his English Schoolmaster," Ath, 2660 (Oct. 19, 1878), 496-7.
Brief biography of Branly and denial that he is the schoolmaster in "WW."

B140 HURD, C. O. "The Logic of Poe's 'Murders'," *Harvard Monthly*, I (1885), 7-10.
Exposes errors in the story: the witnesses should be- lieve that the murderer is speaking their language and that they can not understand the words; the "gens d'armes" should not have suggested the suicide; and "the author's reasons for denying the possibility of a motive for the murder are insufficient."

B141 HURTON, RICHARD. "Poe's Last Poem, 'Lilitha'," *Southern Bivouac*, V (Jun. 1886), 66.
"Lilitha" is a fraud.

B142 INGRAM, JOHN H. Ath, 2606 (Oct. 6, 1877), 426-7.
Discusses several errors in William Gill's *Life of Edgar Allan Poe*. *See* B119.

B143 _____. "The Bibliography of Edgar Allan Poe," Ath, 2544 (Jul. 29, 1876), 145-6.
Concerns rare editions of Poe's work.

B144 _____. "A Disclaimer," Ath, 2516 (Jan. 15, 1876), 89.
Reply to an allegation that he had used material from a lecture by W. F. Gill.

B145 _____. "Edgar Allan Poe," IR, II (Mar. 1875), 145-73.
Biography whitewashing Poe's character.

B146 _____. *Edgar Allan Poe: His Life, Letters and Opinions*. London: J. Hagg, 1860.
Once valuable because it contained previously unpub- lished documents relating to Poe, the biography is now interesting as one of the earliest serious efforts to redeem Poe's reputation.

B147 _____. "Edgar Allan Poe's Early Poems," GM, CCXXXVI, ns. XII (May 1874), 580-8.
Briefly discusses Poe's introduction to the 1831 *Poems*.

*B: 1851-1900*

B148   _____. "Edgar Poe," TB, XLI (Jun. 1874), 375-80. Reprinted in
B1        Ecl, LXXXIII, ns. XX (Aug. 1874).
          Biography, favorably disposed to Poe, charging Griswold
          with maliciousness.

B149   _____. "Edgar Poe and his Biographers," Acad, XXIV (1883), 248.
          Reprinted in TB, LXVIII (1883), 530.
          Defends himself against the attack on his biography in
          TB (Aug. 1883).

B150   _____. "Edgar Poe's 'Raven'," Ath, 2651 (Aug. 17, 1878),
          210.
          Ingram suggests that Albert Pike's "Isadore," New York
          *New Mirror* (Oct. 14, 1843), influenced "The Raven" and
          "Eulalie" and that *Barnaby Rudge* was another source of
          inspiration for Poe.

B151   _____. "The Lunar Hoax," Ath, 2547 (Aug. 19, 1876), 241-2.
          Concerning the influence of "Hans Pfaall" on the "Moon
          Hoax" by Richard Adams Locke.

B152   _____. "Poe's *Politian*," SM-NEM, XVII (Nov. 1875), 588-94.
          Summary of the play.

B153   _____. *"The Raven" With Literary and Historical Commentary.*
          London: George Redway, 1885.

B154   _____. "Recollections of Edgar Allan Poe," Ath, 3248 (Jan. 25,
          1890), 117.
          Regarding Howard Paul's error-ridden reminiscences of
          Poe in *Lambert's Monthly*, I (1890).

B155   _____. "Unknown Correspondence by Edgar Allan Poe," NQM, X
          (Apr. 1870), 1-30.

B156   _____. "Unknown Poetry of Edgar Allan Poe," *Belgravia*, XXIX
          (Jun. 1876), 502-13.
          Reprint of poetry from TOP.

B157   JAMES, HENRY. *Hawthorne.* New York: Harpers, 1879.
          "Poe's collection of critical sketches' of the
          American writers...is probably the most complete and ex-
          quisite specimen of provincialism ever prepared for the
          edification of men. Poe's judgments are pretentions,
          spiteful, vulgar; but they contain a great deal of sense
          and discrimination as well, and here and there, sometimes
          at frequent intervals, we find a phrase of happy insight
          imbedded in a patch of the most fatuous pedantry."

*B: 1851-1900*

B158 _____. "Review of 'Les Fleurs du Mal'," *Nation* (Apr. 27, 1876).
Reprinted in "Baudelaire," *French Poets and Novelists*. New
York and London: Macmillan, 1878. Reprinted in CJ16.
"With all due respect to the very ,original genius of the
author of the 'Tales of Mystery,' it seems to us that to
take him with more than a certain degree of seriousness is
to lack seriousness one's self. An enthusiasm for Poe is
the mark of a decidedly primitive stage of reflection."

B159 JAPP, A. H. "Edgar Allan Poe," BQR, LXII (Jul. 1875), 89-102.
Japp discusses Poe's drinking while accusing Griswold of
slander. In a critical section, he describes the "spirituality" of Poe's works, their "haunting horror," which
sometimes jars with the "clear and graceful music of the
form." Poe differed radically from Hawthorne, who manifests
a "healthy human religious faith" in men and the future.

B160 J.B.G."Poe and his Precursor, T. H. Chivers," Cr, XXX, ns.
XXVII (May 8, 1897), 327.
Chivers' poem "To Allegra Florence in Heaven" is a
source of "The Raven."

B161 JOHNSON, ROSSITER. "Tennyson, Poe, and Admiral Farragut," Cr,
XXI (Oct. 22, 1892), 224.
Brief note on Poe's attitude toward Tennyson in "The
Poetic Principle."

B162 J. R. Y. *Southern Opinion*. Richmond: Mar. 7, 1868.
Brief preface to "O, Tempora! O, Mores!" which the
author claims Poe wrote when he was seventeen.

B163 KENT, MARINER J. "Poe's Last Poem, 'Lilitha'," *Southern
Bivouac,* V (Oct. 1886), 298-9.
"Lilitha" is a fraud.

B164 LAMB, M. J. "Poe's House at Fordham," AppJ, XII (Jul. 18,
1874), 75-6.
Describes a trip to the cottage. Poe was "a man exces-
sively and essentially human, whose infirmities of character and disposition were the bane of his career, and the
occasion of all manner of glorious experiences."  ·

B165 LANG, ANDREW. "Introduction," *The Poems of Edgar Allan Poe*.
London, 1882.

B166 _____. "To Edgar Allan Poe," *Letters to Dead Authors*. London:
Longmans, 1886, 129-39.
Impressionistic remarks about Poe's poverty and hack work.

*B: 1851-1900*

B167 LATHROP, G. P. "Poe, Hawthorne, and Irving," <u>Scrib</u>, XI (Apr. 1876), 799-808.
"...the best of his stories are to the best of Hawthorne's short tales what the most delicate mechanism of metal springs is to an organism filled with the true breath of life." Poe is responsible for the "first agile and determined movement of criticism in this country," but his work is marred by his neurotic impulses and jealousies and conforms more to French than to American or English traditions of literature.

B168 LEA, HENRY C. *Nation*, XXXI (Dec. 9, 1880), 408.
The two hundred fifty copies of <u>TGA</u>, issued by Lea and Blanchard, were not sold out for three years.

B169 LIVINGSTON, LUTHER S. "First Books of Some American Authors," <u>Bkm</u>, VIII (Nov. 1, 1898), 232-4.
Facts about the publication of <u>TOP</u>.

B170 MABIE, HAMILTON W. "Edgar Allan Poe," *Outlook*, LXII (May 6, 1899), 51-62.
Poe's criticism has only historical interest. His reputation depends on his poetry, which completely embodies his aesthetic theory. He is "devoid of humor, that great human quality, which...flows through the greatest imaginative work." In short it fails to represent human life and experience.

B171 _____. "Poe's Place in American Literature," <u>Atl</u>, LXXXIV (Dec. 1899), 733-45.
Believes that Poe's greatest virtue was his detachment from "the time and place in which it made its appearance," a detachment which "was a positive gain for the emancipation of the imagination of the young country...." Like Hawthorne, Poe "gives expression to the ideality of the American mind" and to "the sombre and tragical aspects of experience." His work attests to the existence of "something divine and imperishable in the mind of man,--something which allies him with the creative energy and permits him to share it."

B172 MacKINTOSH, EMILY. "Homes of American Poets," *Peterson's*, XCI (Jan. 1887), 36-7.
Complete fiction.

B173 MANLY, LOUISE. *Southern Literature*. Richmond: B. F. Johnson, 1895.
School text.

B174   MATTHEWS, F. A.   "The Writings of Edgar Allan Poe," *Bachelor of Arts,* III (1896), 328-37.
   Valueless reminiscence.

B175   MAUDSLEY, HENRY, M.D.   "Edgar Allan Poe," *American Journal of Insanity,* XVII (Oct. 1860), 152-198.   Reprinted from *Journal of Mental Science* (Apr. 1860).
   Amusingly windy and impressionistic essay by the Medical Superintendent of The Manchester Royal Lunatic Hospital. Quotes Hawthorne on the subject of inherited moral weakness and concludes that Poe suffered from constitutional defects.

B176   MAULSBY, D. L.   "The Renascence of Poe," *Dial,* XVIII (Mar. 1895), 138-41.
   Brief review of Poe's poor reception in America and objective summary of his contribution to American literature. "...Poe's tales display the conceptions of an idealist, conveyed through the method of a realist." As a critic, "he had at heart the dignity and permanence of American letters." He possessed three characteristics of genius: "intensity, a junction at some point with the infinite, and permanence of power."

B177   MEEHYNS, L. R.   "Poe's Grave in Baltimore," C<u>r</u>, XXXIII (Jul. 1898), 39-45.
   The caretaker of the graveyard reminisces about Poe's funeral.

B178   MINTO, WILLIAM.   FortnR, XXXIV (Jul. 1880), 69.   Reprinted in LLA, CXLVI, Fifth Series XXXI (1880), 690-9; and E<u>cl</u>, XCV (1880), 270.
   Griswold's malicious rumors are difficult to discredit because they are consistent with the general tone of Poe's life. Poe was an "intellectual voluptuary" with a passion for analysis, who squandered his energies solving problems and reviewing second-rate books.

B179   MONROE, H.   "Life and Works," C<u>r</u>, XXVI (Jan. 5, 1895), 215-16.
   Review of Stedman-Woodberry edition of Poe's works. Poe "is the most lyric of our poets, one of the most precious of our literary possessions. His life, moreover, is typical of thousands of hidden tragedies which are continually destroying the flower of American manhood."

B180   MOORE, C. L.   "American Rejection of Edgar Allan Poe," *Dial,* XXVI (Jan. 1899), 40-2; (Apr. 1899), 236.
   Poe is unpopular in America because he was aloof, he indulged in irony, he had no sense of humor or knowledge of

human nature. As a critic of modern English and American masters, he was "almost infallible."

B181  _____. "American Rejection of Edgar Allan Poe," *Dial*, XXVI
B1 (Apr. 1899), 236.
    Answers criticism of his first article on Poe. Poe is not a great world poet, but "he is the most vital and universal force in letters American has yet produced." His poetry is equal in range and execution to Tennyson's, "and the underivable and daemonic spark burns brighter in Poe than in the English poet."

B182  MORAN, DR. JOHN J. *A Defense of Edgar Allan Poe*. Washington D.C.: Boogher, 1885.

B183  MORGAN, APPLETON. "The Personality of Poe," *Munsey's*, XVII (Jun. 1897), 522-30.
    Worthless essay with phrenological bias.

B184  MORSE, JAMES H. "Edgar Allan Poe," Cr, V (Nov. 15, 1884), 229-30.
    Review of Stoddard's edition of Poe's works which mentions Poe's ingenuity, the "growing emptiness of his heart, the grotesque tendency of his imagination, and its total lack of the bias of humanity." Poe lacks the power to draw his creations, "as Hawthorne did, into spiritual regions, for us to admire," or to bring them "home to our bosoms as beings whom we might love or hate."

B185  NELSON, WILLIAM. "Julius Rodman and his Journey: Notes on The Publication in Burton's *Gentleman's Magazine*, " MAH, XXV (Mar. 1891), 255-6.
    Brief history of the story's publication.

B186  NEWCOMER, A. G. "Mr. Sartain and Poe," *Dial*, XXVII (Dec. 16, 1899), 482.
    Note on an error in Angier's review. *See* B66.

B187  NICHOL, JOHN. *American Literature*. Edinburgh: A. and C. Black, 1882.
    Very brief reference.

B188  NOBLE, JAMES A. NQM, VIII (Jul. 1877), 410-27.

B189  ONDERDONK, JAMES L. "Edgar Allan Poe and the Brownings," *Dial*, XIV (Jun. 16, 1893), 353-5.
    Poe's attitude toward Mrs. Browning and the subtle influence of her poetry on "The Raven."

*B: 1851-1900*

B190     \_\_\_\_. "The Lyric Poet of America," *Mid-Continent*, VI (Jun. 1895), 166-73.
    Romantic biography, which emphasizes the narrowness of Poe's work and his themes of destruction and sentience. Within the narrow range, Poe's work is peerless.

B191 O'SULLIVAN, VINCENT. Introduction to *The Raven and The Pit and the Pendulum*. London: Chiswick Press, 1899.
    Poe drank to deaden his feelings of superiority. In addition, drinking protected him against loneliness and the vulgarity of others. "The keystone of Poe's character was his hatred of humanity....Poe, since he could not be an Emperor, went through life solitary, proud, and disconnec-ted, having really...little to do with the community of the earth...."

B192 PAGE, THOMAS NELSON. "Authorship in the South before the War," Lipp, XLIV (Jul. 1889), 112-15.
    Poe's poetry is distinctly Southern in coloring, tone, temper and setting, and is completely original. As a critic, he "installed a new era in criticism" and "lifted literary criticism from the abasement of snivelling imbecility into which it had sunk...[to] a basis founded on the principles of analysis, philosophy and art." Concludes that Poe is the finest writer produced by the Old South.

B193 PANCOAST, HENRY S. *An Introduction to American Literature*. New York: Henry Holt, 1898, 262-74.
    Poe's criticism is of little importance. He was not a scholar, he was involved in petty jealousies, and his poetry is shallow, theatrical and mechanical.

B194 PATTERSON, JOHN. "Some Lyrics of Anacreon or 'Pseudo-Anacreon'," PL, IX (1897), 403.
    The Lyrics are a source of "The Raven."

B195 PAUL, HOWARD. "Recollections of Edgar Allan Poe," *Munsey's*, VII (Aug. 1892), 554-8. Reprinted from *Lambert's Monthly*, I (1890).

B196 PECK, G. W. "Mere Music," LW, L (Mar. 9, 1850), 225-6.

B197 PURVES, JAMES. "Edgar Allan Poe," DUM, LXXXV (Mar. 1875), 336-51.
    Favorable review of Ingram's biography pictures Poe as maligned by jealous, vicious, vengeful critics. "He stood alone, like a church, rich in architecture and noble in appearance, standing off the street of monotonous houses."

B: *1851-1900*

B198   _____. "Edgar Allan Poe's Works," <u>DUM</u>, LXXXVI (Sept. 1875),
B      296-306.
       "Taken altogether, Poe is the most remarkable genius
       that America has yet given birth to.....Many authors have
       excelled him in several departments, but not one has come
       near to him as a poet, a tale writer, an essayist, and a
       critic combined....He is perhaps the greatest universal
       American genius," more powerful than Longfellow, Hawthorne,
       and Lowell.

B199   QUILLER-COUCH, A. T.  "Parodies," <u>Bkm</u>, VII (Aug. 1898), 477.
       Parody of Poe's poetry.

B200   RANKING, B. M.  *Time Monthly Magazine,* VIII (Sept. 1883), 352-
       60.
       Somewhat vague, disorganized essay on Poe's short stories.

B201   REID, CPT. MAYNE.  "A Dead Man Defended," *Onward,* I (Apr.
       1869).

B202   RICE, SARA, ed.  *Edgar Allan Poe, A Memorial Volume.* Baltimore:
       Turnbull Bros., 1877.

B203   RICHARDSON, CHARLES.  "Edgar Allan Poe," *American Literature:
       1607-1885.*  New York: G. P. Putnam's Sons, 1889, 97-137.
       Poe's theme is the eternity of the soul.

B204   ROBERTSON, JOHN.  "Edgar Allan Poe," *Our Corner,* VI (1885),
       154-62, 204-13, 303-10, 346-57.
       Favorable biography with vindication of Poe and general
       discussion of his poetry and prose.

B205   ROSENTHAL, LEWIS.  "Poe Parisian," <u>Cr</u>, V (Jul. 26, 1884), 46-7.
       Poe belonged to Paris, in the environment of an old
       civilization.

B206   SALT, H. S.  "Edgar Allan Poe's Writings," *Progress* (Jul.
       1887).  Reprinted in *Literary Sketches.* London: Swan,
       Sonnenschein, Lowrey, 1888, 104-23.
       Poe's work has value despite its morbidity and narrow
       range.

B207   SARTAIN, J.  "Reminiscences of Edgar Allan Poe," <u>Lipp</u>, XLIII
       (1889), 411-15.
       Explanation of Stoddard's remark that "The Bells" was
       sold three times before it appeared in <u>SUM</u> or <u>GLB</u> and a
       discussion of Poe's confessions that people were plotting
       to kill him over "a woman trouble" and that he had once
       been in Moyamensing Prison.

B208  SCHIPPEN, E.  "Some American Magazine Writers," <u>GLB</u>, CXVI (Apr. 1888), 329-31.
Brief note regarding a new anthology.

B209  SEARS, LORENZO.  *American Literature in the Colonial and National Periods*.  Boston:  E. Benjamin Andrews, 1899, 251-65.
General essay.

B210  SHELDON, CAROLINE.  "Poe's Rejection in America," *Dial*, XXVI (Feb. 16, 1899), 110.
Answers Moore's articles.  Poe had great powers, a "weird and powerful imagination, constructive ability, and exquisite melody of expression."  But his work is shallow.  He fails to "voice in some effective manner the feelings and thoughts common to humanity."  *See* B180 and B181.

B211  SIZER, NELSON.  *How to Study Strangers by Temperament, Face and Head*.  New York, 1895, 83.
Phrenological study of Poe.

B212  SMILES, SAMUEL.  "Edgar Allan Poe," *Brief Biographies*.  Boston: James R. Osgood, 1876.
Focuses on Poe's alcoholism.

B213  SMITH, C. ALPHONSO.  "Repitition in the Poems of Edgar Allan Poe," *Repitition and Parallelism in English Verse*.  New York: University Publishing Co., 1894.

B214  SMITH, E. OAKES.  "Edgar Allan Poe, Autobiographic Notes," *Beadle's*, III (Feb. 1867), 147-56.
Mrs. Seba Smith whitewashes Poe's character by denying that he drank and by revising the story of his death: "At the instigation of a woman, who considered herself injured by him, he was cruelly beaten, blow upon blow, by a ruffian who knew of no better mode of avenging supposed injuries. It is well known that a brain fever followed...."

B215  SMITH, G. BARNETT.  "The Works of Poe," *Tinsley's*, XXVIII (Jan. 1881), 15-32.
Generally favorable biographical and critical essay. Poe's range was narrow and his genius restricted.  But he had genuine inspiration, and his poetry is as musical as Shelley's.

B216  SMYTH, ALBERT.  "Edgar Allan Poe and other Southern Writers," *American Literature*.  Philadelphia: Eldredge and Brother, 1889, 127-33.
Text-book type review.

B217    _____. *The Philadelphia Magazines and Their Contributors:*
        *1741-1850.* Philadelphia: Robert M. Lindsay, 1892.
            Occasional mention of Poe in connection with Philadelphia
        magazines, especially <u>Gr</u>.

B218   SNODGRASS, DR. J. E.   "Facts of Poe's Death and Burial,"
        *Beadle's,* III (Mar. 1867), 283-7.
            Repudiates Mrs. Smith's story and discusses his own
        participation in the events preceding Poe's death. *See* B214.

B219    _____. "Poe-Snodgrass Correspondence," *Baltimore American*
        (Apr. 1881).

B220   SPENCER, EDWARD, ed.   "Poe-Snodgrass Correspondence," *New York*
        *Herald* (Mar. 27, 1881).

B221   STEDMAN, E. CLARENCE.   "Edgar Allan Poe," *Poets of America.*
        Boston:  Houghton Mifflin, 1885, 225-72.

B222    _____. <u>Scrib</u>, XX (May 1880), 107-24.  Reprinted as Introduction
        to his 1880 edition of Poe's works.
            Probably the most comprehensive essay on Poe before 1900.
        Discusses Poe's capricious personality, his drinking habits,
        and the quality of his imagination.  Poe's poetry is ex-
        quisitely lyrical, but he is a "poet of a single mood,"
        who depends too much on metrical devices.  As a short story
        writer, he was with Hawthorne "the last of the romancers,"
        though the New Englander had profounder insights and wrote
        superior prose.  Not a humorist, Poe had great powers of
        irony and satire and made the most out of the romantic
        traditions of the South.  Stedman accepts him "whether as
        poet or romancer, as a pioneer of the art of feeling in
        American literature."

B223   STEVENSON, ROBERT LOUIS.   "The Works of Edgar Allan Poe,"
        <u>Acad</u>, VII (Jan. 2, 1875), 1-2.
            Objects to Poe's portrait, his character and his last
        stories, which he finds "ill-conceived and written care-
        lessly."  In his earlier stories, where horror serves a
        creative purpose, Poe captured perfectly "that region be-
        tween sanity and madness."  The most important question is
        why such subjects interested Poe at all.

B224   STODDARD, RICHARD HENRY.   "Edgar Allan Poe," <u>HNMM</u>, XLV (Sept.
        1872), 557-68.
            Error-filled, angry biography which repeats and em-
        bellishes most of Griswold's slanders.

*B: 1851-1900*

B225   \_\_\_\_. "Edgar Allan Poe," <u>Lipp</u>, XLIII (1889), 107-15.
      Reminiscence of his first meeting with Poe, whom he des-
cribes as "a curious compound of the charlatan and the
courtly gentleman," dishonest and unscrupulous. As a poet,
he was influenced by Coleridge, Scott and Byron, and as a
prose writer, by Brown, Godwin, Hoffmann, and Hawthorne.

B226   \_\_\_\_. "Edgar Allan Poe," *National Magazine,* II (Apr. 1853),
193-200.
      "The radical depravity of a simply analytical mind, the
misfortunes of a broken life, made Poe sometimes a drunkard
....A single glass of wine would intoxicate him; he has
even been known to have been intoxicated by strong coffee."
Much of his poetry is unreadable. In fact, his school of
literature, which is traceable to Goethe, Schiller, Kotze-
bue, Mrs. Radcliff, George Sand, and Hawthorne, "is one
that we thoroughly dislike."

B227   \_\_\_\_. "A Great Man Self-Wrecked," *National Magazine,* I (Oct.
1852), 362-5.
      Fictitious account of Poe's dissipations. "One morning,
the American Minister at St. Petersburgh was summoned to
save a countryman...from the penalties incurred through a
drunken debauch. He came in time to rescue our prodigal
from a prison; and through his influence he was set at
liberty, and enabled to return to the United States."

B228 STUART, ESME and A. LEROY. "Charles Baudelaire and Edgar
Allan Poe," <u>NC</u>, XXXIV (Jul. 1893), 65-80. Reprinted in <u>LLA</u>,
CXCVIII, Fifth Series, LXXXIII (Sept. 16, 1893), 692-703.
      Sympathetic biographies of the two writers to show simi-
larities in their lives and ideas, with a brief discussion
of Poe's influence on the French writer.

B229 SWIGGETT, G. L. "Poe and Recent Poetics," <u>SR</u>, VI (1898), 150-
66.
      Somewhat rambling discussion of Poe's extensive influ-
ence on the Symbolists or Neo-Romanticists.

B230 SWINBURNE, ALGERNON CHARLES. "Letter to Sara Sigourney Rice,"
*New York Daily Tribune* (Nov. 27, 1875), 4. Reprinted in
CJ16.
      On Poe's deserved popularity in England and France.

B231 TABB, JOHN B. "Mr. Stedman's Estimate of Poe," <u>Cr</u>, VII (Nov.
31, 1885), 247.
      Objects to Stedman's remark in *Poets of America* that Poe
can not be considered a great poet because his output is
slender.

*B: 1851-1900*

B232  TALLEY-WEISS, SUSAN ARCHER.  "Last Days of Poe," Scrib, XV
      (Mar. 1878), 707-16.
          Speaks of Poe's kindness and gentleness and asks that
      "more than customary allowance" be made for his faults, in
      view of the "unfavorable circumstances surrounding him from
      his very birth."

B233  THOMAS, M.  *Train*, III (Apr. 1857), 193-8.
          Expresses suspicion of Griswold's biography.

B234  THOMPSON, JOHN R.  "'The Raven' by Edgar Allan Poe," SLM, XXV
      (Nov. 1857), 331-5.
          The poem is a picture of "a man, distracted by grief,
      disordered by long watching, and wild imaginings, wrought
      upon by strange and weird appearances, [who] believes him-
      self in communion with a supernatural being, [and] seeks to
      discover his fate (and that of another dearer to himself)
      in the world to come...."  Two sources of the poem are
      "Noctes Abrosianae," Bl, XLI (Mar. 1829) and Elizabeth
      Barrett Browning's "Lady Geraldine's Courtship."

B235  _____.  "Reminiscences of Poe," Cen., L, ns. XXVIII (Jun. 1895),
      316.
          Editor of SLM recalls his association with Poe in 1848.

B236  TINNON, J. A.  "Poe's 'Ulalume'," Gr, XXXVIII (Feb. 1851), 120-
      2.
          Suggests a correspondence between Poe's poem and Byron's
      "Manfred."

B237  TOLMAN, ALBERT.  "Was Poe Mathematically Correct?" *Dial*, XXVI
      (Mar. 16, 1899), 189-90.
          Shows that measurements in "The Gold Bug" are incorrect.
      *See* CK350.

B238  VAN CLEEF, AUGUSTUS.  "Poe's Mary," HNMM, LXXVIII (Mar. 1889),
      634-40.
          Interview with woman who claimed to have been engaged to
      Poe before he married Virginia.

B239  VICTOR, O. J.  "Some Words of Some Authors," *Ladies' Reposi-
      tory*, XVII (Jun. 1857), 334-36.
          One line note on Poe's "principle of unexpectedness."

B240  WALLACE, HORACE BURNEY.  *Literary Criticisms and Other Papers*.
      Philadelphia:  Parry and McMillan, 1856.
          Praises Poe as an unrivalled critic and short story
      writer.

*B: 1851-1900*

B241 WALLER, W. F. N&Q, V (May 12, 1894), 366.
A source of "Murders" is a story about a monkey's rob-
bery which appeared in *The Annual Register of the Year 1834.*

B242 WATKINS, MILDRED CABELL. *American Literature.* New York:
Literature Primers Series, American Book Co., 1894.
Childish essay on Poe's life and work. Accounts for his
"fickleness, his ugly humor, and his lies" by the fact that
"his imagination was out of proportion to all his other
faculties."

B243 WATTS, THEODORE. "Edgar Poe," Ath, 2549 (Sept. 2, 1876),
306.
Lines from "Eulalie" were borrowed from "Rejected Addresses" (both poems use the word "stagnant"); the source
of "PP" is Mudford's "The Iron Shroud"; and NAGP was inspired by "The Rime of the Ancient Mariner" and "The
Lonely Man of the Ocean," *Monthly Magazine,* LXI.

B244 WELLS, SAMUEL R. *New Physiognomy, or Signs of Characters as
Manifested through Temperament and External Form.* New York,
1875, 527.

B245 WHIBLEY, CHARLES. "Edgar Allan Poe," *New Review* XIV (Jun.
1896), 612-25.
Whibley attacks Poe's maligners and praises his stories
for their originality and ingenuity. He believes, however,
that Poe's impulsive writing methods reduced near master-
pieces to "the lower level of journalism."

B246 WHITMAN, SARAH HELEN. *Edgar Poe and His Critics.* New York,
1860. Reprinted with Introduction and Notes by Oral
Sumner Coad, New Brunswick, 1949.
Defense of Poe against critics, particularly Griswold.
Mrs. Whitman is unabashedly biased in Poe's favor.

B247 _____. *New York Tribune* (Oct. 1875).

B248 WHITMAN, WALT. "Edgar Poe's Significance," (Jan. 1, 1880);
Cr, II (Jun. 3, 1882), 147. Reprinted in *Specimen Days,
Complete Prose Works.* I, New York: New York University
Press, 1892, 230-2. Reprinted in CJ16.
"Almost without the first sign of moral principle, or of
...its heroisms, or the simpler affections of the heart,
Poe's verses illustrate an intense faculty for technical
and abstract beauty, with the rhyming art to excess, an
incorrigible propensity toward nocturnal themes, a demon-
iac undertone behind every page, and, by final judgment,

probably belong among the electric lights of imaginative
literature, brilliant and dazzling, but with no heat."

B249 _____. *Washington Star* (Nov. 18, 1875). Reprinted in CC178.
"For a long while, and until lately, I had a distaste
for Poe's writings. I wanted, and still want for poetry,
the clear sun shining, the fresh air blowing--the strength
and power of health, not of delirium, even amid the storm-
iest passions--with always the background of the eternal
moralities. Non-complying with these requirements, Poe's
genius has yet conquered a special recognition for itself,
and I too have come to fully admit it, and appreciate it
and him."

B250 WILMER, LAMBERT. "Recollections of Edgar Allan Poe," *Baltimore Daily Commercial* (May 23, 1866).

B251 WILSON, JAMES GRANT. "Edgar Allan Poe," *Bryant and his
Friends*. New York: Fords, Howard and Hulbert, 1886, 334-
46.
General biographical remarks which picture Poe as a
maniac dying of delirium tremens. Claims that Bryant agreed with Lowell's description of Poe in *The Fable*.

B252 W. M. G. "Poe's 'Pit and the Pendulum'," <u>Cr</u>, ns. XIV (Jul.
5, 1890), 7.
Poe stole the story from "The Iron Shroud," <u>Bl</u> (Aug.
1830).

B253 WOODBERRY, GEORGE. *The Life of Edgar Allan Poe*. Boston:
Houghton Mifflin, 1885. Reprinted by Biblo & Tanner, New
York, 1905.
Superior to previous biographies but value reduced by
author's unsympathetic attitude to Poe. Woodberry was un-
aware of the extent of Griswold's forgeries and favored
Griswold's judgment. The second edition (1909) is less
hostile to Poe.

B254 _____. "Lowell's Letters to Poe," <u>Scrib</u> (Aug. 1894), 170-6.
Lowell to Poe (Boston, Nov. 19, 1842); (Cambridge, Mar.
6, 1844); Robert Carter to Poe (Cambridge, Jun. 19, 1843).

B255 _____. "Poe in New York," <u>Cen</u>, XLVIII, ns. XXVI (Oct. 1894),
884-96.
Correspondence between Poe and Dr. Charles Anthon,
Horne, Mrs. Browning, Hawthorne, Simms, Cooke, Thomas,
Griswold, and Mrs. Clemm (1844 to 1846).

*B: 1851-1900*

B256 _____. "Poe in Philadelphia," <u>Cen</u>, LVIII, ns. XXVI (1894), 725-37.
    Discussion of Poe's activities in Philadelphia, and a reprint of correspondence between Poe and William Burton, Washington Irving, Philip Pendleton Cooke, Willis, Dickens, and Frederick William Thomas.

B257 _____. "Poe in the South," <u>Cen</u>, XLVIII, ns. XXVI (1894), 572-83.
    Selections from correspondence between Poe and Kennedy, White, Tucker, Paulding, Anthon, and Heath (1834 to 1839).

B258 _____. "Poe's Legendary Years," <u>Atl</u>, LIV (Dec. 1884), 814-28.
Discussion of the various discrepancies among the stories about Poe's life, 1826-1833.

[The following articles, although written after 1900, concern articles about Poe written between 1851 and 1900]

B259 BOYD, ERNEST. *Literary Blasphemies*. New York: Harper and Bros., 1927, 163-85.
    Vague essay on Poe's biographers, especially Griswold, whose slanders increased Poe's reputation and popularity. Completely sympathetic to Griswold.

B260 COOKE, ALICE L. "The Popular Conception of Poe from 1850 to 1890," <u>UTSE</u>, XXII (Jul. 8, 1942), 145-170.
    After reviewing the critical articles about Poe, Cooke concludes that "the great development was not primarily the recognition of his genius but rather the clearing of his name from slanders...."

B261 COYLE, WILLIAM. Essay in *Papers on Poe: Essays in Honor of J. Ward Ostrom*. Springfield, Ohio, 1972.
    Discusses John Frankenstein's unwarranted attack on Poe in 1864.

B262 DAVIS, RICHARD BEALE. "Moncure D. Conway Looks at Edgar Allan Poe Through Dr. Griswold," *Miss Q*, XVIII (Win. 1964-5), 12-18.
    Reprint of Conway's defense of Poe in his unpublished review of Griswold's edition of Poe's works.

B263 FRENCH, WARREN G. "T. S. Arthur: an Unexpected Champion of Poe," <u>TSL</u>, V (1960), 35-41.
    A member of the temperance movement defended Poe.

*B: 1851-1900*

B264 HUTCHERSON, DUDLEY R. "Poe's Reputation in England and America, 1850-1909," AL, XIV (Nov. 1942), 211-33.
Emphasizes the fact that early Poe criticism dealt more
with Poe's personality than with his literature.

B265 MABBOTT, T. O. "An Early Discussion of Poe," N&Q, CXCI (Sept.
7, 1946), 102.
Mabbott finds evidence of early admiration for Poe in
the West. He also cites a reference to Poe in Cpt. L. A.
Norton's *The Restoration: A Metrical Romance of Canada*,
1851.

B266 _____. "Poe and the Artist John P. Frankenstein," N&Q, CLXXXII
(Jan. 17, 1942), 31-2.
Reprint of John Frankenstein's abusive attack on Poe.

B267 WHEELER, PAUL MOWBRAY. *America Through British Eyes: A Study
of the Attitude of the Edinburgh Review Toward the USA from
1802 until 1861*. Rock Hill, South Carlina, 1935.
Brief summary of the ER essay. *See* B15.

*See also* CA8, CC11, CC25, CC112, CC151, CC196, CI1, CI7.

*CA: Articles on the Poe Canon*

CA1   ANON. "Important Unpublished Poe Material," *Bodley Book Shop Catalgue.* No. 1 (1935), p. 38.

CA2   _____. "Local Authority Says New Poe Discovery Rings True," *Richmond News-Leader,* XIII (Apr. 15, 1935).

CA3   _____. "The Manuscript of Poe's 'Eulalie'," BNYPL, XVIII (Dec. 1914), 1461-3.
      Discovery of holograph of Poe's "Eulalie."

CA4   _____. "New Editions of Poe," *Nation,* LXXV (Dec. 4, 1902), 445.

CA5   _____. "Poe's Letters and Manuscripts Found in a Pillow Case," CO, LXX (Jun. 1921), 823-4.
      Discovery of original Poe manuscript.

CA6   _____. "Presentation Copy of The Second Edition of Poe's Conchologist," ATQ, XIV (Spr. 1972), 87.

CA7   BLANCK, JACOB, ed. *Merle Johnson's American First Editions.* 4th ed. Waltham, Massachusetts: Mark Press, 1965.

CA8   BRENNER, EDGAR. "Another Poem Claimed for Poe," Cr, VII (Apr. 10, 1886), 183.

CA9   BRIGHAM, CLARENCE SAUNDERS. "Edgar Allan Poe's Contributions to *Alexander's Weekly Messenger,*" PAAS, ns. LII (Apr. 1942), 45-124. Reprinted by the Poe Society, Worcester, Massachusetts.
      Reprint of Poe's articles on cryptography in AWM with a brief discussion of his contributions to the periodical.

CA10  CAMPBELL, KILLIS. "Bibliographical Notes on Poe," *Nation,* LXXXIX (Dec. 23, 1909), 623-4, 647-8.
      Additions to James Harrison's Bibliography of Poe's writings in the *Virginia Edition,* Vol. 16.

# EDGAR ALLAN POE: AN ANNOTATED BIBLIOGRAPHY

*CA: Articles on the Poe Canon*

CA11 _____. "A Bit of Chiversian Mystification," UTSE, X (1930), 152-5.
  Thomas Holly Chivers, not Poe, probably wrote "The Departed."

CA12 _____. "Gleanings in the Bibliography of Poe," MLN, XXXII (May 1917), 267-72.
  New discoveries in the Poe canon.

CA13 _____. "News for Bibliophiles," *Nation,* XCIII (Oct. 19, 1911), 362-63.
  Seven new items in the Poe canon.

CA14 _____. "The Poe Canon," PLMA, XXVII (1912), 325-53.
  Examination of spurious items in the Poe canon.

CA15 CARLTON, W. N. C. "Authorship of 'English Notes', by Quarles Quickens Reviewed," AC, I (Feb. 1926), 186-90.
  Summary of the issue.

CA16 CHAMBERLAIN, JACOB CHESTER. *First Editions of Ten American Authors.* New York: Anderson Auction Co., 1909.

CA17 CHARVAT, WILLIAM. "A Note on (the Publication of) Poe's *Tales of the Grotesque and Arabesque*," PW,CL (Nov. 23, 1946), 2957-8.
  The edition was limited to 750 copies.

CA18 DAMERON, J. LASLEY. "T. O. Mabbott on the Canon of Poe's Reviews," PN, V (Dec. 1972), 56-7.
  Presents a list of critical essays wrongly attributed to Poe in the Virginia Edition.

CA19 DOHERTY, EDWARD. "'The Spectacles': the Lost Short Story by Edgar Allan Poe," *Liberty,* XV (Sept. 24, 1938), 12-14.
  Author attributes a new short story to Poe.

CA20 EATON, VINCENT L. "Two Poe Rarities," QJCA, XII (1955), 103-5.
  Acquisitions by the Library of Congress.

CA21 ELWELL, T. E. "A Poe Story," TLS, no. 2177 (Oct. 23, 1943), 516.
  Discovery of an 1841 edition of NAGP.

CA22 ENGLEKIRK, JOHN E. "'My Nightmare'--The Last Tale by Poe," PMLA, LII (Jun. 1937), 511-27.
  Francisco Zarate Ruiz probably wrote "M. Pesadille," usually attributed to Poe.

*CA: Articles on the Poe Canon*

CA23 _____. "'The Song of Hollands', an Inedited Tale Ascribed to Poe," NMQR, I (Aug. 1931), 247-70.
    The story was probably written by Aurélian Scholl.

CA24 FRENCH, JOHN C. "Poe and the *Baltimore Saturday Visitor*," MLN, XXXIII (May 1918), 257-67.
    The author discusses the contest and suggests that three poems--"Serenade," "To _____," and "Fanny"--should be added to the canon.

CA25 HALL, CARROLL. *Bierce and the Poe Hoax* with an Introduction by Carey McWilliams. San Francisco: The Book Club of California, 1934.
    Ambrose Bierce, Carroll Carrington and Herman Scheffauer printed Scheffauer's poem "The Sea of Serenity" as a poem by Poe in *The Examiner*.

CA26 HATVARY, GEORGE EGON. "The Whereabouts of Poe's 'Fifty Suggestions'," PN, IV (Dec. 1971), 47.
    Corrects several errors, in Harrison and other books on Poe, on the publication and numbering of "Fifty Suggestions."

CA27 HEARTMAN, CHARLES F. "The Curse of Edgar Allan Poe," ABC, IV (Jul. 1933), 45-9.
    Concerning thefts of a first edition of ATMP.

CA28 _____. *Edgar Allan Poe's Contributions to Annuals and Periodicals*. Metuchen, New Jersey, 1932.

CA29 HEARTMAN, CHARLES F. and JAMES R. CANNY. *A Bibliography of First Printings of the Writings of Edgar Allan Poe*. Rev. ed. Hattiesburg, Mississippi: The Book Farm, 1943.

CA30 HUBBELL, J. B. "'O Tempora! O Mores!'A Juvenile Poem by Edgar Allan Poe," *University of Colorado Studies*, II, Series B (Oct. 1945), 314-21.

CA31 HUTCHERSON, DUDLEY R. "The *Philadelphia Saturday Museum* Text of Poe's Poems," AL, V (Mar. 1933), 36-48.
    The Feb. 25, 1943 PSM contains the only complete edition of Poe's poems before 1843 and the only one supervised by Poe himself. In addition, Poe, not Hirst, wrote the critical biography following the poems.

CA32 JACKSON, JOSEPH. "Dickens in America," *The World's Work* (Jan. 1912).
    Poe is the author of "EN."

*CA: Articles on the Poe Canon*

CA33      \_\_\_\_. "Four of Poe's Critiques in the Baltimore Newspapers,"
      MLN, L (Apr. 1935), 251-6.
        First reprints of critiques by Poe from the SLM men-
      tioned in letters to Thomas Willis White (May 30, 1835;
      Jun. 12, 1835).

CA34  JACKSON, JOSEPH and GEORGE H. SARGENT, eds. *English Notes*.
      New York: Lewis M. Thompson, 1920.
        In the Introduction, Jackson reviews evidence that Poe
      wrote the book.

CA35  LLOYD, J. A. T.  "Who Wrote 'English Notes'?" Cpn, I (Sum.
      1935), 107-18.
        Allusions to Kant, Dr. Aiken and the international copy-
      right problem are evidence that Poe is the author.

CA36  MABBOTT, T. O.  "Additions to 'A List of Poe's Tales'," N&Q,
      CLXXXIII, (Sept. 12, 1942), 163-4.
        Additions to and corrections of John Wyllie's chapter
      in *Humanistic Studies in Honor of John Calvin Metcalf*.
      *See* CA67.

CA37      \_\_\_\_. "Another Spurious Poe," ABC, III (Apr. 1933), 233-4.
        Regarding poems attributed to Poe in a book sale cata-
      logue.

CA38      \_\_\_\_. "Edgar Allan Poe, a Find." N&Q, CL (Apr. 1926), 241.
        Poe published "The Happiest Day" in *The North American*
      (Sept. 15, 1827) and "Dreams" in the same magazine (Oct.
      20, 1827).  He may also have written "The Pirates,"
      signed by William Henry Poe, in *The North American* (Oct.27,
      1827).

CA39      \_\_\_\_. "Newly Found Verses Ascribed to Poe," N&Q, CCI (Mar.
      1956), 122.
        The poem is "Epigram for Wall Street," *New York Evening
      Mirror* (Jan. 23, 1845).

CA40      \_\_\_\_. "Newly-Identified Reviews by Edgar Allan Poe," N&Q,
      CLXIII (Dec. 17, 1932), 441.
        Identifies as Poe's: Reviews of "Orion" and "'Ned Myers
      ...' ed. by J. Fenimore Cooper," Gr (Jan. 1844); "Epes
      Sargent," Gr (Jun. 1844); and "Mysteries of Paris," Gr
      (Feb. 1844).

CA41      \_\_\_\_. "Newly-Identified Verses by Poe," N&Q, CLXXVII (Jul.
      29, 1939), 77-8.
        Poe probably wrote "Lines on Ale" and also the motto
      for the *Stylus* prospectus, signed by Sir Launcelot Canning.

*CA: Articles on the Poe Canon*

CA42 _____. "Palindromes (and Edgar Poe)," N&Q, CXCI (Nov. 30, 1947), 238-9.
Mabbott attributes to Poe some fillers in GM and a Palindrome from *Saturday Evening Post* (Mar. 10, 1827).

CA43 _____. "A Poe Manuscript," BNYPL, XXVIII (Feb. 1924), 103-5.
Concerning the NYPL acquisition of Poe's roll manuscript "Thou Art the Man."

CA44 _____. "Poe and the *Philadelphia Irish Citizen*," New York, 1931. Reprinted from *Journal of the American Irish Historical Society*, XXIX (1930-1), 121-31.
"The Ghost of a Grey Tadpole" is probably by Thomas Dunn English.

CA45 _____. "Poe on Intemperance," N&Q, CLXXXIII (Jul. 18, 1942), 34-5.
Poe did not write "Intemperance," *Sterling's Magazine* (1866).

CA46 _____. "A Poem Wrongly Ascribed to Edgar Allan Poe," N&Q, ns. XIV (Oct. 1967), 367-8.
The poem sent by Mrs. Amelia Poe on Aug. 12, 1912 to Ingram, beginning "then the vessel sinking," is not by Poe.

CA47 _____. "Poe's Essay on the Beet Root," N&Q, CLXVII (Dec. 15, 1934), 420.
On some paragraphs by Poe in AWM (Dec. 18, 1839).

CA48 _____. "Poe's 'Original Conundrums'," N&Q, CLXXXIV (Jun. 5, 1943), 328-9.
Reprint of Poe's "Original Conundrums" from *The Spirit of the Times* and the PSM.

CA49 _____. "Ullahanna--a Literary Ghost," AN&Q, I (Sept. 1941), 83.
Concerning a non-existent poem in the Poe canon.

CA50 NEWCOMER, A. G. "The Editing of Poe," *Dial*, XXX (Mar. 16, 1901), 183.

CA51 NISBET, ADA. "New Light on the Dickens-Poe Relationship," NCF, V (Mar. 1951), 295-302.
The Review of *American Notes* (Bl, Dec. 1842) is by Samuel Warren, not Poe. Samuel Kettell may have written "EN."

# EDGAR ALLAN POE: AN ANNOTATED BIBLIOGRAPHY

*CA: Articles on the Poe Canon*

CA52   \_\_\_\_\_. "Poe and Dickens," NCF, IX (1955), 313.
        Poe wrote all or part of the review of Dickens'
*American Notes* in SLM (Jan. 1843).

CA53   POLLIN, BURTON. "Poe as Probable Author of 'Harper's Ferry',"
      AL, XXXX (May 1968), 164-78.
        Evidence that Poe is the author of the plate article in
*Graham's* (Feb. 1842).

CA54   \_\_\_\_\_. "The Provenance and Correct Text of Poe's Review of
      *Griswold's Female Poets of America*, PN, II (Apr. 1969),
      35-6.

CA55   QUARLES, DIANA. "Poe and the International Copyright," SLM,
      III (Jan. 1941), 4.
        "The Copyright Question" is by Archibald Allison, not
      Poe.

CA56   REDE, KENNETH. "An Unnoted Poe Poem?" ABC, IV (Aug. 1933),
      106-7.
        Poe may be the author of "Home," signed by S. M. S.,
      from a Baltimore magazine (May 1829).

CA57   REECE, JAMES B. "An Error in Some Reprintings of Poe's 1847
      Critique of Hawthorne," PN, IV (Dec. 1971), 47.

CA58   RICHARDS, IRVING. "A New Poe Poem," MLN, XLII (Mar. 1927),
      158-62.
        "The Three Meetings--To Eva," signed "Edgar," Feb. 19,
      1828.

CA59   TAYLOR, BAYARD. "Poe's Last Manuscript," *American Clipper*,
      I (Nov. 1934), 84.

CA60   VARNER, JOHN GREER. *Facsimile reproductions of the "Philadel-*
      *phia Saturday Courier."* Charlottesville: University of
      Virginia, 1933.
        In the Introduction, Varner discusses Poe's association
      with the PSC, revisions of the first texts of his earliest
      tales, and his development into a mature writer and
      burlesque imitator.

CA61   \_\_\_\_\_. "Note on a Poem Attributed to Poe," AL, VIII (Mar.
      1936), 66-8.
        Frances O. Osgood wrote "Impromptu," a poem usually
      attributed to Poe (BJ, Apr. 26, 1845).

# EDGAR ALLAN POE: AN ANNOTATED BIBLIOGRAPHY

## CA: Articles on the Poe Canon

CA62   WALLACE, ALFRED R.   "Leonainie Problem," _FortnR_, ns. LXXV
      (Apr. 1904), 706-11.
         To obtain recognition, James Whitcomb Riley signed
      Poe's name to his own poem.   Later Riley confessed,
      but someone made the poem more "Poesque" in the
      meantime.

CA63   WEBB, HOWARD W. JR.   "A Further Note on the Dickens-Poe
      Relationship," _NCF_, XV (Jun. 1960), 80.
         A letter from Charles Patterson to John Tomlin proves
      that Poe did not write _EN_ or the _Bl._ review of _American
      Notes_.   There was no animosity between Dickens and Poe
      in 1842.

CA64   WHITTY, JAMES H.   "Discoveries in the Uncollected Poems of
      Edgar Allan Poe," _Nation_, CII (Jan. 27, 1916), 105-6.
         Whitty reveals new documents in Poe's handwriting,
      among them a poem, "Life's Vital Stream."

CA65   _____.   "Poeana," _The Step Ladder_ (Poe Anniversary Number),
      XIII (Oct. 1927), 225-43.
        Biographical and bibliographical notes on Poe.

CA66   _____.   "Three Poems by Edgar Allan Poe," _Nation_, CVII (Dec.
      7, 1918), 699-700.
         Reprints of Serenade," "To _____," and "Fanny."

CA67   WYLLIE, JOHN COOK.   "A List of the Texts of Poe's Tales,"
      _Humanistic Studies in Honor of John Calvin Metcalf._
      Charlottesville: _University of Virginia Studies,_ I (1941),
      322-38.

_See also_ CB17, CB18, CC5, CC82, CL449.

## CB: Bibliographies

CB1   ANON.   "The One-Hundred Fiftieth Anniversary of Poe's Birth,"
      _BPLQ_, XI (Apr. 1959), 108-10.
         Bibliography of Library exhibition.

CB2   _____.   Bangs and Co.   Catalogue of an Exceedingly Interesting
      and Valuable Private Library, Comprising the Largest and

# Edgar Allan Poe: An Annotated Bibliography

*CB: Bibliographies*

Most Complete Collection of the Original Editions of the Works of Edgar Allan Poe and of "Poeana." New York: D. Taylor and Co., 1895.

CB3 _____. *Index to Early American Periodical Literature: 1728-1870.* Part II. New York: Pamphlet Distributing Co., 1941.

CB4 ARCHIBALD, R. C. "Music and Edgar Allan Poe," N&Q. CLXXIX (Sept. 7, 1940), 170-1.
　　Additions to Mary Garrettson Evans' *Music and Edgar Allan Poe. A Biographical Study. See* CB12.

CB5 BENTON, RICHARD. "Current Bibliography on Edgar Allan Poe," ESQ, XXXVIII (I Quarter, 1965), 144-47; XLVII (II Quarter, 1967), 84-7.

CB6 _____. "Edgar Allan Poe: Current Bibliography," PN, II (Jan. 1969), 4-18; III (June. 1970), 11-16; IV (Dec. 1971), 38-44.

CB7 BOOTH, BRADFORD ALLEN and CLAUDE E. JONES. *A Concordance of the Poetical Works of Edgar Allan Poe.* Baltimore: The Johns Hopkins Press, 1941.

CB8 BRAGG, CLARA. *Bibliography of Poe.* Columbia Library, 1909.
　　Material by and about Edgar Allan Poe in Columbia University Library.

CB9 DAMERON, J. LASLEY. *Edgar Allan Poe: a Checklist of Criticism: 1942-60.* Charlottesville, SB: BSUV, 1966.

CB10 DEDMOND, FRANCIS B. "A Checklist of Poe's Works in Book Form Published in the British Isles," BB, XXI (1953), 16-20.
　　The list covers the period from 1838 to 1949.

CB11 _____. "Poe in Drama, Fiction, and Poetry," BB, XXI (1954), 107-14.
　　Bibliography of works in which Poe has been criticized or eulogized. "A Wealth of literary criticism, normally overlooked, is to be found in these works...." The plays about Poe are mostly romantic and melodramatic, and the fiction, satiric.

# Edgar Allan Poe: An Annotated Bibliography

CB12 EVANS, MARY GARRETTSON. *Music and Edgar Allan Poe: A Bibliographical Study*. Baltimore: Johns Hopkins Press, 1931.
  Bibliography of Poe's poems set to music. *See* CB4.

CB13 GALE, ROBERT L. *Plots and Characters in the Fiction and Poetry of Edgar Allan Poe*. Hamden, Connecticut: Archon Books, 1970.
  Alphabetical sequences of parts, plot summaries and character identifications.

CB14 GIMBEL, RICHARD. "'Quoth the Raven': A Catalogue of the Exhibition," <u>YULG</u>, XXXIII (Apr. 1959), 139-189.

CB15 GORDON, JOHN D. "Edgar Allan Poe: an Exhibition on the Centenary of his Death, Oct. 7, 1849; A Catalogue of First Editions, Manuscripts, Autographs, letters from the Berg Collection," <u>BNYPL</u>, LIII (1949), 471-91.

CB16 HARASZTI, ZOLTAN. "Poe Centenary," <u>BPLQ</u>, I (Oct. 1949), 151-55.
  Poe materials in the Boston Public Library.

CB17 HEARTMAN, CHARLES and KENNETH REDE. *A Census of First Editions and Source Materials by Edgar Allan Poe in American Collections*. Metuchen, New Jersey: 1932; also in <u>ABC</u>, I (Jun. 1932), 339-43; and II (Jul.-Dec. 1932).

CB18 _____. "A Remarkable Addition to the Poe Census," <u>ABC</u>, III (Apr. 1933), 246.
  Additions to the Heartman-Rede *Bibliography*.

CB19 HUBBELL, JAY B. *Eight American Authors: A Review of Research and Criticism*. ed. by Floyd Stovall. New York, 1956.

CB20 JONES, JOSEPH, *et al. American Literary Manuscripts. A Checklist of Holdings in Academic, Historical and Public Libraries in the United States*. Austin: University of Texas Press, 1960.

CB21 MABBOTT, T. O. "Index to Early American Periodical Literature: 1728-1870," Part II. New York: Pamphlet

*CB: Bibliographies*

Distributing Co., 1941. Reprinted from *The Pamphleteer Monthly,* I (Jan. 1941).

CB22 MARRS, ROBERT L. "Fugitive Poe References: A Bibliography," PN, II (Jan. 1969), 12-16.

CB23 McELDERRY, B. R. JR. "The Edgar Allan Poe Collection," USCLB, no. 4 (Jan. 1948), 4-6.

CB24 MILLER, JOHN CARL. *John Henry Ingram's Poe Collection at the University of Virginia.* Charlottesville, Virginia, 1960.
   A calendar of letters and other manuscripts, photographs, printed matter, and biographical source materials assembled by Ingram, with essay about Ingram as Poe editor and biographer.

CB25 MOSKOWITZ, SAM. *The Man Who Called Himself Poe.* New York: Doubleday, 1969.
   A collection of stories and poems in which Poe appears or in which the author tries to imitate his manner.

CB26 OSOWSKI, JUDY. "Fugitive Poe References: A Bibliography," PN, IV (Dec. 1971), 44-48; III (Jun. 1970), 10-13.

CB27 POLLIN, BURTON (compiler). *Dictionary of Names and Titles in Poe's Collected Works.* New York: Da Capo, 1968.
   Index based on Harrison's edition of Poe's works.

CB28 _____. "Poe and the Computer," *Institute for Computer Research in the Humanities Newsletter (ICRH),* III (1968), 2-3.
   How Pollin used the computer in his compilation.

CB29 QUINN, ARTHUR H. and RICHARD H. HART. *Edgar Allan Poe: Letters and Documents in the Enoch Pratt Free Library,* New York: Scholars' Facsimiles and Reprints, 1941.

CB30 RANDALL, DAVID A. "The J. K. Lilly Collection of Edgar Allan Poe," IUB, no. 4 (Mar. 1960), 46-58.
   Checklist of letters, books, magazines and illustrations in the Lilly Library, Indiana University.

# EDGAR ALLAN POE: AN ANNOTATED BIBLIOGRAPHY

*CB: Bibliographies*

CB31      . *The J. K. Lilly Collection of Edgar Allan Poe: an Account of its Formation*. Bloomington, 1964.

CB32  ROBBINS, J. ALBERT. *Checklist of Edgar Allan Poe*. Columbus, Ohio: Charles E. Merrill Pub. Co., 1969.

CB33  ROBERTSON, JOHN WOOSTER. *Bibliography of the Writings of Edgar Allan Poe*. San Francisco: Russian Hill Private Press; New York: Kraus Reprint Co., 1969.

CB34  SPARKS, ARCHIBALD. "Edgar Allan Poe: Bibliography," N&Q, CLIX (Dec. 27, 1930), 465.
List of Poe Bibliographies.

CB35  TANSELLE, G. T. "The State of Poe Bibliography," PN, II (Jan. 1969), 1-3.
Brief, general essay.

*See also* CL171.

*CC: General Biographical Articles*

CC1  ANON. "Account of a Rare Dumas Manuscript Describing Poe's Visit to Paris in 1832," *New York Times* (Dec. 15, 1929), 19.
A reprint of the Dumas manuscript describing Poe's supposed visit to Paris in 1832.

CC2      . "Connecting Links in Poe's Life," BNM, XXV (Aug. 1907), 804-5.
Brief and uninformative biography.

CC3      . "The Dual Personality of Edgar Allan Poe," CurLit, XLIII (Sept. 1907), 287.
Poe suffered from psychic epilepsy.

CC4      . "Edgar Allan Poe," *Wiley Bulletin*, XXXIII (Win. 1950), 4-5.

CC5      . "Edgar Allan Poe on Professor Anthon," CUQ, XI (Mar. 1909), 207-8.
Reprint of Poe's lecture on Professor Anthon of Columbia University.

CC6      . "Greeley Pays Poe for Contributions to the *Tribune* with a Promissory Note," *Bruno's Weekly*, II (Mar. 4, 1916), 526-8.
Discusses a promissory note from Greeley to Poe in

payment for a story and a letter from Poe to John Thompson, editor of SLM (Jan. 13, 1849) suggesting that he contribute five pages of criticism to that magazine per month.

CC7 _____. "How Poe Must Have Looked," CurLit, XLI (Sept. 1906), 287.
   Discusses Poe's "physical lineaments," with drawings.

CC8 _____. "Lady Editor who Paid Poe Fifty Cents Per Page," CO, LXII (Mar. 1917), 204.

CC9 _____. "A Note on David Poe as Actor," PW, CXVII (Jun. 21, 1930), 3041-2.
   Boston theatrical notices of David Poe.

CC10 _____. *Perspectives, USA*. no. 15 (Spr. 1956), 5-20.

CC11 _____. "Poe a Bricklayer in 1834?" AN&Q, III (Jun. 1943), 36.
   Concerning a suggestion in Cen (1875, p. 142-3) that Poe was a bricklayer.

CC12 _____. "Poe Visited Paris, Dumas Script Says," *New York Times* (Dec. 15, 1929).

CC13 _____. "Souvenirs of Poe's Last Visit to Richmond," PULC, XII (Win. 1951), 83-7.

CC14 ABEL, DARREL, "Literary Consumations I: Massachusetts and Virginia," *American Literature*. New York: Barrons, 1963.
   General Essay on Poe's career.

CC15 ALFRIEND, E. M. "Unpublished Recollections of Edgar Allan Poe," *Literary Era*, ns. VIII (Aug. 1901), 489-91.
   Writer recalls second Mrs. Allan--"refined, educated, woman, with a kind heart, and in every sense a lady, peculiarly gentle and incapable of wrong to anyone."

CC16 ALLABECK, STEVEN. "Mrs. Clemm and Henry Wadsworth Long-fellow," *Harvard Library Bulletin*, XVIII (1970), 32-42.
   Reprints 15 letters from Mrs. Clemm to Longfellow.

CC17 ALLAN, CARLISLE. "Cadet Edgar Allan Poe, USA," AM, XXIX (Aug. 1933), 446-55.
   Poe's career at West Point.

CC18 ARNSTON, HERBERT E. "A Western Obituary of Poe," PN, I (Oct. 1968), 3.
   Appeared in the *Oregon Spectator,* Feb. 7, 1850.

*CC: General Biographical Articles*

CC19    BANDY, W. T.   "The Date of Poe's Burial," <u>PN</u>, IV (Dec. 1971),
        47-8.
            The correct date is Oct. 8.

CC20    BAYLESS, JOY.  *Rufus Wilmot Griswold: Poe's Literary Exec-
        utor.*  Nashville: Vanderbilt University Press, 1943,
        161-200.
            Discussion of Griswold as Poe's literary executor.

CC21    BEWLEY, SIR EDMUND THOMAS.  *The Origin and Early History of
        the Family of Poe.*  Ponsonby and Gibbs, 1906.  Reprinted
        in *New York Genealogical and Biographical Record,* XXXVIII
        (1907), 55-69.

CC22    BINNS, ELIZABETH.  "Daniel Bryan: Poe's Poet of the 'Good Old
        Goldsmith School'," <u>WMQ</u>, ser. 2, XXIII (1943), 465-73.
            Concerns the relationship between Bryan and Poe.

CC23    BIRSS, J. H.  "Poe in Fordham, A Reminiscence," <u>N&Q</u>, CLXXIII
        (Dec. 18, 1937), 440.
            Reminiscence of Poe by Augustine O'Neil.

CC24    BLACK, LADBROKE.  "Edgar Allan Poe," *Some Queer People.*  London:
        Sampson Low, Marston & Co., Ltd., 1931, 136-156.
            Unsympathetic psychological study of Poe's sexual life
        discounts the importance of his childhood (because he
        could not have remembered his early experiences) and sug-
        gests that he completely sublimated his sexual urges.

CC25    BOHNER, CHARLES H.   "The Poe-Kennedy Friendship," <u>PMHB</u>,
        LXXXII (Apr. 1958), 220-22.
            In a letter to Fahnestock (Apr. 13, 1869), John Pendle-
        ton Kennedy stated about Poe, "In his special department
        of thought, our country has produced no poet or prose
        writer superior to him--indeed, I think, none equal to
        him."

CC26    BOND, FREDERICK D.   "The Problem of Mr. Poe," *Open Court,*
        XXXVII (Apr. 1923), 216-23.
            A vindication which attributes all of Poe's problems to
        his marriage to Virginia Clemm.

CC27    BRADDY, HALDEEN.   "Poe and the West--a Comment," <u>PN</u>, I (Oct.
        1968), 31.
            When Poe considered moving to the West.

CC28    BRADSHER, EARL L.  *Mathew Carey, Editor, Author and Publisher:
        a Study in American Literary Development.*  New York:
        Columbia University Press, 1912.

*CC: General Biographical Articles*

CC29    BRUCE, P. A.   "Was Poe a Drunkard?" SAQ, XI (Jan. 1912),3-21.
           The author moves chronologically through Poe's life,
           estimating the amount of liquor he consumed.

CC30    BULLARD, F. LAURISTON.   "Boston Birthplace Not Home of Poe,"
           *New York Times* (Oct. 11, 1931).
           On Boston's neglect of her famous son.

CC31    CAMPBELL, KILLIS.   "The Poe-Griswold Controversy," PMLA,
           XXXIV (Sept. 1919), 436-64.

CC32    _____. "Some Unpublished Documents Related to Poe's Early
           Years," SR, XX (Apr. 1912), 201-12.
           Letters about Poe's youth and relations with John Allan.

CC33    _____. "Who was 'Outis'?" UTSE, VIII (1928), 107-9.
           He is C. C. Felton, a friend of Longfellow.

CC34    CARTER, JOHN F.   "Edgar Allan Poe's Last Night in Richmond,"
           Lipp, LXX (Nov. 1902), 562-6.
           Account of one of Poe's lecture-recitals in Richmond,
           which 13 people attended, and reminiscences about Poe by
           the Dr. whom he visited shortly before he left Richmond.

CC35    CAUTHEN, I. B. JR.   "Lowell on Poe: An Unpublished Comment,"
           AL, XXIV (May 1952), 230-2.
           Reprint of a letter about Poe from Lowell to John H.
           Ingram (May 12, 1879).

CC36    CHAMBERLIN, JOSEPH EDGAR.   "Edgar Allan Poe and His Boston
           Critic, Miss Walter," *Boston Evening Transcript,* Bk.
           Section (Jan. 26, 1924), 2.   Reprinted in *Boston Tran-
           script: A History of Its First Hundred Years.* Boston, 1930.
           Discusses Cornelia Wells Walter's attack on Poe's read-
           ing at the Lyceum.

CC37    CHARVAT, WILLIAM.   *Literary Publishing in America: 1790-1850.*
           Philadelphia: University of Pennsylvania Press, 1959.
           Poe in the publishing business.

CC38    CLARK, C. E. FRAZER, JR.   "Two Unrecorded Notices of Poe's
           Parents," PN, IV (Dec. 1971), 37-8.
           The notices appeared in *The Repertory* (Boston), 1806
           and 1807.

CC39    CLARK, GEORGE P.   "Two Unnoticed Recollections of Poe's Funer-
           al," PN, III (Jun. 1970), 1-2.

*CC: General Biographical Articles*

Reprints recollections by Charles William Hubner and Colonel J. Alden Weston.

CC40 COBURN, FREDERICK W. "Poe as Seen by the Brother of 'Annie'," NEQ, XVI (Sept. 1943), 468-76.
Letters by Amos Bardwell Heywood to Miss Annie Sawyer about Poe's three visits to Lowell.

CC41 COHEN, B. BERNARD and LUCIEN A. "Poe and Griswold Once More," AL, XXXIV (Mar. 1962), 97-101.
Believes that Griswold wrote a negative review of Gr (May 22, 1841) in the *Boston Notion* and that the review was the beginning of the hostility between them.

CC42 COLTON, CULLEN B. "George Hooker Colton and the Publication of 'The Raven'," AL, X (Nov. 1938), 319-30.
A discussion of the Poe-Colton relationship and denial that the two men engaged in a feud.

CC43 COMSTOCK, S. "More About Poe," *Our World Weekly,* III (Nov. 16, 1925), 117.

CC44 COOPER, LETTICE. *Edgar Allan Poe Centenary Commemoration.* Stoke Newington Public Library Committee, 1949.
Inaccurate biography.

CC45 COURTNEY, JOHN F. "Addiction and Edgar Allan Poe," *Resident and Staff Physician* (Jan. 1971), 107-115.

CC46 CRANE, ALEXANDER T. "Reminiscences of Edgar Allan Poe," *Sunday World-Herald,* Omaha (Jul. 13, 1902).

CC47 CULVER, FRANCIS B. "Lineage of Edgar Allan Poe and the Complex Pattern of the Family Genealogy," MyHM, XXXVII (Dec. 1942), 420-2.
Brief discussion of the Poe family tree.

CC48 CUMSTON, CHARLES GREENE, M.D. "The Medical History of Edgar Allan Poe, " *St. Paul Medical Journal* (1909).

CC49 DAMON, SAMUEL FOSTER. *Thomas Holly Chivers, Friend of Poe.* New York and London: Harper Bros., 1903.
Although Damon finally acquits Poe of Chivers' charge of plagiarism, claiming only that Poe made some "crowning appropriations" of Chivers' work, he is clearly biased against Poe, whom he accuses of extorting Chivers financially.

*CC: General Biographical Articles*

CC50  DAVIS, H. C.  "Poe's Stormy Voyage in 1822 is Described,"
      *Charleston* (South Carolina) *News and Courier* (Jan. 5,
      1941).

CC51  DAVIS, RICHARD B.  "Poe and William Wirt," <u>AL</u>, XVI (Nov.
      1944), 212-20.
          Traces the relationship between Poe and Wirt and sug-
      gests that *The Old Bachelor* by David Watson is a source of
      "WW."

CC52  DEDMOND, FRANCIS B.  "Poe's Libel Suit against Thomas Dunn
      English," <u>BPLQ</u>, V (Jan. 1953), 31-7.
          The history of the disagreement and court battle
      between Poe and English.

CC53  _____.  "The War of the Literati: Documents of the Legal
      Phase," <u>N&Q</u>, CXCVIII (Jul. 1953), 303-8.
          Reprints of the declaration of suit against Hiram
      Fuller and Augustus W. Clason, New York Superior Court,
      July 20, 1846, and English's testimony in which he calls
      Poe a "notorious liar, a common drunkard...utterly lost
      to all the obligations of honor." *See* CJ50-CJ51.

CC54  _____.  "Willis and Morris Add a Partner--and Poe," <u>N&Q</u>,
      CXCVIII (Jun. 1953), 253-54.

CC55  DEFOE, M.  "Poe's Instability was the Cause of his Downfall,"
      *Saturday Night*, LXI (Nov. 17, 1945), 20.

CC56  DeGRAZIA, EMILIO.  "Poe's Devoted Democrat, George Lippard,"
      <u>PSt</u>, VI (Jun. 1973), 6-8.
          Discussion of the relationship between the two writers.

CC57  DeTERNANT, ANDREW.  "Edgar Allan Poe and Alexander Dumas,"
      <u>N&Q</u>, CLVII (Dec. 28, 1929), 456.
          The "Paris meeting" of Poe and Dumas.

CC58  DIDIER, EUGENE L.  "Edgar Allan Poe in Society," <u>Bkm</u>, XXVIII
      (Jan. 1909), 455-60.  Reprinted in *The Poe Cult*.
          Romantic account of Poe in society.

CC59  _____.  "The Truth about Edgar Allan Poe," <u>BL</u>, (Mar.-Apr.
      1903), 4.

CC60  DOWDEY, CLIFFORD.  "Poe's Last Visit to Richmond," <u>AH</u>, VII
      (Apr. 1956), 22-6.
          Uninformative and sometimes fictionalized discussion
      of his life.

# Edgar Allan Poe: An Annotated Bibliography

*CC: General Biographical Articles*

CC61　DUFFY, CHARLES.　"Poe's Mother-in-Law: Two Letters to Bayard
　　　　Taylor," AN&Q, II (Jan. 1943), 148.
　　　　　　Two begging letters from Maria Clemm to Taylor.

CC62　EAVES, T. C. DUNCAN.　"Poe's Last Visit to Philadelphia,"
　　　　AL, XXVI (Mar. 1954), 44-51.
　　　　　　New light on Poe's life from Jun. 29 to Jul. 14, 1849.

CC63　EDGERTON, KATHLEEN.　"The Lecturing of Edgar Allan Poe,"
　　　　*Southern Speech Journal*, XXVIII (Sum. 1963), 268-73.

CC64　EHRLICH, HEYWARD.　"Briggs' Dilemma and Poe's Strategy,"
　　　　BNYPL, LXXIII (Feb. 1969), 74-93.
　　　　　　Detailed history of Poe's controversy with Briggs over
　　　　control of the BJ may shed some light on Poe's career with
　　　　other journals.

CC65　EVANS, MARY GARRETTSON.　"Poe in Amity Street," MyHM, XXXVI
　　　　(Dec. 1941), 363-88.
　　　　　　Concerning Poe's experiences in Baltimore.

CC66　EXMAN, EUGENE.　*The Brothers Harper: a Unique Publishing
　　　　Partnership and its Impact Upon the Cultural Life of
　　　　America from 1817-1853.*　New York: Harper and Row, 1965.

CC67　FALCO, NICHOLAS.　"Edgar Allan Poe of the Village of Ford-
　　　　ham," *Bronx County Historical Society Journal,* VI
　　　　(1969), 51-8.
　　　　　　Discusses Poe's life in the Bronx.

CC68　FITZGERALD, BISHOP OSCAR P.　"The Night I Saw and Heard
　　　　Edgar Allan Poe," *Fifty Years,* Nashville and Dallas: M. E.
　　　　Church Pub. House, 1903, 189-201.
　　　　　　Recollections of Poe's lecture shortly before his
　　　　death.

CC69　FLOWER, NEWMAN.　"Two Interesting Sinners," Bkm (London),
　　　　LXXI (Oct. 1926), 16-18.
　　　　　　Emotional account of Poe's terrible life.

CC70　FREEMAN, FRED B. JR.　"Poe's Lowell Trips," PN, IV (Dec.
　　　　1971), 23-4.
　　　　　　The relationship between Poe and Bardwell Heywood,
　　　　Annie Richmond's brother.

CC71　FREEMAN, JOHN.　"Edgar Allan Poe," *London Mercury,* XVI (Jun.
　　　　1927), 162-9.
　　　　　　Biographical remarks, brief and inconsequential.

# EDGAR ALLAN POE: AN ANNOTATED BIBLIOGRAPHY

*CC: General Biographical Articles*

CC72  FRENCH, JOSEPH LEWIS.  "The Closing Scene: An Account of
      Poe's Last Days in Baltimore," BNM, XXV (Aug. 1907), 805-
      10.
          Fictionalized account of Poe's death.

CC73  _____.  "The Day of Poe's Burial," *Baltimore Sun* (Jun. 3,
      1949), 14.

CC74  _____.  "Poe's Literary Baltimore," MyHM, XXXII (Jun. 1937),
      101-12.
          Discusses Poe's experiences in Baltimore and Baltimore
      literary society.

CC75  GARNETT, R. S.  "The Mystery of Edgar Allan Poe," Bl, CCXXVII
      (Feb. 1930), 235-48.
          Discusses the mystery of Poe's visit to Europe.

CC76  GILDER, J. L.  "Biography and Letters," Cr, XLII (Jun. 1903),
      499-502.
          Concerning Harrison's biography of Poe.

CC77  GOODWIN, KATHARINE C.  "Old Documents and their Marketing,"
      *DAR Magazine*, LXVII (Sept. 1933), 539-46.
          Discusses a letter from Maria Clemm requesting a lawyer
      to prosecute her claim against the United States.

CC78  GOUDISS, CHARLES, M.D.  "Edgar Allan Poe: A Pathological
      Study," BNM, XXV (Aug. 1907), 801-4.
          Primitive psychological study suggesting that Poe was
      not a drunkard but a dipsomaniac with disorganized brain
      cells and an unstable nervous system.

CC79  GRAVELY, WILLIAM H. JR.  "Poe and Thomas Dunn English: More
      Light on a Probable Reason for Poe's Failure to Receive
      a Custom-House Appointment," *Papers on Poe's Essays in
      Honor of J. Ward Ostrom*.  Springfield, Ohio, 1972.

CC80  _____.  "Thomas Dunn English's *Walter Woolfe*--A Reply to
      'A Minor Poe Mystery'," PULC, V (1944), 108-14.
          Regarding the Poe-English feud, and specifically the
      parts of the novel containing passages that malign Poe.
      *See* CJ50.

CC81  GRAVES, CHARLES M.  "Landmarks of Poe in Richmond," Cen, LXVII
      (Apr. 1904), 909-20.
          Poe and the Allans.

# EDGAR ALLAN POE: AN ANNOTATED BIBLIOGRAPHY

*CC: General Biographical Articles*

CC82 GRUBB, GERALD. "The Personal and Literary Relationships of Dickens and Poe," <u>NCF</u>, V (Jun., Sept., Dec. 1950), 1-22, 101-20, 209-21.
   Grubb reviews all information concerning the Poe-Dickens relationship, discusses Poe's reviews of Dickens' work and his literary debt to Dickens, and suggests that the review of <u>EN</u> is not authentic.

CC83 GWATHMEY, EDWARD M. "Kennedy, the Patron of Poe," *John Pendleton Kennedy*. New York, 1931, 168-84.
   A brief account of the Poe-Kennedy friendship.

CC84 HALSEY, FRANCIS WHITING, ed. *American Authors and their Homes*. New York: James Pott & Co., 1901.
   A few words concerning Poe's sordid life.

CC85 HARRISON, JAMES A. "New Glimpses of Poe," <u>Ind</u>, LII (Sept. 6, 1900), 2158-61. Reprinted in *New Glimpses of Poe*. New York: M. F. Mansfield and Co., 1901.
   Thomas H. Ellis's recollections of Poe's adoption by the Allans, with other reminiscences by W. Wertenbaker, B. L. Gildersleeve, and O. P. Fitzgerald.

CC86 _____. "A Poe Miscellany," <u>Ind</u>, LXI (Nov. 1, 1906), 1044-51.
   Twenty-two letters about Poe written between 1849 and 1870.

CC87 HARWELL, Richard B. "A Reputation by Reflection: John Hill Hewitt and Edgar Allan Poe," <u>EUQ</u>, III (Jun. 1947), 104-14.
   A review of the life of John Hill Hewitt, a litterateur now remembered chiefly for his antagonism toward Poe.

CC88 HELFERS, M. C. "The Legendary Edgar Allan Poe." *Assembly* (West Point), XXVII (1969), 6-7.
   On Poe in the army.

CC89 HEMSTREET, CHARLES. "Literary Landmarks of New York," <u>Cr</u>, XLII (1903), 237.
   Reminders of Poe in New York.

CC90 HEWITT, JOHN HILL. *Recollections of Poe*. ed. by Richard Barksdale Harwell, Atlanta: The Library, Emory University, 1949.
   Reprint of Hewitt's reminiscences of Poe and a discussion of their friendship. Hewitt was a journalist and man of letters who knew Poe in the 1820's.

*CC: General Biographical Articles*

CC91  HILL, JOHN S.  "The Diabetic Mr. Poe?" PN, I (Oct. 1968), 31.
   Poe was probably a diabetic and died in a diabetic coma.

CC92  HOGREFE, PEARL.  "A Question of Fair Play," EJ, XIV (Feb.
   1925), 151-5.
    Rather inept denial of Poe's dissipations.

CC93  HOOLE, WILLIAM S.  "Poe in Charleston, South Carolina," AL,
   VI (Mar. 1934), 78-80.
    Poe was in Charleston from Nov. 18, 1827 to Dec. 11,
   1828.

CC94  HOWARD, WILLIAM L.  "Poe and his Misunderstood Personality,"
   *Arena*, XXXI (Jan. 1904), 78-83.
    Howard credits Poe, a dipsomaniac and an epileptic, with
   the first definition of dipsomania.

CC95  HUBBELL, JAY B.  "Charles Chauncy Burr: Friend of Poe," PMLA,
   LXIX (Sept. 1954), 833-40.
    A new light on the journalist who defended Poe after
   his death.

CC96  _____.  "Poe's Mother, with a Note on John Allan," WMQ, XXI
   series 2 (Jul. 1941), 250-4.
    Brief note on the career and death of Elizabeth Poe and
   the character of John Allan.

CC97  HURLEY, LEONARD B.  "A New Note on the War of the Literati,"
   AL, VII (Jan. 1936), 376-94.
    In retaliation against Poe's libel suit, English wove
   into his novel *1844: or The Power of the S. F.* six satirical portraits of Poe, accusing him of drunkenness, chronic
   borrowing, pedantry, egotism, and intellectual affecta-
   tions.

CC98  INGRAM, JOHN H.  "Edgar Allan Poe and Some of his Friends,"
   Bkm, XXXV (Jan. 1909), 167-73.
    Very general.  Adds nothing to Poe scholarship.

CC99  _____.  "Edgar Allan Poe's Last Poem: 'The Beautiful Physician'," Bkm, XXVIII (Jan. 1909), 452-4.
    Mrs. Shew constructed the "poem" from Poe's mutterings
   when he was delirious with fever.

*CC: General Biographical Articles*

CC100   J. T. W.  "A Friend of Poe," SRL, X (Sept. 23, 1933), 138.
Uninformative.

CC101   JACKSON, DAVID K.  *Contributors and Contributions to the
Southern Literary Messenger (1834-64).*  Charlottesville,
Virginia: The Historical Pub. Co., 1936.

CC102   _____.  "Poe and the *Messenger*," SLM, I (Jan. 1939), 5-11.
Jackson discusses Poe's editorship of the SLM and
attributes the magazine's fame to Poe's editorial prac-
tices and caustic criticism.

CC103   _____.  *Poe and the Southern Literary Messenger*, with a Foreword by J. H. Whitty, Richmond, Virgina: Press of the
Dietz Printing Co., 1934.
Detailed discussion of Poe's connection with the magazine, a selected bibliography of his contributions in
1835, 1836, and 1837, and the letters of T. W. White to
Lucian Minor, Beverly Tucker, and John M. Speed.  Should
be read in conjunction with Sidney Moss's *Poe's Literary
Battles*.  *See* CJ50.

CC104   _____.  "Some Unpublished Letters of T. H. White to Lucian
Minor," *Tyler's Quarterly Historical and Genealogical
Magazine*, XVII (Apr. 1936), 224-43.
The letters concern the SLM.

CC105   JACKSON, JOSEPH.  "George Lippard: Misunderstood Man of
Letters," PMHB, LIX (Oct. 1935), 376-91.
A passing reference to Poe's kindness to Lippard.

CC106   JACOBS, ROBERT.  "Poe among the Virginians," VMHB, LXVII
(1959), 30-48.
Objective study of Poe's experiences in Virginia.

CC107   JANUARY, JOSEPHINE P.  "Edgar Allan Poe's 'Child Wife': with
an Unpublished Acrostic by Her to Her Husband," Cen,
LXXVIII (Oct. 1909), 894-6.
Facsimiles of documents relating to Virginia Clemm.

CC108   JONES, L. C.  "A Margaret Fuller letter to Elizabeth Barrett
Browning," AL, IX (Mar. 1937), 70-1.
Margaret Fuller describes Poe as "always shrouded in
an assumed character" and discusses his attitude toward
herself.

# EDGAR ALLAN POE: AN ANNOTATED BIBLIOGRAPHY

*CC: General Biographical Articles*

CC109  KOGAN, BERNARD. "Poe, the 'Penn' and the 'Stylus'," SLM, II
       (Aug. 1940), 442-5.
            A discussion of Poe's failure to establish national
       literary magazines.

CC110  KRUTCH, JOSEPH WOOD. "Edgar Allan Poe: Sick Genius in a Harsh
       World," *New York Herald Weekly Book Review* (Dec. 19, 1948).

CC111  LAVERTY, CARROLL. "A Note on Poe in 1838," MLN, LXIV (Mar.
       1949), 174-6.
            The publication of Lambert Wilmer's "Ode XXX--to Edgar
       Allan Poe" *(Saturday Evening Post,* Aug. 11, 1838) might be
       connected with Poe's move to Philadelphia.

CC112  _____. "Poe in 1847," AL, XX (May 1948), 163-8. Reprinted
       from "Recollections of Edgar Allan Poe by an Unknown
       Woman," HJ (Jul. 21, 1860), 754.
            New facts about Poe at Fordham and the composition of
       "Ulalume."

CC113  LEARY, LEWIS. "Miss Octavia's Autograph Album and Edgar
       Allan Poe," *Columbia Library Columns,* XVII (Feb. 1968),
       9-15.
            Poe's poem in Octavia Walton's autograph album gives
       clues that Poe was in Baltimore between Dec. 1826 and
       May 1827.

CC114  LLOYD, J. A. T. "Edgar Allan Poe, FortnR, CXXIX, ns. 124
       (Jun. 1928), 828-40.
            General remarks about Poe's career.

CC115  LOGRASSO, A. H. "Poe's Piero Marconelli," PMLA, LVIII (Sept.
       1943), 780-9.
            Biographical notes on Piero Marconelli, one of Poe's
       Literati.

CC116  MABBOTT, T. O. "Dumas on Poe's Visit to Paris," *New York
       Times* (Dec. 22, 1929), 5.
            Was Dumas truthful about Poe's visit?

CC117  _____. "A Letter of Poe's Sister," N&Q, CLXIX (Dec. 28, 1935),
       457.
            Letter from Rosalie Poe to the editors of the *Newark
       Advertiser* revealing an error in their biography of Poe.

CC118  _____. "A Lost Jingle by Poe," N&Q, CLXXIX (Nov. 23, 1940),
       371.
            Poe recited an impromptu rhyme to a little girl.

*CC: General Biographical Articles*

CC119    _____. "Poe and Ash Upson," N&Q, CLXXII (May 8, 1937), 330-1.
C        Note concerning the friendship between Poe and Upson.

CC120    _____. "Thomas Dunn English's *Walter Woolfe*," PULC, V (1944),
         106-8.
         Concerning the English-Poe relationship and the publi-
         cation of *Walter Woolfe*.

CC121    MACY, JOHN.  "The Biographers of Poe," *The Critical Game*. New
         York: Boni and Liveright, 1922.
         Discusses C. A. Smith's *Edgar Allan Poe: How to Know
         Him* and complains that Poe's biographies are generally
         "thick with moralisms."

CC122    MARBLE, A. R.  "Willis and Poe: A Retrospective," Cr, XLVIII
         (Jan. 1906), 24-6.
         Marble discusses Poe's friendship with Willis and ap-
         plauds him for being the first critic to repudiate Long-
         fellow as a poet and to claim Hawthorne as a genius.

CC123    MARKS, JEANNETTE AUGUSTUS.  "The Poetry of the Outcast,"
         *Genius and Disaster: Studies in Drugs and Genius*. New York:
         Adelphi Co., 1925.
         Error-ridden study of Poe which concludes that his tuber-
         cular stock had a "neurotic significance," that he was
         victimized by a "crude social mechanism," and that he was
         a drug addict.

CC124    MARTIN, E. J. "Edgar Allan Poe," ER, XLVIII (Mar. 1929), 322-
         35.
         Emphasizes Poe's biography and his disgust with the
         provincialism of American letters.

CC125    MASON, LEO.  "More about Poe and Dickens," *Dickensian*, XXXIX
         (Win. 1942/3), 21-8.

CC126    _____. "Poe-Script," *Dickensian*, XLII (Spr. 1946), 79-81.
         All available information on the Poe-Dickens relation-
         ship.

CC127    _____. "A Tale of Three Authors," *Dickensian*, XXXVI (Spr.
         1940), 109-19.
         Rather strained discussion of the Poe-Dickens-Ainsworth
         association.

CC128    MAURICE, ARTHUR B.  "Poe the Man," *Mentor*, X (Sept. 1922),
         10-12.

*CC: General Biographical Articles*

Encourages the reader to pity the mentally unbalanced
dypsomaniac, Poe.

CC129  McCUSKER, HONOR.  "The Correspondence of R. W. Griswold,"
*More Books,* XVI (Mar. through Jun. 1941), 105-16, 152-56,
190-96, 286-89.

CC130  McDOWELL, TREMAINE.  "Edgar Allan Poe and William Cullen
Bryant," PQ, XVI (Jan. 1937), 83-4.
Concerning Poe's appreciation of Bryant and a letter
from Bryant about Mrs. Clemm.

CC131  MENZIES, S. E.  "Editorial Career of Edgar Allan Poe," NCR,
(Jul. 7, 1912), 4.
Brief summary of Poe's career as an editor.

CC132  MILLARD, BAILY.  "Precocity and Genius," Bkm, XLII (Nov.
1915), 342.
Brief note on Poe's youthful genius.

CC133  MILLER, PERRY.  *The Raven and the Whale.*  New York: Harcourt,
Brace, 1956.
A survey of the era of Poe and Melville in New York,
which touches upon Poe's relations with Reynolds, Clark,
Griswold and English, his editorship of the BJ, and other
episodes in his New York career.

CC134  MOORE, RAYBURN S.  "Note on Poe and the Sons of Temperance,"
AL, XXX (Nov. 1958), 359-61.
Poe joined the Shockoe Hill Division, No. 54, Sons of
Temperance, on Aug. 27, 1849.

CC135  MORGAN, DR. APPLETON, ed.  "Edgar Allan Poe in New York,"
*Valentine's Manual of Old New York* (1921), 71-85.
Notes on Poe from previously unpublished papers of the
New York Shakespeare Society.

CC136  MORIARTY, JOSEPH F.  *A Literary Tomahawking, The Libel Action
of Edgar Allan Poe vs. Thomas Dunn English,* typescript in
Columbia University Library, 1963.
Account of the battle between English and Poe, with
reprints of the original libelous articles and trial
transcripts.

CC137  MORRISSEY, W. P.  "Edgar Allan Poe and Mother Mary," *Ave
Maria,* LIII (Mar. 1, 1941), 279-80.

*CC: General Biographical Articles*

CC138  MOSS, SIDNEY.  "Duyckinck Defends Mr. Poe Against New York's
        Penny-A-Liners," *Studies in American Literature,* V (1969),
        supplement, 74-81.
            Discovers an essay on Poe in HJ (Jan. 9, 1847) by
        Evert Duyckinck.

CC139  _____.  "Poe, Hiram Fuller and the Duyckinck Circle," ABC,
        XVIII (1967), 8-18.
            Concerning Fuller's defamation of Poe.

CC140  _____.  "Poe and the Literary Cliques," ABC, VII (Jun. 1957),
        13-19.

CC141  _____.  "Poe and His Nemesis, Lewis Gaylord Clark," AL, XXVIII
        (Mar. 1956), 30-49.
            Detailed and scholarly discussion of the Poe-Clark
        controversy. *See* CJ50.

CC142  _____.  "Poe and the *Norman Leslie* Incident," AL, XXV (Nov.
        1953), 293-306.
            A discussion of Poe's attack on T. S. Fay's novel
        *Norman Leslie* and the recriminations of Fay and his
        supporters. *See* CJ50.

CC143  _____.  "Poe's Infamous Reputation: a Crux in the Biography,"
        ABC, no. 8 (1958), 3-10.
            Excellent discussion of the Poe-English feud and
        Charles Frederick Briggs' involvement in it. *See* CJ50.

CC144  MOYNE, ERNEST JOHN.  "Did Poe Lecture at Newark Academy?"
        *Delaware Notes,* 26 series (1953), 1-19.
            Poe lectured at Newark on Dec. 23, 1843.

CC145  NASH, DR. HERBERT.  "Reminiscences of Poe," *Book of the Poe
        Centenary.* ABUV, Third Series, II (1909), 193-5.

CC146  NEWCOMER, A. G.  "The Poe-Chivers Tradition Reexamined," SR,
        XII (Jan. 1904), 20-35.

CC147  NICHOLS, MARY GOVE.  *Reminiscences of Edgar Allan Poe.* New
        York: Union Square Book Shop, 1931.
            The story of Mrs. Gove Nichols' Visit to Poe at the
        Fordham Cottage.  Reprinted from article in *Six Penny
        Magazine* (Feb. 1863).

CC148  NOLAN, J. BENNETT.  *Israfel in Berkshire: Poe's Visit to
        Reading, Pennsylvania.* Bicentennial of Reading, 1949.

# Edgar Allan Poe: An Annotated Bibliography

*CC: General Biographical Articles*

CC149  OBERHOLTZER, ELLIS P. "Poe's Days in the Quaker City," <u>BNM</u>, XXV (Aug. 1907), 798-801.
    Uninformative study of Poe's days in Philadelphia.

CC150  OELKE, KARL. "Poe at West Point"--a Revaluation," <u>PSt</u>, VI (Jun. 1973), 1-6.
    "This paper will attempt to prove that, in spite of the spartan regimen, Poe had both the time and opportunity for intellectual pursuits other than curriculum-related studies while he was at West Point...."

CC151  OSBORNE, WILLIAM. "Kennedy on Poe: an Unpublished Letter," <u>MLN</u>, LXXV (Jan. 1960), 17-18.
    Kennedy to G. W. Fahnestock: "He was debauched by the most grovelling appetites--and exhalted by the richest conception of genius....In his special department of thought, our country has produced no poet or prose writer superior to him--indeed, I think, none equal to him." (1869)

CC152  OSTROM, JOHN W. "Another Griswold Forgery in a Poe Letter," <u>MLN</u>, LVIII (May 1943), 394-6.
    Griswold changed a postmark from May 29, 1841 to Mar. 29, 1841 to make it appear that Poe tried to force his way into *Poets and Poetry of America*.

CC153  PAINTER, FRANKLIN V. N. "Edgar Allan Poe," *Poets of the South*. New York: American Book Co., 1903.
    Biographical essay which claims that Poe was an amoral genius, who misused and wasted his talent.

CC154  PARTRIDGE, HENRY MORTON. *The Most Remarkable Echo in the World,* privately printed by Cosmo Printing Co., 1933.
    Tries to prove that Mark Twain was really Edgar Allan Poe.

CC155  POE, E. E. "Poe, the Weird Genius," *Cosmopolitan*, XLVI (Feb. 1909), 243-52.
    Romantic account of Poe's background and Virginia's death: "Poe knelt by a dying wife. His ears were sealed to the cheering multitudes outside, he heard only the death-rattle in Virginia's throat. What were the praises of wolves who yesterday had clamored to devour him...?"

CC156  POE, WILLIAM HENRY LEONARD. *The Poems of William H. L. Poe*. Preface, Intro., Facsimiles and Comments by Hervey Allen and T. O. Mabbott. New York: George H. Doran Co., 1926.

*CC: General Biographical Articles*

Biography of Poe and William, with reprint of William's poetry.

CC157 POLLIN, BURTON R. "Poe in the *Boston Notion*," NEQ,XLII (1969) 585-9.
Compares the sketch of Poe's life in the *Boston Notion* (Mar. 4, 1843) with that in the PSM.

CC158 PRUETTE, LORINE. "A Psychoanalytical Study of Edgar Allan Poe," *American Journal of Psychiatry*, XXXI (Oct. 1920), 370-402.
Applies to Poe's life conclusions drawn from a psychiatric study of an only child by A. A. Brill, 1913. Although her approach differs from Bonaparte's, Pruette does link Poe's obsessions with death and his sado-masochistic tendencies to repressed sexual drives; and she examines his work for evidence of sexual sublimation. Valuable chiefly as a pioneer study, the article is limited by its reliance on outdated information.

CC159 PUTNAM, GEORGE P. *George Palmer Putnam: a Memoir.* 1912.

CC160 QUINN, ARTHUR HOBSON. "The Marriage of Poe's Parents," AL, XI (May 1939), 209-12.
The marriage occurred between Mar. 14 and Apr. 9, 1806.

CC161 REDE, WILLYS. "Edgar Allan Poe: Citizen of Baltimore," *Baltimore Sun* (Jan. 17, 1932).

CC162 REDMAN, CATHERINE. "Edgar Allan Poe, Soldier," *Quartermaster Review*, XVI (Jan.-Feb. 1937), 18-21, 73-4.

CC163 REID, CPT. MAYNE. *Edgar Allan Poe.* Ysleta, Texas: Edwin C. Hill, 1933.
Reminiscences of Reid, an intimate friend of Poe.

CC164 RICHARD, CLAUDE. "Poe and 'Young America'," SB: BSUV, XXI (1968), 25-58.
Discusses Poe's years in New York and demonstrates that his advocacy of the Young America Movement explains certain contradictions and erratic judgments in his work at that time, especially his desire to please Duyckinck.

CC165 ROBBINS, J. ALBERT. "Edgar Allan Poe and His Friends: A Sampler of Letters Written to Sarah Helen Whitman," IUB, no. 4 (Mar. 1960), 5-45.
Posthumous opinions about Poe, selected from letters in the Lilly Library.

*CC: General Biographical Articles*

CC166   \_\_\_\_\_. "Edgar Poe and the Philadelphians: a Reminiscence by
a Contemporary," PN, V (Dec. 1972), 45-7.
Reprints some reminiscences of Poe from the *Philadelphia Sunday Dispatch.*

CC167  ROBERTS, W. "A Dumas Manuscript, Did Poe Visit Paris?' TLS,
1929), 978.

CC168  ROSENFELD, ALVIN H. "The Poe-Chivers Controversy," *Books at
Brown,* XXIII (1969), 89-93.

CC169  SAMPSON, GEORGE. "Misfortunes of Poe," Bkm, LXIX (Jan. 1926),
199.

CC170  SARTAIN, WILLIAM. "Edgar Allan Poe: Some Facts Recalled,"
*Art World,* II (Jul. 1917), 320-3.
Reminiscence and some biographical and critical remarks.

CC171  SCHEFFAUER, HERMAN G. "The Baiting of Poe," *Overland
Monthly,* second series 53 (Jun. 1909), 491-4.
Concerning Bliss Carmen's patronizing attitude toward
Poe.

CC172  SCHREIBER, CARL F. "A Close-Up of Poe," SRL, III (Oct. 9,
1926), 165-7.
A discussion of the Poe-English controversy and a
reprint of the deposition against English in Poe's suit
against the *Evening Mirror.*

CC173  \_\_\_\_\_. "The Donkee and the Elephant," YULG, XIX (Jul. 1944),
17-19.
Thomas Dunn English's scurrilous attack on Poe in
*The John-Donkey.*

CC174  SCHWARTZSTEIN, LEONARD. "Poe's Criticism of William W. Lord,"
N&Q, CC, ns. 2 (Jul. 1955), 312.
Poe's charges of plagiarism were groundless.

CC175  SCOTT, W. T. "New England's Newspaper World," SRL (May 22,
1943), 19-20.
Brief discussion of Cornelia Wells Walter's attack on
Poe's performance at the Boston Lyceum.

CC176  SECCOMBE, THOMAS. "Reflections on the Poe Centenary,"
*Cornhill,* ns. XXVI (Mar. 1909), 337-50.
Corny discussion of Poe's life.

*CC: General Biographical Articles*

CC177  SHUMAN, R. BAIRD. "Longfellow, Poe and the Waif," <u>PMLA</u>, LXXVI
(Mar. 1961), 155-6.
On Poe's review of Longfellow's *The Waif* and the subse-
quent controversy.

CC178  SILVER, ROLLO G. "A Note about Whitman's Essay on Poe," <u>AL</u>,
VI (Jan. 1935), 435-6.
Reprint of interview with Walt Whitman at Poe's funeral,
originally appearing in the *Washington Evening Star* (Nov.
18, 1875).

CC179  SLAIGHT, B. H. *Seven Great American Poets.* 1901, 91-146.

CC180  SOMERVILLE, J. A. "The 'Ifs' in Poe's Life," <u>SLM</u>, I (Dec.
1939), 860.
If Poe had been happier, would his work have been the
same?

CC181  SPIVEY, HERMAN E. "Poe and Lewis Gaylord Clark," <u>PMLA</u>, LIV
(Dec. 1939), 1124-32.
A history of the Poe-Clark feud, which began when Clark
refused to publish in <u>Kn</u> the essay "Our Magazine Literature" which Poe finally published in the *New World* (Mar.
11, 1843).

CC182  STARKE, AUBREY. "Poe's Friend Reynolds," <u>AL</u>, XI (May 1939),
152-9.
Biographical supplement to Almy's article on J. N.
Reynolds, <u>Cpn</u>, II (Win. 1937), 227-45.

CC183  STARRETT, VINCENT. "One who Knew Poe," <u>Bkm</u>, LXVI (Oct. 1927),
196-201.
On John Hill Hewitt and his reminiscences of Poe.

CC184  STERN, MADELEINE B. "Poe: 'The Mental Temperament' for
Phrenologists," <u>AL</u>, XL (May 1968), 155-63.
Reviews the interest of nineteenth-century phrenologists in Poe and notes that "Mesmeric Revelation" was
reprinted in *American Phrenological Journal* (Sept. 1845).

CC185  STERN, PHILIP VAN DOREN. Introduction to *The Portable Poe*.
New York: Viking Press, 1945.
Very general biographical information.

CC186  _____. "The Strange Death of Edgar Allan Poe," <u>SRL</u>, XXXII
(Oct. 15, 1949), 8.

*CC: General Biographical Articles*

CC187  STODDARD, RICHARD H. "Reminiscences of Hawthorne and Poe,"
       Ind, LIV (Nov. 20, 1902), 2756-58.
              Poe abused everyone who tried to help him.

CC188  SWINBURNE, CHARLES A. *Letters Chiefly Concerning Edgar Allan
       Poe from Charles A. Swinburne to John H. Ingram,* London:
       Privately Printed, 1910.

CC189  SYMONS, ARTHUR. "On a Certain Misconception of Poe," *Vanity
       Fair* (Oct. 1916).
              Vague comments about Poe's life.

CC190  TANASOCA, DONALD. "A Twentieth Century 'Stylus'," *Secretary's
       News Sheet: Papers of the Bibliographical Society of the
       University of Virginia,* 29 (Oct. 19, 1953), 1-2.
              Brief discussion of Poe's attempt to launch his maga-
       zine.

CC191  TICKNOR, CAROLINE. "Ingram--Discourager of Poe Biographers,"
       Bkm, XLIV (Sept. 1916), 8-14.

CC192  TODD, WILLIAM B. "The Early Issues of Poe's Tales: 1845,"
       LCUT, VII (Fall 1941), 13-18.
              University of Texas acquisitions of Poe's *Tales* with
       previously unrecorded variants.

CC193  TOWNE, CHARLES H. "Where Poe Once Lived and Loved," MAMP,
       ed. by Dorothy Kissling and Arthur Nethercot, Carlyle
       Straub, 1931, 60-64.

CC194  TOWNSEND-WARNER, SYLVIA. "Cross Out Louisa," NSN, ns. VIII
       (Nov. 17, 1934), 730.
              Correction of errors in Dame Una Pope-Hennessy's *Edgar
       Allan Poe: A Critical Biography. See CJ58.*

CC195  TRENT, WILLIAM P. "The Need of Further Study of Poe's Life,"
       ABUV, Third series II (1909), 185-89.
              Discusses holes in the Poe biography.

CC196  TUERK, RICHARD. "John Sartain and Edgar Allan Poe," PSt, IV
       (Dec. 1971), 21-3.
              Discusses Sartain's recollections of his last meeting
       with Poe and reprints the *Boston Evening Transcript*
       version of *Reminiscences.*

CC197  TURNER, ARLIN. Essay in *Papers on Poe: Essays in Honor of J.
       Ward Ostrom.* Springfield, Ohio, 1972.
              Discusses the relations between Poe and Simms.

*CC: General Biographical Articles*

CC198   TYLER, ALICE M.   "Poe's Footsteps Around Richmond," *Richmond Times-Dispatch* (Jan. 17, 1909).

CC199   WATKINS, WALTER KENDELL.   "Where Poe was Born," ABUV, Third series II (1909), 189-93.
A discussion of the Boston acting experiences of Poe's parents.

CC200   WATTS, CHARLES.   "Poe and Chivers," *Thomas Holly Chivers*. Athens: University of Georgia Press, 1956, 138-69.
Detailed account of the Poe-Chivers relationship and of Chivers' charges of plagiarism, "the frustrated orations of one who has been told that he suffered from being guided by a man whom he regarded as a friend and fellow-poet rather than master, and whose pride would never permit outward discipleship."

CC201   WEGELIN, OSCAR.   "Poe's First Printer," AC, III (Oct. 1926), 31.
Biographical note on Calvin F. S. Thomas.

CC202   _____.   "The Printer of Poe's *Tamerlane*, " NYHSQB, XXIV (Jan. 1940), 23-5.
The printer was Calvin F. S. Thomas.

CC203   WEIDMAN, BETTE S.   "*The Broadway Journal:* a Casualty of Abolition Politics," BNYPL, LXXIII (Feb. 1969), 93-113.
Examines Briggs' objectives in founding the *Journal* in the context of the abolition movement.

CC204   WEISS, SUSAN A.   "Reminiscences of Edgar Allan Poe," Ind, LVI, (May 5, 1904), 1010-4; LVII (Aug. 25, 1904), 443-48.
Anecdotes about Poe.

CC205   WHITE, WILLIAM.   "Edgar Allan Poe: Magazine Journalist," JQ, XXXVIII (Spr. 1961), 196-202.
Brief discussion of Poe's journalism career. Contributes no new information.

CC206   WHITING, MARY B.   "The Life Story of Edgar Allan Poe," Bkm (London), XXXV (Jan. 1909), 173-81.
Early, brief, unimaginative.

CC207   WHITTY, J. H.   "Edgar Allan Poe," *Literary Review*, III (1923), 918.

CC208   _____.   "Letters Relating to Poe's Early Life, " NCR, II (Aug. 4, 1912).

*CC: General Biographical Articles*

Poe's Aunt to Mrs. Allan (Feb. 8, 1813); John Allan to William Henry Poe (Nov. 1, 1824); and other papers from the Ellis-Allan papers.

CC209 \_\_\_\_\_. "Letters Touching the Early Life of Edgar Allen Poe," *Nation*, XCV (Jul. 18, 1912), 55.
Hitherto unpublished letters in the Ellis-Allan papers in the Library of Congress.

CC210 \_\_\_\_\_. "The Passing of Poe's English Biographer," *Dial*, LXI (Jun. 22, 1916), 15.
On the death of John H. Ingram.

CC211 \_\_\_\_\_. "Poeana II, A Parrot," Cpn, ns. I (Aut. 1935), 188-90.
Poe owned parrots when he was a boy.

CC212 WILLIAMS, STANLEY T. "New Letters about Poe," YR, XIV (Jul. 1925), 755-73.
Letters, written in the 1850's, concerning Poe, Mrs. Whitman, and Griswold.

CC213 WILLIS, EOLA. "The Dramatic Careers of Poe's Parents," Bkm, LXIV (Nov. 1926), 288-91.

CC214 WILMER, LAMBERT A. *Merlin* (with recollections of Edgar Allan Poe). ed. with Introduction by T. O. Mabbott. New York: Scholars' Facsimiles and Reprints, 1941.
1827 play about Poe with Wilmer's recollections.

CC215 WILSON, JAMES GRANT. "Memorials of Edgar Allan Poe," Ind, LIII (Apr. 25, 1901), 940-2.
Facsimiles of the marriage bond of Poe and Virginia Clemm, with some letters concerning the wedding and Poe's association with the SLM.

CC216 WILSON, JAMES SOUTHALL. "The Young Man Poe,"" VQR, II (Apr. 1926), 238-53.
Concerning Poe and John Allan.

CC217 WROTH, LAWRENCE C. "Poe's Baltimore," JHAM, XVII (Jun. 1929), 299-312.
A description of mid-nineteenth century Baltimore.

CC218 YEWDALE, MERTON. "Edgar Allan Poe, Pathologically," NAR, CCXII (Nov. 1920), 686-96.

# EDGAR ALLAN POE: AN ANNOTATED BIBLIOGRAPHY

*CD: Poe's Correspondence*

CD1   ANON. A checklist (of the library of Mr. William Brewster in which were included some manuscripts and letters of Poe). New York: The Anderson Galleries, 1921.

CD2   _____. "Letter by Poe is Discovered," *Richmond News Leader* (Mar. 16, 1936).

CD3   _____. "Letters of Edgar Allan Poe, 1845-1849," BNYPL, VI (Jan. 1902), 7-11.
Reprint of previously unpublished letters from the Duyckinck Collection in the New York Public Library.

CD4   _____. "Long Letter by Poe to Irving Revealed," *New York Times* I (Jan. 12, 1930), 1.
Poe invites Irving to contribute to Gr (Jun. 21, 1841).

CD5   _____. "New Letter of Edgar Allan Poe," ESQ, LI (II Quarter, 1968), 51-3.
From Poe to Francis Lieber, Jun. 18, 1836. Poe solicits a literary contribution for SLM.

CD6   _____. "New Poe Letter is to be Sold," *Richmond News Leader* (Oct. 5, 1935).

CD7   _____. "Notes on the Genealogy of the Poe Family," *Gulf States Historical Magazine,* I (Jan. 1903), 281-2.
Letter from Poe to William Poe about the family tree.

CD8   _____. "Three New Poe Letters," ATQ, XIV (Spr. 1972), 89-92.
1. Edgar Allan Poe to John Kirk Townsend, Mar. 9, 1843.
2. Edgar Allan Poe to Edgar S. Van Winkle, Nov. 12, 1836.
3. Edgar Allan Poe to Edgar S. Van Winkle, Nov. 26, 1836.

CD9   _____. "An Unpublished Letter from Edgar Allan Poe," *Quarto,* extra no. with no. 19 (Oct. 1949).
Poe soliciting a manuscript from Lewis Cass, former Governor of Michigan Territory (Jul. 4, 1836).

CD10   BIXBY, WILLIAM K. *Some Edgar Allan Poe Letters,* St. Louis, Missouri, 1915.
Reprinted for private distribution from originals in the collection of W. K. Bixby.

CD11   CAMPBELL, KILLIS. Poe Documents in the Library of Congress," MLN, XXV (Apr. 1910), 127-8.
1. Poe to George Watterson (Nov. 1845).
2. Eliza Poe to Mrs. John Allan (Feb. 8, 1813).

*CD: Poe's Correspondence*

        3. John Allan to William Henry Poe (Nov. 1, 1824).
        4. Edward G. Gump to Poe (Mar. 25, 1827).
        5. George Spotswood to John Allan (May 1, 1827).

CD12    \_\_\_\_\_. "Poe and the *Southern Literary Messenger* in 1837," *Nation,* LXXXIX (Jul. 1, 1909), 9-10.
       Reprint of letter from Poe to Mrs. Sarah J. Hale concerning his whereabouts in 1837.

CD13    CHASE, LEWIS. "A New Poe Letter," AL, VI (Mar. 1934), 66-9.
       A letter of biographical and critical interest from Poe to F. W. Thomas (Oct. 27, 1841).

CD14    FIELD, EUGENE. *Some Letters of Edgar Allan Poe to E. A. N. Patterson.* Chicago, 1898.

CD15    HAGEMANN, E. R. "Two Lost Letters by Poe with Notes and Commentary," AL, XXVIII (Jan. 1951), 508-10.
       Letters written in Richmond (Feb. 8, 1836 and Jun. 8, 1936).

CD16    HARBERT, EARL N. "A New Poe Letter," AL, XXXV (Mar. 1963), 80-1.
       Edgar Allan Poe to Mrs. M. St. Leon. Loud (Sept. 18, 1849).

CD17    HARRISON, JAMES A., ed. *Last Letters of Poe to Sarah Helen Whitman.* Published under the auspices of the University of Virginia, New York: G. P. Putnam's, 1909.

CD18    MABBOTT, T. O. "Letters from George W. Eveleth to Edgar Allan Poe," BNYPL, XXVI (Mar. 1922), 171-95.
       Reprint of the letters in the collection at the New York Public Library.

CD19    \_\_\_\_\_. "Letters from Mary E. Hewitt to Edgar Allan Poe," *Christmas Books* (Hunter College, Dec. 1937), 116-21.
       Reprint of Mary E. Hewitt's letters to Poe (Mar. 15, 1845; Mar. 21, 1845; May 29, 1845; Nov. 10, 1845; Dec. 22, 1845; Apr. 15, 1845).

CD20    \_\_\_\_\_. "On Poe's 'Tales of the Folio Club'," SR, XXXVI (Apr. 1928), 171-76.
       Letter from Poe to a Philadelphia publisher (Richmond, 1836), outlining the scheme for the "Folio Club" tales.

CD21    \_\_\_\_\_. "Poe's Letter about 'The Raven'," AN&Q, III (Jan. 1965), 67.

*CD: Poe's Correspondence*

Edgar Allan Poe to Eli Bowen (Oct. 18, 1848). Concerns the holograph of "The Raven."

CD22 _____. "An Unpublished Letter to Poe," N&Q, CLXXIV (May 28, 1938), 385.
Letter, now in the Boston Public Library, from Charles West Thompson to Poe containing information on magazine publishing in America.

CD23 McCORISON, MARCUS A. "Unpublished Poe Letter," AL, XXXII (Jan. 1961), 455-6.
Uninteresting letter from Poe (New York, Apr. 28, 1864) to the University of Virginia.

CD24 MILLER, JOHN C. "A Poe Letter Re-Presented," AL, XXXV (Nov. 1963), 359-61.
Reprints letter from Edgar Allan Poe to Thomas G. Mackenzie, a boyhood friend (Apr. 22, 1843).

CD 25 _____. "An Unpublished Poe Letter," AL, XXVI (Jan. 1955), 560-1.
Letter from Poe to Lewis Jacob Cist (Jun. 3, 1844).

CD26 MOLDENHAUER, JOSEPH J. "Beyond the Tamarind Tree: a New Poe Letter," AL, XLII (Jan. 1971), 468-77.
A letter from Poe to Thomas Wyatt (Apr. 1, 1841) increases our knowledge of Poe's activities in Philadelphia "and invites a thorough investigation of the Poe-Wyatt relationship."

CD27 NEAL, JOHN. *John Neal to Edgar Allan Poe,* Ysleta, Texas: Edwin B. Hill, 1942.
Letters from Neal to Poe (Jun. 8, 1840) and Stedman to Edwin B. Hill (Jul. 1, 1888).

CD28 OSTROM, JOHN W. *A check-list of Letters to and from Poe. University of Virginia Bibliographical Series,* no. 4, Charlottesville: Alderman Library, 1941.

CD29 _____. ed. *The Letters of Edgar Allan Poe.* Cambridge, 1948.

CD30 _____. *The Letters of Poe: Quest and Answer.* Edgar Allan Poe Society of Baltimore, Inc., 1967.
Discusses problems in editing the letters.

CD31 _____. "A Poe Correspondence Re-edited," *Americana,* XXXIV (Jul. 1940), 409-46.
Reprint and discussion of letters to Dr. J. Evan Snodgrass.

# Edgar Allan Poe: An Annotated Bibliography

*CD: Poe's Correspondence*

CD32   \_\_\_\_\_. "Poe's Manuscript Letter to Stella Lewis--Recently Located," PN, II (Apr. 1969), 36-7.
      The letter was found in the British Museum (No. 31897 fl).

CD33   \_\_\_\_\_. "Second Supplement to *The Letters of Poe*," AL, XXIX (Mar. 1957), 79-86.

CD34   \_\_\_\_\_. "Supplement to The Letters of Poe," AL, XXIV (Nov. 1952), 358-66.

CD35   \_\_\_\_\_. "Two 'Lost' Poe Letters," AN&Q, I (Aug. 1941), 68-9.
      Letters to and from George W. Eveleth.

CD36   \_\_\_\_\_. "Two Unpublished Poe Letters," *Americana*, XXXVI (Jan. 1942), 67-71.
      Edgar Allan Poe to Hiram Haines (Apr. 24, 1840 and Aug. 19, 1836).

CD37 POLLIN, BURTON R. "A Spurious Poe Letter to A. N. Howard," PSt, VI (Jun. 1973), 27.
      The forged letter is dated Dec. 7, 1846.

CD38 SHIPMAN, CAROLYN. "A Poet's Library," Cr, XLII (Apr. 1903), 315-19.
      Reproduction of 3rd page of letter from Poe to F. W. Thomas (Sept. 12, 1842) and a letter from Lowell to Poe (Sept. 27, 1844).

CD39 SMITH. "Poe and Kipling," *Literary Digest, International Book Review*, IV (Sept. 1926), 623.
      About the sale of a Poe letter.

CD40 STANARD, MARY N., ed. *Edgar Allan Poe Letters Till Now Unpublished in the Valentine Museum*, Philadelphia: J. B. Lippincott, 1925.

CD41 STOVALL, FLOYD. "An Unpublished Poe Letter," AL, XXXVI (1965), 514-15.
      Poe to E. L. Fancher (Mar. 28, 1846). The letter concerns the lawsuit against English.

CD42 THORP, WILLARD. "Two Poe Letters at Princeton," PULC, X (Feb. 1949), 91-4.
      Poe to Messrs. Carey and Hart (Jan. 21, 1835) and to F. W. Thomas Esq., Treasury Dept. (Nov. 19, 1842).

## CD: Poe's Correspondence

CD43  VARNER, J. G.  "Poe and Miss Barrett," TLS (Apr. 1935), 244.
Changes a date in a Barrett letter.

CD44  WATTS, CHARLES H.  "Poe, Irving and the *Southern Literary
Messenger*," AL, XXVII (May 1955), 249-51.
Reprint of a letter from Poe to Irving (Jun. 17, 1836).

CD45  _____. "Washington Irving and Edgar Allan Poe," *Books at
Brown*, XVIII (May 1956), 11-13.
Reprint of letter from Poe to Irving (Jun. 7, 1836),
soliciting contributions.

CD46  WHITTY, J. H.  "A New Poe Letter: Hitherto Unpublished Note
Deals With Strange Cryptogram," *Richmond Times-Dispatch*
(Jul. 21, 1935), 15.

CD47  WILSON, JAMES SOUTHALL, ed.  "The Letters of Edgar Allan Poe
to George W. Eveleth," ABUV, XVII (Jan. 1924), 34-59.

CD48  _____. "Unpublished Letters of Edgar Allan Poe," Cen, CVII
(Mar. 1924), 652-6.
Correspondence between Poe and Judge Beverly Tucker.

CD49  WOODBERRY, G. E.  "The Poe-Chivers Papers," Cen, LXV (Jan.,
Feb. 1903), 435-47, 545-58.
The Poe-Chivers correspondence is published and their
relationship discussed.

CD50  _____. "Selections from the Correspondence of Edgar Allan
Poe," Cen, XLVIII (1894), 572-83, 725-35, 854-66.
Letters between Poe and John Pendleton Kennedy, T. W.
White, Nathaniel Tucker, James Kirk Paulding, W. E. Burton,
Washington Irving, Henry Wadsworth Longfellow, Charles
Dickens, and others.


## CE: Poe's Career at the University of Virginia

CE1  ALDERMAN, EDWIN A.  "Edgar Allan Poe and the University of
Virginia," VQR, I (Apr. 1925), 78-84.

CE2  BRUCE, PHILIP A.  "Background of Poe's University Life," SAQ,
X (Jul. 1911), 212-26.
Romantic account of Poe's university years.

CE3  CLOYD, E. L.  "Poe's Career at the University," NCR (May 5,
1912), 3.

# EDGAR ALLAN POE: AN ANNOTATED BIBLIOGRAPHY

*CE: Poe's Career at the University of Virginia*

CE4   FORBES, E. A. "Communication to the Editor on Poe at the University of Virginia'," *Dial*, XXXIII (Aug. 16, 1902), 85-6.

CE5   KENT, CHARLES W. "Poe's Student Days at the University of Virginia," <u>Bkm</u>, XIII (Jul. 1901), 430-40. Reprinted in <u>Bkm</u>, XLIV (Jan. 1917), 517-25.
     Denial that Poe was expelled from the University of Virginia.

CE6   STOVALL, FLOYD. "Edgar Poe and the University of Virginia," <u>VQR</u>, XLIII (Spr. 1967), 297-317.
     Summary of familiar facts about Poe as a student.

CE7   TYLER, ALICE M. "Poe at the University of Virginia," <u>BNM</u>, XXV (Aug. 1907), 793-7.

*CF: Poe in the British Isles*

CF1   CAMPBELL, KILLIS. "New Notes on Poe's Early Years," *Dial*, LX (Feb. 17, 1916), 143-6.
     Concerns Poe's London schooling, his trip to England, his 1829 visit to Richmond, and the two years following his expulsion from West Point.

CF2   CHASE, LEWIS. "John Bransby, Poe's Schoolmaster," <u>Ath</u>, no. 4605 (May 1916), 221-2.

CF3   _____. "More Notes on Poe's School in London," *Dial*, LX (May 25, 1916), 499.
     Notes on the Misses Dubourg School in Chelsea, London, which Poe mentions in "Murders."

CF4   _____. "Poe's First London School," *Dial*, LX (May 11, 1916), 458-9.
     Notes on the school of the Misses Dubourg on Sloan St., Chelsea, London.

CF5   _____. "Poe's Playmates in Kilmarnock," <u>Ath</u>, no. 4611 (Nov. 1916), 554.

CF6   _____. "Poe's School at Stoke Newington," <u>Ath</u>, no. 4606 (Jun. 1916), 294.
     Pictures of the school house.

# EDGAR ALLAN POE: AN ANNOTATED BIBLIOGRAPHY

*CF: Poe in the British Isles*

CF7 CONNELY, WILLARD. *Adventures in Biography: A Chronicle of Encounters and Findings.* London: W. Laurie, 1956, 162-83.
Rather superficial discussion of the influence of England on Poe and the relationships between Poe and The English authors Dickens and Elizabeth Barrett Browning.

CF8 WHITTY, J. H. "Edgar Allan Poe, in England and Scotland," Bkm, XLIV (Sept. 1916), 14-21.
Romantic account of Poe abroad.

*CG: Poe and Women*

CG1 ANON. "New Light on Poe's Tragic Love Affair with Sarah Helen Whitman," CO, LXI (Dec. 1916), 416.
No valuable information.

CG2 _____. "The Spectral Loves of Edgar Allan Poe," CurLit. XLIV (Jan. 1908), 48-9.
Brief and romanticized account of Poe's affairs.

CG3 BAILEY, M. E. "Dove and Raven," Atl, CXXXII (Nov. 1923), 647-56.
Very romantic account of the Poe-Whitman affair.

CG4 BLISS, CAREY S. "Poe and Sarah Helen Whitman," *Book Collector*, XII (Win. 1963), 490.

CG5 BRUCE, P. A. "Edgar Allan Poe and Mrs. Whitman," SAQ, XII (Apr. 1913), 129-40.
The account of the first meeting, romance, and final separation of Poe and Mrs. Whitman.

CG6 DIETZ, FRIEDA MEREDITH. "Poe's First and Final Love," SLM, V (Mar. 1943), 38-47.
On Elmira Royster Shelton.

CG7 FREEMAN, FRED B. JR. "The Identity of Poe's 'Miss B'," AL, XXXIX (Nov. 1968), 389-91.
She is Eliza Butterfield, assistant to the Principal at Franklin Grammar School, Lowell, Massachusetts.

CG8 _____. "A Note on Poe's 'Miss B'," AL, XLIII (Mar. 1971), 115-17.
Biographical notes on Miss Butterfield, "one of the last, if not the last, attachments in [Poe's] life."

*CG: Poe and Women*

CG9   HARRISON J. A. and CHARLOTTE F. DAILEY. "Poe and Mrs. Whit-
        man: New Light on a Romantic Episode," Cen, LXXVII (Jan.
        1909), 439-52.
            Reprint of material from Poe-Whitman correspondence.

CG10  INGRAM, JOHN H. "Edgar Allan Poe and 'Stella'," *Albany
        Review,* I (1907), 417-23.
            Discusses the relationship between Poe and Mrs. S. A.
        Lewis, a minor poetess.

CG11  LAUGHLIN, CLARA E. "Poor Poe," *Stories of Authors' Loves.*
        Philadelphia: J. B. Lippincott Co., 1902.

CG12  REDE, KENNETH. "Poe's Annie: Leaves from Lonesome Years,"
        AC, IV (Apr. 1927), 21-8.
            Fanciful discussion of the relationship between Poe and
        Annie Richmond.

CG13  REECE, JAMES B. "A Reexamination of a Poe Date: Mrs. Ellet's
        Letters," AL, XLII (May 1970), 157-64.
            The Ellet incident, incorrectly ascribed to Jun. 1846,
        actually occurred in Jan. 1846, before Poe moved to Ford-
        ham. It explains other incidents in Poe's life at this
        time: the deterioration of his reputation, his banishment
        from the New York literary salons, and his quarrel with
        Thomas Dunn English.

CG14  REED, MYRTLE. "Edgar Allan Poe," *Love Affairs of Literary
        Men.* New York: G. P. Putnam's Sons, 1907, 131-50.
            Frequently inaccurate account of Poe's relations with
        women.

CG15  REIN, DAVID M. "Poe and Mrs. Shelton," AL, XXVIII (May 1956),
        225-7.
            When Poe left Richmond, he was pessimistic about his
        possible marriage to Elmira Shelton, not optimistic, as
        many scholars have suggested.

CG16  ROBBINS, J. ALBERT. "An Addition to Poe's Steamboat Letter,"
        N&Q, CCVIII (Jan. 1963), 20-1.
            Two new sentences in Poe's letter to Sarah Helen Whit-
        man (Nov. 14, 1848) reveal his confusion.

CG17  ROSENFELD, ALVIN. "Wilkins Updike to Sarah Helen Whitman:
        Two New Letters," *Rhode Island History,* XXV (Oct. 1966),
        97-109.
            Mrs. Whitman had a "literary romance" with Poe.

*CG: Poe and Women*

CG18   SMITH, H. "Poe's Child Wife was his Inspiration," *New York Times Magazine* (Dec. 16, 1928).

CG19   SMITH, JULIA. "A New Light on Poe," <u>SLM</u>, I (Sept. 1939), 575-81.
   A new letter about Estelle Anna Lewis (Poe's "Stella") is discovered.

CG20   STOVALL, FLOYD. "The Women in Poe's Poems and Tales," <u>UTSE</u>, V (1925), 197-209.
   Poe's women were either very innocent or beautiful, abnormally intelligent, and passionately in love with one hero. He only loved women who were like him or who were endowed with qualities he desired.

CG21   TICKNOR, CAROLINE. *Poe's Helen*. New York: Scribner's Sons, 1916.
   The biography of Sarah Helen Whitman, with facsimiles of Poe's love letters and the story of the Poe-Whitman relationship.

CG22   VINCENT, H. P. "A Sarah Helen Whitman Letter about Edgar Allan Poe," <u>AL</u>, XIII (May 1941), 162-7.
   In a letter to Griswold (Dec. 12, 1849), Mrs. Whitman defends Poe's work and professes affection for him, despite her friends' efforts to alienate them.

CG23   WHITMAN, SARAH HELEN. *New Letters about Poe*. ed. by Stanley T. Williams, New Haven: Yale University Press, 1925.

*See also* B98, B238, CK220.

*CH. Portraits of Poe and Illustrations of His Work*

CH1   ANON. "Concerning the portrait of 'Edgar'," <u>SLM</u>, II (Dec. 1940), 652.

CH2   _____. "Famous Picture of Poe is Placed on Exhibition," *New York Times* (Oct. 8, 1933).

CH3   _____. "Man in Old Picture May be Poe," *New York Sun* (Apr. 15, 1939).

# EDGAR ALLAN POE: AN ANNOTATED BIBLIOGRAPHY

*CH: Portraits of Poe and Illustrations of His Work*

CH4 _____. "Mystery Painting Shows a new Poe Portrait," *New York Times* (Jan. 19, 1936).
A painting discovered by Richard Gimbel.

CH5 _____. "Portrait of Edgar Allan Poe," *Connoisseur,* LXIX (May 1924), 24.

CH6 BEARDSLEY, AUBREY VINCENT. *Four Illustrations for the Tales of Edgar Allan Poe.* Chicago: H. S. Stone, 1901.

CH7 _____. *Illustrations to Edgar Allan Poe, from drawings by Aubrey Beardsley.* Indianapolis, Privately Printed, 1926.

CH8 BRINTON, CHRISTIAN. "Félix Vallotton," Cr, XLII (Apr. 1903), 333.
Reproduction of his portrait of Poe.

CH9 CAUTHEN, I. B. JR. "Another Mallarmé-Manet Bookplate for Poe's Raven," PN, V (Dec. 1972), 56.

CH10 COBURN, FREDERICK SIMPSON. *Illustrations for the Works of Edgar Allan Poe,* from original paintings by Frederick Simpson Coburn, New York: Putnam, 1902.

CH11 DOWLING, ALBERT W. "The Mystery in the Rue Amity: A 'Sully Portrait of Poe'," *Baltimore Sun Magazine* (Nov. 6, 1966), 11-12.

CH12 FERGUSON, J. DELANCEY. "Charles Hine and His Portrait of Poe," AL, II (Jan. 1932), 465-70.
Was the portrait done from life or copied from a daguerreotype?

CH13 FLOWER, NEWMAN. "Three Interesting Sinners," Bkm, LXIV (Oct. 1926), 152-55.
Fanciful portrait.

CH14 FRASCONI, ANTONIO. *The Face of Edgar Allan Poe,* with a note on Poe by Baudelaire. South Norwalk, Connecticut, 1959.
A book of original woodcuts.

CH15 HEINTZELMAN, ARTHUR W. "Legros' Illustrations for Poe's Tales," BPLQ, VIII (Jan. 1956), 43-8.

# EDGAR ALLAN POE: AN ANNOTATED BIBLIOGRAPHY

*CH: Portraits of Poe and Illustrations of His Work*

CH16 HOWARD, FRANCIS. "On a Portrait of Edgar Allan Poe," *Anglo-Saxon Review,* IV (1900), 95-6.
Regarding a portrait of Poe supposedly painted in England in 1828 by Henry Inman.

CH17 SCHUBERT, LELAND. "James William Carling: Expressionist Illustrator of 'The Raven'," SLM, IV (Apr. 1942), ]73-81.
Concerning the Carling illustrations of Poe's "The Raven" now at the Edgar Allan Poe Foundation in Richmond, Virginia.

CH18 SCHULTE, AMANDA POGUE and JAMES SOUTHALL WILSON. *Facts about Poe.* University of Virginia, 1926.
Includes portraits and daguerreotypes of Poe by Schulte and a brief biography by Wilson.

CH19 SHEPHERD, LILIAN M. "A New Portrait of Edgar Allan Poe," Cen, XCI (Apr. 1916), 906-7.

CH20 TANNENBAUM, LIBBY. "'The Raven' Abroad: Some European Illustrations of the Work of Edgar Allan Poe," *Magazine of Art,* XXXVII (1944), 123-7.
Reproductions and discussion of illustrations of "The Raven" by Edouard Manet, Odilon Redon, Alphonse Legros and others.

CH21 WHITTY, J. H. "Poe Portrait," Cen, XCII (Aug. 1916), 635.
Whitty claims that the portrait in Cen (Apr. 1916) is not authentic. *See CH19.*

*See also* B11, B47, B53, B99, B101, CC7, CJ43.

*CI: Poe Memorial Shrines and Ceremonies*

CI1 ANON. "Actor's Monument to Edgar Allan Poe at Metropolitan Museum," *Frank Leslie's Illustrated Newspaper* (May 2, 1885).

CI2 _____. "Birthplace of Edgar Allan Poe," *Collecting for Profit,* II (Dec. 1931), 1.

CI3 _____. "Celebration of the Centenary of Edgar Allan Poe," *New York Times* (Jan. 31, 1909).

CI4 _____. "Centenary of Poe Tomorrow," and "Poe in New York," *New York Evening Sun* (Jan. 18, 1909).

# Edgar Allan Poe: An Annotated Bibliography

*CI: Poe Memorial Shrines and Ceremonies*

CI5     _____. *The Edgar Allan Poe Club of Philadelphia Honors Phila-delphia's Greatest Genius* (Jan. 19, 1934).
    Consists of leaflets and vignettes.

CI6     _____. "The Edgar Allan Poe Shrine, Richmond," Richmond, Virginia: The Old Stone House, 1923.
    Notes from Woodberry, Armistead C. Gordon, C. Alphonso Smith, George H. Sargeant, Carl Van Doren, Philip Alexander Bruce, James Southall Wilson, J. H. Whitty, Bliss Perry, W. P. Trent.

CI7     _____. "Edgar Allan Poe's Cottage at Fordham," *New York Times Supplement* (Feb. 14, 1897), 14.

CI8     _____. "The Grave of Poe," BNM, XXV (Aug. 1907), 810-11.

CI9     _____. "Find Poe Monument in Museum Discard," *New York Times* (Dec. 31, 1926).

CI10     _____. "Poe Centenary Commemoration," *Pathfinder*, III, no. 7 (Jan. 1909), 127-51.
    Memorial articles in prose and verse by William Ellery Leonard, Carl Holliday, Glen Levin Swiggett, Frank Waller Allen, Cornelius Weygandt.

CI11     _____. *The Poe Cottage: Poe Park and the Shakespeare Society of New York,* 1916.
    Reprints of articles from the *New York Times,* 1905, about efforts of the Shakespeare Society to preserve Poe's cottage at Fordham.

CI12     _____. "Poe Memorial to be Unveiled in Boston, " CSM (Jan. 18, 1924).

CI13     _____. "Unveiling Bust of Edgar Allan Poe," *New York Herald* (Jan. 20, 1909).

CI14     BEAVER, KATE W. "Poe and the Hall of Fame," *Dial*, XXX (Jan 1, 1901), 8.

CI15     BENNETT, PATRICIA. "Poe's Grave in Baltimore Draws New Pilgrim Hosts," *New York Times* (Oct. 11, 1925).

CI16     BLITZSTEIN, MADELIN. "House Where Poe Wrote Restored in his Honor," *New York Times* (Jan. 14, 1934).

CI17     BRUNO, GUIDO. "Poe and O. Henry," *Bruno's Weekly,* III (Jul. 29, 1916), 874-5.

*CI: Poe Memorial Shrines and Ceremonies*

Deplores the fact that $100,000 is being spent on a
memorial to Poe, who died in poverty.

CI18  BUCHHOLZ, HEINRICH EWALD, ed.  *Edgar Allan Poe, A Centenary
       Tribute*.  Baltimore: Edgar Allan Poe Memorial Association,
       Warwick York, 1910.
            Commemoratory articles by Oliver Hackle, William P.
       Trent, John Prentiss Roe, Suzette W. Reese and Mrs. John
       Wrenshall.

CI19  CHAPMAN, JOHN JAY.  "In Memory of Edgar Allan Poe," *New York
       Times Book Review* (Nov. 2, 1924).
            Contest for poem in Poe's memory.

CI20  DEDMOND, FRANCIS B.  "Paul Hamilton Hayne and the Poe West-
       minster Memorial," MyHM, XLV (Jun. 1950), 149-51.
            Concerning Hayne's interest in the Poe Memorial.

CI21  DYSON, ARTHUR THOMAS.  "An appeal for the Preservation of the
       Poe Cottage at Fordham," *New York Times Saturday Review of
       Books* (Aug. 10, 1905).  Reprinted as pamphlet, 1915.

CI22  FOLSOM, MERRILL.  "Poe's Eastern Kingdom," *Ford Times*, LXI
       (1968), 8-12.
            Poe shrines in America.

CI23  HAIGH, D. C.  "Colonial Village of the Dearborn Inn," MHM,
       XXI (1937), 252-5.
            Concerning a replica of Poe's Fordham Cottage at
       Dearborn.

CI24  HUNTER, REX.  "The Grave of Edgar Allan Poe," Bkm (London),
       LXV (Mar. 1924), 292-3.
            Description of his grave.

CI25  IRVING, CARTER.  "Honor for the Mother Poe Never Knew," *New
       York Times Magazine* (Apr. 5, 1925), 4.
            Concerning the stone on Elizabeth Arnold Poe's grave.

CI26  KENT, CHARLES W.  *The Unveiling of the Bust of Edgar Allan
       Poe in the Library of the University of Virginia*.  Lynch-
       burg: J. P. Bell Co., 1901.
            Brief discussion of Poe's association with the Uni-
       versity of Virginia.

CI27  MacCRACKEN, HENRY NOBLE.  "Poe," *Poe Centenary Exercises*.
       TBSAS (Jan. 9, 1909).

*CI: Poe Memorial Shrines and Ceremonies*

CI28 McCABE, LIDA R. "A Pilgrimage to Poe's Cottage," BB, XXV
(Jan. 1903), 592-8.
Rather emotional discussion of the cottage at Fordham.

CI29 MENDOZA, AARON. "A Poe Centennial," *New York Herald-Tribune*
(Mar. 8, 1931).

CI30 NELSON, CHARLES A. "Edgar Allan Poe, Raven Mantel," CUQ, X
(Mar. 1908), 193-4.
Concerning William Hemstreet's donation of the "Poe
Raven Mantel."

CI31 North Side Board of Trade in Commemoration of the One Hund-
redth Anniversary of the Birth of Edgar Allan Poe (Jan.
19, 1909).
Brief tribute from poets and public figures.

CI32 PENDENNIS. "Where Poe Wrote 'The Raven'," *New York Times*
(Aug. 20, 1905).
Regarding the lack of foresight on the part of the New
York Legislature, which purchased the land next to the Poe
cottage, but not the cottage itself.

CI33 STEDMAN, EDMUND CLARENCE. "Poe, Cooper, and the Hall of Fame,"
NAR, CLXXXV (Aug. 1905), 801-12.
Concerning Poe's admission to the Hall of Fame.

CI34 _____. "Poe's Cottage at Fordham," Cen, LXXIII (Mar. 1907),
770-3.

CI35 TRAYLOR, M. G. "'To Keep It in Beauty': The Poe Shrine," SLM,
I (Apr. 1939), 265-8.

CI36 TURNBULL, MRS. L. "New Statue of Edgar Allan Poe by Sir Moses
Ezekiel," *Art and Architecture,* V (May 1917), 306-8.

CI37 WHITTY, J. H. "Poem to Mark the Tomb of Mother," *Richmond
Times-Dispatch* (Oct. 6, 1935), 3.

*See also* B10, B12, B21, B29, B39, B44, B50, B69, B102, B136, CJ30.


*CJ: Full Length Critical and Biographical Studies*


CJ1 ALLEN, HERVEY. *Israfel: The Life and Times of Edgar Allan
Poe.* New York: George H. Doran, 1926.
Allen was the first to examine the Ellis-Allan

*CJ: Full Length Critical and Biographical Studies*

correspondence carefully and to investigate other important
source material. As a result, he unearthed many important
and hitherto unknown facts about Poe. More sympathetic
than Woodberry, but occasionally overworks material and
tends to sentimentalize. Biography is superseded by Quinn.

CJ2 ALLEN, MICHAEL. *Poe and the British Magazine Tradition*. New
York: Oxford University Press, 1969.
Investigates Poe's interest in contemporary British
magazines. Concludes that Poe was a "radically divided
man," whose idealization of the artist as an elite member
of society conflicted with his need to adjust to the demo-
cratizing of literature, with its demand for mass-popular-
ity and mass-producing techniques.

CJ3 ALTERTON, MARGARET. *Origins of Poe's Critical Theory. Uni-
versity of Iowa Humanistic Studies,* II (Apr. 15, 1925);
New York: Russell and Russell, 1965.
Investigates the genesis of Poe's critical theories in
British periodicals, the law, drama, fine arts, philosophy,
and science.

CJ4 ASSELINEAU, ROGER. *Edgar Allan Poe*. University of Minnesota
Pamphlets on American Writers, Minneapolis: University of
Minnesota Press, 1970.
Excellent introduction to Poe. Takes a reasonable
psychological approach in its descriptions of Poe as a
writer driven by neurosis.

CJ5 BARNES, DORA. *Edgar Allan Poe Centenary,* London: Stoke
Newington English PL, 1944.

CJ6 BELL, LANDON. *Poe and Chivers*. London and Columbus: Charles
A. Trowbridge Co., 1931.
Bell defends Poe against Damon's charges of plagiarism
by accusing Chivers of plagiarizing from Poe. Chivers
made such charges against Poe when he was going insane.
*See* CC49.

CJ7 BENET, LAURA. *Young Edgar Allan Poe*. New York: Dodd Mead,
1941.
Fictionalized biography for young readers. Stops with
his editorship of Gr.

CJ8 BITTNER, WILLIAM. *Poe: A Biography*. Boston and Toronto:
Atlantic Monthly Press Book, 1962.
Readable biography, midway between scholarly and popular
types.

# Edgar Allan Poe: An Annotated Bibliography

*CJ: Full Length Critical and Biographical Studies*

CJ9    BONAPARTE, MARIE. *The Life and Works of Edgar Allan Poe:
       A Psychoanalytical Interpretation.* Foreword by Sigmund
       Freud. trans. by John Rodker, London: Imago Pub. Co.,
       1949. Chapter on "Morella" reprinted in CJ16 and in *Art
       and Psychoanalysis,* ed. William Phillips. New York:
       Criterion Books, 1957, 54-88.
           Detailed Freudian interpretation of Poe's work. His
       poetry and tales were created out of "intense emotional
       fixations and painful infantile experiences." His oedipal
       fixation is a motif in all his work.

CJ10   BONDURANT, AGNES MEREDITH. *Poe's Richmond.* Richmond: Garrett
       and Massie, Inc., 1942.
           Although some aspects of the book are highly conjectural,
       such as her discussion of Poe's probable political ac-
       quaintances in Richmond, the author does account for the
       influence of Poe's early environment on his career.

CJ11   BRADDY, HALDEEN. *Glorious Incense: the Fulfillment of Edgar
       Allan Poe.* Washington: Scarecrow Press, 1952.
           Braddy tries to discover the man behind the legend.
       Considers the critical reception of Poe's work, his liter-
       ary revisions, aesthetic models, and his criticism.

CJ12   BROUSSARD, LOUIS. *The Measure of Poe.* Norman: University of
       Oklahoma Press, 1969.
           Reviews Poe's criticism, analyzes Poe's work in terms
       of the ideas in *Eureka,* presents a bibliography of Poe
       criticism. Inadequate in all three areas.

CJ13   BURANELLI, VINCENT. *Edgar Allan Poe.* New York: Twayne Pub-
       lishers, Inc., 1961.
           Treats Poe's aesthetic theories, his flights from
       reality, scientific theories, romanticism, psychology, and
       social criticism. Extensive discussion of his stories and
       poetry.

CJ14   CAMPBELL, KILLIS. *The Mind of Poe and Other Studies.* Cam-
       bridge: Harvard University Press, 1932.
           Discusses Poe's intellectual achievements, his super-
       ficial knowledge, his attachment to facts rather than to
       ideas, his lack of moral and spiritual insight. Poe was
       not isolated from his environment but drew heavily on
       current events for material for his stories. Campbell
       also discusses influences on Poe's work and his con-
       temporary reputation.

# Edgar Allan Poe: An Annotated Bibliography

*CJ: Full Length Critical and Biographical Studies*

CJ15 CARLSON, ERIC W., ed. *Casebook on "The Fall of the House of Usher,"* Columbus, Ohio: Charles E. Merrill Casebook Series, 1971.
Reprints full essays and excerpts from Lawrence, Abel, Spitzer, Wilbur and others. Each essay is listed individually.

CJ16 _____. *The Recognition of Edgar Allan Poe*. Ann Arbor: University of Michigan Press, 1966.
Reprints essays from Lowell, Fuller, James, Matthews, Huxley, Eliot, Auden and others. Each essay is noted individually.

CJ17 CHASE, LEWIS. *Poe and his Poetry*. London: G. G. Harrap, 1913. Reprinted by Folcroft Press, 1969.

CJ18 CHIARI, JOSEPH. *Symbolism from Poe to Mallarmé: The Growth of a Myth*. Foreword by T. S. Eliot, London: Rockliff, 1956.
The book investigates the relationship between Poe and the French symbolists, particularly Mallarmé. Chiari discusses the development of the Symbolist movement in France and Poe's influence on that movement. He concludes that Poe's influence on the French poets is slight, that Mallarmé, Baudelaire and Valéry "saw in Poe an image of [themselves] and of [their] dreams." Whatever influence he did have rested in his attitude toward life and art.

CJ19 CHIVERS, THOMAS HOLLY. *The Life of Edgar Allan Poe,* ed. with Introduction by Richard Beale Davis from manuscript in the Huntington Library, San Marino, California. New York: E. P. Dutton, 1952.

CJ20 CLUTTON-BROCK, A. *Edgar Allan Poe*. London, 1921.

CJ21 CODY, SHERWIN. *Poe: Man, Poet, Creative Thinker*. New York: Boni and Liveright, 1924.
Biography and discussion of Poe as a poet who expressed an ideal of the beautiful. In Poe creative and analytical powers were harmonized.

CJ22 COOPER, L. U. *The Young Edgar Allan Poe*. Toronto, 1964.

CJ23 DAVIDSON, EDWARD. *Poe, a Critical Study*. Cambridge: Belknap Press of Harvard University, 1957. Excerpts reprinted in CJ79.
Discussion of Poe's place in the Romantic tradition. Poe "moved toward what, in terms of literary romanticism,

# Edgar Allan Poe: An Annotated Bibliography

*CJ: Full Length Critical and Biographical Studies*

is known as an organic or unitary principle." He never
emerged, however, from the first stage of Romanticism,
"the young man's private indulgence in solitude and in
terror." Extensive analyses of the poetry and tales.

CJ24 DAVIS, HARRIET E. *Elmira: The Girl Who Loved Edgar Allan Poe*.
New York: Houghton Mifflin, 1966.
Fictional version of the Poe-Royster affair written for
young people.

CJ25 DORSET, GERALD. *An Aristocrat of Intellect*. London: Hornsey
Printers, 1959.
Biographical, bibliographical and critical discussions.
Dorset suggests that Poe's concept of a "new world of
intellect and unity of effect" is a key to the work of
contemporary novelists, especially Camus and Graham Greene.
Fails to develop his suggestion that Poe influenced Tur-
geniev and Dostoevsky.

CJ26 DOUGLAS-LITHGOW, R.A. *Poe's Vindication: the Individuality
of Edgar Allan Poe*. Boston, 1911.

CJ27 DOW, DOROTHY. *Dark Glory*. New York: Farrar and Rinehart,
1931.
Romantic biography.

CJ28 EWERS, HANNS HEINZ. *Edgar Allan Poe*. Trans. by Adele Lewisohn. New York: B. Heubsch, 1917.
A Romantic himself, Ewers believes that art is a means
of exploring areas beyond consciousness. He suggests that
Poe experimented with drugs and liquor to release himself
from consciousness and to create new art values. With an
attitude that approaches the worshipful, Ewers also discusses Poe's Americanism, his influence on French literature, his kinship with Hoffmann and Heine, and his literary experiments.

CJ29 FAGIN, NATHAN BRYLLIAN. *The Histrionic Mr. Poe*. Baltimore:
Johns Hopkins Press, 1949.
Poe was a frustrated actor who turned the world into
a stage and acted out rather than lived his tales. His
characters are masks. He was "a creative actor who throws
himself into a role and proceeds to interpret it by tap-
ping the emotional reservoir within him...and by shaping
it into a unified creation." His identification with
his own character was so complete that for him life and
art were often fused, and the actor became the character.

# Edgar Allan Poe: An Annotated Bibliography

*CJ: Full Length Critical and Biographical Studies*

CJ30   FRAYNE, ANTHONY. *The Rose-Covered Cottage of Edgar Allan Poe in Philadelphia*. Philadelphia: J. Frayne, 1934.

CJ31   GOLDBERG, ISAAC. *Poe as a Literary Critic*. Kansas: Haldeman-Julius Co., 1924.

CJ30   GOSSE, EDMUND W. *Edgar Allan Poe and his Detractors*. London, 1928.

CJ33   HALLIBURTON, DAVID. *Edgar Allan Poe, A Phenomenological View*. Princeton University Press, 1973.
     "I have tried to show that Poe's imaginative writings constitute an overarching unity....The recurrent features in this system include power struggles between beings over who shall survive and on what terms; confrontations between an isolated individual and another human being or between an individual and the material world, or, in cases where he externalizes something that reacts against him, between an individual and himself: a fascination with states or conditions of being...."

CJ34   HARRISON, JAMES A. *The Life and Letters of Edgar Allan Poe*. New York: T. W. Crowell, 1903.
     Interesting primarily as an early biography and whitewash of Poe's character. Superseded by Quinn, Wagenknecht and the critical studies since 1903.

CJ35   HOFFMAN, DANIEL. *Poe Poe Poe Poe Poe Poe Poe*. New York: Doubleday, 1972.
     Psychedelic, egotripping view of Poe, who "wormed his way into my guts and gizzard and haunted my brain and laid a spell upon my soul which this long harangue is an attempt to exorcise." Defies summary, but should be read.

CJ36   HOUGH, ROBERT L. *Literary Criticism of Edgar Allan Poe*. Lincoln, Nebraska, 1965.

CJ37   HOWARTH, WILLIAM L. *Twentieth Century Interpretation of Poe's Tales*. New Jersey: Prentice-Hall, Inc., 1971.
     Reprints essays and excerpts from Levin, Mooney, O'Donnell, Stauffer, Gargano and others. Each essay listed individually.

CJ38   JACOBS, ROBERT D. *Poe: Journalist and Critic*. Baton Rouge: Louisiana State University Press, 1969.
     In what is probably the definitive work on Poe's critical writings, Jacobs traces the influence of eighteenth-century aesthetic theories on Poe and Poe's

*CJ: Full Length Critical and Biographical Studies*

own development as a critic. He shows that "Poe as a
working critic looked backward toward the mechanistic
psychological aesthetic of the previous century and for-
ward to the dynamic organicism of the romantic period."

CJ39  JOYCE, JOHN ALEXANDER. *Edgar Allan Poe*. F. T. Neely Co.,
      1901.
          Popular early biography which relies on personal remin-
      iscences for information. Describes Poe as a literary
      iconoclast.

CJ40  KEILEY, JARVIS. *Edgar Allan Poe: a Probe*. New York: Prome-
      theus Press, 1927.
          Rapt, impressionistic statement, mostly fictitious.

CJ41  KRUTCH, JOSEPH WOOD. *Edgar Allan Poe: a Study in Genius*. New
      York: Alfred Knopf, 1926. Excerpts reprinted in CJ64.
          Early psychoanalytic interpretation describes Poe's
      stories as neurotic fantasies which protected him against
      madness. Poe was impotent and obsessed with the death of
      beautiful women (related to the death of his mother), a
      theme which he elevated to an aesthetic principle. Toward
      the end of his life, he lost the ability to translate his
      fantasies into art.

CJ42  LAUVRIERE, EMILE. *The Strange Life and Strange Loves of Edgar
      Allan Poe*. trans. by Edwin Gile Rich, Philadelphia and
      London: J. B. Lippincott, 1935.
          Poe was a madman with a disordered brain, addicted to
      alcohol and opium. "Towards the end of his career...this
      poor superior degenerate was only a partially reason-
      ing madman, a half-insane person, whose circular, double-
      formed madness permitted the dipsomaniac impulses to graft
      themselves on the phases of melancholic depression, and
      the flights of mystic erotomania on the crises of maniacal
      exaltation."

CJ43  LEIGH, OLIVER. *Edgar Allan Poe: the Man, the Master, the
      Martyr*. Franklin Morris Co., 1906.
          Discusses portraits of Poe, the authenticity of *Lavanta*
      and Poe biographies.

CJ44  LEVINE, STUART. *Edgar Allan Poe: Seer and Craftsman*. Deland,
      Florida: Everett/Edwards, 1972.
          Discusses the importance of the occult tradition in
      Poe's work.

*CJ: Full Length Critical and Biographical Studies*

CJ45   LINDSAY, PHILIP. *The Haunted Man: a Portrait of Edgar Allan Poe*. London: Hutchinson, 1953.
　　　　Fictionalized biography.

CJ46   LLOYD, JOHN ARTHUR THOMAS. *The Murder of Edgar Allan Poe*. London: S. Paul, 1928.
　　　　Emotional, almost hysterical indictment of Griswold and whitewash of Poe's character.

CJ47   LOCARD, EDMOND. *Edgar Allan Poe: Detective*. New York: type-script, 1941.

CJ48   MACY, JOHN A. *Edgar Allan Poe*. Boston: Small, Maynard, 1907.
　　　　General biographical and critical discussions which contribute little to Poe criticism.

CJ49   MORTON, MAXWELL. *A Builder of the Beautiful*. Boston: R. G. Badger, 1928.

CJ50   MOSS, SIDNEY. *Poe's Literary Battles*. Durham: Duke University Press, 1963.
　　　　Indispensible study of Poe's relationships with members of the literary cliques of the 1830's and 40's. Focuses on Poe's contributions to American literary criticism and his problems with Clark, Griswold, Briggs, Longfellow, and others.

CJ51   ＿＿＿＿. *Poe's Major Crisis: His Libel Suit and New York's Literary World*. Durham: Duke University Press, 1970.
　　　　Traces Poe's expulsion from the New York literary world, beginning with his publication of "The Literati" and his libel suit against Hiram Fuller and Augustus Clason. Once again Moss redresses the pictures of Poe as totally self-destructive and insane.

CJ52   NAKAMURA, JUNICHI. *Edgar Allan Poe's Relations with New England*. Hokuseido Press, 1957.
　　　　Superseded by Moss. *See* CJ50, CJ51.

CJ53   OBER, WARREN and others. *The Enigma of Poe*. Boston, 1960.

CJ54   PARKS, EDD WINFIELD. *Edgar Allan Poe as Literary Critic*. Athens: University of Georgia Press, 1964.
　　　　Thesis is that Poe's critical theories were formed by his experiences as a magazine editor and critic and that Poe was concerned with contemporary literary theories. Discusses Poe's articles on Simms, Cooper and Scott.

# EDGAR ALLAN POE: AN ANNOTATED BIBLIOGRAPHY

*CJ: Full Length Critical and Biographical Studies*

CJ55   PHILIPS, MARY ELIZABETH. *Edgar Allan Poe, the Man*.   Chicago
       and Philadelphia: John C. Winston, 1926.
             Contains some indispensible materials on the one hand
       and many factual errors on the other.   According to Wagen-
       knecht, the style is "barbaric"; Hubbell calls it "badly
       written, poorly arranged, and inadequately indexed."

CJ56   POE, ELISABETH ELLICOTT and VYLLA POE WILSON. *Edgar Allan
       Poe, a High Priest of the Beautiful*.  Washington: Stylus
       Publishing Co., 1930.
             Popular biography.

CJ57   POLLIN, BURTON R. *Discoveries in Poe*.   Notre Dame: University
       of Notre Dame Press, 1970.
             New sources, influences, and hypothesis about Poe's
       death.

CJ58   POPE-HENNESEY, UNA. *Edgar Allan Poe: a Critical Biography*.
       London: Macmillan, 1934.
             Factual material is occasionally unreliable and criti-
       cism seldom insightful or original.   Emphasizes the auto-
       biographical element in the stories and poetry. *See*
       CC194.

CJ59   PORGES, IRWIN. *Edgar Allan Poe*.   Philadelphia and New York:
       Chilton Books, 1963.
             Popular, dramatic biography.

CJ60   QUINN, ARTHUR HOBSON. *Edgar Allan Poe*.   New York: Appleton-
       Century-Crofts, 1941.
             Remains the definitive biography of Poe, although it
       should now be supplemented by Moss and by recent biograph-
       ical studies.

CJ61   QUINN, PATRICK F. *The French Face of Edgar Allan Poe*.
       Carbondale: Southern Illinois University Press, 1957.
       Excerpts reprinted in CJ64 and CJ79.
             Reexamination of Poe through French interpretation of
       his work.   Reviews criticism of Bonaparte, Gaston Bache-
       lard, Régis Massac, Marcel Francon and Baudelaire.   Dis-
       cusses the split in Poe's personality between the creative
       and analytical faculties (which leads to the theme of the
       double in his work).   Through his stories, Poe embarked
       on an "imaginative exploration of the frontiers of con-
       scious knowledge."

*CJ: Full Length Critical and Biographical Studies*

CJ62 RANS, GEOFFREY. *Edgar Allan Poe*. Writers and Critics Series,
Edinburgh and London: Oliver and Boyd, 1965.
Broad essay examines Poe's works against the background
of his aesthetics and general philosophy.

CJ63 RANSOME, ARTHUR A. *A Critical Study: Edgar Allan Poe*.
Stephen Swift, 1912.
General interpretation of Poe's poetry and tales emphasizes "his unconcluded search [for]...a philosophy of
beauty that should also be a philosophy of life. He did
not find it, and the unconcluded nature of his search is
itself sufficient to explain his present vitality. Seekers
rather than finders stimulate the imagination."

CJ64 REGAN, ROBERT. *Poe: a Collection of Critical Essays*. New
Jersey: Prentice-Hall, Inc., 1967.
Reprints essays from Quinn, Gargano, Huxley, Stovall,
Tate and others. Each essay is listed in this biblio-
graphy.

CJ65 REIN, DAVID. *Edgar Allan Poe: the Inner Pattern*. New York:
Philosophic Library, 1960.
Analysis of Poe's poetry and tales in terms of the
theory that literary creations, like dreams, reveal the
unconscious desires and fears of the author. The theory is
useful, but Rein applies it indiscriminately and amateur-
ishly. Poe is the hero of all his stories and poems. His
major themes are derived from his guilt (for having neglec-
ted Virginia), fear of death, feelings of persecution and
inadequacy, celibacy, a mother-complex, and masochism.

CJ66 ROBERTSON, JOHN, M.D. *Edgar Allan Poe, a Study*. San Francisco: Bruce Brough, 1921.
Part I is a primitive psychoanalytical study which discusses Poe's inherited nervous disorders and dypsomania.
Accepts Griswold's charges, but believes that Poe's morbid
heredity absolves him of responsibility for his crimes.
Part II is a bibliography of Poe's writings.

CJ67 ROGERS, DAVID. *The Major Poems and Tales of Edgar Allan Poe*.
New York: Monarch Press, 1965.
Typical *Monarch Notes*, competently written.

CJ68 SETON, ANYA. *Dragonwyck*. Philadelphia, 1946.

CJ69 SHANKS, EDWARD. *Edgar Allan Poe*. London: Macmillan, 1937.
Reprinted by Folcroft Press, Folcroft, Pennsylvania, 1969.
Worshipful biography with a discussion of the symbolism
in the tales and poetry.

# Edgar Allan Poe: An Annotated Bibliography

*CJ: Full Length Critical and Biographical Studies*

CJ70    SMITH, CHARLES ALPHONSO. *Edgar Allan Poe: How to Know Him*.
        Indianapolis: Bobbs-Merrill, 1921.
            Treats Poe's reputation and influence in Germany, Russia,
        Spain, Italy and England, denies that he was isolated from
        social and political events of the day, and discusses his
        views on slavery, education, and the literary relationship
        between America and England.

CJ71    STANARD, MRS. MARY MANER PAGE. *The Dreamer: a Romantic
        Rendering of the Life Story of Edgar Allan Poe*.   Phila-
        delphia: Bell Book and Stationery Co., 1909.
            Romanticises Poe's life.

CJ72    STEWARD, ROBERT ARMISTEAD. *The Case of Edgar Allan Poe: a
        Pathological Study Based on an Investigation of Lauvriere*.
        Richmond: Whittel and Shepperson, 1910.

CJ73    STOVALL, FLOYD. *Edgar Poe: Essays New and Old on the
        Man and His Work*.   Charlottesville: University Press of
        Virginia, 1969.
            Reprints several previously published essays.   New
        essays discuss Poe's career, a new Poe discovery, and
        Poe's poetic theories.

CJ74    THOMPSON, JOHN REUBEN. *The Genius and Character of Edgar
        Allan Poe*. ed. and arranged by James H. Whitty and James R.
        Rindfleisch.   Richmond, Virginia: Privately Printed by
        Garrett and Massie, 1929.
            Reprint of Thompson's reminiscences, originally written
        shortly after Poe's death.

CJ75    VELER, RICHARD, ed.  *Papers on Poe: Essays in Honor of J.
        Ward Ostrom*.   Springfield, Ohio: Chantry Music Press at
        Wittenberg University, 1972.
            Seventeen essays on Poe by Ridgely, Griffith, Carlson,
        Gravely, Thompson, and others, listed separately in this
        bibliography.

CJ76    WAGENKNECKT, EDWARD.  *Edgar Allan Poe: The Man Behind the
        Legend*.  New York: Oxford University Press, 1963.
            Surveys Poe's scholarship and tries to distinguish
        between legend and fact. Adds little to Poe criticism.

CJ77    WEISS, SUSAN ARCHER.  *The Home Life of Poe*.  New York: Broad-
        way Publishing Co., 1907.
            Weiss drescribes Poe's "private home-life, domestic and
        social, as she has heard it described by Poe's most
        intimate friends."

*CJ: Full Length Critical and Biographical Studies*

CJ78   WINWAR, FRANCES, pseud. *The Haunted Palace.* New York:
        Harper, 1959.
           Informative popular biography which occasionally sub-
        stitutes intuition for scholarship and sometimes overworks
        materials: "['The Black Cat'] was one of Poe's stories of
        sadistic, reasonless cruelty, perpetrated in fiction for
        the release of some pent-up destructive urge, roused,
        perhaps, by work ill-rewarded, by misery and misfortune
        and a sense of not receiving his just rewards in a world
        that preferred the sham to the genuine and compensated
        genius by poverty and persecution."

CJ79   WOODSON, THOMAS, ed. *Twentieth Century Interpretations of
        "The Fall of the House of Usher,"* New Jersey: Prentice-
        Hall, Inc., 1969.
           Reprints essays by Bonaparte, Lawrence, Abel, Spitzer,
        Cox, Feidelson and others. A note by each entry indicates
        that it has been reprinted in this anthology.

*CK: General Critical Articles*

CK1   ANON. "The Detached Terrorism of Edgar Allan Poe." <u>TLS</u>,
       3595 (Jan. 22, 1971), 95-6.

CK2   _____. "Dreamer of Things Impossible," <u>Acad</u>, LXI (Sept. 1901),
       262-3.
          General remarks on the poetry and tales.

CK3   _____. "Edgar Allan Poe." *Manchester Guardian Weekly,* LXI
       (Oct. 13, 1949), 5.
          Brief note at the centenary of Poe's death.

CK4   _____. "Edgar Allan Poe," *Spectator,* CII (Jan. 23, 1909),
       122-3.
          Poe is immoral and his imagination is unamerican.

CK5   _____. "Israfel in the Laboratory," <u>TLS</u> (Oct. 7, 1949), 648.
          General comments about Poe's poetry.

CK6   _____. "Poe and Other Poets," <u>Acad</u>, LXXVIII (May 14, 1910),
       467-71.
          Brief and unconstructive comparison of Poe with Tenny-
        son and Wordsworth.

CK7   _____. "A Reviewer's Notebook," *Freeman,* V (Apr. 19, 1922),
       142-3.

*CK: General Critical Articles*

CK8 _____. "Satanic Streak in Poe's Genius," <u>CurLit</u>, XLVIII (Jan. 1910), 93-6.

    Poe resembles Milton's Lucifer in his intellectual pride and obsession with the beauty of corruption. He believed in demons; his imagination was absorbed by the preternatural, which found expression in themes of ruin and terror.

CK9 _____. "The Supernatural in Nineteenth-Century Fiction," <u>ER</u>, CLXXXXVII (Apr. 1903), 395-418.

    Supernaturalism supplies the deficit of religious emotion in the nineteenth century. Poe never really relies entirely upon the supernatural--never passes entirely beyond the normal. He occasionally descends to the "sensationalism of physical repulsion" for his effects. Poe makes the nightmare seem real; Hawthorne makes the real seem like a nightmare.

CK10 ABEL, DARREL. "Edgar Poe: A Centennial Estimate," <u>UKCR</u>, XVI (Win. 1949), 77-96.

CK11 ABERNATHY, JULIAN. "Edgar Allan Poe: Literature in the South," *American Literature*. New York: Maynard, Merrill and Co., 1903, 310-23.

    Text-book summary. Poe taught Americans "their first lesson in independent literary criticism, demonstrating the function of taste and literary principles."

CK12 ADAMS, ROBERT M. *Nil: Episodes in the Literary Conquest of Void During the Nineteenth Century*. New York: Oxford University Press, 1966.

    Somewhat familiar generalizations about Poe. Adams discusses the tension between his extreme rationality and his characters' anxieties about the void.

CK13 ADAMS, R. P. "Romanticism and the American Renaissance," <u>AL</u>, XXIII (Jan. 1952), 419-32.

    Discusses Poe in terms of Morse Peckham's definition of the negative Romantic, one who has "rejected the old static mechanistic world order but [has] not...arrived at a satisfactory dynamic and organic metaphysics to replace it." Feelings of guilt, alienation, and fear result from his view of a purposeless universe. Poe is a Romantic in his "partial subscription to an organic theory of form in literature" and in his use of symbolism to express unconscious thoughts, but his Romanticism is negative because he refuses to confront the origin of his inspiration and tries to analyse it as if it were a machine.

# Edgar Allan Poe: An Annotated Bibliography

*CK: General Critical Articles*

CK14  ALTERTON, MARGARET and HARDIN CRAIG.  Introduction to *Edgar Allan Poe: Representative Selections*.  New York: Hill and Wang, 1935.
　　　Extensive essay on Poe which focuses on the development of his ideas about imagination, literary criticism, the metaphysics of *Eureka*.

CK15  ASKEW, MELVIN.  "The Pseudonymic American Hero," <u>BuR</u>, X (Mar. 1962), 224-31.
　　　Discusses the meaning of name changes in American literature, especially "Ligeia."

CK16  AUDEN, W. H. Introduction to *Edgar Allan Poe: Selected Poems and Poetry,* 1950.  Reprinted in *The Recognition of Edgar Allan Poe,* ed. by Eric Carlson, Ann Arbor: University of Michigan, 1966.
　　　Divides Poe's stories into two groups: those "concerned with states of wilful being, the destructive passion of the lonely ego to merge with the ego of another" and those in which "the hero is as purely passive as the I in dreams." In the former group, the "operatic quality of his prose and 'decor' in his tales" preserve the illusions he creates.  Auden also discusses Poe's poetry and criticism and concludes that he "was one of the first to suffer <u>consciously</u> the impact of the destruction of the traditional community and its values, and he paid the heaviest price for this consciousness."

CK17  AUSLANDER, JOSEPH.  "The Poet of Ravens and Lost Ladies," <u>MAMP</u>, ed. by Dorothy Kissling and Arthur H. Nethercot, New York: Carlyle Straub, 1938.
　　　Stresses the frustrations and contradictions of Poe's life that found their way into his poetry and made it the poetry of human experience.

CK18  BABCOCK, MERTEN C.  "The Wizards of Baltimore: Poe and Mencken," *Texas Quarterly,* XIII (1970), 110-15.
　　　Comparison of the two writers.

CK19  BAILEY, J. O.  "Poe's Theory of the Soul," *Carolina Quarterly,* II (Mar. 1950), 38-43.

CK20  BALDWIN, C. S.  "Poe's Invention of the Short Story," *American Short Stories*.  New York, 1904.

CK21  BARCUSE, B.  "Beddoes and Poe," <u>SRL</u>, IX (Jun. 10, 1933), 643.
　　　Useless comparison.

*CK: General Critical Articles*

CK22   BARZUN, JACQUES. "A Note on the Inadequacy of Poe as a
         Proofreader and of His Editors as French Scholars," RR,
         LXI (Feb. 1970), 23-6.
              Points out errors in Poe's written French. *See* CO35.

CK23   BASORE, JOHN W. "Poe as an Epicurean," MLN, XXV (Mar. 1910),
         86-7.
              Poe is Epicurean in his attempts to "rationalize the
         ...conception of materialistic quasi spirits" and in his
         idea that divine nature is unparticled matter.

CK24   BAYM, NINA. "Function of Poe's Pictorialism," SAQ, LXV (1966),
         46-54.
              Poe's main concern is to investigate the nature of the
         imagination, which is symbolized in his stories by the
         setting. Thus, when a character in Poe is overwhelmed by
         his environment, he is really being destroyed by his im-
         agination. For Poe, the journey of the soul into its im-
         agination was not liberating, as it was for the Romantics
         and Transcendentalists, but destructive and maddening.
         *See* Wilbur, CK372, for the opposite view.

CK25   BELL, LONDON. "A Defense of Poe," *Kit-Kat*, V (1916), 1-12.

CK26   BENTON, RICHARD P. "The Study of Poe --Past and Present,"
         ESQ, LX (Fall 1970), 3-4.
              Brief and uninformative.

CK27   BETT, W. R. "Edgar Allan Poe: the Oedipus Complex and Genius,"
         *The Infirmities of Genius*. New York: Philosophical Libra-
         ry, 1952, 69-78.

CK28   BEYER, THOMAS P. "Edgar Allan Poe, a Tribute," *Methodist
         Review*, XCV (Jul. 1913), 536-43.
              Attempt to rescue Poe from barbs of critics, but lacks
         solid scholarship.

CK29   BIER, JESSE. *The Rise and Fall of American Humor*. New York:
         Holt, Rinehart & Winston, 1968, 368-72.
              Discusses Poe's parodies, "diddlings," jokes, spoofs.
         "A great deal of Poe's work may be closer to black humor
         than it is...to the seriously irrational."

CK30   BITTNER, WILLIAM. "Poe and the 'Invisible Demon'," GaR, XVII
         (Sum. 1963), 134-8.
              On Poe's personal and literary use of alcohol.

# Edgar Allan Poe: An Annotated Bibliography

*CK: General Critical Articles*

CK31    BLAKE, WARREN B.    "Edgar Allan Poe, a Centenary Outlook,"
   *Dial*, XLVI (Feb. 16, 1909), 103-5.
    General evaluation of Poe, his debt to Hawthorne and
Hoffmann and his contributions to literature.

CK32    BLANCH, ROBERT.    "Poe's Imagery: an Undercurrent of Childhood
   Fears," *Furman Studies*, XIV (1967), 19-25.
    Poe's imagery suggests that his childhood fears
remained with him through adulthood.

CK33    BLANKENSHIP, RUSSELL.    "The Romantic Movement in Virginia,
   Edgar Allan Poe," *American Literature as an Expression of
   the American Mind*.  New York and London: Henry Holt, 1931.
    Poe escaped from reality by creating a fantasy world
in which the unbelievable and fantastic were normal. He was
the last Gothic Romancer. His weakness was his detachment
from his time and environment. He turned his back on current events and used up his energy "exploiting his purely
imaginative faculty in the realm of mystery and horror."

CK34    BLOCK, L. J.    "Edgar Allan Poe," <u>SR</u>, XVIII (Oct. 1910), 385-
   403.
    Brief treatment of the major phases of Poe's work: his
literary techniques, his influence, his short stories,
humor, and aesthetic theories.

CK35    BOWEN, EDWIN W. "Poe, Fifty Years After," *Forum*, XXXI (Jun.
   1901), 501-10.
    Although acknowledging Poe's greatness, Bowen concen-
trates on Poe's weaknesses as a writer: his narrow political range, his inability to develop characters, and his
abnormally developed imagination.

CK36    BOWRA, C. M.    "Edgar Allan Poe," *The Romantic Imagination*.
   Cambridge: Harvard University Press, 1949, 174-97.
    Poe declared that the supernal, not the phenomenal, is
the only reality, a theory which appealed to Baudelaire
and Mallarmé, who believed with Poe that the task of the
poet is to glimpse the eternal.  Poe went beyond the
Romantics in identifying the real world they sought, "the
world which makes sense of the fragmentary and painfully
actual," and in asserting that beauty is the only concern
of poetry.  The problem with his poems is that their
emotive power is more important than their meaning, for
Poe assumed that his presentation of the supernal world
must be as indefinite as his perception of it.

# EDGAR ALLAN POE: AN ANNOTATED BIBLIOGRAPHY

*CK: General Critical Articles*

CK37    BOYNTON, PERCY H.  "Poe and Journalism," EJ, XXI (May 1932),
        345-52.  Reprinted in *Literature and American Life*.  New
        York: Ginn and Co., 1936.
            Poe's work was influenced by his love of journalism and
        his desire to own a literary magazine.  His interest in
        writing for the popular market (which was a desire for
        fame) accounts for his burlesques of conventional liter-
        ature.  He even considered abusive criticism to be good
        copy.

CK38    BRADDY, HALDEEN.  "Edgar Allan Poe's Princess of Long Ago,"
        *Laurel Review,* IX (1969), 23-31.
            Discusses the "princesse perdue" theme in Poe's poetry.

CK39    _____.  "Poe and Peacock," NMQR, XIX (Aut. 1949), 393-7.
            General critical comments.

CK40    _____.  "Poe's Flight from Reality," TSLL, I (Aut. 1959), 394-
        400.
            Examines Poe's work for symbols of escape.  Poe's use of
        names, his love of the past and future, and his vagueness
        about time and space are indications of his obsession with
        the escape theme.  Braddy concludes that "the single large
        impression that emerges from the body of Poe's art is his
        determined flight from reality."

CK41    BRADLEY, WILLIAM A.  "Edgar Allan Poe's Place in Literature,"
        BNM, XXV (Aug. 1907), 789-92.
            Poe was the first writer to make conscious literary use
        of derangement.  "He narrowed the scope of Romantic
        lyricism" until it lost "its generally human appeal," but
        he intensified it by "divining the moment when the soul
        perceives its dependence on the senses." His stories are
        "symbolic fantasies....poetic renderings of the destiny
        of the soul in life."

CK42    BRADY, CHARLES A.  "Lunatics and Selenophiles," *America* (Jul.
        1958), 448-9.
            Discusses imaginary trips to the moon.

CK43    BREEN, E. J. "A Century of Poe," *Commonweal,* XV (Dec. 9,
        1931), 156.
            Brief notes on Poe's career.

CK44    BRENNER, RICA.  "Edgar Allan Poe," *Twelve American Poets
        Before 1900*.  New York: Harcourt Brace and Co., 1933,
        142-69.
            The hero of Poe's tales is a projection of Poe himself.

*CK: General Critical Articles*

The analytic character is the man Poe thought himself to be, while the disordered personality is Poe "seeking in his imagination an escape from poverty, sorrow, and bitterness."

CK45  BROOKS, CLEANTH.  "Edgar Allan Poe as Interior Decorator," *Venturer*, VIII (1968), 41-6.
   Poe's interiors reflect the dehumanization of his characters.

CK46  BROOKS, VAN WYCK, *America's Coming of Age*.  E. P. Dutton and Co., Inc., 1915.
   Poe is totally isolated from human experience; no moral world exists for him.  In his work, human values are replaced by chemical and mechanical men, emotions, and landscapes.  He is sterile and inhuman, withered at the core, like one of Hawthorne's heroes who has cut himself off from the community.  His work is "the most menacing indictment of a society which is not also an all-embracing organism."

CK47  _____.  "Poe in the South," *The World of Washington Irving*. E. P. Dutton and Co., Inc., 1944, 337-61.
   Brooks' opinion of Poe has matured since he wrote his first essay on him in 1915.  His biographical remarks touch briefly on hereditary and environmental factors that were responsible for Poe's instability.  He now considers Poe an unparalleled literary genius, a skilled craftsman, and a great innovator.  Brooks suggests that Poe tried to assure himself of his sanity by insisting that his stories were calculated.  He also discusses the element of incipient madness and symbolic wish fulfillment in Poe's work and Poe's need to be an intellectual dictator, which accounts for his desire to establish a magazine, for his interest in cryptography and for his creation of Dupin.

CK48  BROPHY, BRIGID.  "Detective Fiction: A Modern Myth of Violence?" HudR, XVIII (1965), 11-30.
   Believes that the French Revolution was "the positive impulsion towards the particular invention of the detective story by Poe and its general adoption as a myth pattern."  The Revolution liberated reason but also "laid human nature under the imputation of blood guilt.  What Poe invented in the first detective story was a hero who delivers the community...from just that imputation...by a better application of reason.

# EDGAR ALLAN POE: AN ANNOTATED BIBLIOGRAPHY

*CK: General Critical Articles*

CK49    BROPHY, LIAM.  "An American and Irish Poet Compared," *Irish Monthly*, LXI (Nov. 1933), 711-14.
    Comparison of Poe and Mangan—similar characteristics of intemperance, depression, morbidity, and a sense of desolation.

CK50    _____.  "Poe and Mangan, Twin Souls," *Ave Maria*, LXX (Jul. 16, 1949), 71-5.

CK51    BROWNELL, WILLIAM C.  "Poe," *American Prose Masters*.  New York: Charles Scribner's Sons, 1909, 207-267; original in Scrib, XLV (Jan. 1909), 69-84.
    Brownell covers every aspect of Poe's work, emphasizing his "perpetual state of warfare with his environment," the artificiality and stageyness of his work, his sensationalism, disinterest in human experience and morality.  He is generally unsympathetic to Poe.

CK52    BRUCE, P.A.  "Certain Literary Aspects of Poe," SR, XXII (Jan. 1914), 38-49.
    Poe had neither a Byronic complex nor a Shelleyan desire for revolt.  His view of art and concentration on the beautiful are Greek.  His work has the morality, purity and reserve of Tennyson, without "the commonplace domestic issues" or "rigid conventionality" of the laureate.

CK53    BUCHHOLTZ, HEINRICH EWALD, ed.  "Edgar Allan Poe: a Centenary Tribute," The Edgar Allan Poe Memorial Association, Baltimore: Warwick York Inc., 1910.
    Includes memorial articles by Oliver Hackle, William P. Trent, John Prentice Roe, Suzette Woodworth Reese, Mrs. John C. Wrenshall.

CK54    BURANELLI, VINCENT.  "Judgment on Poe," AQ, XVII (1965), 259-60.

CK55    BURT, DONALD C.  "Poe, Bradbury and the Science Fiction Tale of Terror," *Mankato State College Series*, III (1968), 76-84.

CK56    BURTON, RICHARD.  "Edgar Allan Poe," *Literary Leaders of America*.  New York: Charles Scribner's Sons, 1904.
    Favorable but general remarks about Poe's poetry.

CK57    BUTTERFIELD, R. W.  "Total Poe," EIC, XXII (Apr. 1972), 196-206.
    Discusses Poe as a "crucially American figure" whose "personal melancholy and desperation find an analogy,

*CK: General Critical Articles*

sometimes conscious, more often unconscious, in his sense
of self-ravage and decay as the pattern of American
history."

CK58   CABELL, JAMES BRANCH.   "To Edgar Allan Poe, Esq.," *Ladies and*
        *Gentlemen.*  New York:   Robert M. McBride & .Co., 1934, 241-
        62.
            "American has produced just one literary genius whose
        existence the world recognizes...." namely, Poe.

CK59   CAIRNS, WILLIAM B.   "Poe's Use of the Horrible," *Dial,* L (Apr.
        1, 1911), 251-2.
            The horror in Poe exists not for its own sake, but to
        dramatize the relationship between the physical and the
        spiritual.

CK60   CAMBON, GLAUCO.   *The Inclusive Flame: Studies in American*
        *Poetry.*  Bloomington: Indiana University Press, 1903.

CK61   CAMPBELL, KILLIS.   "Edgar Allan Poe," *Cambridge History of*
        *American Literature.*  New York: G. P. Putnam's Sons, 1918,
        55-70.
            General survey of Poe which takes the middle road
        between the Griswoldites and whitewashers.  On the positive
        side, Poe had a clear intellect and a great faculty for
        analysis.  Spontaneity and unequalled vividness of imagery
        characterize his poetry.  Although he was the most import-
        ant short story writer before 1850, his tales are often
        flimsy, feeble and humorless, and they suffer from his in-
        ability to develop characters and from his morbidity.

CK62   _____.  Introduction to *Poe's Short Stories.*  New York: Amer-
        ican Authors Series, Harcourt Brace, 1927.

CK63   _____.  "Miscellaneous Notes on Poe," <u>MLN</u>, XXVIII (Mar. 1913),
        65-9.
            Discusses a lecture by Poe, proper names in Poe, and
        sources of "To Science," "The Gold Bug," and "Anastatic
        Printing."

CK64   _____.  "Poe's Treatment of the Negro and the Negro Dialect,"
        <u>UTSE</u>, XVI (1936), 106-14.
            Poe said very little about the Negro, was not actively
        involved in abolition, did not reproduce the Negro dialect
        accurately, generally depicted the Negro as stupid, and
        believed that slavery is the best solution to the Negro
        question.

*CK: General Critical Articles*

CK65    \_\_\_\_. "The Relation of Poe to his Times," <u>SP</u>, XX (Jul. 1923), 293-301.
     Although his work contains no distinctively American themes or traditions, Poe was not isolated from contemporary events and ideas. *Politian,* for example, is based on the tragedy of anti-bellum Kentucky, and his other work contains allusions to aerial navigation, mesmerism, and cholera. In addition, his book reviews reveal his profound concern for literary standards of the day.

CK66   CANBY, HENRY SEIDEL. "Poe," *Classic Americans.* New York: Harcourt, Brace and Co., 1931, 263-308.
     Canby regards Poe primarily as a journalist whose attitudes about literature were shaped by his interest in journalism. This essay is a catalogue of Poe's deficiencies: his lack of humor, "fudge," meretriciousness, and technical trickery. Also discusses Poe's split personality: his neurotic desire to escape to a subliminal world vs. his powerful sense of order and passion for science. The whole man functioned only when his "dreams sprang from deep intuitions...or when they crystalized about an idea in an order prepared by his logical mind." Too often, however, the technical overpowered the poetical sense.

CK67   CARGILL, OSCAR. "The Decadents," *Intellectual America, Ideas on the March.* New York: The Macmillan Co., 1941, 176-185.
     In a discussion of Poe's neurotic attitude toward love and sex, Cargill suggests that his need to defend Mrs. Allan against her promiscuous husband led him to champion an intense purity and chastity. Obviously "highly sexed," he used up his sexual energy remaining chaste. His belief that the death of a beautiful woman is a subject for poetry had its source in his sublimation of sexual energy into the worship of ideal Beauty. Finally, Cargill traces Poe's "entire aesthetic" to necrophilia.

CK68   CARLSON, ERIC T. "Charles Poyen Brings Mesmerism to America," *Journal of the History of Medicine and Allied Science,* XV (Apr. 1960), 121-32.

CK69   CARLSON, ERIC W. "Poe's Vision of Man," *Papers on Poe: Essays in Honor of J. Ward Ostrom.* Springfield, Ohio, 1972.
     Poe's major theme is "the quest for rebirth of mind and soul and thereby the realization of a new unity of being," and <u>not</u> "an essentially unsound emphasis on death and destruction."

CK70   CARTER, H. HOLLAND. "Some Aspects of Poe's Poetry," *Arena,*

XXXVII (Mar. 1907), 281-5.
Brief discussion of the melancholy strain in Poe's poetry, of his poetic principles, odd names, and weird effects.

CK71  CARY, RICHARD.  "Poe and the Great Debate," TSLL, III (Sum. 1961), 223-33.
Discusses Poe's role in encouraging the development of American literature.  Should be read in conjunction with Moss.  *See* CJ50.

CK72  CASALE, OTTAVIO M.  "Poe on Transcendentalism," ESQ, L (I Quarter 1968), 85-97.
An analysis of Poe's attitudes toward New England concludes that despite his contempt for New England ideas, Poe "had no quarrel with the metaphysical substance of transcendentalism."

CK73  CECIL, L. MOFFITT.  "Poe's 'Arabesque'," CL, XVIII (Win. 1966), 55-70.
Study of the historical meanings of "Arabesque," Cecil believes that Poe used the term in its strictly etymological sense to mean "Arabian" as well as in its stylistic or genre sense.  The Eastern influences on Poe account for his use of the term in its first sense.

CK74  _____.  "Poe's Wine List," PN, V (Dec. 1972), 41-2.
Discusses the importance of wine in some of Poe stories including "The Cask," and "Thou Art the Man."  Concludes that Poe was not a wine expert and that when he wrote about wine, he was almost always ridiculing those characters who pretended to be connoisseurs.

CK75  CHANDLER, ALICE.  "'The Visionary Race': Poe's Attitude Toward his Dreamers," ESQ, LX (Fall 1970), 73-82.
Traces the development of Poe's philosophy from a belief in a "dualistic universe in which the ideal can only be achieved through the destruction of the real" to an acceptance of a "monistic world, in which art is both creative and redemptive."  Most of Poe's major stories are discussed in this context.

CK76  CHARVAT, WILLIAM.  "Poe: Journalism and the Theory of Poetry," *Aspects of American Poetry: Essays Presented to Howard Mumford Jones*. ed. Richard Ludwig.  Columbus: Ohio State University Press, 1962.  Reprinted in *The Profession of Authorship in America, 1800-1870*. ed. Matthew J. Bruccoli, Columbus: Ohio State University Press, 1968, 84-98.

*CK: General Critical Articles*

Traces Poe's publishing ventures, his effort to become a popular writer. Sees *Eureka* as his effort to create a modern epic, "to journalize scholarship to make knowledge and theory diverting."

CK77  CHESTERTON, G. K. "Best Detective Story," *Chesterton's Weekly,* XIX (May 24, 1934), 180.

CK78  CHRISTOPHER, J. R. "Poe and the Detective Story," *Armchair Detective,* II (1968), 49-61.

CK79  CHURCHILL, WILLIAM. "Edgar Allan Poe," *The Marvelous Year.* New York: Heubsch, 1909, 23-6.
       General essay on Poe, the voice of protest against the commonplace.

CK80  CLOUGH, WILSON O. "The Use of Color Words by Edgar Allan Poe," PMLA, XLV (Jun. 1930), 598-613.
       A discussion of Spengler's and Havelock Ellis's theories of color symbolism and the possibility of applying these theories to Poe's work.

CK81  COAD, ORAL. "The Gothic Element in American Literature before 1835," JEGP, XXIV (1925), 72-93.
       Examines American literature for traces of Gothic terror before Poe.

CK82  CODY, SHERWIN. "Poe's Contribution to American Literary History," *Dial,* XXXV (Sept. 16, 1903), 161-2.
       General statement which considers Poe first as a poet, second as a writer of short stories, and third as a critic anxious to educate the American public to appreciate good literature.

CK83  COHEN, J. M. "The Dream World of Edgar Allan Poe," *Listener,* XLII (Sept. 1949), 540-1.
       Discusses Poe as a precursor of surrealism.

CK84  COWIE, ALEXANDER. "Edgar Allan Poe," *The Rise of the American Novel.* New York: American Book Company, 1948, 300-06.
       Poe is important primarily as a reviewer and critic.

CK85  COWLEY, MALCOLM. "Aidgarpo," NR, CXIII (Nov. 5, 1945), 607-10.
       Except for his mechanical attitude toward literature and his eagerness to create effects, Poe is outside the mainstream of American life and literature. He was the first to develop theories of symbolism that were destined for popularity in France.

# Edgar Allan Poe: An Annotated Bibliography

*CK: General Critical Articles*

CK86   \_\_\_\_\_. "The Edgar Allan Poe Tradition," *Outlook*, CXLIX (Jul. 1928), 497-9.
    Accounts for the American underestimation of Poe and the recent excesses in psychological interpretations of his work. Poe's most serious flaw was "his lack of visualization; his inability to see, or to make the reader see the background of his stories." In spite of his faults, however, he was probably the most important American man of letters, with a wide range of intellectual interests and a great hostility to specialization.

CK87   COX, ELETHEA. "Lecture on Edgar Allan Poe," Typescript (Feb. 16, 1905), in Columbia University.
    Summary of Poe's life and general comments on his work.

CK88   COX, JAMES. "Edgar Poe: Style as Pose," VQR, XLIV (Win. 1968), 67-89. Reprinted in CK79.
    Attempts to rescue Poe from charges of vulgarity and contrivance by demonstrating that the postures and impersonations of his narrators are essential to the meaning. "Poe's 'art'...reveals that terror is the illusory life into which man perpetually flees....This larger terror...is the recognition which Poe's form enacts" through impersonation.

CK89   CUNLIFF, MARCUS. "Edgar Poe," *The Literature of the United States*. London and Baltimore: Penguin Books, 1954.
    General discussion of Poe concludes that he was a lesser man of letters than Irving and Cooper, neurotic, childlike, more interesting to read about than to read.

CK90   CURTI, MERLE. "The American Exploration of Dreams and Dreamers," JHI, XXVII (1966), 391-416.

CK91   DALY, C. D. "The Mother Complex in Literature," *Yearbook of Psychoanalysis,* IV (1948), 172-210.
    The "Menstruation Complex" is the source of tension in Poe's stories.

CK92   DANDRIDGE, DANSKE. "Poe on Happiness," PL, XV (Dec. 1904), 108-10.
    Describes Poe's conditions for bliss.

CK93   DANIEL, ROBERT. "Poe's Detective God," *Furioso*, VI (Sum. 1951), 45-54. Excerpts reprinted in CJ37.
    Daniel extends More's idea that Poe's horror stories are substitutes for Christian myths. In a world in which crime has replaced good and evil, Dupin becomes the essential God, a gifted individual, a worker of miracles, "the

*CK: General Critical Articles*

most enduring religious substitute in the imagination...
of a century of hero-worship." *See* CO30.

CK94 DANNER, RICHARD. "The Poe-Matthews Theory of the American
Short Story," <u>BSUF</u>, VIII (Win. 1967), 45-50.
Brander Matthews popularized Poe's theory of the short
story.

CK95 DARNALL, F. M. "The Americanism of Edgar Allan Poe," <u>EJ</u>, XVI
(Mar. 1927), 185-92.
An analysis of American characteristics of individual-
ism, romance, and idealism and how they are reflected in
Poe's work.

CK96 DAVIDSON, EDWARD H. *Introduction to Selected Writings of
Edgar Allan Poe*. Boston: Houghton Mifflin Co., 1956.

CK97 DAVIS, DAVID B. *Homicide in American Fiction, 1798-1860:
a Study in Social Values*. Ithaca, New York: Cornell
University Press, 1957, *passim*.

CK98 DAVIS, MALCOLM. "Poets at Midnight," <u>YLM</u>, LXXV (Dec. 1909),
144-8.

CK99 DeLaMARE, WALTER. "A Revenant," *The Wind Blows Over*. London:
Farber and Farber, 1936, 185-235.
Disorganized, uncritical little essay in imaginary
setting.

CK100 DICKINSON, THOMAS H. *The Making of American Literature*. New
York: Appleton-Century Co., 1932.
Few superficial pages on Poe.

CK101 DIDIER, EUGENE L. "The Poe Cult," <u>Bkm</u>, XVI (Dec. 1902), 336-
40. Reprinted in *The Poe Cult*.
Brief essay on Poe's popularity and the value of Poe
editions.

CK102 DINAMOV, S. "The Scientifico-Fantastic Novels of Edgar
Poe," *Literature and Marxism* (Moscow), III (1931), 51-64.
Dinamov believes that Poe's stories embody a Marxist
conflict (a struggle between the landowning South and
manufacturing North) and thus expose the inadequacy of
capitalism.

CK103 DOUGLAS, NORMAN. "Edgar Allan Poe, From an English Point of
View," *Putnam's*, V (Jan. 1909), 433-8.
Vague, general assessment and vindication of Poe.

*CK: General Critical Articles*

CK104  DOUGLAS-LITHGOW, R. A. "Poe's Place in American Literary
        History," *Massachusetts Magazine,* IV (Apr. 1911), 75-81.
        Brief but laudatory remarks.

CK105  DOYLE, SIR ARTHUR CONAN. *New York World* (Jan. 21, 1923).
        Doyle discusses Poe's contributions to literature, in-
        cluding the detective story, the semi-scientific story,
        the horror and buried treasure stories.  He also acknow-
        ledges his own debt to Poe.

CK106  _____. *Through the Magic Door.*  London: Smith, Edler, 1907,
        p. 114.
        Considers Poe the "supreme original" short story writer
        to whom all writers of detective fiction are indebted.

CK107  DURICK, JEREMIAH.  "The Incorporate Silence and the Heart
        Divine," *American Classics Reconsidered*. ed. by Harold C.
        Gardiner, New York: Charles Scribner's Sons, 1958, 176-92.
        Takes issue with many common assumptions about Poe,
        especially that he created under the influence of stimu-
        lants and was isolated from the world.  Believes that
        *Eureka* is as idealistic as it is materialistic and that
        Poe's philosophy of nature is as pantheistic as Emerson's.
        Poe saw the universe as "a plot of God" and life as a
        human tragedy in which "the conquerer worm" is the hero.

CK108  ELIOT, T. S.  "American Literature and American Language."
        Address at Washington University, *Washington University
        Studies*, ns. 23 (Jun. 9, 1953).
        Poe is an "enigma, a stumbling block for the critic."
        He had a negligible influence on English and American
        literature but a great influence in France.  The dream
        world he created was conditioned by the real world of
        Baltimore, Philadelphia and Richmond.

CK109  _____. "From Poe to Valéry," HudR, II (Aut. 1949), 327-42.
        Excerpts reprinted in CJ16.
        Eliot discusses Poe's weaknesses as a writer--his
        "slip-shod and careless" choice of words, his immaturity,
        and his isolation--and his effect on Baudelaire, Mallarmé,
        and Valéry.  Poe "appears to yield himself completely to
        the idea of the moment; the effect is that all his ideas
        seem to be entertained rather than believed.  What is
        lacking is not brainpower, but the maturity of intellect
        which comes only with the maturing of the man as a whole,
        the development and coordination of the various emotions."
        Nevertheless, Eliot is convinced "of the importance of
        Poe's work as a whole."

# Edgar Allan Poe: An Annotated Bibliography

*CK: General Critical Articles*

CK110     \_\_\_\_. "The Influence of Landscape Upon the Poet," *Daedelus*, LXXXIX (Spr. 1960), 420-8.

CK111   ELKINS, W. R. "The Dream World and the Dream Vision: Meaning and Structure in Poe's Art," *Emporia State Research Studies*, XVII (Sept. 1968), 5-17.
    Biographical reading of Poe's work.

CK112   EVANS, OLIVER. "Infernal Illumination in Poe," <u>MLN</u>, LXXV (Apr. 1960), 295-7.
    Poe was obsessed with the idea of illumination, and two types appear in his work: rays of light cast downward from above (beneficent) and "a supernatural source of light which emanated <u>upward</u> from the infernal regions (destructive).

CK113   F. M. D. "A Greater Place for Poe," <u>SLM</u>, III (Sept. 1941), 359.

CK114   FAGIN, N. BRYLLION. "Edgar Allan Poe," <u>SAQ</u>, LI (Apr. 1952), 276-85.
    Discusses the incantory element in Poe's poetry and prose, his technical skills, his experiments with form, and his contributions to psychological realism.

CK115   FEIDELSON, CHARLES JR. "Four American Symbolists: Poe," *Symbolism and American Literature*. Chicago: University of Chicago Press, 1953, 35-43. Reprinted in CJ79.
    Explores Poe's literary themes of irrationality. Poe's "primary aim is the destruction of reason." His characters try to create a new world by destroying the old and finally understand "that horror and extinction are the necessary means to the new vision." Unlike Emerson and Whitman, he was at war with himself, not with a rationalistic society. On the other hand, his "materialistic idealism" corresponds to the "transcendentalist psychophysical world."

CK116   FIEDLER, LESLIE A. "Edgar Allan Poe and the Invention of the American Writer, <u>ChiR</u>, XIII (Win. 1959), 480-6.
    Essay adapted from *Love and Death in the American Novel* describes Poe as an alienated artist whose life was a work of art. He comes to represent "an advocate of the id against a world imprisoned in its own rigidified ego-ideals." He acts out the ideals and values which society has rejected, and by punishing him for doing so, society frees itself of its repressed longings and secret guilt.

*CK: General Critical Articles*

CK117 _____. *The Return of the Vanishing American*. New York: Stein
     & Day, 1968.
       Poe failed to write a "Western" novel because he could
not assimilate Western myths into the Southern gothic tradition. Only in NAGP did he approach "the essential Western myth of male companionship triumphing over hostility
between the races and death itself."

CK118 FITCH, GEORGE HAMLIN. *Great Spiritual Writers of America*.
     San Francisco: Paul Elder and Co., 1916.
       Very general essay.

CK119 FLANAGAN, THOMAS. "The Life and Early Death of the Detective
     Story," *Columbia University Forum*, I (Win. 1957), 7-10.

CK120 FLETCHER, JOHN GOULD. Foreword to MAMP. ed. by Dorothy Kiss-
     ling and Arthur H. Nethercot, Carlyle Straub Pub. (Apr.
     1938), 16-28.
       Emphasizes Poe's romanticism, analytical powers, and
habits of introspection.

CK121 FLORY, WENDY S. "Rehearsals for Dying in Poe and Emily Dick-
     inson," ATQ, XVIII (Spr. 1973), 13-19.
       Compares the authors' fascination with the experience
of dying and the prospect of their own death.

CK122 FOXE, DR. ARTHUR N. "Poe as Hypnotist," *Psychoanalytic
     Review,* XXVIII (Oct. 1941), 520-5.
       Credits Poe with great psychological insights, with
writing an excellent description of a hypnotic state, and
suggests that Poe actually carried out hypnosis on himself
and on others.

CK123 FRAIBERG, LOUIS. "Joseph Wood Krutch: Poe's Art as an Ab-
     normal Condition of the Nerves," *Psychoanalysis and Amer-
     ican Literary Criticism.* Detroit: Wayne State University
     Press, 1960.
       Krutch discusses Poe's psychic necessity to write what
he wrote and applies to Poe's work the theory of sublimation and the fact that unconscious conflicts can be
embodied in fantasies. There are many weaknesses in
Krutch's thesis. He failed to probe Poe's drinking problem and his ideas about his real mother and father, and he
makes only a superficial connection between his impotence
and his mother fixation, between his dreams and literature.
In addition, he describes the neurosis, but not its sources.
Finally, Krutch believes that since Poe wrote out of

*CK: General Critical Articles*

psychic necessity, and not for social or moral reasons,
his work is not valuable.

CK124 FRANKLIN, H. BRUCE. *Future Perfect: American Science Fiction
of the Nineteenth Century*. New York: Oxford University
Press, 1966, 93-103.
Discusses Poe as a science-fiction writer.

CK125 FRUIT, JOHN PHELPS. "Obsession of Edgar Allan Poe," <u>PL,</u> XII
(Jan. 1900), 42-58.
An examination of *Eureka* and Poe's ideas about immor-
tality and the absolute.

CK126 FUSSELL, EDWIN. *Frontier: American Literature and the American West*. New Jersey: Princeton University Press, 1965.
Believes that Poe identified "his own troubled destiny
...with the Western myth." Poe's narratives of exploration
and discovery have distinctly Western settings, details,
and devices (especially <u>NAGP</u> and "Masque"). Some Poe
protagonists who are in a limbo between life and death are
actually "in a border situation metaphorically comparable
to the American sense and definition of the Western frontier." In many tales, Poe has made a "daring attempt to
translate the generic cultural experience of the actual
Westward Movement into parallel psychological and individual terms...."

CK127 GALLOWAY, DAVID. "Introduction," *Selected Writings of Edgar
Allan Poe*. Baltimore: Penguin, 1967.
General essay on Poe's value.

CK128 GARGANO, JAMES W. "The Question of Poe's Narrators," <u>CE</u>, XXV
(Dec. 1963), 177-81. Reprinted in CJ16 and CJ64.
Suggests that Poe's narrators are dupes of their own
passions. "Through the irony of his characters' self-
betrayal" and through the structure of his stories, Poe
suggests ideas never considered by his narrators, who
expose their insanity through hysterical style and language. Poe is a Romantic, but "he is also a chronicler of
the consequences of Romantic excesses which lead to psychic
disorder, pain, and disintegration."

CK129 GARRISON, JOSEPH M. JR. "The Function of Terror in the Work
of Edgar Allan Poe," <u>AQ</u>, XVIII (Sum. 1966), 136-50. Excerpts reprinted in CJ16.
Considers the existence of artistic integrity in Poe's
work and suggests how it may resolve "the ostensible tension between his acknowledged committment to 'Supernal

*CK: General Critical Articles*

Beauty' as the poetic idea" and his preoccupation with
insanity, terror, and "those demonic influences which
paralyze personality." He concludes that the horror tales,
such as "FHU," can be viewed as consistent with Poe's view
of poetry as a means of elevating the soul "in providing
therapeutic contrast." That is to say, they "teach his
reader to navigate the tempests of human condition without
losing the 'spiritualizing' principle that enables him to
repudiate 'Vice solely on the ground of her deformity--
her disproportion--her animosity...to Beauty'."

CK130   GARY, LORENA M. "The Poet who Dwells in the Valley of Nis,"
        PL, XLVII (1941), 59-63.
        Brief, uninformative look at Poe.

CK131   GATES, LEWIS. "Edgar Allan Poe," *English Studies and Appre-
        ciations*. New York and London: Macmillan, 1900, 110-29.
        Interesting early essay, though Gates fails to develop
        his most provocative ideas. Poe's heroes are forerunners
        of the modern decadents in their moodiness, refined sens-
        ibility, shades of feeling, and self-absorption. His tales
        are really romantic prose-poems of the terror of a dis-
        eased mental life. His tales of ratiocination are like his
        horror stories in their remoteness from reality and their
        shallow treatment of life. His world is an artificial one,
        where all human beings are monomaniacs.

CK132   GOLDBERG, ISAAC. "Poe and Mencken, A Literary Divertisement,"
        *Stratford Monthly,* ns. I (May 1924), 137-45.
        Obvious similarities noted between the two men: they
        both drank, were pedantic, negative critics, suspicious of
        creative abandon. No instructive conclusions are drawn.

CK133   GOLDHURST, WILLIAM. "Poe-esque Themes," *Papers on Poe:
        Essays in Honor of J. Ward Ostrom*. Springfield, Ohio,
        1972.
        Defines eight Poe subjects: Appearance and Reality, the
        Double, the Devil on the Loose, Compulsive Self-Betrayal,
        Plastic Space and Time, Buried Alive, the Supernal One-
        ness, the Novel Experience.

CK134   GOSSE, EDMUND. "The Centenary of Poe," *Contemporary Review*
        (Literary Supplement), LXXXXV (Feb. 1909), 1-8.
        Poe was isolated from the "community of good taste"
        which condemned his poetry as immoral and worthless. He
        was a master of form, sound, and prosody and a pioneer in
        replacing didacticism in poetry with feeling and beauty.

133

He restored a primitive faculty to poetry and "insisted upon mystery and symbol."

CK135 _____. *Some Diversions of a Man of Letters*. London: William Heinemann, 1919, 101-43. Published as separate volume, *Centenary of Edgar Allan Poe,* 1920.
  Sees Poe as a pioneer in the art of symbolism, "a primitive faculty of which civilization seemed successfully to have deprived her [poetry]....He was the discoverer and founder of symbolism."

CK136 GRANT, VERNON W. *Geat Abnormals: The Pathological Genius of Kafka, Van Gogh, Strindberg, and Poe*. New York: Hawthorn Books, 1968.

CK137 GRAY, JOHN W. "The Public Reading of Edgar Allan Poe," *Southern Speech Journal*, XXVIII (1963), 109-15.

CK138 GREEN, A. W. "The Weekly Magazines and Poe," *English Studies in Honor of James Southall Wilson*. Charlottesville, 1951.

CK139 GREENLAW, EDWARD. "Poe in the Light of Literary History," JHAM, XVIII (Jun. 1930), 273-90.
  Vague and general remarks with an attempt to discover analogies between ideas of Poe and writers of the early English Renaissance.

CK140 GREER, LOUISE. *Browning and America*. Chapel Hill: University of North Carolina Press, 1952.
  Brief remarks on the attitude of the Brownings to Poe.

CK141 GREGORY, HORACE. "Within the Private View," PR, X (May and Jun. 1943), 263-4. Reprinted in *Shield of Achilles*. New York: Harcourt, Brace.
  Gregory discusses Poe's services as an opposer of "dull-witted authority" in America and compares him to Melville, who also penetrated and exposed private worlds of human experience. His best poetry discovers the root of "human evil and super-human joy" among the terrors of childhood, terrors which he expressed more vividly than any other poet. "He associates a lack of security...so often felt...by the sensitive and unhappy child with the conviction of being prematurely doomed, of being predestined for madness or for Hell."

CK142 GREY, JAMES. "Poe, Whitman and Twain Singled out as the Great," *New York Sun* (Sept. 2, 1933).

# EDGAR ALLAN POE: AN ANNOTATED BIBLIOGRAPHY

*CK: General Critical Articles*

CK143   GRIFFITH, CLARK.   "Caves and Cave Dwellers: a Study of the
        Romantic Imagination," JEGP, LXII (Jul. 1963), 551-68.
            Discusses cave imagery in Emerson, Melville, Hawthorne,
        and Poe.   In Poe imagery is generally concerned with "the
        progressive disintegration of the human mind."   Poe's
        protagonists discover that "despite [their] pretense of
        aloofness, the outer world can impinge upon [them], can
        take advantage of some psychic flaw within [them], and has
        the power to drive [them] mad."

CK144   _____.   "'Emersonianism' and 'Poeism': Some Versions of the
        Romantic Sensibility," MLQ, XXII (Jun. 1961), 125-34.
            Compares the Romanticism of Emerson and Poe.   The Emer-
        sonian weakness "for ignoring psychological realities
        while generalizing reality into philosophical concepts" is
        "Poeism" strength.   Sees Hawthorne as the chief adherent
        to the Poeist position in their shared passion for psycho-
        logizing.

CK145   _____.   "Poe and the Gothic," *Papers on Poe: Essays in Honor
        of J. Ward Ostrom*.   Springfield, Ohio, 1972.
            Poe's contribution to the Gothic was to turn from ex-
        terior to interior material.

CK146   HAGOPIAN, JOHN V. and W. GORDON CUNLIFFE.   *Insight,* I (1964?),
        203-7.

CK147   HALE, E. E. JR.   "Edgar Allan Poe," *Reader,* V (Mar. 1905),
        487-90.
            Very general essay on Poe's poetry and the quality of
        his imagination.

CK148   HALFEY, JAMES.   "Malice in Wonderland," ArQ, XV (1959), 5-12.
            Discusses Poe as one of many artists alienated from
        society in America, where art is an alternative to life.
        Poe's "Oval Portrait" dramatizes the conflict.

CK149   HAMILTON, ROBERT.   "Poe and the Imagination," QRL, CCLXXXVIII
        (Oct. 1950), 514-25.
            Poe possessed remarkable imagination, reason, and
        sensibility, but his emotions were morbid.   He was a
        descriptive rather than a narrative genius and actually
        experienced the terror of his tales.

CK150   HAMMOND, ALEXANDER.   "A Reconstruction of Poe's 1833 *Tales of
        the Folio Club*," PN, V (Dec. 1972), 25-32.
            Demonstrates that "the contents, ordering, and overall
        design of the eleven-story version of *Tales of the*

*CK: General Critical Articles*

*Folio Club*...can be recovered with considerable cer-
tainty on the basis of available bibliographic and textual
evidence."

CK151   HANCOCK, A. E. "Poe and the Dual Personality in Literature,"
        <u>BL</u>, II (1903), 355.

CK152   HAYCRAFT, H. "From Poe to Hammett," *Wilson Library Bulletin,*
        XII (1937), 371-7.

CK153   _____. "Time: 1841--Place: America," *Murder for Pleasure:
        the Life and Times of the Detective Story.* New York and
        London: Appleton-Century Co., 1941, 1-27.
           Believes that Poe foretold the entire evolution of the
        detective romance as a literary form.

CK154   HAYTER, ALETHEA. "Poe," *Opium and Romantic Imagination.*
        Berkeley: University of California Press, 1968, 132-51.
           Discusses Poe "as a theorist of the use of opium as an
        effect in literature" and describes the narrator of
        "Ligeia" as an opium addict.

CK155   HERTZ, ROBERT M. "English and American Romanticism," <u>Person,</u>
        XLVI (1965), 81-92.
           Brief comparison of Poe and Emily Bronte.

CK156   HOFRICHTER, LAURA. "From Poe to Kafka," <u>UTQ</u>, XXIX (Jul.1960),
        405-19.
           Poe's work embodies the split between reality and the
        imagination, between the "external object and the inner
        vision of the artist" and between art and science, art and
        life, and beauty and life. It is a spiritual autobiography,
        "the insistence on the objective and general validity of
        the inner world of the poet." For Poe, reality is the
        servant of the imagination; for Kafka, "imagination has
        devoured reality and all that is left."

CK157   HONIG, EDWIN. "In Defense of Allegory," <u>KR</u>, XX (Win. 1958),
        1-19.

CK158   HOUGH, GRAHAM. "Edgar Allan Poe," *Studies in the Arts: Pro-
        ceedings of the St. Peter's College Literary Society.* ed.
        by Frances Warner, Oxford: Basil Blackwell, 1968, 82-98.

CK159   HOWE, M. A. DeWOLFE. "Edgar Allan Poe," *American Bookman.*
        New York: Dodd, Mead and Co., 1902, 76-99.
           Very general remarks about Poe's life and works.

# EDGAR ALLAN POE: AN ANNOTATED BIBLIOGRAPHY

*CK: General Critical Articles*

CK160  HOWELLS, WILLIAM DEAN. "Edgar Allan Poe," <u>HW</u>, LIII (Jan. 16, 1909), 12-13.
    Poe has some merit as a poet though none as a novelist. His stories are mechanical, his characters are agents of repugnant deeds, and he himself is a horror-monger. He had the making of a genius, but "he never got it out," and his work is now outdated.

CK161  _____. "One Hundred Years of American Verse," <u>NAR</u>, CLXXII (Jan. 1901), 148-60.
    General remarks on the supernatural and "supernature-worship" which begins and ends with Poe.

CK162  HUBBELL, JAY B. "Edgar Allan Poe," *The South in American Literature*. Part V, Duke University Press, 1954, 528-50.
    Hubbell treats Poe's southern background, his relations with southern writers, and his "southern" attitudes (his glorification of women, for example). He also examines his work for a southern point of view and concludes that Poe's classicism, elusive intensity, rhetoric, rejection of didactic literature and indifference to reform are traceable to the whig (conservative) influence in Richmond.

CK163  _____. "Edgar Allan Poe and the Southern Literary Tradition," <u>TSLL</u>, II, (Sum. 1960), 151-71. Reprinted in *South and Southwest,* Durham, North Carolina: Duke University Press, 1965.
    Hubbell chiefly discusses Poe's "southern" attitudes toward literature (a preoccupation with verbal melody) and women (a religion of Beauty), his influence on Southern writers such as John Gould Fletcher, Cabell, Aiken, Faulkner, Warner and Wolfe.

CK164  _____. "The Literary Apprenticeship of Edgar Allan Poe," <u>SLJ</u>, II (1969), 99-106.

CK165  _____. *Who Are the Major American Writers?* Duke University Press, 1972, 51-57.
    General essay on Poe's career and reputation.

CK166  HUBNER, CHARLES. "Poe and Some of his Critics," *Representative Southern Poets*. New York and Washington: Neal Publishing Co., 1906, 194-205.
    Attacks Poe's critics.

CK167  HUGHES, DAVID. "The Influence of Poe," <u>FortnR</u>, CLXXII, ns. 166 (Nov. 1929), 342.
    Poe is readable because of his "seediness" (lack of

*CK: General Critical Articles*

responsibility), his unity of effect, and his decadence. He is so emotional, however, that we rarely desire to read him a second time.

CK168 HUNGERFORD, EDWARD. "Poe and Phrenology," AL, II (Nov. 1930), 209-13.
Hungerford traces the development of Poe's interest in phrenology and suggests ways in which the science influenced Poe's criticism and character analysis. In "Ligeia," for example, Poe drew on phrenology to explore the heroine's will to live and her gift for languages.

CK169 HUXLEY, ALDOUS. *Vulgarity in Literature.* London: Chatto and Windus, 1930, 26-36. Excerpts reprinted in CJ16 and CJ64.
The substance of Poe's work is refined, but its form—that part which the French cannot truly appreciate—is vulgar. He is a gentleman with bad taste; his poetry is too poetical, too musical, to be pleasant.

CK170 INGRAM, JOHN. "Variations in Poe's Poetry," *Bibliophile,* II (May 1909), 128-36.

CK171 JACKSON, HOLBROOK. "Estimates of Edgar Allan Poe," *All Manner of Folk.* London: Grant Richards Ltd., 1912, 91-103.
General, rather vague essay which pictures Poe as a spiritual foreigner in America, a child of feudalism and heraldry, the first English-speaking decadent. His work foreshadows that of the pre-Raphaelites, Symbolists, Realists.

CK172 JACOBS, ROBERT D. "Campaign for a Southern Literature: *Southern Literary Messenger,*" SLJ, II (1969), 66-88.
Poe's contribution to the SLM is discussed.

CK173 _____. "Poe and the Agrarian Critics," *Hopkins Review,* V (1952), 43-54.
Discusses similarities between Poe's social and political ideas and those in *I'll Take My Stand.* For example, Poe and the agrarians have a classical world view, affirm "the limitations of man and the supremacy of nature," and believe "that the universe is for the artist." They consider modern civilization an era of spiritual decay, doubt the possibility of human perfectability, and work out the "dislocation of modern sensibility" as a literary theme. They part company when Poe "deviates first into romanticism...and then into science."

# Edgar Allan Poe: An Annotated Bibliography

*CK: General Critical Articles*

CK174   \_\_\_\_\_. "Poe as a Literary Critic--a Teaching Approach,"
ESQ, XXXI (II Quarter 1963), 7-11.
    Suggests that Poe should be taught as a book reviewer.

CK175   \_\_\_\_\_. "Poe in Richmond, the Double Image," *The Dilemma of
the Southern Writer*. ed. by Richard Meeker. Farmville,
Virginia, 1961.

CK176   \_\_\_\_\_. "Poe's Earthly Paradise," AQ, XII (Fall 1960), 404-13.
    Poe's attempt to construct an earthly paradise in some
stories and his interest in the archetypical story of man's
fall from innocence are evidence of his belief that the
artists' function is to arrange chaotic nature into artistic and intelligible order, to adapt the raw materials of
nature to the limitations of man's senses, which are other-
wise unaware of the perfectability of nature.

CK177   \_\_\_\_\_. "Rhetoric in Southern Writing: Poe," GaR, XII (Spr.
1958), 76-9.
    Poe's theory of effect and even his style were influ-
enced by the Southern rhetorical tradition and particularly by William Wirt, who felt that oratory should elicit a
"sympathetic response in the minds and emotions of the
audience."

CK178 JOHNSON, C. F. *Outline History of English and American Literature*. New York: American Book Co., 1900.
    Text-book summary which emphasizes Poe's gloom, melan-
cholia and amorality. Poe was an impressionist who "fixed
his attention on one aspect of his subject (preferably an
abnormal one), and intensifies that aspect, and rigidly
excludes everything not in harmony with it."

CK179 JONES, HOWARD MUMFORD. "Poe, 'The Raven,' and the Anonymous
Young Man," WHR, IX (1955), 127-38. Reprinted in *History
and the Contemporary: Essays in Nineteenth Century Literature*. Madison: University of Wisconsin Press, 1964.
    Poe was interested more in general ideas about man than
in the destructive tendencies of the individual ego, and
so his stories commence like contes and end like tales.
That is, they begin with symbolic anonymity and wind up in
terms of "generalized human experience." His central
character is a standard nineteenth century hero who moves
from sanity to monomania in "prosodic devices so powerful
that nobody has since dared to imitate them."

# Edgar Allan Poe: An Annotated Bibliography

*CK: General Critical Articles*

CK180 KANE, MARGARET. "Edgar Allan Poe and Architecture," <u>SR</u>, XL (Jan.-Mar. 1932), 149-60.
Poe's Gothic architecture was influenced by eighteenth-century English conventions: use of interiors to create atmosphere, tower rooms, draperies, difficulty of access, artificial light, melancholy, gloom, underground vaults.

CK181 KATSURADA, RIKICHI. "Notes on a Study of Poetry by Coleridge and Poe," *Studies in English Literature* (Hosei University), No. 4 (Mar. 1961), 14-20.

CK182 KAUN, ALEXANDER. "Poe and Gogol: a Comparison," *Slavonic and East European Review,* XV (Jan. 1937), 389-99.
Both Poe and Gogol experienced abnormal childhoods and probably suffered from organic defects making normal sexual relations impossible. Both sought a refuge from reality and the masculine world in the creation of ideal women, and their sense of inferiority led them to develop traits of egotism, a tendency to distort and exaggerate, and a craving for fame and success. Neurotics and depressives, they died because they lost the will to live.

CK183 KAYSER, WOLFGANG. *The Grotesque in Art and Literature.* Trans. by Ulrich Weisstein, Bloomington: Indiana University Press, 1963.
Distinguishes between Poe's use of the terms "grotesque" and "arabesque." Argues that Poe uses "grotesque" in its traditional meaning, that it implies more than comic and burlesque.

CK184 KIERLY, ROBERT. "The Comic Masks of Edgar Allan Poe," *Umanesimo,* I (1967), 31-4.

CK185 KNAPP, GEORGE L. <u>Lipp</u>, LXXXIII (Jan. 1909), 74-81.
Poe was isolated because he did not share common American assumptions about the inferiority of American literature and because Puritanical America regarded weakness and self-indulgence as sins. He wasted his genius.

CK186 KNIGHT, GRANT. *The Critical Period in American Literature.* Chapel Hill: University of North Carolina Press, 1951, 38-41.
Bierce "revealed none of the somber, sexual necrophilia of Poe...had no fondness for the fact or appearances of death....did not share Poe's passion for the pictorial opportunities of the funereal...had no infatuation with the trappings, the atmosphere and vestments, and the housings of those who had died or were about to die."

*CK: General Critical Articles*

CK187  KRAMER, AARON. *The Prophetic Tradition in American Poetry: 1835-1900*. Rutherford, New Jersey: Fairleigh Dickinson University Press.
Discusses Poe's contempt for the politics of his country.

CK188  KREYMBORG, ALFRED. "The Weary Wayworn Wanderer," *A History of American Poetry*. New York: Tudor Publishing Co., 1934.
General remarks on Poe's poetry. Some mention of his sources and of his influence on twentieth-century American poetry via French Symbolists.

CK189  KRUTCH, JOSEPH WOOD. "A Baleful and Self-Consuming Meteor," *New York Times Book Review* (Aug. 6, 1944), 6.
General remarks.

CK190  _____. "His Nightmares Go on Forevermore," *New York Times Book Review*, XVIII (Jan. 18, 1959), 1.
Rather general remarks about Poe's achievements.

CK191  _____. "The Strange Case of Mr. Poe," AM, VI (Nov. 1925), 349-56.
Krutch discusses Poe's misanthropy and his thirst for notoriety, characteristics which explain his contemptuous criticism, his pretenses to strange passions and esoteric knowledge, and his interest in cryptograms. Poe's interest in tales of ratiocination and his attempts to provide rational explanations for his imaginative writing were his means of proving to himself that he was sane.

CK192  KURTZ, LEONARD. *The Dance of Death: The Macabre Spirit in European Literature*. New York: Columbia University Press, 1934, 263-5.
Brief discussion of death dances in Poe.

CK193  LANIER, EMILIO. "The Bedlam Patterns East of Greece," *East-West Review*, III (1966-7), 1-22.

CK194  LATIMER, GEORGE D. "The Tales of Poe and Hawthorne," NEM, XXX (Aug. 1904), 692-703.
Poe and Hawthorne were attracted to the weird, the gruesome, the morbid. Hawthorne, however, was a moralist, while Poe was interested primarily in form and technique. His characters have no moral nature and are high-strung neurotics, but in one supreme moment, they appear "in the grasp of bitter circumstances, wretched, despairing creatures, victims of their fierce passion, caught in the toils of their own weaving."

# Edgar Allan Poe: An Annotated Bibliography

*CK: General Critical Articles*

CK195　LAVERTY, CARROLL D.　"Poe in his Place--in his Time," ESQ, XXXI (II Quarter 1963), 23-5.
　　Discusses the extent to which Poe used contemporary scientific material in his work.

CK196　LAWRENCE, D. H.　"Edgar Allan Poe," *Classic American Literature*. New York: Doubleday, 1951, 73-92. Originally published in 1922. Reprinted in CJ15, CJ16 and CJ74.
　　Lawrence emphasizes Poe's interest in the disintegration of the consciousness. Poe desired the continual experience of spiritual love, complete unity with another human being; and he pursued this unity beyond the grave. Believing that physical possession is not enough, the heroes try to possess the souls of their women. In "Ligeia" the heroine wills herself to death in complete submission to her husband's will and then wills herself back to life to complete the process of unity. The incest theme is useful to Poe because the unity of two close relatives is not obstructed by physical resistance.

CK197　LAWSON, LEWIS.　"Poe's Conception of the Grotesque," MissQ, XIX (Fall 1966), 200-206.
　　Believes that "grotesque" meant to Poe "the known stretched to the point of originality" or to its "ultimate limit." It was therefore "a form of the ideal, a result of pure imagination."

CK198　＿＿＿＿. "Poe and the Grotesque: a Bibliography, 1695-1965," PN, I (Apr. 1968), 9-10.
　　Bibliography of source work on the concept of the grotesque.

CK199　LEARY, LEWIS.　"Edgar Allan Poe: The Adolescent as Confidence Man," SLJ, IV (Spr. 1972), 3-21.
　　Graceful essay on "America's first great writer of the second rank." Concludes that Poe "does not speak to us, or for us....As a trickster, he delights; but the longer we know him, the greater slackens our confidence."

CK200　LEBEL, ROBERT.　"Quidor and Poe: or the American Loneliness," VVV, no. 2-3 (Mar. 1943), 55-6.
　　Poe and Quidor are similar "in their simultaneous rebellion against the tedious and the rational, in their passionate search for poetic substances."

CK201　LERNER, ARTHUR.　*Psychoanalytically Oriented Criticism of Three American Poets: Poe, Whitman and Aiken.* Rutherford, New Jersey: Fairleigh Dickinson Press, 1970.

*CK: General Critical Articles*

Discusses the positives and negatives of psychological criticism.

CK202 LEVIN, HARRY. *The Power of Blackness*. New York: Vintage Books, 1960, 101-65. Excerpts reprinted in CJ37 and CJ79.
Ranges through most of Poe's stories offering psychological, philosophical, and autobiographical interpretations. Emphasizes Poe's obsession with death and death symbolism and suggests that "his hero is modern man, caught in a mechanical life and propelled toward death."

CK203 LEWIS, C. L. "Edgar Allan Poe and the Sea," SLM, III (Jan. 1941), 5-10.
Discusses Poe's experiences on the sea and the sea imagery in his poetry and prose.

CK204 LEWISOHN, LUDWIG. "The Troubled Romancers," *Expressionism in American Literature*. New York: Harper, 1932, 153-68.
Considers Poe a hopeless neurotic (psychopathic type) for whom literature was a means of escape from an intolerable reality. Denies the value of most of his work.

CK205 LIEBMAN, SHELDON W. "Poe's Tales and his Theory of the Poetic Experience," SSF, VII (Fall 1970), 582-97.
Believes that Poe's stories objectify what for Poe are two central events of the poetic experience: the pursuit of Beauty and Knowledge and the making of a poem.

CK206 LIND, ROBERT. "The Poetry of Poe," NSN, XVIII (Mar. 25, 1922), 704-6.
General remarks on Poe's poetry. Treats him as a brilliant novice whose talent equalled his genius only in "To Helen."

CK207 LOMBARD, CHARLES. "Poe and French Romanticism," PN, III (Dec. 1970), 30-35.
Poe's views on the French Romantics are discussed.

CK208 LOVECRAFT, HOWARD. "Edgar Allan Poe," *The Recluse, The Outsiders and Others*. Sauk City: Ben Abramson, 1939. Reprinted in *Supernatural Horror in Literature,* 1945.
Poe advanced, perhaps perfected, the modern horror story with his consummate craftsmanship, his impersonal approach, and his insistence on psychological realism.

CK209 LUCAS, FRANK L. "Romanticism and Decay," *Literature and Psychology*. London: Cassell, 1951.

*CK: General Critical Articles*

CK210  LYNCH, JAMES. "The Devil in the Writings of Irving, Haw-
        thorne, and Poe," NYFQ, VIII (Sum. 1952), 111-31.
            In his comparison of the treatment of the devil by
        three American authors, Lynch concludes that Poe "con-
        ceives of his devil in terms of the grotesque with an ad-
        mixture of grisly and clumsy humor, to which are added a
        satirical and debunking attitude." In "The Devil in the
        Belfry," for example, the devil is "the element of chaos
        that is apt to upset overly-regulated lives."

CK211  LYNEN, JOHN F. "The Death of the Present: Edgar Allan Poe,"
        *The Design of the Present*. New Haven: Yale University
        Press, 1969.
            A survey of Poe's fiction in relation to the central
        theories of *Eureka*. Concludes that Poe "'never resolves'
        the polarity of unity and separation in time; instead all
        values tend to be absorbed into the sense of 'annihilation'
        present in *Eureka*." (from PN, 1969, p. 13)

CK212  LYONS, NATHAN. "Kafka and Poe--and Hope," MinnR, V (May-
        Jul. 1965), 158-68.
            Compares the authors' work in terms of theme, language,
        structure, and adjustment to the world. Kafka's "accept-
        ance of responsibility for the world" is the opposite of
        "Poe's preoccupation with an isolated human perversity."
        Both develop themes of "inexorable loneliness."

CK213  MABIE, HAMILTON WRIGHT. "Poe," *Poe Centenary Exercises*,
        TBSAS, New York: The Society (Jan. 9, 1909).
            Considers Poe a unique writer, far ahead of his time.

CK214  _____. "'To Helen' and 'Israfel'," *Outlook*, XCI (Apr. 24,
        1907), 955-7.
            Poe's individual poetry lacks range, passion and real-
        ity, but it shows "individuality of conception and dis-
        tinction of workmanship."

CK215  MacDONALD, DWIGHT. "Masscult and Midcult," PR, XXVII (Spr.
        1960), 203-33; (Fall 1960), 589-631.
            Illustrates the difference between masscult--culture
        manufactured for the market--and high culture by com-
        paring the detective stories of Earl Stanley Gardner with
        Poe's. The former lack personal tone and their prose
        style is poor. Poe's stories, on the other hand, communi-
        cate a sense of the neurotic personality.

CK216  MACY, JOHN. "The Fame of Poe," Atl, CII (Dec. 1908), 835-43.
            Negative essay dwelling on Poe's total isolation from

*CK: General Critical Articles*

the community. Denies the connection between his
emotional problems and his work.

CK217 _____. "Poe," *The Spirit of American Literature*. New York:
Doubleday, Page and Co., 1913, 123-55.
    Amplifies earlier essay. Believes Poe's writing lags
far behind great contemporary literature, is "creepy and
fascinating and subtle." His achievements lie in the
areas of criticism and philosophy, and he was "the single
voice of protest against a transcendent cosmology."

CK218 MARCHAND, ERNEST. "Poe as Social Critic," <u>AL</u>, VI (Mar. 1934),
28-43.
    Poe was not isolated from his environment. He was a
literary satirist, an office-seeker during Tyler's Presi-
dency, and an outspoken critic of political corruption
in New York. He opposed anything that threatened the
integrity of the individual. He held typically southern
views regarding women, social reforms, and slavery, and
he was concerned about the effects of mechanization on
society.

CK219 MARKHAM, EDWIN. "Poe," <u>MAMP</u>, ed. by Dorothy Kissling and
Arthur H. Nethercot. New York: Carlyle Straub, 1938, 40-57.
    Discussion of Poe's short stories, literary themes and
theories, and his interest in abnormality. His value as
a critic lies in his fight against the "literary tinsel"
of the day.

CK220 _____. "The Poetry of Poe," *Arena*, XXXII (Aug. 1904), 170-5.
Reprinted in *American Writers on American Literature*. ed.
by John Macy, New York: Horace Liveright, 1931.
    General essay which touches briefly on each of Poe's
major poems and on their connection with the death of Mrs.
Stanard.

CK221 MARSHALL, THOMAS P. "The Poet and the Symbol," *Three Voices
of The American Tradition: Edgar Allan Poe, Herman Melville, Ernest Hemingway*. Athens, 1955, 15-30.
    Poe's influence on the short story.

CK222 MARTIN, TERENCE. "The Imagination at Play," <u>KR</u>, XXVIII
(1966), 195-8. Excerpts reprinted in CJ37.
    Poe, who had a liberated imagination, who took a-social
and anti-social postures, was alienated from a convention-
al society **that** "refused to live by the imagination."

*CK: General Critical Articles*

CK223  MATHERLY, ENID P.  "Poe and Hawthorne as Writers of the Short
       Story," *Education,* XL (Jan. 1920), 294-306.
           Usual and obvious comparison between Poe, the pictorial,
       analytical and technical writer, lacking humor and human
       sympathy, and Hawthorne, the writer interested in character
       development, human emotions, symbolism and moral problems.

CK224  MATTHEWS, BRANDER.  *The Philosophy of the Short Story,* New
       York:  Longmans, Green and Co., 1901.
           Brief comparison of Poe and Hawthorne.  Although both
       wrote fantasy, Hawthorne's weird and strange effects
       symbolize the moral and psychological struggles of the
       characters; whereas the ethical is absent from Poe's work.
       They are both American in their sympathy with Oriental
       thought.

CK225  _____.  "Poe and the Detective Story," Scrib, XLII (Sept.
       1907), 287-93.  Reprinted in CJ16.
           Poe's theory that the effectiveness of the detective
       story rests in the time lag between the revelation of the
       crime and the detective's elucidation of it brought psycho-
       logical interest to the genre: "the application of human
       intelligence to the solution of a mystery."  His develop-
       ment of the second character, to whom the clues are
       revealed, also added interest.

CK226  _____.  "Poe's Cosmopolitan Fame," Cen, LXXXI (Dec. 1910),
       271-5.
           General remarks about the failure of Americans to
       respond to Poe because he failed as a human being, because
       he was never afraid to show his true feelings, and because
       he had little to say.

CK227  MATTHIESSEN, F. O.  "Poe," SR (Spr. 1946), 175-205.  Reprinted
       in LHUS. ed. by Robert E. Spiller, Willard Thorpe, etc., I,
       New York: Macmillan, 1948, 321-42.
           Broad and revealing essay considering every facet of
       Poe's development, particularly his influence on French
       symbolists and modern criticism, his humor, his interest
       in contemporary landscape, and his critical methods.

CK228  MAUCLAIR, CAMILLE.  "Edgar Allan Poe as Inspirer of Ideas,"
       FortnR, trans. by Catherine Phillipps, CXX, ns. CXIV (Sept.
       1923), 474-85.
           Poe studied perversity and projected the split in his
       own personality into his writings.  He was a complete poet
       and mystic, who understood the relationship between the

*CK: General Critical Articles*

physical and moral worlds. His knowledge of science and psychology is only now being verified.

CK229  MAXWELL, D. E. S.  "Introduction," *The Major Poems and Tales of Edgar Allan Poe*. New York, 1965.

CK230  _____. "Poe and the Romantic Experiment," *American Fiction: the Intellectual Background*. London: Routledge and Kegan, 1963, 53-96.

CK231  MAYERSBERG, PAUL.  "The Corridors of the Mind," *Listener*, LXXIV (1965), 959-960.
On the fantasies in Poe's horror stories.

CK232  McDOWELL, T.  "Poe and William Cullen Bryant," PQ, XVI (Jan. 1937), 83-4.
Poe had a favorable opinion of William Cullen Bryant.

CK233  McELDERRY, B. R. JR.  "Poe's Concept of the Soul," N&Q, CC, ns. 2 (Apr. 1955), 173-4.
Poe defined soul as something apart from the heart or intellect--close to the imagination.

CK234  McLEAN, FRANK.  "The Conditions Under Which Poe Did his Imaginative Work," SR, XXXIV (Apr. 1926), 184-95.
To create, Poe required leisure and purpose--purpose being the achievement of fame and the ownership of a literary magazine. When he realized that he would never succeed, he became confused and aimless.

CK235  McLUHAN, H. M. "Edgar Allan Poe's Tradition," SR, LII (Jan. 1944), 24-33.
McLuhan distinguishes between the New England literary tradition of Hawthorne and Melville, which was Calvinistic, scholastic, autocratic and isolatory, and the southern tradition, to which Poe belonged. Poe projected his southern experience in symbols of alienation and inner conflict, representing the Byronic tradition "of the aristocratic rebel fighting for human values in a subhuman chaos of indiscriminate appetite." The tradition was concerned not with innate depravity but with a split between society and personality."...by defining on his own and projecting the inner emotional drama of his time ...[Poe] probably did as much as Jefferson to energize American life."

*CK: General Critical Articles*

CK236   MENCKEN, H. L.   "The Mystery of Poe," *Nation,* CXXII (Mar. 17,
         1926), 289-90.
              "Strapped to the water-wagon, with a ton of Bibles to
         hold him down, he would have been precisely the same Poe."
         Discusses the tragedy of Poe's life, his absurd stories,
         bombastic criticism, and jingle-like poetry.  Nevertheless,
         Poe's "titanic" tragedy breaks through his "nonsensical
         theories and idle pedantries...and gives an austere dignity
         to even his worst jingles."

CK237   MENGELING, MARVIN and FRANCES.   "From Fancy to Failure," UR,
         XXXIII (Sum. 1967), 293-98; XXXIV (Aut. 1967), 31-6.
              Whether a Poe character succeeds in solving or fails to
         solve a problem depends upon whether he uses his fancy or
         his imagination.  The character who employs fancy is
         doomed to failure.

CK238   MILLER, JAMES E. JR.   *Quests Surd and Absurd: Essays in Amer-
         ican Literature.*  Chicago:  Chicago University Press, 1967.
              Brief, scattered comments of Poe's treatment of the
         journey theme.

CK239   _____.  "Uncharted Interiors: The American Romantics Revis-
         ited," ESQ, XXXV (II Quarter 1964), 34-9.
              Familiar essay on Poe.  "In many ways the entire work
         of Poe can be seen as a probing of the dark 'chambers and
         magazines' of the soul or mind....All of Poe's imaginative
         writing represents in some sense an exploration of hidden
         labyrinths of the interior...."

CK240   MILTON, W. F.   "Poe's Mechanical Poems," *Texas Review* (Jan.
         1918), 133-8.

CK241   MOLDENHAUER, JOSEPH J.   "Murder as a Fine Art: Basic Connec-
         tions Between Poe's Aesthetics, Psychology, and Moral
         Vision," PMLA, LXXXIII (May 1968), 284-97.
              Elaborate and overconceived essay on unity in Poe.
         "Unity, the essential condition and supreme value of art,
         is the condition likewise of death, as pursued by Poe's
         fictional characters through destructive acts which are
         vicariously and finally suicidal....In killing others
         [Poe's protagonists] impose unity upon the diverse and
         particular, assimilating into themselves which were tan-
         gible reflections of their own beings...."

CK242   MONROE, HARRIET.   "Poe and Whistler," PL, XXI (Sept. 1910),
         391-6.
              Discussing similarities between the two artists.

# Edgar Allan Poe: An Annotated Bibliography

*CK: General Critical Articles*

CK243  MONTROSE, J. M.  "A Southern Mystery," *Literature of the South*.  New York: Thomas Crowell, 276-95.

CK244  MOONEY, STEPHEN.  "Poe's Gothic Wasteland," SR, LXX (Spr.1962), 261-83.  Excerpts reprinted in CJ16 and CJ37.
　　　　Mooney develops Tate's idea that Poe discovered the modern subject of the disintegration of the personality. His achievement was his expression of the dehumanizing forces of human life in Gothic terms (the literary mode of the day) and his success in penetrating the tinsel of nineteenth century American life and discovering where the community failed to nourish individual consciousness.  His images of anxiety-ridden nineteenth-century man foreshadow the wasteland, the literary theme of the twentieth century.  *See* CK34.

CK245  _____.  "The Comic Intent in Poe's Tales: Five Criteria," MLN, LXXVI (May 1961), 432-4.
　　　　Any upward flight, group action, use of machines or mechanical motions, and avoidance of unity and proportion are signals of comic intent on Poe's stories.

CK246  MOORE, CHARLES L.  "The Case of Poe and His Critics," *Dial*, XLII (Nov. 16, 1909), 367-70.
　　　　Unsuccessful attempt to rescue Poe from his reputation.

CK247  MORDELL, ALBERT.  *The Erotic Motive in Literature*.  New York: Coller Books, 1962.  Reprinted from 1919 edition.
　　　　Finds Poe to be a frustrated lover, drunkard, sadist, masochist, a man who suffered from "a damming of the libido," who was "so absorbed in his dreams that he never tried to take an interest in reality.  Hence we will find no moral note in Poe's work."

CK248  MORE, PAUL ELMER.  "A Note on Poe's Method," SP, XX (Jul. 1923), 302-9.  Reprinted in *The Demon of the Absolute. New Shelburne Essays*.  I, Princeton: Princeton University Press, 1928, 77-8.
　　　　Poe was interested in analysis and the dissection of sensation rather than in morality and ethics.  He differed from other "masters of unearthly reverie" in his consciousness of logical analysis, which he raised to the level of art.  His limitations were caused by his identification of truth with didacticism.

CK249  MORRISON, CLAUDIA.  *Freud and the Critic: The Early Use of Depth Psychology in Literary Criticism*.  Chapel Hill: University of North Carolina Press, 1968.

*CK: General Critical Articles*

Analysis of Joseph Wood Krutch's psychoanalytical study, *Edgar Allan Poe: A Study in Genius*.

CK250  MOSS, SIDNEY.  "Poe's Apocalyptic Vision," *Papers on Poe: Essays in Honor of J. Ward Ostrom*.  Springfield, Ohio, 1972.
Discusses Poe's fiction in terms of a central theme of "alienation and victimization...that man is totally helpless in a universe he has abandoned all hope of understanding."

CK251  MUCHNICK, HELEN.  *The Unhappy Consciousness: Gogol, Poe, Baudelaire*.  Northampton, Massachusetts: Smith College, 1967.
The three writers have "unhappy consciousnesses": they are alienated and yearn for a transcendent world.

CK252  MURCH, A. E.  *The Development of the Detective Novel*.  New York: Philosophical Library, 1958, 67-83.
Touches upon sources, method, and influence of Poe's detective fiction.

CK253  MURPHY, GEORGE D.  "Source for Ballistics in Poe," <u>AN&Q</u>, IV (Mar. 1966), 99.
Poe was the first practitioner of detective stories to employ ballistics.

CK254  NELSON, LOUISE A.  "Arabesque and Grotesque Stories of Edgar Allan Poe," *Calcutta Review* (Calcutta), XXXVI (Jul. 1930), 10-19.
General essay on Poe's stories.

CK255  NETHERY, WALLACE.  "Poe and Charles Lamb," <u>PN</u>, III (Dec. 1970), 38.
Brief discussion of Poe's references to Lamb.

CK256  NEUMANN, J. H.  "Poe's Contribution to English," <u>AS</u>, XVIII (Feb. 1943), 73-4.
List of words which the Oxford English Dictionary cites as original with Poe.

CK257  NEWCOMER, A. G.  "Romance," *American Literature*.  Chicago: Scott, Foresman, 1901, 112-27.
Text-book type of summary.

CK258  NORWOOD, G.  "Going Native," *Saturday Night,* LVIII (Oct. 10, 1942), 33.

*CK: General Critical Articles*

CK259 O'BRIEN, EDWARD J. H. *The Advance of the American Short Story*. New York: Dodd Mead and Co., 1923, 65-88.
Discusses Poe's objectivity and powers of analysis, his split personality, and his several personae. Two sides of his personality appear in his stories: Poe himself and the character he desired to be.

CK260 OLIVERO, FREDERICO. "Symbolism in Poe's Poetry," *Westminster Review*, CLXXX (Apr. 1913), 201-7.
Discusses several of Poe's poems as symbolic of psychological states. Poe's conception of nature as a symbolic representative of ideas and feeling is embodied in "Ulalume." In the first two stanzas there is a correspondence between landscape and soul: the moon is love, the lake is forgetfulness or death, and the rosemary is remembrance.

CK261 OLNEY, CLARK. "Edgar Allan Poe: Science-Fiction Pioneer," GaR, XII (Win. 1958), 416-21.
Poe was the first writer of "science-centered fiction to base his stories on a rational kind of extrapolation, avoiding the supernatural." He was also a pioneer in realism and logic.

CK262 OLYBRIUS. "The Character of Hamlet," N&Q, CLXXXIX (Sept. 22, 1945), 130.
Discusses Poe's views on Hamlet.

CK263 OSGOODE, JOSEPH. "Edgar Allan Poe," *Tell It in Gath*. Sewanee: University Press of Sewanee, 1918, 140-182.
Overzealous in admiration for Poe, who "died drugged and poisoned by certain public-spirited citizens whose patriotic zeal easily outran their discretion, and not as the outcome of a drunken debauch...."

CK264 OSOWSKI, JUDY. "T. S. Eliot on 'Poe the Detective'," PN, III (Dec. 1970), 39.
Discusses Eliot's admiration for Poe's detective stories.

CK265 PARKES, HENRY. "Poe, Hawthorne, Melville: An Essay in Sociological Criticism," PR, XVI (Feb. 1949), 157-65.
The three writers viewed the individual as isolated from society and they failed to see the "natural universe as an ordered unity which harmonizes with human ideals." Poe carries isolation, which Hawthorne regards as sinful, to its limits. All his characters are isolated, and they also have an intense will to power. They foreshadow the neurotic personality of the twentieth century.

# EDGAR ALLAN POE: AN ANNOTATED BIBLIOGRAPHY

*CK: General Critical Articles*

CK266  PARRINGTON, VERNON L.  *Romantic Revolution in America: Main Currents in American Thought*.  II, New York: Harcourt Brace, 1927, 57-9.
    "The problem of Poe, fascinating as it is, lies quite outside the main current of American thought, and it may be left with the psychologist and the belletrist with whom it belongs.  It is for abnormal psychology to explain his neural instability...his irritable pride, his quarrelsomeness, his unhappy persecution complex, his absurd pretensions to a learning he did not possess ...."

CK267  PARRY, ALBERT.  "The Lone One," *Garrets and Pretenders: a History of Bohemianism*.  New York: Covici, Freide, 1933, 3-14.
    Poe laid the foundations for American bohemianism.  His mad, unconventional personality was moulded by heredity and environment; alcohol was his means of escaping from a painful social position.

CK268  PATTEE, FRED L.  *The Development of the American Short Story*.  New York: Harper, 1923.
    Denies that Poe invented the short story but believes that he was the first to outline the techniques for the genre.  Discusses satirical elements in the stories, the source of Poe's Gothicism, and the artificiality and amorality of his work.  Poe capitalized on horror not because it was in his soul, but because it was marketable.

CK269  PEARCE, ROY HARVEY.  "Poe," *The Continuity of American Poetry*.  Princeton: Princeton University Press, 1961, 141-53.
    Discusses the egocentrism of Poe's poems, the fact that their value "lies primarily in their over-insistent exhibition of an imagination trying in vain to demonstrate its power to reach beyond itself."  In the end, Poe "is more of a culture hero than an artist."

CK270  PERRY, BLISS.  "Poe and Whitman," *The American Spirit in Literature*.  New Haven: Yale University Press, 1920, 187-206.
    Brief discussion of Poe as an egotist and a Romantic.

CK271  PERRY, WILBUR.  "Edgar Allan Poe," *Birmingham-Southern College Bulletin*, XXI (Jun. 1928), 29-34.
    General appreciation of Poe.

CK272  PICKETT, LA SALLE CORBELL.  "Poet of the Night," *Literary Hearthstones of Dixie*, Philadelphia: J. P. Lippincott Co., 1912, 11-41.
    Romantic, unscholarly approach to Poe's work.

*CK: General Critical Articles*

CK273 PITTMAN, DIANA. "Key to the Mystery of Edgar Allan Poe,"
_SLM_, III (Aug. 1941), 367-71.
The key to Poe's work is the English Reform Bill of
1832, which is allegorized in all of Poe's short stories
and poems.

CK274 POLLARD, PERCIVAL. _New York Times_ (Jan. 10, 1909).

CK275 POLLIN, BURTON R. "Byron, Poe and Miss Matilda," _Names,_ XVI
(1968), 390-414.
The appearance of the figure Matilda in the works of
Byron and Poe.

CK275 _____. "'Delightful Sights,' a Possible Whitman Article in
Poe's _Broadway Journal,_" _WWR_, XV (1969), 180-87.

CK277 _____. "New York City in the Tales of Poe," _Bronx County
Historical Society Journal,_ II (Jan. 1965), 16-22.
Notes references to New York City in Poe's tales.

CK278 _____. "Poe as Scriblerian," _Scriblerian,_ I (1969), 30-1.

CK279 PORTE, JOEL. _The Romance in America: Studies in Cooper, Poe,
Hawthorne, Melville and James_. Middletown: Wesleyan University Press, 1969, 53-94.
Poe is a serious writer, who sees romance as a way of
exploring the "secret soul of man." At the heart of the
"underground experiences" in Poe is usually the darkest
aspect of sexuality. Porte discusses "FHU" as a story of
incest and "Ligeia" and "Berenice" as erotic fantasies.
Also discusses _NAGP_.

CK280 POULET, GEORGES. _The Metamorphosis of the Circle_. trans.
Carley Dawson and Elliott Coleman. Baltimore: Johns Hopkins Press, 1966, 182-202. Reprinted in CJ79.
Elusive essay on Poe's "poetic of limitation." Poe
"does not go beyond limits" but rather "measures the
span of the human enclosure."

CK281 _____. "Time and American Writers," _Studies in Human Time_.
Trans. Elliot Coleman, 1956. Excerpts reprinted in CJ16.
Believes that the center of the literary work is the
author's sense of time, which in Poe's dream world is a
"perpetual present," symbolized by the sunken city. The
dream for Poe "ends in death but not in total extinction."

*CK: General Critical Articles*

CK282   PRAZ, MARIO.  "Poe and Psychoanalysis," SR, LXVIII (Sum.1960),
374-90. Trans. by B. M. Arnett.
Examines psychoanalytic theories and Bonaparte's attempt
to view Poe's work in the light of these theories.  He concludes that they are invalid because no matter whose hand
the psychoanalyst is playing, he always holds the trump
card--he can always make the stories fit his theory.

CK283   PRUETTE, LORINE.  "A Psychoanalytical Study of Edgar Allan
Poe," *The Literary Imagination: Psychoanalysis and the
Genius of the Writer*. ed. Hendrick Ruitenbeck. Chicago:
Quadrangle Books, 1965, 391-432.
Misleading psychoanalytic interpretation of Poe.

CK284   PUGH, GRIFFITH T.  "Poe, an Induction," EJ, XLV (Dec. 1956),
509-16.

CK285   QUINN, ARTHUR HOBSON.  "Beauty and the Supernatural," *Literature of the American People*.  New York: Appleton-Century-
Crofts, 1951, 292-307.
Quinn ranges over Poe's life and work, touching briefly
on most of his short stories, his poetry, and his influence
in America and Europe.  His remarks about the short story
are limited chiefly to their supernatural aspects. Valuable
chiefly as a survey.

CK286   QUINN, PATRICK F.  "Four Views of Edgar Allan Poe," JA,V
(1960), 138-46.
Examines different approaches to Poe's work and concludes that his stories are more than strange "yarns" and
"psychological allegories." They "represent his participa-
tion in a great and endless debate about one of the basic
issues in western thought, the relationship between the
two realms of Existence and Essence," between actual life
as we live it and "the realm of abstraction, of imagination, where there are no problems but only solutions,
where there is permanence rather than change."

CK287   RAGO, HENRY.  "Sociology of Composition," *Commonweal*, XLVI
(Jul. 18, 1947), 336-8.
Poe's importance as a modern writer lies in his interest in a highly conscious literature, in his perception
that the central tendency of American writing is subjective, and in his desire to involve his society in his neurosis.  In him we see "the concentration of a pathology in
the social organism."

# Edgar Allan Poe: An Annotated Bibliography

*CK: General Critical Articles*

CK288 RANSOME, ARTHUR. "Edgar Allan Poe," <u>TB</u>, CXXXIV, ns. II (Dec. 1906), 481-96.
    General essay emphasizing analysis as the predominant passion of Poe's mind and describing Dupin as "the embodiment of the analytical spirit of all mankind....one of the attitudes of man's brain."

CK289 RASCOE, BURTON. "Poe the Inventor," <u>MAMP</u>. ed. by Dorothy Kissling and Arthur H. Nethercot, New York: Carlyle Straub, 1938, 109-12.
    The only imitator of Poe in America was Henry James. His English imitators were Carlyle and Stevenson.

CK290 RAYAN, KRISHNA. "Edgar Allan Poe and Suggestiveness," *British Journal of Aesthetics,* IX (1969), 73-9.

CK291 REID, WHITELAW. "The Poe Centenary," *London Commemorations.* London: Harrison and Sons, 1909.
    Brief and general essay on Poe's achievements.

CK292 REILLY, JOHN E. "Ermina's Gales: The Poems Jane Locke Devoted to Poe," *Papers on Poe: Essays in Honor of J. Ward Ostrom.* Springfield, Ohio, 1972.

CK293 REIN, DAVID M. "Poe and Virginia Clemm," <u>BuR</u>, VII (May 1958), 207-16.
    Autobiographical interpretation of Poe's tales.

CK294 _____. "Poe's Dreams," *London Magazine,* II (Apr. 1962), 42-58.
    Applies Freudian dream analysis to several stories. Superficial and valueless essay.

CK295 RICHARDSON, CHARLES F. "Edgar Allan Poe, World Author," <u>Cr</u>, XLI (Aug. 1902), 138-49.
    General essay on Poe's reputation and on his value as a poet and writer of short stories.

CK296 RIDING, LAURA. "The Facts in the Case of Monsieur Poe," *Contemporaries and Snobs.* London: Jonathan Cape, 1928, 201-55.
    Poe was insignificant--five-fifths fudge, slipshod, vulgar, artificial, illogical, and egotistical. He pretended to be paranoid to build his reputation.

CK297 ROMAN, ROBERT C. "Poe on the Screen," *Films in Review,* XII (Oct. 1961), 462-74; with additional note by George Turner, XIII, p. 62.

# Edgar Allan Poe: An Annotated Bibliography

For Poe scholars who are also film buffs, Roman discusses the first film of Poe's life (1909), directed by D. W. Griffith, and the history of Poe's works on the screen.

CK298 ROURKE, CONSTANCE. *American Humor: a Study of the National Character*. New York: 1931, 145-9 and passim. Excerpts reprinted in CJ16.
Poe was not dependent solely upon inner sources for his material but was influenced by native American forces, such as the Negro and Western traditions of comic story-telling, the stories of adventurers who passed through his father's store, and the "broad grotesque myth-making" of Longstreet's *Georgia Scenes*. His instinct for comedy and hoax were part of the American literary tradition, specifically the tradition of Western story-tellers "who described wild and perverse actions with blank and undisturbed countenances, and whose insistent use of the first person brought them to the brink of inner revelation."

CK299 RUBIN, LOUIS D. JR. "Edgar Allan Poe: a Study in Heroism," *The Curious Death of the Novel: Essays in American Literature*. Baton Rouge: Louisiana State University Press, 1967, 47-66.

CK300 RYAN, JOHN K. "Growth of a Judgment," CER, XLV (Feb. 1947), 85-96.
Traces the development of Poe's idealism through four versions of his poem "Imitation."

CK301 SAINTSBURY, GEORGE. "Edgar Allan Poe," *Dial*, LXXXIII (Dec. 1927), 451-63. Reprinted in *Prefaces and Essays*. ed. by Oliver Elton. London: Macmillan, 1933, 314-24. Reprinted in CJ16.
Essay seems pregnant with meaning, but never quite gives birth.

CK302 SALE, MARIAN M. "Poe," *Commonwealth*, XXXIII (Apr. 1966), 28-37.

CK303 SANFORD, CHARLES L. "Edgar Allan Poe: A Blight on the Landscape," AQ, XX (1968), 54-66. Revision of article in *Rives*, No. 18 (Spr. 1962), ]-9. Reprinted in CJ16.
Places Poe in the tradition of the American Adam. "...the cycles of aspiration and disillusionment which shape his work relate to the cultural drive for a paradisiacal fulfillment in the New World. His major theme then becomes the dispossession from Paradise...."

# Edgar Allan Poe: An Annotated Bibliography

*CK: General Critical Articles*

CK304  SCHELL, STANLEY.  "Edgar Allan Poe, a Literary Study," *Werner's Magazine,* XXV (Mar. 1900), 151-66.
General essay on Poe's work.

CK305  SCHWABER, PAUL.  "On Reading Poe," *Literature and Psychology,* XXI (1971), 81-99.
Somewhat vague essay, which concludes: "Because of his neuroses, resources and situation in life, Poe as an artist could sense the agony that attends a technocratic, middle-class ascendency.  He presents perverse realities that can be felt and believed, and therefore feared."

CK306  SCHWARTZ, ARTHUR.  "The American Romantics: an Analysis," ESQ, XXXV (II Quarter, 1964), 39-44.
Brief remarks comparing Poe with other American Romantics.  Sees two Poes: "one who seeks escape from self... and one who analyses and calculates the chances for survival,"  Also suggests that Poe may be anti-Romantic in that he had no awareness of the "cumulative experiential progress toward definition of the self."

CK307  SEELYE, JOHN.  "Edgar Allan Poe," *Tales of the Grotesque and Arabesque.  Landmarks in American Writing.*  ed. Hennig Cohen.  New York, London: Basic Books, 1969.
Discusses Poe's American themes of containment, unity and alienation.

CK308  SHAPIRO, KARL.  "Is Poetry an American Art?" CE, XXV (Mar. 1964), 395-405.
Refers to Poe as "still one of the great destructive forces of literature," responsible for "successfully and scientifically disintegrating the psyche."

CK309  SHAW, GEORGE BERNARD.  "Edgar Allan Poe," *Pens Portraits and Reviews,* XXVII of *Works.*  London: Constable and Co., 1932, 220-36.  Originally in *Nation* (Jan. 16, 1909).  Reprinted in CJ16.
General essay on Poe's achievements and on the failure of American critics to appreciate his genius.  Americans can not appreciate Poe because they wallow in sensuality, because he begins "just where the world, the flesh, and the devil leave off."

CK310  SHULMAN, ROBERT.  "Poe and the Powers of the Mind," ELH, XXXVII (1970), 245-62.
Poe's stories display "real insight into that basically irrational strategy by which the mind attempts to preserve

itself from its own forces of madness, disease, and
disintegration...."

CK311 SIMPSON, LEWIS P. "Touching 'The Stylus': Notes on Poe's
Vision of Literary Order," *Studies in American Literature*,
Waldo McNeir and Lee Levy, eds. Baton Rouge, 1960.

CK312 SLICER, THOMAS R. "Edgar Allan Poe, the Pioneer of Romantic
Literature in America," *From Poet to Primer*. London and
New York: Grolier Society, 1909, 3-41.
Slightly hysterical discussion of Poe's poetry. Poe
was a pioneer of Romantic literature in America, but he was
also a drunkard, a dope addict, and a neurotic--"a sigh
that lingers in the air and finally expires in a sob."

CK313 SMART, CHARLES A. "On the Road to Page One," <u>YR</u>, XXXVII (Win.
1948), 242-56.
Passing reference to Poe.

CK314 SMITH, BERNARD. "The Quest of Beauty in Romance: Poe,"
*Forces in American Criticism*. New York: Harcourt Brace,
1939, 185-202.
Views Poe as a product of the Romantic movement, from
which he acquired ideas about sensationalism, the value of
pure imagination, and self-absorption. He accepted the
myths of the agrarian south, banished didacticism from
literature, and "formulated sanctions" for artists who
wished to isolate themselves from experience. "In sum,
his critical writing was narrow, special, and usually perverse. Its only value was in calling attention to the
pleasurable aspects of literature during an overly moralistic and intellectual time."

CK315 SMITH, C. ALPHONSO. "The Americanism of Poe," <u>ABUV</u>, Poe
number III, third series (Apr. 1909). Reprinted in *Kit-
Kat*, V (1915), 13-19.
Although half of Poe's brain was haunted by spectors,
the other was intellectual and made him "the greatest
constructive force in American literature." His interest
in technique and structure was very American.

CK316 _____. "The Haunted Poet," *Mentor*, X (Sept. 1922), 3-8.
Development of earlier essay.

CK317 _____. "Poe's Place in the World of Letters," <u>NCR</u> (May 5,
1912).
Discussion of Poe's four contributions to literature:
he was a discoverer in the realm of meter and rhythm, a

pioneer in the short story, the exponent of self-consciousness in literature, and the revealer of a distinctive Americanism.

CK318   SNELL, GEORGE.   "Poe--the Terror of the Soul," *Shapers of American Fiction*.   New York: E. P. Dutton, 1947, 45-60.
            Poe's stories anticipate Freud and belong to the mainstream of American literature in that they reflect "the dark strain of Calvinism," Puritan repression, and "the sense of decay or dissolution...of the new world." "MSFB" is a parable of man's life, and "Ligeia" an allegory about obsessive love.

CK319   SNYDER, EDWARD D.   "Bowra on Poe: Corrections," MLN, LXVII (Jun. 1952), 422-3.
            Correction of three errors in *The Romantic Imagination*.

CK320   SPANNUTH, JACOB E. and T. O. MABBOTT, eds.   *Doings of Gotham: Poe's Contribution to the "Columbia Spy."*   Pottsville, Pennsylvania, 1929.
            Mabbott introduces the volume with a discussion of Poe's sketches of New York.

CK321   SPENCER, BENJAMIN.   "'Beautiful Blood and Beautiful Brain': Whitman and Poe," ESQ, XXXV (II Quarter 1964), 45-50.
            Speculates on the Preface Poe and Whitman might have written for the American Romantic movement if they had lived at the same time.   Then discusses their differences.   Poe would have disagreed with most of the 1855 Introduction.   Unlike Whitman, he lost his desire to remain in the Romantic Weltanschaung of German, English, and American idealists.   Whitman is an organicist; Poe an atomist; Whitman a seer; Poe a histrio; Whitman devoted to the imagination, Poe to the intellect.

CK322   SPILLER, ROBERT E.   "The American Literary Dilemma and Edgar Allan Poe," *The Great Experiment in American Literature*.   ed. by Carl Bode.   New York: Praeger, 1961, 3-25.
            Poe was "the first to furnish an adequate statement of the American literary dilemma: the necessity...for creating a past in which ideal form could be recognized, applied to the anarchy of the present, and presented in a

*CK: General Critical Articles*

native language of literary form and style." He is the
source of "that literature which deals with the inner
realities and builds for them symbolic and structural
forms to satisfy the cravings of the aesthetic faculties."

CK323   STANARD, MARY.  "Was Poe Never Ethical?" *Nation*, XCII (May 25,
1911), 527.
Poe's stories often have moral themes.  "FHU," for example, concerns a man who has allowed his soul to die
through egoism.

CK324   STAUFFER, DONALD B.  "Poe's Views on Nature and the Function
of Style," ESQ, LX (Sum. 1970), 23-30.
Discusses Poe's attitude toward language, grammar,
sentence structure, word choice.

CK325   _____. Essay in *Papers on Poe: Essays in Honor of J. Ward
Ostrom*.  Springfield, Ohio, 1972.
Discusses phrenology in Poe's writings.

CK326   STEBBING, W.  *Poets: Geoffrey Chaucer to Alfred Tennyson*.
London, 1927, 198-206.
Brief remarks on Poe's weirdness.

CK327   STEVENSON, ROBERT LOUIS.  "The Works of Edgar Allan Poe,"
*The Works of Robert Louis Stevenson*. South Seas Edition,
XXIV. New York: Charles Scriber's Sons, 1925, 107-18.
Unsympathetic view of Poe's stories.

CK328   STOCKETT, LETITIA.  "Poe's Backgrounds," JHAM, XX (Jan. 1932),
123-33.
Emphasizes Poe's involvement with the literary issues
of his day, especially romanticism, and his influence on
modern writers in the area of the bizarre and the occult.

CK329   STONE, EDWARD.  "Poe In and Out of his Time," ESQ, XXXI (II
Quarter 1963), 14-18.
General discussion of the link between Poe's characters
and "the despairing spirit of modern man."

CK330   _____. "The Devil is White," *Essays on Determinism in American Literature*. ed. Sidney J. Krause. *Kent Studies in
English*. Vol. I, Kent State University Press, 1964.
Traces the tendency in American literature "to assoc-
iate whiteness with an anti-religious concept of the universe." Mentions NAGP, "PP," "Berenice" very briefly.

# Edgar Allan Poe: An Annotated Bibliography

*CK: General Critical Articles*

CK331　STOVALL, FLOYD.　"The Conscious Art of Edgar Allan Poe," CE,
　　　　XXIV (Mar. 1963), 417-21.　Reprinted in CJ64.
　　　　　　Accuses critics in recent decades of misunderstanding
　　　　Poe's poetry by disliking him so much that they fail to
　　　　see what is really there (Yvor Winters); analyzing his
　　　　work like psychologists doing clinical work-ups (Lawrence,
　　　　Krutch, Bonaparte); liking him unwillingly (Tate); dis-
　　　　liking him unwillingly (Eliot).

CK332　_____.　"Introduction to the *Poems of Edgar Allan Poe*. Char-
　　　　lottesville: University Press of Virginia, 1965.
　　　　　　Offers brief biography, general view of his poetry,
　　　　reputation and achievement.

CK333　_____.　"Poe as a Poet of Ideas," UTSE, XI (1931), 56-62.
　　　　　　Examines Poe's poetry for the development of his aes-
　　　　thetic theories.　Denies that Poe advocated art for art's
　　　　sake and suggests that his repudiation of truth in poetry
　　　　was really a repudiation of didacticism in art.

CK334　STRANDBERG, VICTOR.　"Poe's Hollow Men," UR, XXV (1969),
　　　　203-12.
　　　　　　Poe's characters suffer from "moral depravity and meta-
　　　　physical despair."

CK335　STRICKLAND, SIR WALTER.　"The Numerical Element in Edgar
　　　　Allan Poe's Twelve Great Poems," *The Great Divide*. I,
　　　　New York: B. Westerman Co., Inc., 1931.
　　　　　　Tries to fathom the numerical mysticism in Poe's poetry
　　　　"to see how subtly numerical mysticism and particularly
　　　　that of the two key numbers 7 and 8, and especially that
　　　　of 7 in its 3 and 4 binary procreations, has been inter-
　　　　woven with the texture of the twelve great poems in
　　　　question."

CK336　SWIGG, RICHARD.　"Waste and Idealism in the *Tales* of Edgar
　　　　Allan Poe," *Lawrence, Hardy and American Literature*. New
　　　　York: Oxford University Press, 1972, 189-201 and *passim*.
　　　　　　Discusses the *Tales* as assertations of individualism
　　　　and spiritual distinctiveness.　The American artist finds
　　　　that his "authority of self" is eroded by "the hurly-burly
　　　　of a democratic consciousness, by an external crowding and
　　　　distortion of spiritual feeling."

CK337　SWIGGETT, G. L.　"Plea for Poe," PL, XIII (Jul. 1901), 379-86.
　　　　　　Plea for greater recognition of Poe.

# EDGAR ALLAN POE: AN ANNOTATED BIBLIOGRAPHY

*CK: General Critical Articles*

CK338  TANASOCA, DONALD.  "Poe and Whitman," *Walt Whitman Birthplace Bulletin,* II (Apr. and Jul., 1959), 3-7, 6-11.

CK339  TARBOX, RAYMOND.  "Blank Hallucinations in the Fiction of Poe and Hemingway," AI, XXIV (1967), 312-43.
Discusses manic-depressive states and hallucinatory states common to the fiction of Poe and Hemingway.

CK340  TATE, ALLEN.  "The Angelic Imagination: Poe and the Power of Words," KR, XIV (Spr. 1952), 455-75.  Reprinted in *The Forlorn Demon.*  Chicago, 1953; in *The Man of Letters in the Modern World* (as "The Angelic Imagination: Poe as God"); in *Collected Works.*
Tate questions Eliot's theory that Poe entertained rather than experienced ideas.  He sees Poe as a transitional figure with a traditional attitude toward "a disorder that has since become typical."  Poe discovered the great modern subject, the disintegration of the personality (treated in "The Conversation of Eiros and Charmion," "The Colloquy of Monos and Una," "The Power of Words," and *Eureka*), but he dealt with the theme in an ordered, unified language rather than in a correspondingly disintegrated grammar and rhetoric.  Tate also discussed Poe's failure to harmonize his faculties among different orders of experience, to experience disintegration himself.  *See* CJ16 and CK109.

CK341  _____.  "Our Cousin Mr. Poe," PR, XVI (Dec. 1949), 1207-1217.  Reprinted in *Collected Essays.*  Denver: A Swallow, 1959; and in *The Man of Letters in the Modern World.*  New York: Meridian Books, 1955; and in CJ15 and CJ64.
Poe wrote as if the Classical and Christian traditions had already been lost.  His subject was "dehumanized man," man "alone in the world, and thus dead to it."  The characters are monsters of sensation, locked into the self, "feeding upon the disintegration of [their] objects and absorbing them into the void of the ego."

CK342  _____.  "The Poetry of Edgar Allan Poe," SR, LXXVI (Spr.1968), 214-25.  Essay also appears as the Introduction to the Signet edition of *The Complete Poems and Selected Criticism of Edgar Allan Poe,* New American Library.
Discusses Poe as the discoverer of Existentialism in Americans in his poetry of aloneness and isolation.  He is the "type of the alienated poet, the outcast, the poète maudit--the poet accursed," and he consciously exploited this role.

*CK: General Critical Articles*

CK343 _____. "Three Commentaries: Poe, James and Joyce," <u>SR</u>, LVIII (Win. 1950), 1-15.

In insisting upon unity of effect, Poe anticipated James. He also transformed Gothic machinery into serious art, so that Roderick Usher "becomes the prototype of the Joycean and Jamesian hero who cannot function in the ordinary world," who suffers from a split personality and from want of a moral sense. Unlike Joyce, however, Poe never achieved direct impressions in his work. In "FHU," for example, there is a complete lack of dramatized detail, and the unity of tone is never woven directly into the action of the story. Everything is described; nothing shown. Symbolism is "external and lyrical" rather than "intrinsic and dramatic." Poe was unable to "combine incident with his gift for insight symbolism."

CK344 TAYLOR, N. "The Supernatural in Nineteenth-Century Fiction," <u>ER</u>, CXCVII (Apr. 1903), 401-6.

General discussion of the supernatural element in Poe's fiction.

CK345 TAYLOR, WILLIAM FULLER. "Edgar Allan Poe," *The Story of American Letters*. Chicago: Henry Regnery Co., 1956, 110-19.

General survey of Poe's life and work. Concludes that he was the "first generally fine professional critic.... [who] formulated the first important body of aesthetic theory in America," saw the aesthetic possibilities of the short story, and discovered sources of terror in abnormal psychology.

CK346 THOMPSON, G. R. "Introduction," *Great Short Works of Edgar Allan Poe*. New York: Harper and Row, 1970.

CK347 _____. "Poe and 'Romantic Irony'," *Papers on Poe: Essays in Honor of J. Ward Ostrom*. Springfield, Ohio, 1972.

Poe's Gothic tales "can be demonstrated to have at least three simultaneous levels of meaning: supernaturalistic, psychological, and absurdist."

CK348 _____. "Unity, Death and Nothingness--Poe's Romantic Scepticism," <u>PMLA</u>, LXXXV (1970), 297-301.

Analyzes Moldenhauer's brilliant but mistaken theories on Poe. Poe is in the end a skeptic and a nihilist. *See* CK241.

# EDGAR ALLAN POE: AN ANNOTATED BIBLIOGRAPHY

*CK: General Critical Articles*

CK349   TINKER, CHAUNCEY. "Poetry and the Secret Impulse," <u>YR</u>, XVI
      (Jan. 1927), 275-86.
         Attacks the psychoanalytical approach to Poe, partic-
      ularly Freudian-oriented essays of Krutch and Mordell.

CK350   TOLMAN, ALBERT H. "Was Poe Accurate?" *The Views About Ham-
      let and Other Essays*. Boston and New York: Houghton
      Mifflin, 1904, 397-403.
         Pedantic discussion of mathematical errors in "The
      Gold Bug."

CK351   TRENT, WILLIAM. "The Centenary of Poe," *Longfellow and
      Other Essays*. New York: T. Y. Crowell, 1910, 211-44.
         Calls on American critics to abandon their prejudices
      toward Poe.

CK352   _____. "Edgar Allan Poe," *Critical Writers of America*. New
      York: H. Holt, 1912, 97-110.
         Poe's work symbolizes the search for an eternal order.
      He is the prophet of his own doom.

CK353   _____. "Edgar Allan Poe," *A History of American Literature,
      1601-1865*. New York: D. Appleton, 1905, 366-83.
         Discusses Poe's alienation from the contemporary lit-
      erary scene, his anti-Puritanism and anti-didacticism.

CK354   TRIEBER, J. MARSHALL. "The Scornful Grin: A Study of Poesque
      Humor," <u>PN</u>, IV (Dec. 1971), 32-4.
         Sees Poe's humor in terms of Poe's "delight in over-
      coming others."

CK355   VAN DOREN, CARL. *American Literature: An Introduction*. Los
      Angeles: United States Library Association, 1933.
         Few general words.

CK356   VARNER, CORNELIA. "Notes on Poe's Use of Contemporary Mate-
      rials in Certain of his Stories," <u>JEGP</u>, XXXII (Jan. 1933),
      77-80.
         Gives seven examples of Poe's use of periodicals in
      short stories "The Man," "Loss of Breath," "Thousand-and-
      Second Tale of Scheherazade," "Conversation of Monos and
      Una," and "The Spectacles."

CK357   WAGGONER, HYATT H. "Transcendental Despair," *American Poets
      from the Puritans to the Present*. Boston: Houghton
      Mifflin, 1968, 130-146.
         Discussion of Poe as a possible Transcendentalist.

*CK: General Critical Articles*

"Intending to affirm the reality of the transcendent Ideal, he made of Transcendentalism a doctrine of negation and despair."

CK358 WARFEL, HARRY. "Mathematics of Poe's Poetry," CEA Critic, XXXI (May 1959), 5-6.

CK359 WASSERSTROM, WILLIAM. "The Spirit of Myrrha," AL, XII (Win. 1956), 455-72.
On father-daughter relationships in literature.

CK360 WEBB, HOWARD W. "Contributions to Poe's *Penn Magazine*," N&Q, CCIII, ns. 5 (Dec. 1958), 447-8.
A list of probable contributions to Poe's ill-fated magazine. Concludes that it would not have lived up to Poe's conception of it because the contributions were second-rate.

CK361. WEBER, JOHN-PAUL. "Edgar Poe on the Theme of the Clock," *La Nouvelle Revue Francais,* 68 and 69 (Aug. and Sept. 1958), 301-11, 498-508; trans. Claude Richard and Robert Regan for *Poe: a Collection of Critical Essays.* ed. by Robert Regan, New Jersey: Prentice Hall, 1967.
Discusses the clock symbol in "The Devil," "The Raven," "Masque," "FHU," "Descent," "MSFB," "TTH," "PP." Decides that Poe witnessed sexual relations ("nocturnal romps") between his parents, which he interpreted as a struggle. "...in the unconscious of the neurotic the rhythm of the clock is frequently associated with the sex act."

CK362 WEISS, MIRIAM. "Poe's Catterina," MissQ, XIX (Win. 1965-6), 29-33.
Discussion of Poe's devotion to cats. In his literature, "cats are generally cats, not sex symbols, love objects, mother figures, or anything else but cats which behave like cats."

CK363 WEISSBUCH, TED N. "Edgar Allan Poe: Hoaxer in the American Tradition," NYHSQB, XLV (July 1961), 291-309.
Discusses Poe as a literary hoaxer interested in discovering literary techniques to achieve sucess. "Hans Pfaall" moves from "burlesque to an almost plausible account of a balloon voyage." "Balloon Hoax" was an attempt to outdo R. A. Locke's "Moon Hoax," which received more publicity than "Hans Pfaall." Other hoaxes are NAGP, "Facts," "Ragged Mts.," and "Baron Von Kempelen and his Discovery."

*CK: General Critical Articles*

CK364  WELLS, Henry.  "Discoveries in Imagination," *The American Way of Poetry*.  New York: Columbia University Press, 1943, 19-28.
        Poe was "New Worldish" in his tragic disillusionment and despair, American in his loneliness and hostility, "the first martyr of the decadent American society.  He experienced the clash between the profoundly romantic and spiritual temperament and a profoundly materialistic and pragmatic society."

CK365  WELLS, ROSS.  "College 'Lit.' First to Recognize Poe." *Richmond Times-Dispatch*, VI (Oct. 6, 1935).

CK366  WENDELL, BARRETT.  "Edgar Allan Poe," *A Literary History of America*.  New York: Charles Scribner's Sons, 1900, 204-19.
        General remarks on Poe's career as a critic, on his predilection for hoaxes, on the lack of "actuality" in his work.  Unsympathetic to Poe, believing that Poe was inferior because of the circumstances of his birth.

CK367  ____.  "Nationalism of Poe," *Book of the Poe Centenary*. ed by Charles W. Kent and John S. Patton, Charlottesville: University of Virginia (Jan. 19, 1909).
        Poe's isolation and romanticism were contemporary American characteristics.

CK368  WERTZ, S. K. and LINDA.  "On Poe's Use of 'Mystery'," PSt, IV (Jun. 1971), 7-10.
        Rather pretentious little essay which examines "Poe's descriptions and discussions of mystery and [calls] upon the assistance of the philosophers who have discussed mystery at some length."  After attempting to distinguish between "mystery" and "problem," the authors conclude that "mystery..., for Poe, is best depicted as that which involves the subject and the reader in preternatural or abnormal speculations--in astute analysis of the bizarre."

CK369  WHITESIDE, MARY BRENT.  "Poe and Dickinson," MAMP, ed. by Dorothy Kissling and Arthur H. Nethercot, New York: Carlyle Straub, 1938.  Reprinted in Person, XV (Oct. 1934), 315-26.
        An uninstructive comparison in which both poets are believed to have had self-revelations and intense emotions, to have composed "in a single lightening flash of inspiration," to have been concerned with truth, immortality, love, and death.

# EDGAR ALLAN POE: AN ANNOTATED BIBLIOGRAPHY

*CK: General Critical Articles*

CK370 WHITTY, J. H. "Poe's Writings Influenced by Richmond Gardens," *Richmond News-Leader* (Apr. 24, 1937).

CK371 WIGFALL, GREEN A. "The Weekly Magazines and Poe," *English Studies in Honor of James Southall Wilson*. Charlottesville: University of Virginia, 1951.
  Discussion of the various weekly magazines Poe contributed to: BJ, HJ, YBLG.

CK372 WILBUR, RICHARD. "The House of Poe," Lecture at the Library of Congress under the auspices of the Gertrude Clarke Whittall Poetry and Literary Fund, *Anniversary Lectures*, 1959. Reprinted in CJ15, CJ16, CJ64.
  Poe's fundamental plot describes the effort of the poetic soul to escape from the mundane physical world into a world of pure spirit, dream, poetic intuition. The enclosure is always a sign of the poet escaping into dreams, into his mind. Applying this theory to "FHU," Wilbur concludes that the story is "triumphant," that Usher escapes earthly attachments and becomes "all soul."

CK373 _____. *Major Writers in America*. New York, 1962.

CK374 _____. ed. *Poe: The Laurel Poetry Series*. New York: Dell, 1959.
  Poe's poetry is not "a protest against the separation of mind and world but an extreme assertion of that separation, [which]...aspires...to that isolate freedom of the imagination we enjoy in dreams." Consequently, it is not a report of Beauty but "an account of the process of aspiration, and a rational of the soul's struggle to free itself of earth and move toward the supernal."

CK375 WILLIAMS, VALENTINE. "The Detective in Fiction," FortnR, CXXXIV, ns. 128 (Sept. 1930), 381-92.
  Poe, the original amateur detective, was the first to solve crimes by ratiocination.

CK376 WILLIAMS, WILLIAM CARLOS. "Edgar Allan Poe." *In the American Grain*. New York: A. C. Boni, 1925, 216-34. Excerpts reprinted in CJ16 and CJ37.
  Poe's genius was shaped by "the necessity for a new beginning" in American literature, by his desire to eliminate all "colonial imitation," and by "the immediate effect of the locality upon the first." 'Poe achieved the exposure of American "makeshifts, self deceptions and grotesque excuses." He perceived and captured "the grotesque inappropriateness of the life about him."

*CK: General Critical Articles*

His insights penetrated his theory of poetry, an artistic effort to "lay low the 'maiseries' of form and content with which his world abounded," and to restore the spirit of originality to a slavish and banal country. "He was the first to realize that the hard, sardonic, truculent mass of the New World, hot, angry--was, in fact, not a thing to paint over, to smear, to destroy--for it would not be destroyed, it was too powerful,--it smiled!"

CK377 WILSON, EDMUND. "Poe at Home and Abroad," *Shores of Light*. New York: Farrar, Straus and Young, 1952, 179-90 (essay dated Dec. 8, 1926). Reprinted in CJ16.
Describes Poe as a typical nineteenth-century Romantic whose stories embody his confused sexuality and his rebellion against social and moral orders. He contributed an original aesthetic discipline to Romanticism, and "no one understood better than Poe that the deepest psychological truth may be rendered through phantasmagoria."

CK378 WILSON, JAMES SOUTHALL. "The Devil was in It," AM, XXIV (Oct. 1931), 215-20.
Many of Poe's tales, especially those intended as Folio Club Tales, are unrecognized satires and burlesques. Poe tried to teach himself how to write by burlesquing the fashionable literature of the day--the epigrammatic cleverness of Bulwer, the extravagances of BJ, and the style of the Transcendentalists.

CK379 _____. "Personality of Poe," VMHB, LXVII (Apr. 1959), 131-42.
Objective study of Poe, free of moral judgments and psychological excesses.

CK380 _____. "A Poe Society," SRL, III (Apr. 2, 1927), 706.
Brief description of the Edgar Allan Poe Society of Baltimore.

CK381 WILT, NAPIER. "Poe's Attitudes Toward his Tales, a New Document," MP, XXV (Aug. 1927), 101-5.
Since Poe confessed that he modeled "Berenice" after stories in popular magazines, his tales can not be read as revelations of his neuroses.

CK382 WINTERS, IVOR. "Edgar Allan Poe, A Crisis in the History of American Obscurantism," AL, VII (Jan. 1937), 379-401. Reprinted in CK16 and CK37.

# EDGAR ALLAN POE: AN ANNOTATED BIBLIOGRAPHY

*CK: General Critical Articles*

Poe misunderstood the poetry of previous ages, was inferior in matters of taste, was guilty of vulgar sentimentalism, believed that the poetic mood is governed by narrow rules, failed to comprehend the spiritual act responsible for great poetry, was oblivious to the function of the intellect in poetry, did not recognize the great satirical and didactic masters of literature, failed to grasp the real distinction between truth and beauty, reduced poetry to a position of triviality, sought isolated fragments of human experience, was childish, amoral, and obscure.

CK383 WOOD, CLEMENT. "The Stricken Eagle," <u>MAMP</u>, ed. by Dorothy Kissling and Arthur H. Nethercot. New York: Carlyle Straub, 1938, 68-102.
Poe's stories reveal his oedipal complex, his excessive adoration for his dead mother. In marrying a cousin, he came as close as possible to consummating his love with his mother.

CK384 WOODBERRY, GEORGE EDWARD. "The Poe Centenary," *The Torch and Other Addresses*. New York: Harcourt Brace and Howe, 1920. General remarks, favorable to Poe.

CK385 WYLD, LIONEL D. "The Enigma of Poe: Reality vs L'Art Pour L'Art'," *Lock Haven Bulletin*, series 1, no. 2 (1960), 34-8.
Purports to examine the extent to which Poe's poems were related to genuine personal experience, but never gets to the subject.

CK386 WYLIE, CLARENCE P. "Mathematical Allusions in Poe," *Scientific Monthly*, LXIII (Sept. 1946), 227-35.
"From the nature and frequency of his mistakes and misconceptions, both in *Eureka*...and in his other essays... it seems abundantly clear that Poe was not a poor mathematician but simply no mathematician at all."

CK387 YEATS, WILLIAM BUTLER. "Letter to W. T. Horton," *Letters of W. B. Yeats*. ed. by Alan Wade. New York, 1955.
Reveals a dislike for Poe (except for his "sometimes profound" critical essays). Poe generally vulgar, commonplace, and insincere.

CK388 YOUNG, PHILLIP. "The Early Psychologists and Poe," <u>AL</u>, XXII (Jan. 1951), 442-54.
The author discusses early psychological criticism of Poe.

# Edgar Allan Poe: An Annotated Bibliography

*CL: Interpretations of Individual Works*

### "Al Aaraaf"

CL1  CAIRNS, WILLIAM B.  "Some Notes on Poe's 'Al Aaraaf'," MP, XIII (May 1915), 35-44.
    Discusses the history of the poem's publication, various interpretations and sources.  The poem shows that the absence of knowledge is a blessing.  "It is the idea of beauty which the Deity disseminates throughout the universe as his special message, and which is to keep the worlds from tottering in the guilt of man."  Excesses of truth or knowledge are enemies of this beauty.

CL2  CHURCH, HENRY W. and HERVEY ALLEN.  "Poe and Nature," SRL, XI (Apr. 6, 1935), 598.
    Regarding the source of flower names in "Al Aaraaf."

CL3  MABBOTT, T. O.  "'Al Aaraaf,' Part II, 1-8," Expl, XVI, Q4 (Nov. 1957).
    Query.

CL4  PETTIGREW, RICHARD C. and MARIE M.  "A Reply to Floyd Stovall's Interpretation of 'Al Aaraaf'," AL, VIII (Jan. 1937), 439-45.
    Discusses holes in Stovall's belief that Al Aaraaf is God's instrument in the destruction of the world.

CL5  STOVALL, FLOYD.  "An Interpretation of Poe's 'Al Aaraaf'," UTSE, IX (1929), 106-33.
    Stovall believes that the poem dramatizes God's rule by power, rather than his rule by Beauty.  There are three separate threads in the poem: a religious motif concerned with man's relation to God's authority, an astronomical motif, which explains "prophecy in terms of observed phenomenon," and an apocalyptic motif in which "Al Aaraaf is a material star that becomes the instrument of God in the destruction of the world."

### "Alone"

CL6  CAUTHEN, I. B.  "Poe's 'Alone': Its Background, Source, and Manuscript," SB:BSUV, III (1950), 284-91.
    The source is Byron's *Manfred*.

*See also* B96.

# EDGAR ALLAN POE: AN ANNOTATED BIBLIOGRAPHY

*CL: Interpretations of Individual Works*

### "Angel of the Odd"

CL7   BANDY, W. T.   "More on 'The Angel of the Odd'," <u>PN</u>, III (Jun. 1970), 22.

CL8   GERBER, GERALD.   "Poe and 'The Manuscript'," <u>PSt</u>, VI (Jun. 1973), 27.
"The Angel of the Odd" was influenced by "Conversations with Thomas Paine," *Manuscript*, II, 33-64 and by "The Providential Release," 65-88. "The Oblong Box" was influenced by a story in the same periodical, II, 1-16.

CL9   _____. "Poe's Odd Angel," <u>NCF</u>, XXIII (1968), 88-93.
"'The Angel of the Odd' burlesques both the ideal of perfectibility and those reformers whose schemes were calculated to improve mankind."

CL10  MABBOTT, T. O.   "The Origins of Poe's 'Angel of the Odd'," <u>N&Q</u>, CLX (Jan. 3, 1931), 8.
The origin is a paragraph in the *Philadelphia Public Ledger* (Jun. 5, 1844).

CL11  RICHARD, CLAUDE.   "Arrant Bubbles: Poe's 'The Angel of the Odd'," <u>PN</u>, II (Oct. 1969), 46-8.
Sees the tale as another episode in the war between the literati and as a satire on New England and the transcendentalists.

### "Annabel Lee"

CL12  BOOTH, BRADFORD A.   "The Identity of 'Annabel Lee'," <u>CE</u>, VII (Oct. 1945), 17-19.
She is Sarah Elmira Royster.

CL13  BROWN, WALLACE C.   "The English Professor's Dilemma," <u>CE</u>, V (Apr. 1944), 380-85.
Should students read "Annabel Lee," a worthless but popular poem, or "To Helen," one of the great English lyrics?

CL14  EMPRIC, JULIENNE H.   "A Note on 'Annabel Lee'," <u>PSt</u>, VI (Jun. 1973), 26.
Believes that the narrator's perspective has remained unchanged since he was a child.

CL15  GROSS, SEYMOUR L.   "The Reflection of Conrad Aiken's 'Strange Moonlight'," <u>MLN</u>, LXXII (Mar. 1957), 185-89.
Aiken's story is an ironic comment on "Annabel Lee."

*CL: Interpretations of Individual Works*

CL16  LAW, ROBERT A. "A Source for 'Annabel Lee'," <u>JEGP</u>, XXI (Oct.
2, 1922), 341-6.
The source is "The Mourner" from the *Charleston Courier*
(Dec. 4, 1807).

CL17  MELTON, W. F.  "Some Autobiographical Notes in Poe's Poetry,"
<u>SAQ</u>, XI (Apr. 1912), 175-9.
The author reads "Annabel Lee" and "Eleonora" in the
light of Poe's marriage.

*See also* B1, B116, CL528.


"The Assignation:

CL18  BENTON, RICHARD P.  "Is Poe's 'The Assignation' a Hoax?" <u>NCF</u>,
XVIII (Sept. 1963), 193-7.
Discusses the tale as a parody inspired by the Byron-
Guiccioli romance, "a Poesque attempt to deceive those
readers of Poe's time who were ordinarily shocked by the
Byronic message."  The narrator is Byron's friend, the
Irish poet Thomas Moore.

CL19  DIXON, JEANNE.  "Poe: a Borrowing from Goldsmith," <u>N&Q</u>,
CLXIII (Nov. 12, 1932), 350.
A situation in "The Assignation" comes from *The Vicar
of Wakefield*.

CL20  ENGSTROM, ALFRED G.  "Chateaubriand's *Itineraire de Paris a
Jerusalem* and Poe's 'The Assignation'," <u>MLN</u>, LXIX (Nov.
1954), 506-7.
Part of Poe's story is a paraphrase of a section in
Chateaubriand's work dealing with the Altar of Laughter.

CL21  WHITT, CELIA.  "Poe and *The Mysteries of Udolpho*," <u>UTSE</u>,
XVII (1937), 124-31.
Poe borrowed many aspects of Mrs. Radcliffe's story for
"The Assignation": situation, character, poison, use of
venetian glass.

*See also* CO14.


"Autography"

CL22  HAMMOND, ALEXANDER.  "The Hidden Jew in Poe's 'Autography',"
<u>PN</u>, II (Oct. 1969), 55-6.

*CL: Interpretations of Individual Works*

Concerning a hitherto undetected cryptographic riddle
in "Autography," which is an anti-Semitic joke.

CL23 MABBOTT, T. O. "Poe's Obscure Contemporaries," <u>AN&Q</u>, I (Feb.
1942), 166-7.
A list of unidentified names from "Literati" and
"Autography."

CL24 O'CONNOR, ROGER. "Letters, Signatures and 'Juws' in Poe's
'Autography'," <u>PN</u>, III (Jun. 1970), 21-2.
An alternative suggestion to Hammond's idea that Poe's
riddle is an anti-Semitic joke.


"Balloon Hoax"

CL25 BRIGHAM, CLARENCE SAUNDERS. *Poe's "Balloon Hoax."* Metuchen,
New Jersey, 1932. Reprinted in <u>ABC</u>, I (Feb. 1932), 94-5.
Concerning the appearance of "Balloon Hoax" in the *New
York Sun* (April 13, 1844).

CL26 FALK, DORIS. "Thomas Low Nichols, Poe, and the 'Balloon
Hoax'," <u>PN</u>, V (Dec. 1972), 48-9.
Discusses and reprints Nichols' account of the balloon
hoax episode in *Forty Years of American Life: 1821-1861*.

CL27 JACKSON, JOSEPH. ed. *The Philosophy of Animal Magnetism.*
Philadelphia, 1928.
In the Foreward, Jackson reviews the contemporary sci-
entifiar achievements familiar to Poe when he wrote "Balloon Hoax," and discusses the evidence for authorship of
the *The Philosophy of Animal Magnetism*.

CL28 MABBOTT, T. O. "Poe's 'Balloon Hoax'," *New York Sun* (Jan.
23, 1943), 6.
The source is an article in *Gentleman's Magazine* on
aereonotics.

CL29 NORRIS, W. B. "Poe's Balloon Hoax," *Nation,*XCI (Oct. 27,
1910), 389-90.
Poe relied on Monck Mason's account of his balloon
trip.

CL30 SCUDDER, H. H. "Poe's 'Balloon Hoax'," <u>AL</u>, XXI (May 1949),
179-90.
Discusses similarities between Poe's tale and Monck
Mason's account of his Nov. 1836 balloon trip(Theodore
Foster, pub., New York, 1837).

*CL: Interpretations of Individual Works*

CL31  WILKINSON, RONALD S.  "Poe's 'Balloon-Hoax' Once More," <u>AL</u>,
　　　　XXXII (Nov. 1960), 313-17.
　　　　　　A source is the anonymous pamphlet Monck Mason distrib-
　　　　uted at an exhibition of his model dirigible balloon at
　　　　the Royal Adelaide Gallery in London.

CL32  WIMSATT, W. K. JR.  "A Further Note on Poe's 'Balloon Hoax',"
　　　　<u>AL</u>, XXII (Jan. 1951), 491-2.
　　　　　　Poe's "Balloon Hoax" (*New York Sun*, Apr. 13, 1844) was
　　　　followed by a complimentary postscript probably drafted by
　　　　Poe himself.  A copy of the publication is owned by the
　　　　American Antiquarian Society and was reprinted by C. S.
　　　　Brigham, <u>ABC</u> (Feb. 1932) and in a pamphlet, *Poe's Balloon
　　　　Hoax*.  Metuchen, New Jersey, 1932.

*See also* CK363, CL532.


"The Bells"

CL33  BIRSS, JOHN H.  "Emerson and Poe: a Similitude," <u>N&Q</u>, CLXVI
　　　　(Apr. 21, 1934), 279.
　　　　　　Similarity between line 10 of "The Bells" and "Wood-
　　　　notes," 165.

CL34  CAMERON, KENNETH.  "Poe's 'The Bells': A Reply to Schiller
　　　　and Romberg?" <u>ESQ</u>, XXXVIII (I Quarter 1965), 2-73.
　　　　　　Reprints the music and score of Schiller and Romberg's
　　　　"Song of the Bells," a source of Poe's poem.

CL35  _____.  "Poe's 'Bells' and Schiller's 'Das Lied von der
　　　　Glocke'," <u>ESQ</u>, XIX (II Quarter 1960), 37.
　　　　　　Source of the poem is a passage from Madame de Stael's
　　　　*Germany,* which discusses Schiller's poem.

CL36  COOPER, C. B.  "Tintinnabulation," <u>MLN</u>, XLI (May 1926), 318.
　　　　　　The word is repeated five times in John Hookham Frere's
　　　　edition of *Monks and Giants,* Canto III (1817).

CL37  DEDMOND, FRANCIS B.  "The Word 'Tintinnabulation' and a
　　　　Source for Poe's 'The Bells'," <u>N&Q</u>, CXCVI (Nov. 24, 1951),
　　　　520-1.
　　　　　　Poe probably saw the word "tintinnabulatory" in "Mira-
　　　　bilia Exempla, No. IV," <u>GM</u> (Apr. 1838), which is also a
　　　　source of the poem.

CL38  DOLSON, E. C.  "A Foote Note on Poe," <u>NEM</u>, ns. XXXV (Sept.
　　　　1906), 79-80.

*CL: Interpretations of Individual Works*

Poe originally sent *Sartain's* an 18 line poem. Six months later he enlarged and revised it; and three months after that, he sent the final draft.

CL39   DuBOIS, ARTHUR E.   "The Jazz Bells of Poe," <u>CE</u>, II (Dec. 1940), 230-44.
    Although Poe never searched for an organic American theme, in "The Bells" he came closer than any other American of his time to an organic rhythm. His themes are purely personal, representing a world of escape, a limbo between life and death, the real and ideal. The bells represent the real world and the world of the unconscious and remind Poe of death and of a life which cheated him and drove him insane. The poem's rhythm and sounds develop this theme of madness.

CL40   DUDLEY, FRED A.   "'Tintinnabulation': And a Source of Poe's 'The Bells'," <u>AL</u>, IV (Nov. 1932), 296-300.
    Sources are DeQuincey's *Confessions of an English Opium-Eater;* "A Dozen Nuisances of London--by a Pedestrian," *Fraser's,* II (Nov. 1830), 450; "The First Man I was Near Seeing Hanged," *Frasers,* IX (Jun. 1834), 711; a review of *The Hunchback of Notre Dame, Fraser's,* XII (Jul. 1885), 97; "A Letter to the Bels of a Parish Church in Italy," cited in *New England Dictionary.*

CL41   MABBOTT, T. O.   "Poe's Word 'Tintinnabulation'," <u>N&Q</u>, CLXXV (Nov. 26, 1938), 387.
    Cites use of word in letter from William Wilberforce Lord.

CL42   _____.  "Writing of Poe's 'The Bells'," <u>AN&Q</u>, II (Oct. 1942), 110.
    The story that Poe wrote the poem in a Judge's office is probably specious.

CL43   THOMPSON, G. R.  "Poe's Readings of *Pelham:* Another Source for 'Tintinnabulation' and Other Piquant Expressions," <u>AL</u>, XLI (May 1969), 251-55.
    A source for the word is "tintinnabulary," which appears in Bulwer-Lytton's *Pelham.*

CL44   TURNER, ARLIN.  "Writing of Poe's 'The Bells'," <u>AN&Q</u>, II (Aug. 1942), 73.
    Discusses the legend that Poe wrote the poem in a Judge's office.

*CL: Interpretations of Individual Works*

CL45 _____ and T. O. MABBOTT. "Two Poe Hoaxes by the Same Hand,"
AN&Q, II (Jan. 1943), 147-8.
Concerning hoaxes involving "The Bells" and the "New
Orleans *Raven*."

CL46 WILLIAMS, PAUL O. "A Reading of Poe's 'The Bells'," PN, I
(Oct. 1968), 24-25.
"...the poem enforces the familiar Poe theme, even
moral, that discord and death alone are triumphant."

*See also* A5, A62, A190, B132, B207, CN4, CN6.


"Berenice"

CL47 ABEL, DARREL. "Coleridge's 'Life-in-Death' and Poe's 'Death-
in-Life'," N&Q, CC, ns. 2 (May 1955), 218-20.
Although Poe frequently insisted that the coexistence
of life and death in a person is an illusion and can be
explained by natural causes, he also employed the supernatural method--the invasion of a natural object or person by something supernatural. The model of both "Berenice" and "Ligeia," stories in which a ghost invades and
supplants the real spirit of the body, is "The Rime of the
Ancient Mariner."

CL48 DAVIDSON, FRANK. "A Note on Poe's 'Berenice'," AL, XI (May
1913), 212-13.
Describes the plot of "Manuscript Found in a Madhouse,"
E. L. Bulwer, which Poe cited as a popular contemporary
story like "Berenice."

CL49 FORCLAZ, ROGER. "A Source for 'Berenice' and a Note on Poe's
Reading," PN, I (Oct. 1968), 25-27.
Two sources are "An Event in the Life of a Dentist,"
*New York Mirror*, X (Apr. 6, 1833), 313-14, and "The Death's
Head," *Phantasmagoriana*.

CL50 SLOAN, DAVID E. E. "Gothic Romanticism and Rational Empiricism in Poe's 'Berenice'," ATQ, XIX (Summer 1973), 19-26.
Believes that the tale is concerned with the tension
between the empiricism of the Enlightenment and Romantic
Gothicism. After proving that tooth extraction was accepted as a cure for many diseases, Sloane suggests that
"the application of a medical cure by Poe's psychologi-
cally deranged Romantic hero, Egaeus, becomes a statement
on the dangers of empiricism in an illusory physical

*CL: Interpretations of Individuals Works*

world--a working out in fiction of the theme of Poe's
'Sonnet--to Science'."

*See also* A75, CK279, CK330, CK381, C57.


"The Black Cat"

CL51 \_\_\_\_. "Another Poe Letter for Sale," <u>ESQ</u>, LXIII (Spr. 1971),
37.
Edgar Allan Poe to Ezra Holden Esq. or Andrew McMakin
(Aug. 26, 1843) reveals that Poe sold "The Black Cat" for
twenty dollars.

CL52 BONAPARTE, MARIE. "'The Black Cat'," trans. by John Rodker,
<u>PR</u>, XVII (Nov. 1950), 834-60.
Freudian interpretation of the story suggests that its
main theme is fear of castration. The cat, symbolizing
the female genitals, is a totem of Poe's mother, whom Poe
hates because she is a castrated and castrating being.
Castration occurs when he puts out the cat's eyes. Primitive weaning and separation anxieties of childhood are also symbolized in the story.

CL53 FRUSHELL, RICHARD C. "'An Incarnate Night-Mare': Moral
Grotesquerie in 'The Black Cat'," <u>PN</u>, V (Dec. 1972),
43-4.
Investigates the "'Moral' undercurrent implicit in the
narrator's degeneration by stages into the condition of
grotesque perversity."

CL54 GARGANO, JAMES W. "'The Black Cat': Perverseness Reconsidered," <u>TSLL</u>, II (Sum. 1960), 172-8. Excerpts reprinted in CJ37.
"The cat symbolizes the multiple personality of the
narrator, who turns against himself and tries to obliter-
ate his vision of the good." Dramatic irony consists in
his denial of a moral order while the reader observes it
in operation. Finally, his efforts to prove himself superior to that order cause his downfall.

CL55 KRAPPE, E. S. "A Possible Source for Poe's 'Tell-Tale Heart'
and 'The Black Cat'," <u>AL</u>, XII (Mar. 1940), 84-88.
The source is Dickens' "The Clock-Case: a Confession
Found in a Prison in the Time of Charles the Second,"
from *Master Humphrey's Clock*.

*See also* CK362, CL82, CL449, CR12.

# Edgar Allan Poe: An Annotated Bibliography

*CL: Interpretations of Individual Works*

"The Cask of Amontillado"

CL56  ADLER, JACOB H.  "Are There Flaws in 'The Cask of Amontilla-
       do'?" N&Q, CXCIX (Jan. 1954), 32-4.
           The reader can never be certain whether Montresor is a
       detached foreign observer or an Italian.

CL57  APPEL, ALFRED JR.  PN, V (Dec. 1972), 51.
           Claims that Nabokov personally denied having parodied
       "The Cask of Amontillado" in *Lolita*. *See* CL60 and CL61.

CL58  BALES, KENT.  "Poetic Justice in 'The Cask of Amontillado',"
       PN, V (Dec. 1972), 51.
           Poe's "Protestant Christian audience...can indulge
       their ideological hatreds by justly condemning Montresor
       to hell on the strength of his professed beliefs which,
       in this matter, they share."  Herein lies the irony.

CL59  CAMPBELL, KILLIS.  "Three Notes on Poe," AL, IV (Jan. 1933),
       385-8.
           1. The title "Journey into the Blue Distance" was prob-
       ably a free rendering of the secondary title of Tieck's
       "Das Alte Buch: oder Reise ins Blaue Hinein," reviewed in
       Bl, 1837.
           2. The plot of "The Cask of Amontillado" is similar to
       a passage in Bulwer's *Last Days of Pompeii*.
           3. Most of Poe's review of *Astoria* is paraphrased from
       Irving's Astoria itself.

CL60  CLARK, GEORGE P.  "A Further Word on Poe and *Lolita*," PN, III
       (Dec. 1970), 39.
           Notes a parody of "The Cask of Amontillado" in Chapter
       35 of *Lolita*.

CL61  _____.  PN, V (Dec. 1972), 51.
           Nabokov's parody of "The Cask of Amontillado" in *Lolita*
       was unconscious.  It is irrelevant that he denied it.  *See*
       CL57 and CL60.

CL62  DEDMOND, FRANCIS B.  "An Additional Source of Poe's 'The Cask
       of Amontillado'," N&Q, CXCVII (May 10, 1952), 212-14.
           The source is "The Tun of Red Wine," GM (May 1838).

CL63  _____.  "'The Cask of Amontillado' and the War of the Litera-
       ti," MLQ, XV (1954), 137-46.

*CL: Interpretations of Individual Works*

The story is a sublimation of Poe's desire to take revenge on Hiram Fuller and Thomas Dunn English. Poe is
Montresor; Fortunato is English; and Luchesi, the real
butt of sarcasm in the story, is Fuller.

CL64 DOXEY, WILLIAM S. "Concerning Fortunato's 'Courtesy'," SSF,
IV (Spr. 1967), 266-7.
Argues against Rea's contention that Fortunato exhibits
"the courtesy of the uncomplaining." Fortunato's weakness
is pride. *See* CL81.

CL65 FELHEIM, MARVIN. "'The Cask of Amontillado,'", N&Q, CXCIX
(Oct. 1954), 447-8.
Both requirements of Montresor's revenge are fulfilled:
he punishes with impunity, and he makes Fortunato aware
that he is being punished because he is a Mason. Montresor considers himself a priest acting out an elaborate,
sacrificial ritual--the vaults and wine becoming blas-
phemous sacramental properties. Fortunato, the snake in
Montresor's crest, becomes the traditional religious serpent of evil.

CL66 FOOTE, DOROTHY N. "'The Cask of Amontillado'," Expl, XX,
item 27 (Nov. 1961).
Disputes Fossum's interpretation. Montresor knows that
he has "violated the seconds of his desiderator of revenge."

CL67 FOSSUM, RICHARD H. "Poe's 'The Cask of Amontillado'," Expl,
XVII, item 16 (Nov. 1958).
The story is doubly ironic. Fortunato is unaware of
Montresor's real motivation for inviting him to the wine
cellar; and Montresor, who needs peace himself, hopes
that his victim will rest in peace. He pleads to the
bones to free him from guilt.

CL68 FREEHAFER, JOHN. "Poe's 'The Cask of Amontillado': a Tale of
Effect," JA, XIII (1968), 134-42.
Stresses the irony and unity of effect in the tale and
concludes that "'The Cask of Amontillado' is the ultimate
horror story of a perfect crime of revenge, in which the
revenger enjoys the mastery and impunity of the goddess
Nemesis and demands admiration for the artistry and sang-
froid with which he has sacrificed his victim."

CL69 GARGANO, JAMES W. "'The Cask of Amontillado': a Masquerade
of Motive and Identity," SSF, IV (Win. 1967), 119-26.

179

*CL: Interpretations of Individual Works*

Like other self-deceived narrators in Poe, Montresor has projected "his internal confusions into the external world," into Fortunato, "who symbolizes Montresor's lost estate, his agonizing remembrance of lapsed power and his present spiritual impotence."

CL70  GOLDHURST, WILLIAM.  PN, V (Dec. 1972), 51.
     Disagrees with Clark.  Montresor feels no guilt over the murder.  *See* CL60.

CL71  HARKEY, JOSEPH H.  "A Note on Fortunato's Coughing," PN, III (Jun. 1970), 22.
     Pointed satire on Poe's criticism.

CL72  HARRIS, KATHRYN MONTGOMERY.  "Ironic Revenge in Poe's 'The Cask of Amontillado'," SSF, VI (Spr. 1969), 333-6.
     Analyzes the Catholic-Masonic elements in the story and its ironic ending.

CL73  HENNINGS, F. J.  "The Bouquet of Poe's Amontillado," SAB, XXXV (Mar. 1970), 35-40.
     Regarding the unpredictable endings of Poe's stories.

CL74  MABBOT, T. O.  "Poe's 'The Cask of Amontillado'," Expl, XXV, item 30 (Nov. 1966).
     Medoc, the wine Montresor offers Fortunato, is thought to have therapeutic value.  This is an example of "superb irony."

CL75  MOON, SAM.  "'The Cask of Amontillado'," N&Q, CXCIX, ns. I (Oct. 1954), 448.
     Poe treats the tale of revenge ironically, for Montresor fails.  By the end of the story, Fortunato "has gone 'for [because of] the love of God'."  In addition, Montresor has failed to punish with impunity, for he has not rested in peace for fifty years.

CL76  NEVI, CHARLES N.  "Irony and 'The Cask of Amontillado'," EJ, LVI (Mar. 1967), 461-3.
     Discusses the importance of teaching the irony of the tale.

CL77  PEARCE, DONALD.  "'The Cask of Amontillado'," N&Q, CXCIX, ns. I (Oct. 1954), 448-9.

*CL: Interpretations of Individual Works*

The story is similar to the étude, whose theme is torture, betrayal and revenge. It is a "profane rite, a sort of Black Mass, or parody of archetypal events and themes in Holy Scripture," manifested in Montresor's mephistophelean costume, the serpent theme, and elements of the Passion.

CL78 POLE, JAMES. <u>AL</u>, VI (Mar. 1934), 21.
Disputes Schick's theses. *See* CL84.

CL79 RANDALL, JOHN H. "Poe's 'The Cask of Amontillado' and the Code of the Duello," *Studia Germanica Gandensia*, V (1963), 175-84.
The tale is about "an extreme version of the gentleman's code," which includes the right to avenge any affront to the honor of the gentleman.

CL80 RASOR, C. L. "Possible Sources of 'The Cask of Amontillado'," *Furman Studies*, XXXI (Win. 1949), 46-50.

CL81 REA, J. "In Defense of Fortunato's Courtesy," <u>SSF</u>, IV (Spr. 1967), 267-9.
Defends against Doxey's essay. *See* CL64 and CL82.

CL82 _____. "Poe's 'The Cask of Amontillado'," <u>SSF</u>, IV (1966), 57-69.
Poe's theory of the perverse, which includes the idea that we wish to harm someone <u>because</u> he has been good to us, operates in "The Cask of Amontillado," "FHU," and "The Black Cat."

CL83 ROCKS, JAMES E. "Conflict and Motive in 'The Cask of Amontillado'," <u>PN</u>, V (Dec. 1972), 50-51.
Believes that previous critics have "tended to dismiss the question of Montresor's motive in killing Fortunato" and explores the Catholic-Masonic conflict in the tale. Montresor kills Fortunato because he believes that "he must protect God's word and His Church against His enemies and [he] demonstrates his 'love' of God in this deed of sacrifice."

CL84 SCHICK, JOSEPH. "The Origin of 'The Cask of Amontillado'," <u>AL</u>, VI (Mar. 1934), 18-21.
Poe combined two sources: Joel Tyler Headley's *Letters from Italy* and items from work by Bulwer-Lytton.

*CL: Interpretation of Individual Works*

CL85  SNOW, EDWARD R.  "The Roving Skelton of Boston Bay," *Yankee*
      (Dublin, New Hampshire), XXV (Apr. 1961), 52-5, 109-10.
          Possible source for "The Cask of Amontillado" is the
      Massie legend of Boston.


CL86  STEELE, CHARLES W.  "Poe's 'The Cask of Amontillado'," Expl,
      XVIII, item 43 (Apr. 1960).
          The word "Amontillado" is related to the Italian
      "ammontare," meaning "collected or formed into little
      heaps" and is a pun by Montresor.


CL87  WATERMAN, ARTHUR E.  "Point of View in Poe," *CEA Critic*,
      XXVII (1965), 5.
          The basic irony of the story is that in taking revenge,
      Montresor has damned himself.

*See also CL384, CR40.*

                    "The City in the Sea"

CL88  AMACHER, RICHARD E.  "Poe's 'The City in the Sea'," Expl,
      XIX, item 60 (May 1961).
          Denies Richard Wilbur's suggestion that the poem is
      pictorial and that evidence of its meaning can only be
      found in Poe's later prose works.  He also describes the
      poem's structure, dramatic movement, and pictorial
      quality.


CL89  BAKER, CHRISTOPHER.  "Spenser and 'The City in the Sea',"
      PN, V (Dec. 1972), 55.
          Sources of "The City in the Sea" in *The Faerie Queene*.


CL90  BASLER, ROY P.  "Poe's 'The City in the Sea'," Expl, IV, item
      30 (Feb. 1946).  Reprinted in *Sex, Symbolism and Psychol-
      ogy*.  New Brunswick: Rutgers University Press, 1948,
      192-5.
          The city is on the water, not beneath it, although it
      is about to sink into the sea as "when the unconscious
      dream sinks from the dream world into the oblivion of
      absolute unconsciousness--death."  It symbolizes "the
      creative power of the psyche--a last recapitulative
      vision in the moment of death."  The allusions are not
      morally relevant, but symbolize "sinful beauty destroyed
      (Freudian repressions of desire)."

*CL: Interpretations of Individual Works*

CL91  BELDEN, H. M.  "Poe's 'The City in the Sea' and Dante's 'City
     of Dis'," <u>AL</u>, VII (Nov. 1935), 332-4.
        Descriptions of the landscape are similar in these
     works.

CL92  CLAUDEL, ALICE M.  Essay in *Papers on Poe: Essays in Honor of
     J. Ward Ostrom*.  Springfield, Ohio, 1972.
        Discusses the classical and religious symbolism in "The
     City in the Sea."

CL93  CLOUGH, WILSON O.  "Poe's 'The City in the Sea' Revisited."
     *Essays on American Literature in Honor of Jay B. Hubbell,*
     edited by Clarence Gohdes.  Durham: Duke University Press,
     1967, 77-89.
        The city symbolizes Poe's idea of the void or nothing-
     ness which will result when the cosmos returns to unity.

CL94  DRISKELL, DANIEL.  "Lucretius and 'The City in the Sea'," <u>PN</u>,
     V (Dec. 1972), 54-5.
        Parallels between Lucretius' *De Rerum Natura* (V) and
     "The City in the Sea."

CL95  H. H. J.  "Edgar Allan Poe, an Unnoticed Plagiarism," <u>Acad</u>,
     LXXVIII (Jun. 25, 1910), 612-13.
        Poe's doomed city may be Babylon.

CL96  J. R. C.  "'The City in the Sea'," <u>Expl</u>, III Q17 (Apr. 1945).

CL97  KEEFER, T. FREDERICK.  "'The City in the Sea': A Reexamina-
     tion," <u>CE</u>, XXV (Mar. 1964), 436-9.
        Critics misunderstand the word "in" in the title; it
     means "surrounded by," not "under."  The poem is simply a
     picture of a dead city, and its purpose is not to commu-
     nicate ideas but to create images of lifelessness, dread,
     and horror.

CL98  MABBOTT, T. O.  "Poe's 'The City in the Sea'," <u>Expl</u>, IV,
     item I (Oct. 1945).
        Requests information about the poem.

CL99  PITTMAN, DIANA.  "Key to the Mystery of Edgar Allan Poe: 'The
     Doomed City,' 'The City of Sin,' 'The City in the Sea',"
     <u>SLM</u>, III (Dec. 1941), 549-52.  *See* CK273.

CL100 POUND, LOUISE.  "On Poe's 'The City in the Sea'," <u>AL</u>, VI
     (Mar. 1934), 22-7.

*CL: Interpretations of Individual Works*

Possible sources of Poe's doomed city are: Babylon, Isaiah and Revelations, the Dead Sea, Helike (described by Ovid, Pliny and Strabo), and the Lisbon earthquake of 1775.

CL101 _____. "Poe's 'The City in the Sea' Again," <u>AL</u>, VIII (Mar. 1936), 70-1.
The city of Tyre, doomed for its sins, is referred to from the pulpit as "the city in the sea."

CL102 ROSE, MARILYN. "Poe's 'The City in the Sea': a Conjecture," <u>ESQ</u>, L (I Quarter 1968), 58-9.
Recognizing the viol in the poem as a pun on the French "viol" encourages one to conjecture that the cause of the disaster is the behavior of the dwellers who "worship at shrines which consecrate the sexual surrender necessary for human life, the very life which Poe's work consistently discredits."

CL103 STOCKTON, ERIC W. "Celestial Inferno: Poe's 'The City in the Sea'," <u>TSL</u>, VIII (1963), 99-106.
The poem fuses the images of Heaven and Hell and is thus reminiscent of Poe's life-in-death paradox.

*See also* CL398.


"A Descent into the Maelstrom"

CL104 BANDY, WILLIAM T. "A New Light on the Source of Poe's 'A Descent into the Maelstrom'," <u>AL</u>, XXIV (Jan. 1953), 534-7.
The source is "The Maelstrom: A Fragment," *Fraser's,* X (1834), 276-81.

CL105 MURPHY, CHRISTINA. "The Philosophical Pattern of 'A Descent into the Maelstrom'," <u>PSt</u>, VI (Jun. 1973), 25-6.
Both "Descent" and *Eureka* "are built upon opposites, particularly contrary cognitive states, reconciled only through moments of direct, personal, aesthetic, or intuitive apperception."

CL106 SHUMAN, R. BAIRD. "Norway mile: a Linguistic Note," <u>N&Q</u>, CCII (Sept. 1953), 398.
Term used in "A Descent into the Maelstrom" means "four and half English Miles."

CL107 SWEENEY, GERARD M. "Beauty and Truth" Poe's 'A Descent into the Maelstrom'," <u>PSt</u>, VI (Jun. 1973), 22-25.

*CL: Interpretations of Individual Works*

Discusses two levels of narration in the tale," ...the
sailor's narrative illustrates Poe's thesis that, as regards the chaotic mysteries of nature, aesthetic intuition
is far more important than science."

CL108 TURNER, ARLIN. "Sources of Poe's 'A Descent into the Maelstrom'," JEGP, XLVI (Jul. 1947), 298-301.
The sources are "Le Maelstrom" *(Le Magasin Universal,*
Apr. 1836) and *The Mariner's Chronicle: Containing Nar-*
*ratives of...Disasters at Sea,* 1834.

CL109 YONCE, MARGARET. "The Spiritual Descent into the Maelstrom:
A Debt to 'The Rime of the Ancient Mariner'," PN, II
(Apr. 1969), 26-9.
Similarities in subject matter, detail and theme (the
process of spiritual transcendence).

*See also* CK361.


"Diddling Considered as One of the Exact Sciences"

CL110 POLLIN, BURTON R. "Poe's 'Diddling Considered as One of the
Exact Sciences': the Sources of Title and Tale," SLJ, II
(Fall 1969), 106-11.
The source is "Raising the Wind" by James Kenney.

CL111 RICHARD, CLAUDE. "Poe and the Yankee Hero: an Interpretation
of 'Diddling Considered as One of the Exact Sciences',"
MissQ, XXI (Spr. 1968), 93-109.
The story was originally one of the *Tales of the Folio*
*Club.* Originally, Poe meant it to be a satire against
John Neal, but in 1843 he revised it to satirize "the
treatment of Yankee heroes by Yankee writers," or speci-
fically, Sam Patch.


"Domain of Arnheim:

CL112 HESS, JEFFRY A. "Sources and Aesthetics of Poe's Landscape
Fiction," AQ, XXII (Sum. 1970), 177-89.
Analyzes "The Landscape-Garden," "The Domain of Arnheim," and "Landor's Cottage," and concludes that these
stories "refute a belief in artistic perfectibility" since
the Garden is an ambiguous symbol, a symbol of ideality
but also of human perfectibility.

*CL: Interpretations of Individual Works*

CL113  JEFFREY, DAVID K.  "The Johnsonian Influence: *Rasselas* and
        Poe's 'The Domain of Arnheim'," PN, III (Dec. 1970), 26-9.
        Believes that Poe drew the descriptions in the tale
        from Chapter I of *Rasselas* and that Poe's story "is both
        a voyage toward death and a return to the womb."

*See also* CL424.


                          "Dream-Land"

CL114  BASLER, ROY P.  "Dream-Land," *Sex, Symbolism and Psychology
        in Literature*.  New Brunswick: Rutgers University Press,
        1948.
        The imagery is the unconscious symbolism of disquietude
        and the recognition of a profound sense of peace in the
        unconscious.


                       "Duc de L'Omelette"

CL115  CARSON, DAVID L.  "Ortolans and Geese: Origin of Poe's 'Duc
        de L'Omelette'," CLAJ, VIII (Mar. 1965), 277-83.
        Believes the story to be based on a West Point experi-
        ence and concludes that "traditional critical appraisals
        of his writings--including those which are obviously
        humorous--give him credit for having been a great deal
        more serious in his intentions than he actually was."

CL116  DAUGHRITY, K. L.  "Poe's Quiz on Willis," AL, V (Mar. 1933),
        55-62.
        In "Duc de L'Omelette" Poe satirizes Willis.

CL117  HIRSCH, DAVID.  "Another Source for Poe's 'The Duc de L'Om-
        elette'," AL, XXXVIII (Jan. 1967), 532-36.
        Poe's parody of Disraeli's novel *The Young Duke* was
        prompted not only by the novel itself but by a "subjec-
        tive and meretricious review" of it in *Westminster Review*
        (Oct. 1831), which Poe was trying to parody.

CL118  HUDSON, RUTH LEIGH.  "Poe and Disraeli," AL, VIII (Jan. 1937)
        402-16.
        Poe's Tales "King Pest," "Duc de L'Omelette," "The Bar-
        gain Lost," and "Bon-Bon" are satires of the grotesque and
        extravagance of characterization of Benjamin Disraeli's
        novels.

*See also* A55, A95, A163, CL301.

# EDGAR ALLAN POE: AN ANNOTATED BIBLIOGRAPHY

*CL: Interpretations of Individual Works*

### "Eldorado"

CL119  CARLSON, ERIC.  "Poe's 'Eldorado'," <u>MLN</u>, LXXVI (Mar. 1961), 232-3.

    The last stanza is not ironic or pessimistic.  The poem is an "expression of Poe's lifelong attachment to an absolute ideal," a renewed vow.

CL120  COAD, O. S.  "The Meaning of Poe's 'Eldorado'," <u>MLN</u>, LIX (Jan. 1944), 59-61.

    The poem probably symbolizes the coming death of the poet--the land of gold.  Any idealistic interpretation is inconsistent with Poe's personality.

CL121  MABBOTT, T. O.  "The Sources of Poe's 'Eldorado'," <u>MLN</u>, LX (May 1945), 312-14.

    The poem, which harmonizes literary allusions, personal interests, contemporary events, and the "universal comment" was influenced by the anonymous "Tom-a-Bedlam Song" by Henry B. Hirst's "The Unseen River" and by Moore's *Epicurean*.

CL122  SANDERLIN, W. STEPHAN.  "Poe's 'Eldorado' Again," <u>MLN</u>, LXXI (Mar. 1956), 189-92.

    The key word is "shadow," which has a different meaning in each stanza.  The poem, which reveals "constant undertones of sombreness, darkness, and death," is far less optimistic than most critics have believed.  The "pilgrim shadow" is actually the Angel of Death.

### "Eleonora"

CL123  BASKETT, SAM S.  "A Damsel with a Dulcimer: an Interpretation of Poe's 'Eleonora'," <u>MLN</u>, LXXIII (May 1958),332-8.

    "Eleonora" is an allegory of Poe's idea that the poet (the narrator) "is inspired by the beauty, grace, and love of woman" to achieve a vision of supernal beauty and by the awareness that the vision is transitory.  To some extent the Beauty is beyond man's reach.  The relationship between Eleonora and Ermengarde suggests Poe's ideas about the difference between fancy and the imagination, for Ermengarde is a symbol of unattained supernal beauty.

CL124  BENTON, RICHARD P.  "Platonic Imagery in Poe's 'Eleonora'," <u>NCF</u>, XXII (1967), 293-97.

    Poe's tale is based on the Platonic concept of the Twin Venuses.

# Edgar Allan Poe: An Annotated Bibliography

*CL: Interpretations of Individual Works*

CL125  POLLIN, BURTON R.  "Poe's Use of the Name Ermengarde in
        Eleonora'," N&Q, ns. XVII (Sept. 1970), 332-33.
        The source is *The Betrothed* by Scott.

CL126  SNOW, SINCLAIR.  "The Similarity of Poe's 'Eleonora' to Ber-
        nardin de Saint-Pierre's *Paul et Virginie*," *Romance Notes*,
        V (Aut. 1963), 40-44.

*See also* CL17, CL187.

## Eureka

CL127  BOND, FREDERIC DREW.  "Poe as an Evolutionist," PSMo, LXXI
        (Sept. 1907), 267-74.
        A review of Poe's theories in *Eureka* and an attempt to
        connect his ideas about evolution with those of Herbert
        Spencer.

CL128  CONNER, FREDERICK W.  "Poe and John Nichol: Notes on a Source
        of *Eureka*," *All These to Teach: Essays in Honor of C. A.
        Robertson*, edited by Robert Bryan and others.
        The source is Nichol's *Architecture of the Heavens*,
        1837.

CL129  _____.  "Poe's *Eureka*: the Problem of Mechanism," *Cosmic Op-
        timism: a Study of the Interpretation of Evolution by
        American Poets from Emerson to Robinson*.  Gainsville Uni-
        versity of Florida Press, 1949, 67-91.

CL130  DeCASSERES, BENJAMIN.  "Poe's Metaphysical Work Yet May Rank
        with Efforts of the Great Evolutionists," *Sun and New York
        Herald* (Feb. 1920).
        Review of Poe's life when he wrote *Eureka*.

CL131  HOAGLAND, CLAYTON.  "The Universe of *Eureka*: A Comparison of
        the theories of Eddington and Poe," SLM, I (May 1934),
        307-13.
        Similarities between *Eureka* and Sir Arthur Eddington's
        "The Expanding Universe."

CL132  HOLMAN, HARRIET.  "Hog, Bacon, Ram, and Other 'Savans' in
        *Eureka*: Note toward Decoding Poe's Encyclopedic Satire,"
        PN, II (Oct. 1969), 49-55.
        Investigates the possibilities of satire in *Eureka*.

CL133  _____.  "Splitting Poe's 'Epicurean Atoms': Further Specula-
        tion on the Literary Satire of *Eureka*," PN, V (Dec. 1972),
        33-37.

*CL: Interpretations of Individual Works*

Reads Poe's conceit of Epicurean Atoms in space as a satire on the Transcendentalists "and presumably all metaphysicians and arch romantics who regarded themselves as the center of a sensate existence and for whom the only test of reality, truth, was their own feeling."

CL134  LAFLEUR, L. J. "Edgar Allan Poe as Philosopher," Person, XXII (Oct. 1951), 401-5.
In *Eureka* Poe showed that he misunderstood the Newtonian theory of gravitation, failed to explain the development of the individual personality, and wrote inconsistently about God.

CL135  MADDISON, CAROL HOPKINS. "Poe's *Eureka*," TSLL, II (Aut. 1960), 350-67.
Poe examined the universe for verification of his aesthetic theories and found it to be an example of the absolute principle of the unity which controls all creative work. He drew an analogy between God and the artist, between the universe and the art product, but in developing the analogy, he violated the principles of unity--particularly in his defense of intuition, in his rhapsodic summation at the end of the work, in his shift of emphasis from the universe to man and in his dogmatism. He was influenced by contemporary scientific publications, by the Leibnizian doctrine of morals, pantheism, Hinduism, and transcendentalism.

CL136  NORDSTEDT, GEORGE. "Poe and Einstein," *Open Court*, XLIV (Mar. 1930), 173-80.
Both Poe and Einstein viewed the universe as limited and spherical in shape, both recognized the existence of other universes, and Poe approached Einstein's curvilinear closed four-dimensional continuum.

CL137  QUINN, PATRICK F. "Poe's *Eureka* and Emerson's *Nature*, ESQ, XXXI (II QUARTER 1963), 4-7.
Notes similarities between the works, especially in their perception "that diversity is transient and relative," that Truth and Beauty are one, and that a universal soul impells man's life. The differences lie in Emerson's "warm feeling for reality," and Poe's "cold excitment, aloof, and almost trans-human." *Nature* is a poem of life: *Eureka* death.

CL138  RAMAKRISHNA, D. "Poe's *Eureka* and Hindu Philosophy," ESQ, XLVII (II Quarter 1967), 28-32.

*CL: Interpretations of Individual Works*

Compares several philosophical positions of Poe to assertions in the Vedanta and Bhagavad Gita. Shows that Poe's philosophy was similar to Hindu thought.

CL139  SMITHLINE, ARNOLD.  "*Eureka*: Poe as Transcendentalist," ESQ, XXXIX (II Quarter 1965), 25-8.
Poe's affinity with transcendentalism lies in his advocacy, in *Eureka*, of the intuitive method over the rational, his idea that the universe was originally a unity, and his vision of the final unity of man and God.

CL140  VAN NOSTRAND, A. D.  *Everyman His Own Poet: Romantic Gospels in American Literature*.  New York: McGraw Hill, 1968.
Rather confused and confusing essay concentrating on *Eureka*, which "least of all presents the evangelical strain of American idealism."

CL141  WALLACE, ALFRED RUSSELL.  *Edgar Allan Poe*.  New York: privately printed, 1930.
Letters between Wallace and Ernest Marriott concerning scientific accuracy in *Eureka* and the question of the authorship of *Leonainie*.

CL142  WEINER, PHILIP.  "Poe's Logic and Metaphysics," Person, XIV (Oct. 1933), 268-74.
Brief discussion of *Eureka* and of Poe's reliance on intuition rather than on induction or deduction.

*See also* A24, A148, B80, B93, CJ12, CK14, CK76, CK107, CK125, CK211, CK340, CK386, CL106, CL148, CL435, CO41, CS45, CS47.


"Evening Star"

CL143  KILBURN, P. E.  "Poe's 'Evening Star'," Expl, XXVIII (May 1970), Item 76.
Disputes Wilbur's "backwards" reading of the poem.  The poet actually rejects the moon for its coldness (chastity-Diana) and prefers Venus (love).


"Facts in the Case of M. Valdemar"

CL144  FALK, DORIS V.  "Poe and the Power of Animal Magnetism," PMLA, LXXXIV (May 1969), 536-46.

*CL: Interpretations of Individual Works*

Analysis of "The Facts in the Case of M. Valdemar," "A
Tale of the Ragged Mountians," and "Mesmeric Revelation"
in terms of Poe's understanding of animal magnetism and
mesmerism.  Connects these usually isolated tales to certain central Poe themes about the imagination or states of
intensified consciousness.

CL145  MABBOTT, T. O.  "English Publication of Poe's 'Facts in the
Case of M. Valdemar'," N&Q, CLXXXIII (Nov. 21, 1942),
311-12.
Mabbott discusses the English publication of the story
and suggests that a possible source is "Seeress of
Prevorsity" (1845).

*See also* CK363, CL461.


"The Fall of the House of Usher"

CL146  ABEL, DARREL.  "A Key to the House of Usher," UTQ, XVIII
(Jan. 1949), 176-85.  Reprinted in CJ15 and CJ79.
Analyzes the symbols in the story which dramatize the
encroachment of evil on good.  The story is a psychological allegory of the struggle between life-reason and
death-madness for possession of Usher's soul.

CL147  BAILEY, J. O.  "What Happens in 'The Fall of the House of
Usher'?" AL, XXXV (Jan. 1964), 445-66.  Reprinted in CJ15.
Suggests that the Usher family is devitalized by a vampire and that finally Madeline herself becomes a vampire.
Usher and the narrator represent two sides of Poe's personality: the man who has "dreamed into life his Arabesque
tales of terror" and the rational man.  Ironically, "Roderick, psychic and intuitive, sees truth that the narrator can not see."  Yet the narrator alone is saved.  Poe
solved the identity problem in M. Dupin, in whom reason
and intuition coalesce.

CL148  BEEBE, MAURICE.  "The Fall of the House of Pyncheon," NCF, XI
(Jun. 1956), 1-17.
Poe and Hawthorne shared an organic view of nature and
of art and believed that the artist is Godlike.  The
structural basis of "The Fall of the House of Usher" is
the view of the universe in *Eureka*: in both, atoms radiate
outward and struggle to return to unity.

*CL: Interpretations of Individual Works*

All the elements in "The Fall of the House of Usher" reflect one another, and Roderick, the dramatic center of
the story, must radiate a diffusing power (symbolized by
his art) to keep everything from turning back to him.  The
unifying tendency finally overcomes him, breaking down the
distinction between matter and spirit.  The same unity
exists in *The House of the Seven Gables*.

CL149 _____. "The Universe of Roderick Usher," Person, XXXVII
(Spr. 1956), 147-60.  Reprinted in *Ivory Towers and Sacred
Founts*.  New York: New York University Press, 1964.  Reprinted in CJ64.
    Attempts to correlate Poe's theory of the short story
with his cosmology.  The artistic creation is for Poe a
creative power which disperses elements previously ordered
by God and reassembles them into new unities or totalities.
"The Fall of the House of Usher" is an example of a story
in which this correlation occurs, for Roderick, "a prototype of the artist as God," is motivated by a desire to
return to unity.

CL150 BONAZZA, BLAZE AND EMIL ROY.  "'The Fall of the House of Usher'," *Instructor's Manuel to Accompany "Studies in Short
Fiction."*  New York: Harper Row, 1965.

CL151 BOOTH, WAYNE C.  *The Rhetoric of Fiction*.  Chicago: University of Chicago Press, 1961, 200-4.  Reprinted in CJ79.
    Uses "Premature Burial" and "The Fall of the House of
Usher" to demonstrate that the information and the mood in
a literary work must be dramatized and not merely stated
by the author in his own voice.

CL152 BROOKS, CLEANTH AND R. P. WARREN.  "'The Fall of the House of
Usher': Edgar Allan Poe," *Understanding Fiction*.  New
York: Appleton-Century Croft, 1943, 184-205.  Excerpts reprinted in CJ79.
    The story lacks theme, moral, and the struggle essen-
tial for tragedy.  In addition, the characters have been
denied freedom of will.  Poe's interest in the story was
a morbid interest in horror for horror's sake.

CL153 COHEN, HENNIG.  "Roderick Usher's Tragic Struggle," NCF, XIV
(Dec. 1959), 270-2.
    Disputes the Brooks and Warren allegation that Roder-
ick's struggle is not tragic.  Roderick struggles to live,
but the price he pays is his madness and Madeline's agony.
She can not die unless he dies also.  Roderick knows that
Madeline is alive in the tomb; and when she confronts him,

*CL: Interpretations of Individual Works*

begging for death, he is overwhelmed with pity and yields.

CL154 CRONIN, JAMES. "Poe's Vaults," N&Q, CXCVIII (Sept. 1953), 395-96.
    Believes that some details in the tale are irrelevant to the final effect.

CL155 DAVIS, JEFF. "The Lady Madeline as a Symbol," *Annotator* (Purdue University), no. 2. (Apr. 1954), 8-11.
    Davis discovers parallels between "WW" and "The Fall of the House of Usher": both takes place within the mind or symbolize mental states. Madeline symbolizes Roderick's insanity, and her burial is his temporary effort to suppress his madness.

CL156 DAVIS, RICHARD BEALE. "Haunted Palace and Haunted Place," N&Q, CCIV (Sept. 1959), 336-7.
    The motto at the head of Chapter XI in Cooper's *Wing-and-Wing* suggests the spirit of Poe's poem.

CL157 GARMON, GERALD. "Roderick Usher: Portrait of the Madman as an Artist," PSt, V (Jun. 1972), 11-14.
    "Roderick is a man whose temperament is a development of the very sensations which must destroy him, and he is struggling against his environment and his heredity." He hopes to break the "limits of his individuality" by breaking his bond with Madeline, but he fails, destroyed by his sensitivity, "which simultaneously makes him long for freedom and...incapable of achieving it."

CL158 GOLD, JOSEPH. "Reconstructing the 'House of Usher'," ESQ, XXXVII (IV Quarter 1964), 74-6.
    Madeline is a "factitious embodiment" of Usher's fear of being buried alive. He dies when this fear rises up and "confronts him with himself."

CL159 GOODWIN, K. L. "Roderick Usher's Overrated Knowledge," NCF, XVI (1961), 173-5.
    Hennig Cohen's statement that "The Fall of the House of Usher" is tragic, and his description of Roderick's struggle run counter to the pervasive gloom of the story. If Usher is the source of this gloom, as the story suggests, it would be inconsistent for him to struggle against death, a concomitant of gloom. Actually, however, there is no struggle because Usher has no will to live.

CL160 GORDON, CAROLINE AND ALLEN TATE. *The House of Fiction*. New York: Charles Scribner's Sons. Reprinted in CJ79.

*CL: Interpretations of Individual Works*

Credits Poe with creating in Roderick Usher the "archetypal hero of modern fiction" but shows that his techniques are primitive, that he is unable to make the symbolism intrinsic and dramatic.

CL161  GUILDS, JOHN C. JR. "Poe's Vaults Again," N&Q, CCII, ns. 4
(May 1957), 220-1.
Roderick Usher's intention to bury his sister alive is
revealed in his painting: "a madman's phantasmagoric conception of his anticipated crime."

CL162  HALFEY, JAMES. "A Tour of the House of Usher," ESQ, XXXI
(II Quarter 1963), 18-20
Discusses "The Fall of the House of Usher" in terms of
its comment on Poe's own culture: "it is with the terrify-
ing irrational phenomenon of everyday life itself that the
story is concerned; it is his own real world of Baltimore
and Richmond and Philadelphia that Poe, looking imagina-
tively at the mundane, discovers to be a nightmare of decadence, of death in life and death devouring life."

CL163  HARTLEY, LODWICK. "From Crazy Castle to the House of Usher:
a Note Toward a Source," SSF, II (Spr. 1965), 256.
The source is John Hall Stevenson's residence in York-
shire.

CL164  HILL, ARCHIBALD A. "Principles Governing Semantic Paral-
lels," TSLL, I (Aut. 1959), 356-65.
Statistical analysis of "The Fall of the House of
Usher."

CL165  HILL, JOHN. "Dual Hallucination in 'The Fall of the House of
Usher'," SWR, XLVIII (Aut. 1963), 396-402. Excerpts reprinted in CJ37.
Madeline's appearance from the tomb is really a hallucination of the narrator and Roderick, who are both going
insane.

CL166  _____. "Poe's 'The Fall of the House of Usher' and Frank
Norris' Early Short Stories," HLQ, XXVI (1962), 111-12.

CL167  HOFFMAN, MICHAEL J. "The House of Usher and Negative Romanticism," *Studies in Romanticism*, IV (1965), 158-68.
Poe is a Negative Romantic. The House of Usher, a symbol of the Enlightenment, collapses of internal weakness,
leaving the narrator, the "questing Romantic hero," the
"new post-Enlightenment man," alienated in a meaningless
world.

*CL: Interpretations of Individual Works*

CL168. KENDALL, LYLE.   "The Vampire Motif in 'The Fall of the House of Usher'," CE, XXIV (Mar. 1963), 450-3.  Reprinted in CJ79.
   The story is purely Gothic.  Madeline is a vampire, and Usher, who has pernicious anemia, is her final victim.  The theme is "the active existence of malignant evil in our world."  Poe believes that "evil in the long run feeds incestuously upon itself."

CL169  MABBOTT, T. O.  "Poe's 'The Fall of the House of Usher'," Expl, XV (Nov. 1956), 7.
   Cites an incident in Poe's life that suggests that the story had a basis in reality.

CL170  _____.  "Poe's Vaults," N&Q, CXCVIII (Dec. 1953), 542-3.
   Roderick, Madeline, and the house share the same soul.  When one dies or is destroyed, the other must follow--a confirmation of the sentience of inorganic things.  Roderick knows that his sister is alive when he first buries her in the tomb.

CL171  MARRS, ROBERT L.  "'The Fall of the House of Usher' A Checklist of Criticism Since 1960," PSt, V (Jun. 1972), 23-4.

CL172  MARSH, JOHN L.  "The Psycho-Sexual Reading of 'The Fall of the House of Usher'," PSt, V (Jun. 1972), 8-9.
   Analyzes "The Fall of the House of Usher" as "a story of moral (sexual) perversion" in which Roderick and Madeline are engaged in an incestuous relationship.

CL173  MARTINDALE, COLIN.  "Archetype and Reality in 'The Fall of the House of Usher'," PSt, V (Jun. 1972), 9-11.
   Usher is attempting, with the narrator's help, "to escape from a regressive state of consciousness."  His escape is "symbolized by Madeline's burial.  When Usher attempts to modulate this all-or-none repression of the feminine, unconscious components of his personality," the narrator tries to assist (gives advice in the form of "The Mad Tryst").  Usher is finally too weak to mature, and his ego is ultimately overwhelmed by his unconscious.

CL174  MOFFETT, H. Y.  "Applied Tactics in Teaching Literature, 'The Fall of the House of Usher'," EJ, XVII (Sept. 1928), 556-9.
   Discussion of how to present the story to a classroom.

CL175  MORLEY, CHRISTOPHER.  "The Allergy of Roderick Usher," TLS (Apr. 9, 1949), 233.

*CL: Interpretations of Individual Works*

Humorous note that Usher had an allergy and the house "fell" because of "pollinous, hyperaesthetic rhinitis," "allergic dermatoris," and migraine.

CL176 NORMAN, H. L. "Possible Source of E. A. Butti's 'Castello del Sogno'," MLN, LII (Apr. 1937), 256-8.
The source is Poe's "The Fall of the House of Usher."

CL177 OLSON, BRUCE. "Poe's Strategy in 'The Fall of the House of Usher'," MLN, LXXV (Nov. 1960), 556-59. Reprinted in CJ15.
The story dramatizes Poe's theory that man's Intellect, Taste and Moral Sense are separate faculties and that pure Intellect can not comprehend the creative process. The merging of Usher with the house and the theme of sentience demonstrate the superiority of imagination over intellect.

CL178 PHILLIPS, H. WELLS. "Poe's Usher: Precursor of Abstract Art," PSt, V (Jun. 1972), 14-16.
Poe predicted modern abstract art in "The Fall of the House of Usher."

CL179 PHILLIPS, WILLIAM. "Poe's 'The Fall of the House of Usher'," Expl, IX, Item 29 (Feb. 1951). Reprinted in CJ15.
Discusses events in the story, not mentioned by Darrel Abel, that foreshadow the tragedy and "link Usher's over-developed and introverted sensibility to the action which tragically results from it."

CL180 PITTMAN, DIANA. "'The Fall of the House of Usher'," SLM, III (Nov. 1941), 502-9.
"With a perfection found in few of his other tales, Edgar Allan Poe permeated 'The Fall of the House of Usher' with the figurative speech of all his British Reform allegory. Here is the decline of the British Constitution and the separation of Church and State symbolized by the twin brother and sister. Undoubtedly Poe is picturing the turbulent Parliamentary Reform era which culminated in the passage of the Reform Bill in 1832...." *See* CK273.

CL181 POCHMANN, HENRY A. *German Culture in America.* Madison: University of Wisconsin Press, 1957.
The plot of "The Fall of the House of Usher" is close to that of "The Lords of Entail" ("Die Majoratsherren") by Achim von Arnim, 1820.

*CL: Interpretations of Individual Works*

CL182  POLLIN, BURTON R.  "Poe's Pen of Iron," ATQ, II (II Quarter 1969), 16-18.
  The source of "The Mad Tryst" by Sir Launcelot Canning and the source of the pseudonym itself (from "The Fall of the House of Usher") may be William Canynge "who encouraged...Thomas Rowley to write the poems and prose actually written by Thomas Chatterton."  Another source may be Tennyson's *The Lady of Shalott*, part 3.

CL183  RAMSEY, PAUL J.  "Poe and Modern Art," *College Art Journal*, XVIII (Spr. 1959), 210-15.
  Roderick's paintings are precursors of modern art.

CL184  ROBINSON, E. ARTHUR.  "Order and Sentience in 'The Fall of the House of Usher'," PMLA, LXXVI (Mar. 1961), 68-81.
  Examines the patterns of order and disorder in the house, Usher, and Madeline.  The organization of the "House" (meaning both the decay of the building and the dilapidation of the ancestral line of Usher) has resulted in sentience.

CL185  ROSE, MARILYN GADDIS.  "Usher as Myth in Green's *Minuit*," *Romance Notes*, V (1964), 110-114.

CL186  SAMUELS, CHARLES T.  "Usher's Fall: Poe's Rise," GaR, XVIII (Sum. 1964), 208-16.
  Somewhat confused essay on "The Fall of the House of Usher" and "Ligeia."  Poe demonstrates the great American theme that "purity is purchased by crime," that "virtue is egoism, that a desire for purity is a desire for self...."

CL187  SERONSY, CECIL C.  "Poe and 'Kubla Khan'," N&Q, CCII (May 1957), 219-20.
  Traces the influence of "Kubla Khan" on "The Fall of the House of Usher" and "Eleonora."

CL188  SMITH, HERBERT F.  "Usher's Madness and Poe's Organicism; a Source," AL, XXXIX (Nov. 1968), 379-89.
  Discusses Roderick's belief in the "inorganic metaphor," the idea that "apparently inorganic matter is only an inert form of larger life."  Smith traces the idea in the contemporaneous writings of Richard Watson.

CL189  SPAULDING, K. A.  "'The Fall of the House of Usher'," Expl, X, Item 52 (Jun. 1952).  Reprinted in CJ15.
  A discussion of Roderick's failure to rescue Madeline once he realizes that he has buried her alive.

# EDGAR ALLAN POE: AN ANNOTATED BIBLIOGRAPHY

*CL: Interpretations of Individual Works*

CL190  SPITZER, LEO.  "A Reinterpretation of 'The Fall of the House of Usher'," CL, IV (Aut. 1952), 351-63.  Reprinted in *Essays on English and American Literature*.  ed. Anna Hatcher.  Princeton University Press, 1963.  Reprinted in CJ 15 and CJ79.
      The story dramatizes deterministic ideas of Poe's time, specifically the belief that atmosphere influences the personality.  The story also illustrates the idea that "fear, by anticipating terrible events, has a way of bringing about prematurely those very events."

CL191  ST. ARMAND, BARTON LEVI.  "Usher Unveiled: Poe and the Metaphysic of Gnosticism," PSt, V (Jun. 1972), 1-8.
      "...Poe's metaphysic derives precisely from those very unorthodox and even heretical doctrines which were current at the beginnings of Christianity itself and then suppressed...by the actions of such dogmatic Church councils as that of Nicea.  It was from the philosophical tree of peculiar images and mystic speculations which flourished at Alexandria and in Egypt of the first and second centuries A. D. that Poe drew most of his imagery."  In this context, 'The Fall of the House of Usher,' when viewed in Gnostic terms, can be seen as a tale precisely about what Jung called the 'retrogressive liberation of a soul from the character imprinted by the Archons'."

CL192  STEIN, WILLIAM BYSSHE.  "Twin Motif in 'The Fall of the House of Usher'," MLN, LXXV (Feb. 1960), 109-11.  Reprinted in CJ15.
      Madeline "is a visible embodiment of the alter ego.  She stands for the emotional or instinctive side of her brother's personality which has stagnated under the dominion of the intellect..." and which must revolt.  "In sum, the outraged unconscious swallows up all conscious authority."  Thus the twin motif occupies two levels of the story: the literal and the psychological.

CL193  STONE, EDWARD.  "Usher, Poquelin and Miss Emily: Progress of the Southern Gothic," GaR, XIV (Win. 1960), 433-43.
      Compares Poe's "The Fall of the House of Usher," Cable's "Jean-ah Poquelin," and Faulkner's "A Rose for Miss Emily."  Cable advances beyond Poe in mixing the Gothic with local color and characterization and Faulkner advances even further in his understanding of the pathological personality.

*CL: Interpretations of Individual Works*

CL194   THOMPSON, G. R.   "The Face in the Pool: Reflections on the Doppelgänger Motif in 'The Fall of the House of Usher'," PSt, V (Jun. 1972), 16-21.
"What I offer as progressive to our understanding of the tale is principally addenda to [Abel's interpretation] in terms of a reconsideration of the principal symbols of the tale within the primary structural context proposed-- that is, the structure wherein the subjectivity of the narrator provides the basic system of structures holding in tension all the others.   I shall attempt to demonstrate the pervasiveness of the primary structure principally by reference to the pattern of the double and its redoubled manifestations."   *See* CL146.

CL195   TYTELL, JOHN.   "Anais Nin and 'The Fall of the House of Usher'," *Under the Sign of Pisces: Anais Nin and her Circle*, I (1970), 5-11.
Poe's influence on Anais Nin.

CL196   WALKER, I. M.   "The 'Legitimate Sources' of Terror in 'The Fall of the House of Usher'," MLR, LXI (Oct. 1966), 585-92.   Excerpts reprinted in CL37.
In the nineteenth century scientists believed that gasses emanating from stagnant water and decaying matter caused physical and mental illnesses.   Roderick's insanity thus has a "legitimate" cause.   Eventually the narrator succumbs to Roderick's fantasy.

CL197   WARFEL, H. R.   "Poe's Dr. Percival: A Note on 'The Fall of the House of Usher'," MLN, LIV (Feb. 1939), 129-31.
Poe's Dr. Percival must be Dr. Thomas Percival (1740-1804), who was mentioned by Watson in *Chemical Essays*.

CL198   WILCOX, EARL J.   "Poe's Usher and Ussher's Chronology," PN, I (Oct. 1968), 31.
The name may have been derived from the Irish divine, Bishop James Ussher (1581-1656), who published *Annales Veteris et Novi Testamenti*.

Excerpts on "The Fall of the House of Usher" from Bonaparte reprinted in CL79.

*See also* A81, B106, CK88, CK128, CK279, CK323, CK343, CK361, CK372, CL82, CL224, CO9, CR15, CR37, CR48.

"A Farewell to Earth"

CL199   NEVINS, G. S.   "Poe's 'A Farewell to Earth'," N&Q, CXCIV (Mar. 5, 1949), 106.
Query.

*CL: Interpretations of Individual Works*

"For Annie"

CL200  HOGUE, L. LYNN.  "Eroticism in Poe's 'For Annie'," ESQ, LX
(Fall 1970), 85-87.
The personna, who is not Poe, experiences an explicit
sexual relationship with Annie.  Poe, "in the throes of
apparent suicidal impulse and unfulfilled desires,...
turn[s] to erotic wish fulfillment through poetry."  The
sexual passion is consumed through the personna in the
poem.

"The Gold Bug"

CL201  BLANCH, ROBERT J.  "The Background of Poe's 'The Gold Bug',"
*English Record,* XVI (Apr. 1966), 44-8.
The sources of the tale are both literary (Irving's
*Tales of the Traveller*) and experiential.

CL202  GOLDHURST, WILLIAM.  "Edgar Allan Poe and the Conquest of
Death," *New Orleans Review,* II (1969), 316-19.
Discusses the "will against death" theme and LeGrand's
progression in the tale as a progression from heaven to
hell to death to resurrection.

CL203  GRAVELY, W. H. JR.  "An Incipient Libel Suit Involving Poe,"
MLN, LX (May 1945), 308-11.
Concerning charges by the *Philadelphia Spirit of the
Times* and the *New York Herald* that Poe plagiarized "The
Gold Bug" and conspired with the publishers of the *Dollar
Newspaper* to defraud the public.

CL204  HASSELL, J. WOODROW JR.  "The Problem of Realism in 'The Gold
Bug'," AL, XXV (May 1953), 179-92.
The story is "a product of the collaboration of the
Poet and the Reasoner."  In "The Gold Bug" realism and
fantasy blend nicely although they occasionally conflict.
Poe's art is revealed in his ability to conceal the con-
flict and make fantastic elements appear realistic.

CL205  HOLSAPPLE, C. K.  "Poe and Conradus," AL, IV (Mar. 1932), 62-
8.
A Source of "The Gold Bug" may be David Arnold Conradus' article on cryptography, GM, XII (1842), 241-2,
473-5.

CL206  LAVERTY, CARROLL.  "The Death's-Head on the Gold Bug," AL,
XII (Mar. 1940), 88-91.

*CL: Interpretations of Individual Works*

Poe synthesized notes and pictures of the death-head moth into the gold bug.

CL207  MABBOTT, T. O.  "The Source of Poe's Motto for 'The Gold Bug'," N&Q, CXCVIII (Feb. 1953), 68.
A Source is Frederick Reynolds' "The Dramatist," Act IV, sc. 2.

CL208  SMYTH, ELLISON A.  "Poe's 'The Gold Bug' From the Standpoint of an Entomologist," SR, XVIII (Jan. 1910), 67-72.
Attempts to identify the beetle.

CL209  ST. ARMAND, BARTON LEVI.  "Poe's 'Sober Mystification': The Uses of Alchemy in 'The Gold-Bug'," PSt, IV (Jun. 1971), 1-7.
Hassell is incorrect in charging the story with inconsistencies and implausibilities. It will prove to be aesthetically whole when examined for traditional alchemic signs, symbols, philosophy. *See* CL204.

CL210  STOCKTON, ERIC.  "Poe's Use of Negro Dialect in 'The Gold Bug'," *Studies in Honor of Charles Carpenter Fries,* University of Michigan Press, 1964.

*See also* B24, B237, CK63, CK350, CL449, CS16.

"Hop Frog"

CL211  HOUK, ANNELLE S. AND CARLOTTA L. BOGART.  eds. "'Hop Frog'," *Understanding the Short Story,* 31-41.

"How to Write a Blackwood Article"

CL212  GERBER, GERALD.  "The Coleridgean Context of Poe's *Blackwood* Satires," ESQ, LX (Fall 1970), 87-91.
Analyzes the Coleridgean materials and concludes that Poe admired Coleridge as an artist of integrity because he refused to become a hack writer.

CL213  _____.  "Milton and Poe's 'Modern Woman'," PN, III (Dec. 1970) 25-26.
Discusses Miltonic qualities in "How to Write a Blackwood Article" and "A Predicament," especially the character of Zenobia, who resembles Eve of *Paradise Lost.*

CL214  McCLARY, BEN HARRIS.  "Poe's 'Turkish Fig-Pedler'," PN, II (Oct. 1969), 56.

*CL: Interpretations of Individual Works*

The sources of the motto of "How to Write a Blackwood Article" are works by Sir Walter Scott and Lord Asquith-and-Oxford.

CL215  McELRATH, JOSEPH R. JR.  "Poe's Conscious Prose Technique," *NEMLA Newsletter*, II (1970), 34-43.
Elements of self-parody in "How to Write a Blackwood Article" and "A Predicament" demonstrate "how keenly conscious [Poe] was of the characteristic traits of his own craftsmanship."

CL216  McNEAL, THOMAS H.  "Poe's *Zenobia*: an Early Satire on Margaret Fuller," MLQ, XI (Jun. 1950), 205-16.
Discussion of Margaret Fuller as the "Psyche Zenobia" of Poe's satire.

CL217  POLLIN, BURTON R.  "Figs, Bells, Poe and Horace Smith," PN, III (Jun. 1970), 8-10.
The source of Poe's motto for "How to Write a Blackwood Article" is the tenth article in *Rejected Addresses* by James and Horace Smith.

CL218  _____. Essay in *Papers on Poe: Essays in Honor of J. Ward Ostrom*. Springfield, Ohio, 1972.
Discusses the allusions in Poe's Psyche Zenobia stories.

CL219  SCHUSTER, RICHARD.  "More on the 'Fig-Pedler'," PN, III (Jun. 1970), 22.
On the sources and meaning of the motto of Poe's "How to Write a Blackwood Article."

CL220  TAYLOR, WALTER F.  "Israfel in Motley," SR, XLII (Jul. to Sept. 1934), 330-40.
Poe satirized the pedantic moralism of his age "How to Write a Blackwood Article" is a satire on transcendentalism) and burlesques his own grotesque genre, which he had developed not because he was "an abnormal neurotic" but because he wished to satisfy public tastes.

*See also* CL273, CR25, CR51.

"The Imp of the Perverse"

CL221  KANJO, EUGENE R.  "'The Imp of the Perverse': Poe's Dark Comedy of Art and Death," PN, II (Oct. 1969), 41-44.

*CL: Interpretations of Individual Works*

"...the tale is as much about the creative mechanism in man as it is about the destructive--indeed, the tale is typically Romantic in its conception of the paradoxically intertwined relationship of the creative and the destructive.

"Introduction"

CL222   REIN, DAVID.   "Poe's Introduction," <u>Expl</u>, XX, Item 35 (Sept. 1961).
In lines headed "Introduction," published in 1831, Poe is complaining that all that he loved had gone out of his life.

"The Island of the Fay"

CL223   MILLER, F. DeWOLFE.   "The Basis for Poe's 'The Island of the Fay'," <u>AL</u>, XIV (May 1942), 135-40.
Poe wrote the story to accompany John Sartain's mezzotint, <u>Gr</u>.

"Israfel"

CL224   CAMPBELL, KILLIS.   "Poe, Stevenson, and Béranger," *Dial*, XLVII (Nov. 16, 1909), 374-5.
Poe may have written "Israfel" under the inspiration of the lines from Béranger, which he later used at the beginning of "The Fall of the House of Usher."

CL225   DAVIDSON, GUSTAV.   "Poe's 'Israfel'," *Literary Review* (Fairleigh Dickinson), XII (1968), 86-91.

CL226   FRIESNER, DONALD NEIL.   "Ellis Bell and 'Israfel'," *Bronte Society Transactions*, XIV (1964), 11-18.

CL227   K. N. V.   "Israfel," <u>Expl</u>, II, Q5 (Oct. 1943).
Query.

CL228   MABBOTT, T. O.   "Poe's 'Israfel'," <u>Expl</u>, II, Item 57 (Jun. 1944).
The poem answers Shelley's "Skylark," and there is a tenuous connection between it and "Exegi Monumentum" of Horace, Dryden's "Alexander's Feast," and Collins' "The Passions."

*CL: Interpretations of Individual Works*

CL229  WERNER, W. L.  "Poe's 'Israfel'," Expl, II, item 44 (Apr.
          1944).
              "Israfel" illustrates Poe's use of irregular stanza
          patterns and rhymes at "unusual and unanticipated inter-
          vals."

*See also* CK214.


                    "The Journal of Julius Rodman"

CL230  CRAWFORD, POLLY P.  "Lewis-Clark's *Expedition* as a Source of
          Poe's 'The Journal of Julius Rodman'," UTSE, XII (1932),
          158-70.
              Discusses the extent of Poe's borrowings from *The His-*
          *tory of the Expedition Under the Command of Lewis and*
          *Clark* (Philadelphia 1814).

CL231  KIME, WAYNE R.  "Poe's Use of Irving's *Astoria* in 'The Jour-
          nal of Julius Rodman'," AL, XL (May 1968), 215-22.
              Attempts to demonstrate the "nature and extent" of the
          influence of *Astoria* on Poe's tale.

CL232  _____.  "Poe's Use of MacKenzie's *Voyages* in 'The Journal of
          Julius Rodman'," *Western American Literature,* III (Spr.
          1968), 61-67.

CL233  LEVINE, STUART.  "Poe's 'The Journal of Julius Rodman,' Juda-
          ism, Plagiarism, and the Wild West," *Midwest Quarterly,*
          I (Spr. 1960), 245-59.

CL234  TURNER, ARLIN.  "A Note on Poe's 'The Journal of Julius Rod-
          man'," UTSE, X (1930), 147-51.
              Discusses Poe's debt to Washington Irving, particularly
          for "The Journal of Julius Rodman," passages of which he
          borrowed from *The Adventurers of Captain Boneville.*

CL235  _____.  "Another Source of Poe's 'The Journal of Julius Rod-
          man'," AL, VIII (Mar. 1936), 69-70.
              Poe borrowed a passage from Alexander MacKenzie's
          *Voyages.*

*See also* A102, B185.


                         "The Lake: To--"

CL236  MORRISON, ROBERT.  "Poe's 'The Lake: To--'," Expl, VII, item
          22 (Dec. 1948).
              The lake is Lake Drummond in Virginia.

*CL: Interpretations of Individual Works*

### "Landor's Cottage"

CL237 MABBOTT, T. O. "Landor's Cottage," N&Q, CCV (Aug. 1960), 314.
Query.

CL238 ROSENFELD, ALVIN. "Description in Poe's 'Landor's Cottage'," SSF, IV (Spr. 1967), 264-6.
The description is "naturalistic, with emphasis placed primarily on composition."

### "Lenore"

CL239 BRODERICK, JOHN C. "Poe's Revisions of 'Lenore'," AL, XXXV (Jan. 1964), 504-10.
Discusses the history of the revisions and demonstrates the superiority of the final version of the poem.

### "Ligeia"

CL240 BASLER, ROY R. "The Interpretation of 'Ligeia'," CE, V (Apr. 1944), 363-72. Reprinted in *Sex, Symbolism and Psychology*. New Brunswick: Rutgers University Press, 1948, 143-59. Excerpts reprinted in CJ64.
The main character is the narrator, who is insane, whose story can not be taken at face value. In "Ligeia" Poe treats obsession and "the power of frustrate love to create an erotic symbolism and mythology in compensation for sensual disappointment."

CL241 _____. "Poe's 'Ligeia'," PMLA, LXXVII (Dec. 1962), 675.
Defense of his article against Schroeter. *See* CL261.

CL242 DAVIS, JUNE and JACK L. "An Error in Some Recent Printings of 'Ligeia'," PN, III (Jun. 1970), 21.
Incorrect printing of "my" for "her" in several editions changes the meaning of the tale.

CL243 _____. "Poe's Ethereal Ligeia," *Bulletin of the Rocky Mountain MLA*, XXIV (1970), 170-76.
Lady Ligeia is possibly a delusion of the narrator.

CL244 FISHER, BENJAMIN FRANKLIN IV. "Dickens and Poe: *Pickwick* and 'Ligeia'," PSt, VI (Jun. 1973), 14-16.
Explores the influence of "A Madman's Manuscript," a tale in Chapter II of *Pickwick Papers*.

*CL: Interpretations of Individual Works*

CL245 GARGANO, JAMES W. "Poe's 'Ligeia', Dream and Destruction," CE, XXIII (Feb. 1962), 337-42.
    "Ligeia" concerns a man who hopes to inhabit the ideal because he is disillusioned with a stagnant reality. Finally, through sheer will, he imposes his vision of the ideal upon reality by resurrecting Ligeia, the apotheosis of the poetic vision, "a huge metaphor for the narrator's romantic version of a Platonic 'heaven'....Poe knows only too well that the wages of protracted romantic self-indulgence are self-deception and ultimate madness."

CL246 GARRETT, WALTER. "The Moral of 'Ligeia' Reconsidered," PN, IV (Jun. 1971), 19.
    The "moral undercurrent" of the story develops "when Ligeia is resurrected [and] allegorically God and the universe are reunited."

CL247 GARRISON, JOSEPH JR. "The Irony of 'Ligeia'," ESQ, LX (Fall 1970), 13-18.
    Builds Stauffer's assumptions to different conclusions. The narrator is on an "epistemological quest," but makes a "devasting error: he does not see the discrepancy between that which he would know and the process by which he would know it." That is, he fails because he tries to "fathom [the will] as if it were a reasonable entity." *See* CL263.

CL248 GRIFFITH, CLARK. "Poe's 'Ligeia' and the English Romantics," UTQ, XXIV (Oct. 1954), 8-25. Excerpts reprinted in CJ37.
    The story is a veiled joke, a satire of Transcendentalism and of English Romanticism, which feeds on but is uninspired by German sources. Rowena symbolizes the "impoverished English Romanticism, as yet 'unspiritualized' by German cant," while the narrator is the "prototype of Poe's favorite whipping boy...whose intellectual pretensions are bolstered by gleanings from the German."

CL249 HALIO, JAY L. "The Moral Mr. Poe," PN, I (Oct. 1968), 23-4.
    Poe was opposed not to moralizing in poetry, but to "reason and preach of virtue." "Morella," for example, is a story of retribution, and "Ligeia" shows "Poe's deeply moral, though hardly didactic, concern with the effects of a Faustian will rivaling God's."

CL250 HAMILTON, CLAYTON. *Manual of the Art of Fiction*, 1918.
    "Ligeia" is a tale of the supernatural. The main character is Ligeia, who struggles to overcome death.

*CL: Interpretations of Individual Works*

The narrator is merely an eyewitness and a means of mea-
suring Ligeia's superhuman will.

CL251 HOFFMAN, DANIEL. "I Have Been Faithful to You in My Fashion:
the Remarriage of Ligeia's Husband," *Southern Review*, VIII
(Jan. 1972), 89-106.
    Ligeia represents knowledge which she seems to promise
her husband. The story falls within the Fall of Man but
not the Fortunate Fall archetype.

CL252 HUDSON, RUTH. "Poe recognizes 'Ligeia' as his Masterpiece,"
*English Studies in Honor of James Southall Wilson*. Charlottesville: University of Virginia, 1951, 35-44.
    Poe considered "Ligeia" his best tale, the one which
most completely embodies his ideal of effect.

CL253 KOSTER, DONALD. "Poe, Romance and Reality," ATQ, XIX (Sum.
1973), 8-13.
    Strangely dated analysis of "Ligeia" which claims that
Poe was "intensely interested in abnormal human behavior"
and that abnormal behavior is more interesting than con-
ventional behavior. Also alleges that the narrator killed
Ligeia.

CL254 LAUBER, JOHN. "'Ligeia' and its Critics: a Plea for Literal-
ism," SSF, IV (Fall 1966), 28-33. Excerpt reprinted in
CJ37.
    Argues in line with Schroeter and the "traditional"
view that the narrator's story must be accepted without
qualification, that he is not self-deluded or lying.
Those critics who argue that Poe hated Gothic grotesquerie
"have tried to create a new work more in accord with contemporary values and standards of taste." *See* CL261.

CL255 LUBBERS, KLAUS. "Poe's 'The Conquerer Worm'," AL, XXXIX
(Nov. 1968), 375-79.
    Applies the "scena vitae" or "theatrum mundi" topos to
the poem. The theatre is the universe in which men are
"lumped together as pitiable pantominists in a farce."
God has withdrawn. The Elizabethan cosmic order has been
destroyed. "Formless things" and "crawling shapes" now
have God's power. The worm itself may personify Death.

CL256 MORRISON, CLAUDIA C. "Poe's 'Ligeia': an Analysis," SSF, IV
(Spr. 1967), 234-45.
    Psychoanalytic analysis of "Ligeia," a "wish fantasy"
for the return of the lost mother involving repressed incestuous desires and vampirism.

*CL: Interpretations of Individual Works*

CL257 RAMAKRISHNA, D. "The Conclusion of Poe's 'Ligeia'," ESQ,
XLVII (II Quarter 1967), 69-70.
Poe leaves the reader confused as to whether Ligeia's
resurrection is meant to be sublime, lofty, or horrible.

CL258 _____. "Poe's 'Ligeia'," Expl, XXV, item 19 (Oct. 1966).
Denies West's allegorical reading of the tale as a repudiation of Gothic romance. The "enveloping atmosphere
in the tale...is not supernal beauty but Gothic horror."

CL259 REA, JOY. "Classicism and Romanticism in Poe's 'Ligeia',"
BSUF, VIII (Win. 1967), 25-29.
"Ligeia" is a story of the struggle between Classicism
and Romanticism.

CL260 REED, KENNETH T. "'Ligeia': The Story as Sermon," PN, IV
(Jun. 1971), 20.
The five-part structure of "Ligeia' is based upon the
five-part sermon formula recommended in nineteenth-century treatises on homiletics.

CL261 SCHROETER, JAMES. "A Misreading of Poe's 'Ligeia'," PMLA,
LXXVI (Sept. 1961), 397-406.
Summarizes past critical interpretations and accepts
the traditional readings of the story that the narrator's
statements must be taken at face value. The major theme
of the story is the human will's capacity to triumph over
death. *See* CL240.

CL262 _____. "Poe's 'Ligeia'," PMLA, LXXVII (Dec. 1962), 675.
Answers Basler. *See* CL241.

CL263 STAUFFER, DONALD B. "Style and Meaning in 'Ligeia' and
'William Wilson'," SSF, II (Sum. 1965), 316-31. Excerpts
reprinted in CJ37.
The purpose of the essay is "to describe the elements of
style found in each story; and...to analyse the function
of these elements...to see what relationship exists between the style of the tale and its meaning."

CL264 SWANSON, DONALD R. "Poe's 'The Conquerer Worm'," Expl, XIX,
item 52 (Apr. 1961).
Discusses the structure and dramatic aspects of the
poem. Like the man in the poem, Ligeia pursues a transcendent or eternal life but cannot catch it. The audience
ironically accepts the worm, a symbol of death, as a hero.

# Edgar Allan Poe: An Annotated Bibliography

*CL: Interpretations of Individual Works*

CL265   WEST, MURIEL.  "Poe's 'Ligeia'," <u>Expl</u>, XXII, item 15 (Oct. 1963).
    The story allegorizes Poe's hatred of having to write prose pot-boilers.  The Gothic-Romantic conflict is at the heart of the tale.  Rowena is a bad Gothic prose tale which comes to life when Poe's muse transforms it into a prose poem.

CL266   _____.  "Poe's 'Ligeia' and Isaac D'Israeli," <u>CL</u>, XVI (Win. 1964), 19-28.
    West interprets the story according to D'Israeli's suggestion that Ligeia is an ideal presence, a poetic muse who guides the poet in his quest for truth and beauty. Rowena symbolizes Poe's occupation when he gave up writing.  West also connects the tale with D'Israeli's *Mejnorin and Leila*.

*See also* CK15, CK128, CK154, CK168, CK279, CL47, CL186, CL436, CL454, CL525, CL528.


"The Lighthouse"

CL267   MABBOTT, T.O.  "Poe's Tale, 'The Lighthouse'," <u>N&Q</u>, CLXXXII (Apr. 25, 1942), 226-7.
    Reprint with notes of Poe's last and unfinished tale.


"Lionizing"

CL268   ARNOLD, JOHN.  "Poe's 'Lionizing': The Wound and the Bawdry," *Literature and Psychology*, XVII (1967), 52-54.
    Discussion of Poe as the first American writer to define "the requisite conditions for the development of the wounded man--the alienate--the impotent--the anti-hero--as hero....to define the first American Lion whose Lionship derives from his sexual impotence."

CL269   BENTON, RICHARD P.  "Poe's 'Lionizing': A Quiz on Willis and Lady Blessington," <u>SSF</u>, V (Spr. 1968), 239-45.
    The "quiz" aims not only at Willis but also at Lady Blessington, whose London literary receptions were famous and at Willis' first two letters to the *New York Mirror* in which he describes the Lady and her circle.

CL270   _____.  "Reply to Professor Thompson," <u>SSF</u>, VI (Fall 1968), 97.

*CL: Interpretations of Individual Works*

Controversy over whether the hero of "Lionizing" is "ingratiating like Willis" or "*arrogant* like Bulwer, or like Bulwer's 'fashionable' characters in *Pelham*." *See* CL271.

CL271   THOMPSON, G. R.   "On the Nose--Further Speculations on the Sources and Meaning of Poe's 'Lionizing'," SSF, VI (Fall 1968), 94-7.
    The sources are a remark in the *Edinburgh Review*, XLVII, 190 and Bulwer's *Pelham* (1828). One object of the satire is the duel at Chalk Farm in 1806 between Thomas Moore and Francis Jeffrey, editor of *Edinburgh Review*.

*See also* A77, CL442.


"The Literary Life of Thingum Bob, Esq."

CL272   ENGSTROM, ALFRED G.   "Poe, Leconte de Lisle, and Tzara's Formula for Poetry," MLN, LXXIII (Jun. 1958), 434-36.
    Poe's Thingum Bob, Esq. was a dadaist born before his time. His "pepper-castor" deserves a place with Tristan Tzara's "Sac."

CL273   POLLIN, BURTON R.   "Poe's Dr. Ollapod," AL, XLII (Mar. 1970), 80-2.
    Poe's Dr. Ollapod (from "A Predicament") was a character in "The Poor Gentleman," a favorite American farce. The character, a charlatan, was originally played by William E. Burton. Poe changed the name to Dr. Morphine when he was associated with Burton's *Gentleman's Magazine*.

CL274   _____.   "Poe's Literary Use of 'Oppodeldoc' and Other Patent Medicines," PSt, IV (Dec. 1971), 30-2.
    "Oppodeldoc" was the name of a well-known patent medicine. Poe resented the inventors of quack remedies because they often made undeserved fortunes, and he frequently made fun of them.

CL275   ROCHE, A. JOHN.   "Another Look at Poe's Dr. Ollapod," PSt, VI (Jun. 1973), 28.
    The source of the name is a column by Willis Gaylord Clark in the *Knickerbocker,* signed "Ollapod."

CL276   WHIPPLE, WILLIAM.   "Poe, Clark, and 'Thingum Bob'," AL, XXIX (Nov. 1957), 312-16.
    "Thingum Bob," a satire on Willis Clark, is a key to the Poe-Clark relationship. Poe studied the *Knickerbocker* editorials for his materials.

*CL: Interpretations of Individual Works*

CL277   _____. "Poe's Political Satire," UTSE, XXXV (1956), 81-95.
      Whipple traces the development of Poe's political sat-
ire, concluding that "Four Beasts in One" and "King Pest"
are satires of Jackson and his government; "The Devil in
the Belfry" satirizes Van Buren's dandyism; "The Man" aims
at Vice President Richard M. Johnson; and "The Sphinx" and
"Mellonta Tauta" satirize democracy.


"Maezel's Chess Player"

CL278 WIMSATT, W. K. JR. "Poe and the Chess Automaton," AL, XI
    (May 1939), 138-51.
      Poe owes most of his overrated essay "Maelzel's Chess-
Player" to Sir David Brewster's *Letters on Natural Magic*.
The value of the essay lies in the clear, concise prose
and the logic of the arguments; but it is not an example
of original thinking.


"The Man That Was Used Up"

CL279 ABEL, DARRELL. "Le Sage's Limping Devil and Mrs. Bullfrog,"
    N&Q, CXCVIII (Apr. 1953), 165-66.
      Chapter III of Le Sage's *The Devil Upon Two Sticks* is a
source of Poe's "The Man That was Used Up."

CL280 MABBOTT, THOMAS O. "Poe's 'The Man That Was Used Up'," Expl,
    XXV, item 70 (Apr. 1967).
      The name "Sinivate" is Cockney for "insinuate." Sini-
vate is supposed to have "definite information" for the
narrator, not mere insinuations.

CL281 WETZEL, GEORGE. "The Source of Poe's 'The Man That Was Used
    Up'," N&Q, CXCVIII (Jan. 1953), 38.
      The source is Le Sage's *The Devil Upon Two Sticks*,
Chapter 3.

*See also* CK356, CL277, CL313, CL452, CS80.


"Marginalia"

CL282 HATVARY, GEORGE EGON. "Poe's Borrowings from H. B. Wallace,"
    AL, XXXVIII (1966), 365-72.
      Poe's borrowings from Wallace's novel *Stanley* in
"Marginalia."

*CL: Interpretations of Individual Works*

CL283  O'NEILL, E. H.  "The Poe-Griswold-Harrison Texts of the Mar-
         ginalia'," AL, XV (Nov. 1943), 238-50.
C                Griswold omitted several items from his edition of the
         "Marginalia" and added others to Poe's original text.
         Stoddard used Griswold's text as a basis for his edition;
         Stedman and Woodberry started from scratch for theirs.
         Harrison's text agrees with Poe's.  O'Neill prints twenty-
         six items cited by Griswold but not by Harrison.


                "The Masque of the Red Death"

CL284  BENTON, RICHARD P.  "'The Masque of the Red Death'--The
         Primary Source," ATQ, I (I Quarter 1969), 12-13.
                The source is Willis' account of a masked ball he
         attended in Paris, *New York Mirror*, IX (June. 2, 1832),
         330.

CL285  CARY, RICHARD.  "'The Masque of the Red Death' Again," NCF,
         XVII (Jun. 1962), 76-8.
                A source is an item in the *New York Expositer* (May
         1839) regarding a corpse who came to a masquerade ball in
         Russia.

CL286  GERBER, GERALD E.  "Additional Sources for 'The Masque of the
         Red Death'," AL, XXXVII (1965), 52-4.
                Discusses sources in *The Canons of Good Breeding,* an
         etiquette book which Poe reviewed.

CL287  GONZALES, JOSEPH F.  "A Scrim for Poe's Screams," EJ, LIII
         (1964), 531-2.
                On teaching "The Masque of the Red Death."

CL288  HOLSAPPLE, C. K.  "'The Masque of the Red Death' and 'I Pro-
         mesi Sposi'," UTSE, XVIII (1938), 137-9.
                Manzoni's "I Promesi Sposi" is a source of Poe's story.

CL289  MOHR, FRANZ K.  "The Influence of Eichendorff's 'Ahnung und
         Gegenwart' on Poe's 'The Masque of the Red Death'," MLQ,
         X (Mar. 1949), 3-15.
                Detailed review of several possible sources and a dis-
         cussion of the connection between Poe's story and Eichen-
         dorff's.

CL290  POLLIN, BURTON R.  "Notre Dame de Paris in Two of Poe's
         Tales," RLV, XXXIV (1968), 354-65.
                Hugo's influence on "The Masque of the Red Death."

*CL: Interpretations of Individual Works.*

CL291 _____. "Poe's 'Shadow' as a Source of his 'The Masque of the
         Red Death'," *SSF*, VI (Fall 1968), 104-7.
             Pollin discusses the extent to which "Shadow--A Para-
         ble" "resembles a dress rehearsal for 'The Masque of the
         Red Death'."

CL292 _____. "Victor Hugo and Poe," *RLC*, XLII (Oct.--Dec. 1968),
         494-519.
             Victor Hugo's Influence on "Masque" and "PP."

CL293 REECE, JAMES B.  "New Light on Poe's 'The Masque of the Red
         Death'," *MLN*, LXVIII (Feb. 1953), 114-5.
             Thomas Campbell's *Life of Petrarch* (1841) is a possible
         source.

CL294 ROPPOLO, JOSEPH.  "Meaning and 'The Masque of the Red
         Death'," *TSE*, XIII (1963), 59-69.  Reprinted in CK64.
             Reviews past critical interpretations of the story and
         offers further suggestions.  The story is "a parable of
         the inevitability and universality of death," which is to
         say a parable "of the human condition, of man's fate, and
         of the fate of the universe."  Man invests death with his
         own terror, and this terror can kill.  The intruder is
         thus "man's...self-aroused and self-developed fear of his
         own mistaken concept of death."

CL295 VANDERBILT, KERMIT.  "Art and Nature in 'The Masque of the
         Red Death'," *NCF*, XXII (Mar. 1968), 379-89.
             Sees the story as a fable "of nature and art," drama-
         tizing "the tensions of the 'Romantic' artists in Ameri-
         ca."  Prospero is the "artist-hero" who fails "to control
         and transform the corrosive elements of nature and to
         gain...the artist's triumph over death."  In "The Domain
         of Arnheim" Ellison succeeds, where Prospero fails "to re-
         concile the higher claims of ideal beauty and truth with
         the lower demands of utility...."

*See also* CK126, CK361, CL384, CR48.


"Mellonta Tauta"

CL296 POLLIN, BURTON.  "Politics and History in Poe's 'Mellonta
         Tauta': Two Allusions Explained," *SSF*, VIII (Fall 1971),
         627-31.
             Identifies the inscription on the marble slab as the
         cornerstone to the unbuilt monument to George Washington
         in New York and "the great American poet Benton" as

*CL: Interpretations of Individual Works*

Senator Thomas Hart Benton.  The story expresses Poe's
"disenchantment with the rule of common man, whose abortive
monuments have been buried and whose pretentions have
collapsed, like the balloon 'Skylark'."

CL297  TAFT, KENDALL.  "The Identity of Martin Van Buren Mavis," <u>AL</u>,
XXVI (Jan. 1954), 562-3.
   The character in Poe's preface to "Mellonta Tauta" is
Andrew Jackson Davis, the "Poughkeepsie Seer."

*See also* CL277.

"Metzengerstein"

CL298  FISHER, BENJAMIN F.  "Poe's 'Metzengerstein': Not a Hoax,"
<u>AL</u>, XLII (Jan. 1971), 487-94.
   Believes that the story is without comic intention.  A
comparison of early and final versions show that Poe "refined away crudities...to cull out extremes" to produce an
effective Gothic rather than humorous story.

CL299  MELCHIORI, BARBARA.  "The Tapestry Horse: 'Childe Roland' and
'Metzengerstein'," *English Miscellany*, XIV (1963), 185-
193.

CL300  SMITH, G. P.  "Poe's 'Metzengerstein'," <u>MLN</u>, XLVIII (Jun.
1933), 356-9.
   The animal motif is not pure folklore.  Poe's direct
model was probably Hoffmann's *Die Elixiere des Teufels,*
and the origin of the horse's malevolence is probably the
water-horse of Celtic folklore.  Poe's horse is animated
by the avenging spirit of Baron of Berlifitzing.

CL301  THOMPSON, G. R.  "Poe's 'Flawed' Gothic: Absurdist Techniques
in 'Metzengerstein' and the *Courier* Satires," <u>ESQ</u>, LX
(Fall 1970), 38-58.
   Discusses five *Courier* tales ("DL'O," "A Tale of
Jerusalem," "Bon-Bon," "Loss of Breath," and "Metzengerstein") as burlesques and satires in which form and meaning are unified.

*See also* CL444.

"Morella"

CL302  HOLT, PALMER C.  "Poe and H. N. Coleridge's *Greek Classic
Poets:* 'Pinakidia,' 'Politian' and 'Morella' Sources,"<u>AL</u>,
XXXIV (Mar. 1962), 8-30.

*CL: Interpretations of Individual Works*

From H. N. Coleridge's *Introductions to the Study of the Greek Classic Poets, Designed Principally for the Use of Young Persons at School and College:* London, Poe borrowed the motto of "Morella," two quotations in *Politian,* an uncredited quotation for a book review, a magazine filler and ten items in "Pinakidia."

CL303  MABBOTT, T. O.  "The Source of the Title of Poe's 'Morella'," N&Q, CLXXII (Jan. 9, 1937), 26-7.
The source is a story about Juliana Morella in *Godey's* (Sept. 1834), 144.

CL304  NEALE, WALTER G.  "The Source of Poe's 'Morella'," AL, IX (May 1937), 237-9.
The source is Henry Glassford Bell's "The Dead Daughter," *Edinburgh Literary Journal,* V (Jan. 1, 1831), 4-6.

CL305  RICHMOND, LEE J.  "Edgar Allan Poe's 'Morella': Vampire of Volition," SSF, IX (Win. 1972), 93-5.
The narrator's identity has been submerged in Morella's so that she might achieve metempsychosis.

Essay on "Morella" from Bonaparte reprinted in CJ16.

*See also* A76, CL421, CO41.


"Manuscript Found in a Bottle"

CL306  GUILDS, JOHN C. JR.  "Poe's 'Manuscript Found in a Bottle': a Possible Source," N&Q, CCI (Oct. 1956), 452.
William Gilmore Simms' "A Picture of the Sea," SLG (Dec. 1828), 208-15 is the source.

CL307  POLLIN, BURTON R.  "Poe's Use of Material from Barnardin de Saint-Pierre's *Etudes,"* *Romance Notes,* XII (1971), 1-8.
Source study for "Manuscript Found in a Bottle."

CL308  RICHARD, CLAUDE.  "'Manuscript Found in a Bottle' and the Folio Club," PN, II (Jan. 1969), 23.
On the place in the original group of *Tales* which Poe intended "Manuscript Found in a Bottle" to occupy.

CL309  STAUFFER, DONALD BARLOW.  "The Two Styles of Poe's 'Manuscript Found in a Bottle'," *Style,* I (Spr. 1967), 107-120.
The mixture of two styles, the "plausible" and the "arabesque," provides "psychological depth by marking the progression of the narrator's disintegration of mind with a corresponding progression of style."

*See also* A12, A48, A79, CR39.

# Edgar Allan Poe: An Annotated Bibliography

*CL: Interpretations of Individual Works*

"The Murders in the Rue Morgue"

CL310  BANDY, W. T.  "Who was Monsieur Dupin?" <u>PMLA</u>, LXXIX (Sept. 1964), 509-510.

"The Murders in the Rue Morgue" is very probably the most widely read and imitated work of fiction that has come out of this hemisphere for almost a century and a quarter." Dupin's name is derived from the names of two friends of Poe: C. Auguste Dubouchet and S. Maupin.

CL311  BOLL, ERNEST.  "The Manuscript of 'The Murders in the Rue Morgue', and Poe's Revisions," <u>MP</u>, XL (May 1943), 302-15.

Discussion of the condition of the manuscript and the revisions, which illustrate Poe's "struggle towards the flawless ideal."

CL312  DISKIN, PATRICK.  "Poe, LeFanu and the Sealed Room Mystery," <u>N&Q</u>, ns. XIII (1966), 337-9.

Sources of "The Murders in the Rue Morgue" are LeFanu's "Passage in the Secret History of an Irish Countess" (1838) and Mangan's "The Thirty Flasks" (1838).

CL313  HATVARY, GEORGE E.  "Introduction," *A Photograph Facsimile Edition of Poe's Prose Romances: "Murders in the Rue Morgue" and "The Man That Was Used Up."* ed. George Hatvary and T. O. Mabbott, *New York,* 1968.

CL314  HAWKINS, JOHN.  "Poe's 'The Murders in the Rue Morgue'," <u>Expl</u>, XXIII, item 49 (Feb. 1965).

The story is "the account of an attempted proof of the superiority of the mental powers involved in a chess game as opposed to those involved in a draughts game," or the superiority of acumen (draughts) over concentration (chess).

CL315  HOLMAN, HARRIET R.  "Longfellow in the Rue Morgue," <u>ESQ</u>, LX (Fall 1970), 58-60.

The "very little fellow [who] would do better for the Théâtre des Variétés" is a reference to Longfellow.

CL316  MOORE, JOHN ROBERT.  "Poe, Scott and 'The Murders in the Rue Morgue'," <u>AL</u>, VIII (Mar. 1936), 52-8.

The fact that Poe borrowed the idea of the orang-outang from Scott's *Count Robert of Paris* shatters Hervey Allen's argument about his psychosis, a thesis which he based on the "abnormal" imagery of the story.

# EDGAR ALLAN POE: AN ANNOTATED BIBLIOGRAPHY

*CL: Interpretations of Individual Works*

CL317 OUSBY, Ian V. K. "'The Murders in the Rue Morgue' and 'Doctor D'Arsac': a Poe Source," <u>PN</u>, V (Dec. 1972), 52.
The source is "Doctor D'Arsac" by "J. M. B."

CL318 RYAN, SYLVESTER. "A Poe Oversight," <u>CE</u>, XI (Apr. 1950), 408.
Poe failed to record the presence of blood in the room where the murders occurred.

CL319 WILBUR, RICHARD. "The Poe Mystery Case," *New York Review of Books* (Jul. 13, 1967), 16, 25-8.
In "The Murders in the Rue Morgue" the characters are all elements of a single personality represented by Dupin. "Allegorically, the action of the story has been the soul's fathoming and ordering of itself, its 'apprehension' of that base or evil force within it (the orangutan) which would destroy the redemptive principle embodied in Mme. Espanaye and her daughter."

*See also* B140, B241, CL147, CR46.

"The Mystery of Marie Roget"

CL320 BENTON, RICHARD P. "'The Mystery of Marie Roget'--A Defense," <u>SSF</u>, VI (Win. 1969), 144-52.
"There is, finally, another unusual feature of the structure of this story that ought not to go unappreciated. This is Poe's anticipation of an important technique used in modern thinking - model building. The construction of theoretical models is a popular investigative technique in mathematics and in the natural and social sciences today. Leo Apostel defines model building as follows: 'Any subject using a system A that is neither directly nor indirectly interacting with a system B to obtain information about the system B, is using A as a model for B.'...Poe made literary history by anticipating the modern practice of model building."

CL321 HATVARY, GEORGE EGON. "Horace Binney Wallace: A Study in Self Destruction," <u>PULC</u>, XXV (1964), 137-49.
The reference to Landor in "The Mystery of Marie Roget" is not to Walter Savage Landor but to Wallace's pseudonym "Landor." Wallace's novel *Stanley* influenced several Poe tales.

CL322 PAUL, RAYMOND. *Who Murdered Mary Rogers?* New Jersey: Prentice Hall, 1971.
Mary's fiance Daniel Payne is the culprit.

*CL: Interpretations of Individual Works*

CL323  SAYERS, DOROTHY L.  "'The Mystery of Marie Roget'," *The Art of the Mystery Story*. ed. Howard Haycraft. New York, 1946, 83.
　　　　This tale differs from the other two Dupin stories in that it is not a sensational thriller but a purely intellectual work.

CL324  WALSH, JOHN.  *Poe the Detective: The Curious Circumstances Behind "The Mystery of Marie Roget."* New Brunswick: Rutgers University Press, 1968.
　　　　Studies newspapers and other primary sources in a re-examination of Poe's treatment of the murder of Mary Rogers.

CL325  WIMSATT, W. K. JR.  "Mary Rogers, John Anderson, and Others," AL, XXI (Jan. 1950), 482-4.
　　　　Wimsatt discusses Worthen's article, feels that new evidence confirms the possibility that Mary died from an abortion, and discusses the implication of John Anderson.

CL326  ＿＿＿.  "Poe and 'The Mystery of Marie Roget'," PMLA, LVI (Mar. 1941), 230-48.
　　　　Wimsatt reviews Poe's treatment of the story, his divergence from newspaper reports, his logic and inconsistencies. He believes that Poe's most valuable suggestion is that the naval officer was implicated.

CL327  WORTHEN, SAMUEL C.  "Poe and the Beautiful Cigar Girl," AL, XX (Nov. 1948), 305-12.
　　　　The author discusses the actual facts of the murder and describes Poe's neglect of these facts, his faulty logic, and his failure to solve the mystery.

CL328  ＿＿＿.  "A Strange Aftermath of 'The Mystery of Marie Roget'," PNJHS, LX (Apr. 1942), 116-23.
　　　　Worthen discusses Poe's mishandling of the story and the court case, Laurel Appleton vs. New York Life Insurance Co. and F. A. Hammond.


"Mystification"

CL329  POLLIN, BURTON R.  "Poe's 'Mystification': Its Source in Fay's *Norman Leslie*," MissQ, XXV (Spr. 1972), 111-30.
　　　　Analysis of Poe's story "Mystification" as a burlesque of Theodore Sedgwick Fay's *Norman Leslie*.

# EDGAR ALLAN POE: AN ANNOTATED BIBLIOGRAPHY

*CL: Interpretations of Individual Works*

*The Narrative of Arthur Gordon Pym*

CL330   ALMY, ROBERT F.   "J. N. Reynolds: a Brief Biography with Particular Reference to Poe and Symmes," <u>Cpn</u>, ns. II (Win. 1937), 227-45.
        Poe borrowed his theory of the hollow earth and polar apertures from Reynolds, who had found it in Symmes.

CL331   BAILEY, J. O.   "An Early American Utopian Fiction," <u>AL</u>, XIV (1942), 285-93.
        The essay discusses *Symzonia,* a novel about an adventure into the hollow earth, probably by Cpt. John Cleves Symmes.

CL332   _____.   "Sources of Poe's *The Narrative of Arthur Gordon Pym* and "Hans Pfaal" and Other Pieces," <u>PMLA</u>, LVII (1942), 513-35.
        Among the sources listed are *Symzonia* by Captain Adam Seaborn, source for *The Narrative of Arthur Gordon Pym;* George Tuckers's *A Voyage to the Moon,* a source of "Hans Pfaal."

CL333   BEZANSON, WALTER E.   "The Troubled Sleep of Arthur Gordon Pym," *Essays in Literary History.* ed. by Rudolpf Kirk and C. F. Main, New York: Russell and Russell, 1965, 149-77.
        Bezanson extends Quinn's idea that Poe's genius lay in the creation of dream symbolism and morbid fantasies to the theory that his tales are often psychological projections "from the mind of a troubled sleeper who wakes and then drops back into the self's midnight." He cites as dream forms Pym's vision of himself on the hull of the ship, the Uriel incident, the entombment of Pym in the *Grampus,* Pym's masquerade as a corpse, the cannibal affair and the last journey into the unknown. "In Poe we must settle for the visual and latent force of the oneiric projection, the disturbing painting nailed to the mind's wall." *See* CL355.

CL334   CAMPBELL, JOSIE P.   "Deceit and Violence: Motifs in *The Narrative of Arthur Gordon Pym,*" <u>EJ</u>, LIX (Feb. 1970), 206-12.
        In Poe's tales, "violence either prefixes or follows the deception and occasionally merges with it."

CL335   CANDELARIE, CORDELIA.   "On the Whiteness at Tsalal: A Note on *Arthur Gordon Pym,*" <u>PSt</u>, VI (Jun. 1973), 26.

*CL: Interpretations of Individual Works*

Believes that the Tsalalians fear white because their only acquaintance with the color has been with the "freezing death" of the snow surrounding them.

CL336 CECIL, L. MOFFITT. "Poe's Tsalal and the Virginia Springs," NCF, XIX (Mar. 1965), 398-402.
The source of the extraordinary water of Tsalal in NAGP is the Virginia Springs.

CL337 _____. "Two Narratives of Arthur Gordon Pym," TSLL, V (Sum. 1963), 232-41.
NAGP is two stories. The first one, that of the boy stowaway on the *Grampus*, is abandoned with the death of Augustus. The second is a fantasy about a polar exploration on the *Jane Guy*. Poe, determined to publish them together, hoped to bridge the gap by claiming that *he* wrote the first part and Pym, the second. Pym's claim that the styles differ means simply that the point of view and tone change.

CL338 COVICI, PASCAL JR. "Toward a Reading of Poe's *The Narrative of Arthur Gordon Pym*," MissQ, XXI (Spr. 1968), 111-118.
Discusses the white-black-red iconography in the story. Dirk Peters is a "mediating force between the destructive anarchy bodied forth in blackness [the cook] and the seductive disintegration that Poe attributes to things white [Pym]."

CL339 DUNLOP, G. B. "A Poe Story," TLS (Jan. 15, 1944), 36.
NAGP was first published in 1838, in England, by Wiley and Putnam.

CL340 ELWELL, T. E. "A Poe Story," TLS (Oct. 23, 1943), 516.
On an English publication of NAGP.

CL341 HELMS, RANDEL. "Another Source for Poe's *The Narrative of Arthur Gordon Pym*," AL, XLI (Jan. 1970), 572-75.
The source is Jane Porter's *Sir Edward Seaward's Narrative of His Shipwreck*.

CL342 HINZ, EVELYN J. "Tekeli-li: *The Narrative of Arthur Gordon Pym* as Satire," *Genre*, III (1970), 379-97.
The tale is a "Mennippean Satire" in which the hero is a self-deceived fictional character who cannot comprehend reality.

CL343 HUNTRESS, KEITH. "Another Source for Poe's *The Narrative of Arthur Gordon Pym*," AL, XVI (Mar. 1944), 19-25.
The source is R. Thomas's *Remarkable Events and*

220

*CL: Interpretations of Individual Works*

*Remarkable Shipwrecks,* which had as its own source Archibald Duncan's *The Mariner's Chronicle.*

CL344 KAPLAN, SIDNEY. Introduction to *The Narrative of Arthur Gordon Pym.* New York: American Century Series, Hill and Wang, 1960. Reprinted in CJ64 and CJ79.
Kaplan reviews various interpretations and suggests that the story reflects Poe's resentment and racial phobia toward the Negro. Poe was a "Biblical fundamentalist," prophesying the damnation of the black race.

CL345 LaGUARDIA, DAVID. "Poe, Pym and Initiation," ESQ, LX (Fall 1970), 82-5.
Pym, the "archetype of initiates in American literature," early demonstrates a propensity for destruction leading to a series of ritualistic deaths. He moves "from a world of syllogistic precision to one of imagination and illusion." Eventually, he is out of place in a society of pat solutions.

CL346 LEE, GRACE F. "The Quest of Arthur Gordon Pym," SLJ, IV (Spr. 1972), 22-33.
Discusses NAGP as a "two-pronged dream quest into the unknown," an archetypal descent into hell which "utilizes the structure of a sea voyage, a familiar post-Jungian image of the collective unconscious, to voyage into the recesses of the human psyche and to journey backward in time to the origins of creation."

CL347 LEE, HELEN. "Possibilities of 'Pym'," EJ, LV (Dec. 1966), 1149-54.
In NAGP Poe "uses artistic order to demonstrate the disorder of human life."

CL348 LEVINE, RICHARD A. "The Downward Journey of Purgation: Notes on an Imagistic Leitmotif in *The Narrative of Arthur Gordon Pym,*" PN, II (Apr. 1969), 29-31.
Discusses NAGP as a "narrative of man's journey of purgation." The story contains themes of conflict, discomfiture and restoration, which are "myth of life," components. Poe's journey takes him "from shadow to light to salvation."

CL349 McKEITHAN, D. M. "Two Sources of Poe's *The Narrative of Arthur Gordon Pym,*" UTSE, XIII (1933), 116-37.
The sources are *The Mariner's Chronicle* by Archibald Duncan and *A Narrative of Four Voyages* by Benjamin Morrell.

*CL: Interpretations of Individual Works*

CL350 MOLDENHAUER, J.J. "Imagination and Perversity in *The Narrative of Arthur Gordon Pym*," TSLL, XIII (Sum. 1971), 267-80.

CL351 MOSS, SIDNEY P. "A Conjecture Concerning the Writing of *Arthur Gordon Pym*, SSF, IV (Fall 1966), 83-6.
Poe probably didn't palm off two separate tales as though they were one. Rather, he saw a chance to develop the first two episodes of NAGP, already published in SLM, in such a way as to satisfy Harper's condition for a full-length book. *See* CL337 and CL359.

CL352 _____. "*Arthur Gordon Pym,* or the Fallacy of Thematic Interpretation," UR, XXXIII (Sum. 1967), 298-306.
After discussing the separate episodes in NAGP, Moss chastises critics who hunt for themes without considering narrative details, "a fallacious and irresponsible procedure indeed."

CL353 O'DONNELL, CHARLES. "From Earth to Ether: Poe's Flight Into Space," PMLA, LXXVII (Mar. 1962), 85-9. Reprinted in CJ37.
Most of Poe's stories dramatize "the absurd tug of war between human soul and flesh," between unity ("the giving up of the struggle") and the desire to live in man's present condition on earth. Analyzes NAGP in these terms and attempts to prove ("grant[ed] that it isn't obvious") that at various moments in the story Poe describes how Pym is later rescued.

CL354 PEDEN, WILLIAM. "Prologue to a Dark Journey: the 'Opening' to Poe's *The Narrative of Arthur Gordon Pym*," *Papers on Poe: Essays in Honor of J. Ward Ostrom*. Springfield, Ohio, 1972.
Pym's adventures on the *Ariel* foreshadow the violence and terror of the rest of the novel. Peden discusses the book from an existential point of view.

CL355 QUINN, PATRICK F. "Poe's Imaginary Voyage," HudR, IV (Win. 1952), 562-85.
Emphasizes the themes of revolt and deception in the story, the constant struggle between appearance and reality, and its "development from pedestrian fact to a haunting dream-like world." The story unmasks the real world as fraudulent and deceitful. Quinn also compares NAGP with *Moby Dick* and reviews Bonaparte's and Bachelard's interpretations.

CL356 REDE, KENNETH. "Notes from an Investigator's Notebook," AL, V (Mar. 1933), 49-54.
1. Notes on copyright and title-page of NAGP.

*CL: Interpretations of Individual Works*

    2. Appearance of "The Raven" in *Parker's Fourth Reader*.
    3. Extracts from "Al Aaraaf," then unpublished, appearing
       in *The Baltimore Gazette and Daily Advertiser* (May 18,
       1892).
    4. Reprint of Poe's legal papers.

CL357  RHEA, R. L.  "Some Observations on Poe's Origins," <u>UTSE</u>, X
       (1930), 135-46.
         Traces similarities between "Some Words" and *The Medi-
       cal Repository,* ns. V (Jan. 1820), 109; and <u>NAGP</u> and
       Captain Cook's *Voyages* and Reynolds' address on the explor-
       ation to the Pacific Ocean and the South Seas, 1836.

CL358  RIDGELY, J. V.  "The Continuing Puzzle of *The Narrative of
       Arthur Gordon Pym*," <u>PN</u>, III (Jun. 1970), 5-6.
         Discusses discrepancies in the first three editions of
       <u>NAGP</u>, hitherto unnoticed sources from Irving's *Astoria* and
       Benjamin Morrell's *A Narrative of Four Voyages* and the
       language of Tsalal, which Ridgely believes may have been
       derived from Malayo-Polynesian languages.

CL359  _____.  "The End of Pym and the Ending of *Pym*," *Papers on Poe:
       Essays in Honor of J. Ward Ostrom.*  Springfield, Ohio, 1972.
         Discusses historical and philological evidence which
       suggests that the final discovery, never disclosed by Pym,
       was that an ancient race of white people had reached the
       southernmost part of the globe.

CL360  _____ and IOLA S. HAVERSTICK.  "Chartless Voyage: The Many
       Narratives of Arthur Gordon Pym," <u>TSLL</u>, VII (Spr. 1966),
       63-80.
         Demonstrates that the story was composed in five stages
       (not two as Cecil suggests), and that it is internally dis-
       organized and incoherent, "lacks a controlling theme and has
       no incontrovertible serious meaning--symbolic, pschoanalyti-
       cal, existentialist, racist, or otherwise." *See* CL336.

CL361  SEELYE, JOHN.  "Introduction," *The Narrative of Arthur Gordon
       Pym, Benito Cereno and Related Writings.*  Lippincott, 1967.
         Discusses the failure of <u>NAGP</u> as a work of art and
       compares it to *Moby Dick*.

CL362  SHEEHAN, PETER J.  "Dirk Peters: a New Look at *Pym*," *Laurel
       Review,* IX (1969), 60-70.
         Discusses the role of Peters, who represents rationality
       (Pym represents imagination).

*CL: Interpretations of Individual Works*

CL363  STROUPE, JOHN H.  "Poe's Imaginary Voyage: Pym as Hero," SSF,
       IV (Sum. 1967), 315-22.
           Disputes Quinn's contention that Pym is not the hero
       and describes Pym's adventures as "a pattern of heroic
       withdrawal" and return out of which ultimately comes an
       affirmation of life.

CL364  TYNAN, DANIEL.  "J. N. Reynolds' *Voyage of the Potomac:* Another
       Source for *The Narrative of Arthur Gordon Pym*," PN, IV
       (Dec. 1971), 35-37.
           Discusses the borrowings.

*See also* A40, A94, B61, B243, CA21, CK126, CK279, CK330, CK363, CR13.

""Never Bet the Devil Your Head"

CL365  GLASSHEIM, ELIOT.  "A Dogged Interpretation of 'Never Bet the
       Devil Your Head'," PN, II (Oct. 1969), 44-5.
           The story "is a rough sketch of the weakness in the
       Transcendental Idealist position (Toby), the materialist
       and literalist position (the devil) and the conventional
       social or moralistic position (the narrator)."

"The Oblong Box"

CL366  CARLEY, C. V.  "A Source for Poe's 'The Oblong Box'," AL,
       XXIX (Nov. 1957), 310-13.
           Newspaper accounts of the Colt-Adams murder (Sept. 17,
       1847) are sources.

CL367  VIERRA, CLIFFORD CARLEY.  "Poe's 'Oblong Box': Factual
       Origins," MLN, LXXIV (Dec. 1959), 693-95.
           The events of Poe's story parallel an actual murder
       which occurred on Sept. 17, 1841, the murder of Samuel
       Adams by John Colt.

*See also* CL8.

"The Oval Portrait"

CL368  DOWELL, RICHARD W.  "The Ironic History of Poe's 'Life in
       Death': a Literary Skeleton in the Closet," AL, XLII (Jan.
       1971), 478-86.
           The original version of "The Oval Portrait," a chaotic
       confused tale, was written and published before Poe's

*CL: Interpretations of Individual Works*

review of *Twice-Told Tales,* in which he expounded on
his unity of effect theory.

CL369 GROSS, SEYMOUR. "Poe's Revision of 'The Oval Portrait',"
MLN, LXXIV (Jan. 1959), 16-20.
Gross concludes that Poe was not the victim of a disordered imagination. In revising "The Oval Portrait," he
expunged those macabre elements which threatened the
thematic coherence and effect of the story.

CL370 TANSELLE, G. THOMAS. "Unrecorded Early Reprintings of Two
Poe Tales," PBSA, LVI (II Quarter 1962), 252.
"The Purloined Letter" and "The Oval Portrait" were
reprinted in the *New York Weekly News* (Jan. 25, 1845 and
May 10, 1845, respectively). The July 5, 1845 issue also
contains a review of the 1845 edition of *Tales.*

CL371 THOMPSON, GARY R. "Dramatic Irony in 'The Oval Portrait': a
Reconsideration of Poe's Revisions," ELN, VI (Dec. 1968),
107-114.
The theme of the tale is self-deception. The narrator
is so taken in by his own hallucinations that he may also
trick the unwary reader (like Gross: CL369) into believing
this to be a Gothic tale without a moral.

*See also* CK148, CO14.


"Palaestine"

CL372 BAILEY, J. O. "Poe's Palaestine'," AL, XIII (Mar. 1941),
44-58.
Comparison of Poe's essay "Palaestine" with an article
on Palestine from Rees' *Cyclopaedia.*


"Pinakidia"

CL373 ADAMS, PERCY. "Poe a Critic of Voltaire," MLN, LVII (Apr.
1942), 273-5.
Cites two errors in Poe's criticism of Voltaire's *La
Mort de César,* in "Pinakidia," SLM (Aug. 1836).

CL374 GRIGGS, EARL LESLIE. "Five Sources of Poe's 'Pinakidia',"
AL, I (May 1929), 196-9.
The sources are: Disraeli's *Curiosities of Literature,*
Baron Brelfeld's *Elements of Universal Erudition,* Jacob
Bryant's *Mythology,* James Montgomery's *Lectures on*

*CL: Interpretations of Individual Works*

*Literature* and Cooper's *Excursions in Switzerland.*
Griggs also lists many secondary sources.

CL375  JACKSON, DAVID K.  "Poe Notes: 'Pinakidia' and 'Some Ancient
Greek Authors', <u>AL</u>, V (Nov. 1933), 258-67.
Believes that Poe intended to publish items from "Pinakidia" in the <u>SLM</u>. At least nine items were borrowed from
A. W. Schlegel's *Lectures on Dramatic Arts,* while a source
of Poe's "Some Ancient Greek Authors" is Charles Anthon's
revised edition of J. Lemprière's *Classical Dictionary.*

CL376  KNOWLTON, EDGAR C.  "Poe's Debt to Father Bouhours," <u>PN</u>, IV
(Dec. 1971), 27-9.
Discussion of Poe's use of Father Dominique Bouhours'
*La Manière de bien Penser* as a source for "Pinakidia."

CL377  MABBOTT, T. O.  "'Antediluvian Antiquities': A Curiosity of
American Literature and a Source of Poe's," <u>AC</u>, IV (Jul.
1927), 124-6.

*See also* CL302.


"The Pit and the Pendulum"

CL378  ALTERTON, MARGARET.  "An Additional Source for Poe's "The Pit
and the Pendulum'," <u>MLN</u>, XLVIII (Jun. 1933), 349-56.
The source is Juan Antonio Llorente's *History of the
Spanish Inquisition.*

CL379  CLARK, DAVID L.  "The Source of Poe's 'The Pit and the Pendu-
lum'," <u>MLN</u>, XLIV (Jun. 1929), 349-56.
The sources of the four instruments of torture are:
William Mudford's "The Iron Shroud," <u>Bl</u> (Aug. 1830); "The
Man in the Bell," <u>Bl</u>; "The Involuntary Experimentalist,"
<u>Bl</u> (Dec. 1837).  The victim also bears a resemblance to the
protagonist of *Edgar Huntley,* chapter 16.

CL380  HIRSCH, DAVID H.  "Another Source for 'The Pit and the Pendulum'," <u>MissQ</u>, XXIII (Win. 1969-70), 35-43.
The source is "Singular Recovery from Death," <u>Bl</u> (Sept.
1821).

CL381  _____.  "The Pit and the Apocalypse," <u>SR</u>, LXXVI (Oct.-Dec.
1968), 632-52.
Analyzes the story in existential terms.  The narrator
"desires only to be free.  Yet he realizes at the same time
that freedom is not possible in the face of death.  And for

him death is the *sine qua non* of the human condition; for him, truly, death is there as the only reality" and human freedom can only be absurd. Sees Poe as a precursor of Kafka and Camus.

CL382   LUNDQUIST, JAMES.   "The Moral of Averted Descent: the Failure of Sanity in 'The Pit and the Pendulum'," PN, II (Apr. 1969), 25-6.
          The main character has one of the few integrated personalities in Poe fiction, but his sanity is more terrifying than madness because it reveals his hopelessness. He "represents mankind condemned by a vindictive power for an almost forgotten sin."

CL383   MARTUZA, ATHAR.   "An Arabian Source for Poe's 'The Pit and the Pendulum'," PN, V (Dec. 1972), 52.
          The source is George Sale's translation of and commentary on the Koran.

CL384   SOLOMONT, SUSAN AND RITCHIE DARLING.   *Four Stories by Poe.* Norwich, Vermont: Green Knight Press.
          Discusses "PP," "Masque," "Cask," and "TTH."

*See also* B243, B252, CK330, CK361.

### "The Poetic Principle"

CL385   RUBIN, JOSEPH J.   "John Neal's Poetics as an influence on Whitman and Poe," NEQ, XIV (Jun. 1941), 359-62.
          Poe's "Poetic Principle" was influenced by Neal's "What is Poetry?"

### *Politian*

CL386   ARNDT, KARL J.   "Poe's *Politian* and Goethe's 'Mignon'," MLN, XLIX (Feb. 1934), 101-4.
          On Goethe's influence on Poe's play.

CL387   GATES, WILLIAM B.   "Poe's *Politian* Again," MLN, XLIX (Dec. 1934), 561.
          The opening lines of Byron's *The Bride of Abydos* are a source of the play.

CL388   JILLSON, WILLARD.   "The Beauchamp-Sharp Tragedy on American Literature," *Register of the Kentucky State Historical Society*, XXXVI (1938),

*CL: Interpretations of Individual Works*

Discusses the historical event and books which deal with
it.

CL389 KIMBALL, WILLIAM J. "Poe's *Politian* and the Beauchamp-Sharp
Tragedy," PN, IV (Dec. 1971), 24-7.
Claims that the real case "directly generated some
parts of *Politian*."

CL390 KIRKLEY, DONALD. "Edgar Allan Poe's Play, *Politian,* Given at
Goucher," *Baltimore Sun* (Feb. 19, 1933).
Very negative review of the play, claiming it lacks
dramatic force and is a hodgepodge of romantic conventions.

CL391 MABBOTT, T. O. "Another Source of Poe's Play 'Politian',"
N&Q, CXCIV (Jun. 25, 1949), 279.
A source of the finale is Victor Hugo's *Hernani*.

CL392 _____. "The Text of Poe's Play 'Politian'," N&Q, CLXXXIX
(July 14, 1945), 14.
Mabbott corrects an error in his published text of
Poe's play.

*See also* A27, A88, A162, B152, CK65, CL302.


"The Premature Burial"

CL393 BANDY, W. T. "A Source of Poe's 'The Premature Burial'," AL,
XIX (May 1947), 167-8.
The source is "The Life-Preserving Coffin" by Mrs. Seba
Smith.

*See also* CL151, CL444.


"Purloined Letter"

CL394 HAYCRAFT, HOWARD. "Poe's 'Purloined Letter'," PBSA, LVI
(1962), 486-7.
First publication of the story was *The Gift: 1845.*
Philadelphia: Carey and Hart, 1845.

CL395 VARNADO, S. L. "The Case of the Sublime Purloin: or Burke's
*Inquiry* as the Source of an Anecdote in 'The Purloined
Letter'," PN, I (Oct. 1968), 27.

*See also* CL370.

# EDGAR ALLAN POE: AN ANNOTATED BIBLIOGRAPHY

*CL: Interpretations of Individual Works*

"The Raven"

CL396 ANON. "The Croak of the Raven," TLS, 3230 (Jan. 23, 1964), 6.

CL397 ADAMS, JOHN F. "Classical Raven Lore and Poe's Raven," PN, V (Dec. 1972), 53.
Discusses traditions associated with the bird which "broaden the ironic dimension and range of application of the private symbol."

CL398 BAKER, HARRY T. "Coleridge's Influence on Poe's Poetry," MLN, XXV (Mar. 1910), 94-9.
Cites similarities between "The Raven" and "Christabel" and between "City" and "The Rime of the Ancient Mariner."

CL399 BAYLESS, JOY. "Another Rufus W. Griswold as a Critic of Poe," AL, VI (Mar. 1934), 69-72.
"The Raven" was published by Rufus White Griswold in *Hartford Weekly Gazette,* not by Rufus Wilmot Griswold.

CL400 BEIDY, H. ALOIS. *Mysterie of Poe's "The Raven,"* New York: H. A. Beidy, 1956.

CL401 BURCH, FRANCIS F. "Clement Mansfield Ingleby on Poe's 'The Raven': An Unpublished British Criticism," AL, XXXV (Mar. 1963), 81-3.
Summarizes the manuscript in the Folger Shakespeare Library (ms. N.a. 117).

CL402 CARGILL, OSCAR. "A New Source for Poe's 'The Raven'," AL, VIII (Nov. 1936), 291-4.
The source is a translation of Bürger's "Lenore" from Sir Walter Scott's "Ballad's, Translated or Imitated from the German" and William Taylor's *Historic Survey of German Poetry.*

CL403 COLWELL, JAMES L. AND GARY SPITZER. "'Bartelby' and 'The Raven': Parallels of the Irrational," GaR, XXIII (1969), 37-43.
Discusses similarities in "mood, content, method and structure."

CL404 COURSON, DELLA. "Poe and the Raven," *Education,* XX (May 1900), 566-70.
Analysis of "The Raven" as an allegory of the soul struggling with Remorse over lost innocence.

*CL: Interpretations of Individual Works*

CL405  DAMERON, J. LASLEY.  "Another 'Raven' for Edgar Allan Poe,"
       N&Q, CCVIII (Jan. 1963), 21-2.
       A possible source is "The Raven" by G. F. W., *Bentley's
       Miscellany* (May 1, 1838).

CL406  FORSYTHE, ROBERT S.  "Poe's 'Nevermore': a Note," AL, VII
       (Jan. 1936), 439-52.
       The author traces the word in Shelley, Lowell, and
       Tennyson and discusses sources of "The Raven" in poetry
       by Chivers, Philip Pendleton Cooke, Longfellow, Paulding,
       and Felicia Dorothea Hermans, a popular English poetess.

CL407  FUSSELL, EDWIN.  "Poe's 'Raven'; or How to Concoct a Popular
       Poem from Almost Nothing at All," ELN, II (Sept. 1964),
       36-9.
       Believes the poem was inspired from *The Duchess of
       Malfi,* Act V, scene iii.

CL408  GRANGER, BYRD HOWELL.  "Devil Lore in 'The Raven'," PN, V
       (Dec. 1972), 25-6.
       Discusses the folklore patterns in the poem.  "When one
       sells his soul to the Devil, the first manifestation is
       the loss of one's own shadow, for it has united with all
       that is the Devil's."

CL409  GRAVELY, WILLIAM H. JR.  "Christopher North and the Genesis
       of 'The Raven'," PMLA, LXVI (Mar. 1951), 149-61.
       Gravely discusses several sources of the poem: *Barnaby
       Rudge,* Mrs. Browning's *Lady Geraldine's Courtship,*
       John Wilson's "Noetes Ambrosianae," and "A Glance over
       Selby's Ornithology."

CL410  GREEN, ANDREW.  "Essays in Miniature: 'The Raven'," CE, IV
       (Dec. 1942), 194.
       Rather garbled discussion of the relationship between
       "The Raven" and "The Philosophy of Composition."

CL411  GREEN, GEORGE.  "The Composition of 'The Raven'," *Aberystwyth
       Studies* (Wales), XII (1932), 1-20.
       Considers "The Philosophy of Composition" a hoax and
       applies J. Livingston Lowes' method in *Road to Xanadu* to
       the composition of "The Raven."  He concludes that "the
       genesis of 'The Raven' is...to be discovered in the prob-
       ably unwitting desire to return to infancy. The room
       itself, which is depicted in the poem, is at the same time
       the retreat from the world of the present, and also the
       womb and tomb sanctuary, the unknown world of metaphysics
       whose gates are life and death."  Entering the world

*CL: Interpretations of Individual Works*

means surrendering the ego. The cry "Nevermore" is "an assurance of the preservation of the ego."

CL412  GRIFFIS, WILLIAM ELLIOT.  "Behind the Mystery of Poe's 'Raven'," *New York Times Book Review* (Jan. 20, 1924).

CL413  JACKSON, JOSEPH.  "Poe's Signature to 'The Raven'," SR, XXVI (Jul. 1918), 272-5.
       Poe's use of the pseudonym "Quarles" is discussed.

CL414  JONES, JOSEPH.  "'The Raven' and 'The Raven': Another Source of Poe's Poem," AL, XXX (May 1958), 185-93.
       The source of Poe's poem was probably "The Raven: or the Power of Conscience, an Old Border Legend," *Fraser's* (Mar. 1839).

CL415  KERLIN, R. T.  "*Weiland* and 'The Raven'," MLN, XXXI (Dec.1916), 503-5.
       The author cites passages in the novel that Poe's poem resembles.

CL416  KING, CLEMENT.  "Poe's 'The Raven'," *Mentor,* X (Sept. 1922), 9.
       The Raven is emblematic of "'the Irreparable, the guardian of pitiless memories, whose burden ever recalls the days that are no more'."

CL417  LEES, DANIEL E.  "An Early Model for Poe's 'Raven'," *Papers on Language and Literature,* VI (1970), 92-5.
       The source is "The Owl," Bl, XX.

CL418  LEGLER, H. E.  *Poe's "The Raven": Its Origin and Genesis: a Compilation and Survey.* Wausau, Wisconsin, 1907.

CL419  MABBOTT, T. O.  "First Publication of Poe's 'Raven'," BNYPL, XLVII (Aug. 1943), 581-4.
       "The Raven" was first published in *A Plain System of Elocution,* Second Edition, George Vandenhoff, 1845.

CL420  _____.  "Poe's 'The Raven': First Inclusion in a Book," N&Q, CLXXXV (Oct. 9, 1943), 225.

CL421  McCARTHY, KEVIN M.  "Another Source for 'The Raven': Locke's *Essay Concerning Human Understanding,*" PN, I (Oct. 1968), 29.
       The source is a passage from Locke which Poe discusses in "Morella."

*CL: Interpretations of Individual Works*

CL422  McVICKER, CECIL DON.  "Poe and 'Anacreon': A Classical
    Influence on 'The Raven'," PN, I (Oct. 1968), 29.

CL423  MOORE, JOHN ROBERT.  "Poe's Reading of *Anne of Geirstein*," AL,
    XXII (Jan. 1951), 493-96.
        Concerning the influence of this work on "The Raven" and
on "The Domain of Arnheim."

CL424  MORGAN, MRS. EDMUND.  "The Poe Revival," BL (Apr. 1903).
    New edition of "The Raven" is mentioned.

CL425  NORSTEDT, GEORGE.  "Prototype of 'The Raven'," NAR, CCXXIV
    (Dec. 1927), 692-701.
        "The Raven" is compared to a poem called "Evermore."

CL426  ORVELL, MILES D.  "'The Raven' and the Chair," PN, V (Dec.
    1972), 54.
        Discusses a biographical source of Poe's interest in
ravens--a chair in the dining suite of the John Allan
family.

CL427  RICHARD, CLAUDE.  "Another Unknown Early Appearance of 'The
    Raven'," PN, I (Oct. 1968), 30.
        The poem appeared in the *New York Morning News* (Feb. 3,
1845).

CL428  STEIN, ALLEN F.  "Another Source for 'The Raven'," AN&Q, IX
    (1971), 85-7.
        The source is Cornelius Mathew!s novel, *The Career of
Puffer Hopkins*, printed in *Arcturus* (Jun. 1841-May 1842).

CL429  STEWARD, CHARLES D.  "A Pilfering by Poe," Atl, CCII (Dec.
    1958), 67-8.
        Poe is a plagiarist because he neglected to acknowledge
*Barnaby Rudge* as a source of "The Raven" in "The Philosophy
of Composition."

CL430  TANSELLE, G. THOMAS.  "Two More Appearances of 'The Raven',"
    PBSA, LVII (II Quarter 1963), 229-30.
        "The Raven" appeared in the *Pennsylvania Inquirer*
(Feb. 15, 1845) and the *London Journal* (Mar. 21, 1846).

CL431  _____.  "An Unknown Early Appearance of 'The Raven'," SB:BSUV,
    XVI (1963), 220-3.
        A previously unrecorded appearance in *New York Weekly
News* (Feb. 8, 1845), with a list of twenty early appearances of the poem from Jan. 29, 1845 to Nov. 3, 1849.

*CL: Interpretations of Individual Works*

CL432  TRIPLETT, E. B.  "A Note on Poe's 'The Raven'," <u>AL</u>, X (Nov. 1938), 339-41.
       Similarities between "The Raven" and W. Falconer's "The Dervish."

CL433  VARNADO, S. L.  "Poe's Raven Lore: a Source Note," <u>AN&Q</u>, VII (1968), 35-7.
       The source is *The Darker Superstitions of Scotland* by Sir John Graham Dalyell.

CL434  WHITTY, J. H.  "The First and Last Publication of Poe's 'The Raven'," <u>PW</u>, CXXX (Oct. 17, 1936), 1635,
       The poem was published in *The Examiner* (Sept. 25, 1849).

*See also* A60, A66, A69, A91, A99, A103-4, A132, A191, B9, B47, B91, B116, B132, B150, B153, B160, B194, B234, CG42, CO21, CH9, CH17, CH20, CK361, CL356, CL528, CN4, CR9, CR10, CR16, CR54, CS5, CS17, CS50, CS58, CS94.


"Shadow--A Parable"

CL435  DeFALCO, JOSEPH.  "The Sources of Terror in Poe's 'Shadow--A Parable'," <u>SSF</u>, VI (Fall 1969), 643-9.
       The story "presents a vivid portrait of the shock to human sensibilities that results in the awareness of the loss of individual identity after death." As such, it previews Poe's conclusions on life, death and afterlife described in *Eureka*.


"Silence--A Fable"

CL436  BASLER, ROY P.  "Poe's Dream Imagery," *Sex, Symbolism and Psychology in Literature*. New Brunswick: Rutgers University Press, 1948, 177-200.
       Like "Ligeia," a symbolic drama of insanity, "Silence--A Fable" is "an evocation of the loneliness and desolation of the realm of the unconscious inhabited by a fear-stricken, cynical, world-weary Psyche."

CL437  CLAUDEL, ALICE M.  "What has Poe's 'Silence--A Fable' to Say?" <u>BSUF</u>, X (1969), 66-70.
       The tale describes "the death of poetry in a kind of wasteland under the aegis of a controlling elite."

CL438  PITTMAN, DIANA.  "'Silence--A Fable'," <u>SLM</u>, III (1941), 418-22.

*CL: Interpretations of Individual Works*

CL439  THOMPSON, G. R. "'Silence--A Fable' and the Folio Club: Who
were the 'Psychological Autobiographists'?" PN, II (Jan.
1969), 23.
The story satirizes a school of writing which Poe
labeled "the manner of psycholgical autobiographists."


"The Sleeper"

CL440  HUNTER, W. B. "Poe's 'The Sleeper' and *Macbeth*," AL, XX (May
1948), 55-7.
The image of the mystic moon echoes the witches' scene,
11, v.

CL441  MABBOTT, T. O. "Poe's 'The Sleeper' Again," AL, XXI (Nov.
1949), 339-40.
The poem, which contains an allusion to the virus lunare,
is similar to Moore's *Lalla Rookh*. The irony of the poem
is that the powerful and beneficent virus lunare was too
late for the lady.

*See also* CL516.


"Some Ancient Greek Authors"

CL442  JACKSON, DAVID K. "'Some Ancient Greek Authors': A Work of
Poe," N&Q, CLXVI (May 26, 1834), 368; AL, V (Nov. 1933),
263-7.
Poe is indebted to Charles Anthon's revised edition of
J. Lemprière's *Classical Dictionary* for "Some Ancient Greek
Authors" and "Lionizing."


"Some Words With a Mummy"

CL443  CAMPBELL, KILLIS. "Source of Poe's "Some Words With a Mummy',"
*Nation*, XC (Jun. 23, 1910), 625-6.
The source is R. M. Bird's *Sheppard Lee*, Philadelphia,
1836.

CL444  KING, LUCILLE. "Notes on Poe's Sources," UTSE, X (1930), 128-
34.
"Premature Burial" from "The Buried Alive," Bl (Oct.
1821); "Metzengerstein" from *The Castle of Otranto;* "Some
Words" from "Letter from a Revived Mummy," *New York
Evening Mirror* (Jan. 21, 1832) and *The Encyclopedia
Americana*, IX (1854), 89.

# EDGAR ALLAN POE: AN ANNOTATED BIBLIOGRAPHY

*CL: Interpretations of Individual Works*

CL445  POLLIN, BURTON R.  "Poe's 'Some Words With a Mummy' Recon-
       sidered," ESQ, LX (Fall 1970), 60-67.
           Several sources are mentioned, including John Gliddon's
       *Ancient Egypt* in *New York World* (Apr. 1843), 68; James
       Silk Buckinham's *Egyptian Lectures;* and *The Mummy: or The
       Liquor of Life: a Farce in One Act.*

*See also* CL357.


## "Song"

CL446  ADKINS, N. F.  "Poe's Borrowings," N&Q, CLXVII (Jul. 28,1934),
       67-8.
           Adkins suggests a connection between Poe's "Song" and
       Fitz-Greene Halleck's "To...."


## "Sonnet--An Enigma"

CL447  BANDY, W. T.  "Poe's 'An Enigma' (or 'Sonnet'), 4." Expl, XX,
       item 35 (Dec. 1961).
           The "Naples bonnet" is an Italian Straw hat.


## "Sonnet--To Science"

CL448  JACKSON, DAVID K.  "A Typographical Error in the B Version of
       Poe's 'Sonnet -- To Science'," PN, III (Jun. 1970), 21.
           Suggests that "Nais" may be a typo for "Naiad" since
       there is another typo in the B version.

CL449  MABBOTT, T. O.  "A Few Notes on Poe," MLN, XXXV (Jun. 1920),
       372-4.
           "Sonnet--Silence" first appeared in PSC (Jan. 4, 1840);
       Poe wrote a note on the meaning of "agit rem" in GM (Jul.
       1840); "The Black Cat" appeared in the Boston *Pictorial
       National Library* (Nov. 1848); Willis printed "The Bells"
       in HJ (Oct. 27, 1849); "The Gold Bug" was dramatized in
       1843. Also mentions new reviews discovered in the PSM.

CL450  MONTEIRO, GEORGE.  "Edgar Allan Poe and the New Knowledge,"
       SLJ, IV (Spr. 1972), 34-40.
           "Sonnet--To Science" dramatizes two different poetic
       responses to the conflict between Romanticism and Science:
       a capitulation to Science and a resistance to the "scien-
       tific" invasion of the private reaches of his imagination.

*See also* CK63, CL50, CL484.

*CL: Interpretations of Individual Works*

"Sonnet--To Zante"

CL451 POLLIN, BURTON R. "Poe's 'Sonnet--To Zante': Sources and Associations," CLS, V (Sept. 1968), 303-15.
    The sonnet was inspired by certain phrases in his own poem "Al Aaraaf," which in turn came from Chateaubriand's *Itineraire,* the biography of Byron, and Keats' "Ode to a Nightingale."

"The Spectacles"

CL452 MOONEY, STEPHEN L. "The Comic in Poe's Fiction," AL, XXXIII (Jan. 1962), 433-41.
    Applies Bergson's theory of the comic to "Four Beasts in One," "Hop-Frog," "The Man," "The Spectacles," "Tarr and Fether"--with special emphasis on comic progression. "Poe's comedy is allied to vaudeville and farce, and is directed toward the exposure of a society in which heroes and rulers are shown to be deluded or irresponsible and their subjects a dehumanized, sycophantic mass."

CL453 POLLIN, BURTON R. "'The Spectacles' of Poe--Sources and Significance," AL, XXXVII (1965), 187-90.
    The source is "The Mysterious Portrait," an anonymous tale in *New Monthly Belle Assemblée.* Pollin also discusses the biographical aspects of the tale.

CL454 SALZBERG, JOEL. "Preposition and Peaming in Poe's 'The Spectacles'." PN, III (Jun. 1970), 21.
    "The Spectacles" is "in part, a comic variant on 'Ligeia,' and Poe characterizes the protagonist as a ludicrous version of the transcendentally inclined husband." Also notes an error in the Modern Library Edition.

*See also* CK356.

"Stanzas"

CL455 HINDIN, MICHAEL. "Poe's Debt to Wordsworth: a Reading of 'Stanzas'," *Studies in Romanticism,* VIII (1969), 109-20.
    Influence of "Ode: Intimations on Immortality" on Poe.

"The System of Dr. Tarr and Prof. Fether"

CL456 BENTON, RICHARD P. "Poe's 'The System of Dr. Tarr and Prof.

*CL: Interpretations of Individual Works*

Fether': Dickens or Willis?" PN, I (Apr. 1968), 7-9.
 The original source of the story was Willis' "The Madhouse of Palermo," not Dickens' *American Notes* as Whipple
asserts. Benton also suggests a political interpretation
of the story.

CL457 WHIPPLE, WILLIAM. "Poe's Two-Edged Satiric Tale," NCF, IX
 (Nov. 1954), 121-33.
 "Tarr and Fether" is a satire of the "soothing system"--
lenient methods employed in treating the insane--and of
Charles Dickens, who visited a mental hospital in Boston
to observe such methods.

*See also* CL452.


"Tale of Jerusalem"

CL458 VARNER, J. G. "Poe's 'Tale of Jerusalem,' and *The Talmud*,"
 ABC, VI (Feb. 1935), 56-7.
 In "A Tale of Jerusalem," which he borrowed from "The
Talmud," Poe burlesques Horace Smith's *Zillah, A Tale of
Jerusalem*.


"A Tale of the Ragged Mountains"

CL459 CARTER, BOYD. "Poe's Dept to Charles Brockden Brown," PrS,
 XXVII (Sum. 1953), 190-6.
 Certain elements in "A Tale of the Ragged Mountains,"
such as character relationships, harmony or atmosphere,
and descriptions, are similar to those in *Edgar Huntley*,
although Poe invested them with a rich and original
symbolism.

CL460 ISANI, MUKHTAR ALI. "Some Sources for Poe's 'A Tale of the
 Ragged Mountains'," PN, V (Dec. 1972), 38-40.
 Believes that the Indian episode is "a spoof upon the
current taste for Orientalism." Also discusses a source
of the story, Hastings' *A Narrative of the Late Transations
at Benares*.

CL461 LIND, SIDNEY. "Poe and Mesmerism," PMLA, LXII (Dec. 1947),
 1077-94.
 Discusses the history of mesmerism and Poe's use of it
in "Facts" and "A Tale of the Ragged Mountains." Poe
regarded mesmerism as a valid science. In the second story,

*CL: Interpretations of Individual Works*

the metempsychotic implications exist in the mind of Dr. Templeton, who holds Bedloe in a hypnotic trance.

CL462  PITTMAN, DIANA. "'A Tale of the Ragged Mountains'," SLM, III (Sept. 1941), 422-31.

CL463  THOMPSON, G. R. "Is Poe's 'A Tale of the Ragged Mountains' a Hoax?" SSF, VI (Sum. 1969), 454-60.
　　　　Sees three levels of irony in the story: "first, a 'scientific' explanation of the apparently supernatural events, which leads, second, to a very different 'psychological' explanation...and to, third, an insinuated burlesque (under the whole structure of explanations) of a Gothic novel by Charles Brockden Brown."

*See also* CK363, CL144, CO14, CS52.


"Tamerlane"

CL464  BAXTER, NANCY N. "Thomas Moore's Influence on 'Tamerlaine'," PN, II (Apr. 1969), 36.
　　　　Poe's poem was derived from Moore's tale "The Veiled Prophet of Khorassan" in *Lalla Rookh*.

CL465  LOBERGER, GORDON J. "Poe's Use of 'Page' and 'Lore' in 'Tamerlane'," PN, III (Dec. 1970), 37-38.
　　　　The "page of early lore" refers to the face of the beautiful woman in the previous lines.

CL466  SHOCKLEY, M. S. "*Timour the Tartar* and Poe's 'Tamerlane'," PMLA, LVI (Dec. 1941), 1103-6.
　　　　Source study of "Tamerlane."

*See also* CL528.


"The Tell-Tale Heart"

CL467  CANARIO, JOHN W. "The Dream in 'Tell-Tale Heart'," ELN, VII (Mar. 1970), 194-97.
　　　　The narrator is "the deranged victim of a hallucinatory nightmare" about death. In his dream, the narrator believes that he has destroyed his own body (the old man) and has thus escaped death.

CL468  GARGANO, JAMES W. "The Theme of Time in 'Tell-Tale Heart'," SSF, V (Sum. 1968), 378-82.

*CL: Interpretations of Individual Works*

The self-deceived narrator projects his fear of
mortality onto the old man.  He believes that by destroying the symbol of his fear, he can free himself from it;
but his real enemy is time.

CL469   POLLIN, BURTON R.  "Bulwer Lytton and 'Tell-Tale Heart',"
        AN&Q, IV (Sept. 1965), 7-8.
            Bulwer Lytton's "Monos and Daimonos" is a source of
        Poe's "Tell-Tale Heart."

CL470   REILLY, JOHN E.  "The Lesser Death-Watch and 'The Tell-Tale
        Heart'," ATQ, II (II Quarter 1969), 3-9.
            The narrator, a paranoid schizophrenic with symptoms
        of perceptual disturbance, really hears the rapping of
        the death-watch insect. In "the moral or allegorical
        dimensions of the story...the innocuous sound of an insect
        becomes a measure of time under the aspect of death, a kind
        of metaphor binding together three tokens of man's
        mortality: the process of nature, the beating of the human
        heart, and the ticking of a watch."

CL471   ROBINSON, E. ARTHUR.  "Poe's 'Tell-Tale Heart'," NCF, XIX
        (Mar. 1965), 369-78.  Excerpts reprinted in CJ37.
            Discusses the architectural principle of thematic
        repetition and variation of incident in the tale, and
        demonstrates how two aspects of the story--the psycho-
        logical handling of time and the "murderer's psychological
        identification with the man he kills"--are common to other
        tales by Poe.  The theme of "TTH" is "self-destruction
        through extreme subjectivity marked paradoxically by both
        an excess of sensitivity and temporal solipsism."

CL472   _____.  "Thoreau and the Deathwatch in Poe's 'Tell-Tale
        Heart'," PSt, IV (Jun. 1971), 14-16.
            Poe's source for the deathwatch may have been Thoreau's
        *Journal* entry Aug. 10, 1838, later published in "The
        Natural History of Massachusetts," *Dial,* 1842.

CL473   SENELICK, LAURENCE.  "Charles Dickens and 'Tell-Tale Heart',"
        PSt, VI (Jun. 1973), 12-14.
            Suggests that a Dickens pot-boiler, "A Confession Found
        in a Prison," *Master Humphrey's Clock* (I) inspired Poe's
        tale.

*See also* CK361, CL55, CL384.

*CL: Interpretations of Individual Works*

"Three Sundays in a Week"

CL474   CHERRY, FANNYE N.   "The Source of Poe's 'Three Sundays in a
         Week'," <u>AL</u>, II (Nov. 1930), 232-5.
              Two possible sources are "Three Thursdays in One Week,"
         *Philadelphia Public Ledger* (Oct. 29, 1841) and an article
         in the *Ledger* (Nov. 10, 1841).

CL475   MABBOTT, T. O.   "Poe and Dr. Lardner," <u>AN&Q</u>, III (Nov. 1943),
         115-7.
              Dorton Dubble L. Lee, of "Three Sundays" is probably
         Dionysius Lardner, LL.D.   Poe borrowed many ideas from
         Lardner's lectures.

CL476   TAYLOR, ARCHER.   "Poe's Dr. Lardner and 'Three Sundays in a
         Week'," <u>AN&Q</u>, III (Jan. 1944), 153-5.
              A survey of the expression "When three Sundays fall in
         a week."


"To Helen"

CL477   BAUM, PAULL F.   "Poe's 'To Helen'," <u>MLN</u>, LXIV (May 1949),
         289-97.
              The author discusses Poe's relationship with Mrs. Jane
         Stanard, the supposed Helen of the poem, and suggests that
         three figures are fused into a lyrical composition: Mrs.
         Stanard, Mrs. Allan, and Homer's Helen.

CL478   BEACH, JOHN.   "A Perfumed Sea," <u>CJ</u>, XXIX (Mar. 1934), 454-6.
              The classical references in "To Helen" suggest that
         "the perfumed sea" is the Mediterranean.

CL479   CLAUDEL, ALICE MOSER.   "Poe as Voyager in 'To Helen'," <u>ESQ</u>,
         LX (Fall 1970), 33-8.
              Analysis of the Christian symbolism in the poem, the
         hyacinth hair (a rebirth symbol), the statue and the agate
         lamp.   Poe tried to find supernal beauty in a fusion of
         Greek-Roman-Christian-Oriental-Byzantine culture.

CL480   D'AVANZO, MARIO L.   "'Like Those Nicéan Barks': Helen's
         Beauty," <u>PSt</u>, VI (Jun. 1973), 26-7.
              The "Nicéan Barks" simile may have been drawn from a
         tradition in Greek art called "Nike"--"a beautiful woman
         standing on a boat prow, or bark."

CL481   DURHAM, F. M.   "A Possible Relation between Poe's 'To Helen'
         and Milton's *Paradise Lost*, Bk IV," <u>AL</u>, XVI (Jan. 1945),
         340-3.

*CL: Interpretations of Individual Works*

Three allusions in Poe's poem--"Nicean Barks,"
"hyacinth hair," and "perfumed sea"--appear in *Paradise
Lost*, Bk IV.

CL482    GARGANO, JAMES.  "Poe's 'To Helen'," MLN, LXXIX (Dec. 1960),
652-53.
Helen is a savior who leads the narrator, a Ulyssean
wanderer, to a spiritual home.

CL483    HAVELOCK, E. A.  "Homer, Catullus and Poe," CW, XXXVI (Apr. 12,
1943), 248-9.
Shows twelve words and phrases from Catullus and Homer
which influenced "To Helen."  Helen's sexual powers, the
return of Odysseus to Ithica, and Catullus' journey from
Asia Minor to Sirmio are motifs in Poe's poem.

CL484    HOLT, PALMER.  "Notes on Poe's 'To Science,' 'To Helen,' and
'Ulalume'," BNYPL, LXIII (Nov. 1959), 568-70.
A source of "To Science" is Bernadin de St. Pierre's
*Studies in Nature*, trans. by Henry Hunter, Philadelphia,
1808; "Nicean" comes from the Greek NIKH, used in
Plutarch's *Life of Nicias*, translated by John and William
Langhorne, 1770; "Ulalume" is a combination of Turkish
words meaning "light of the dead" or "dead star."

CL485    JONES, JOE J.  "Poe's 'Nicean Barks'," AL, II (Jan. 1931),
433-8.
The author discusses Poe's knowledge of Catullus and
suggests that he borrowed "Nicean" from Catullus' poems,
4, 10, 31, 46.

CL486    KUMMER, GEORGE.  "Another Poe-Coleridge Parallel?" AL, VIII
(Mar. 1936), 72.
"The weary way worn wanderer" is similar to Coleridge's
"...minister refreshment to the tired way-wanderer" ("The
Destiny of Nations").

CL487    LIPSCOMB, HERBERT.  "Poe's 'Nicean Barks' Again," CJ, XXIX
(Mar. 1934), 454.
Discusses the source of the term "opens more readily
magic casements on perilous seas."

CL488    LORD, JOHN B.  "Two Phonological Analyses of Poe's 'To
Helen'," *Language and Style*, III (1970), 147-58.
Technical discussion of the connection between sound
patterns, distinctive feature clusters and phonetics on
the one hand and meaning on the other.

*CL: Interpretations of Individual Works*

CL489  MABBOTT, T. O.  "Poe's 'To Helen'," Expl, I (Jun. 1943), 60.
       Poe has combined three classical stories in the poem:
       Helen's appearance as a lover of those who consult her
       dream oracle; Bacchus' return from peaceful conquest of
       the East; and Psyche's attempt to awaken Cupid with oil
       from her lamp.  The poem tells the reader that "spiritual
       love leads man to beauty."

CL490  MIEROW, H. E.  "A Classical Allusion in Poe," MLN, XXXI (Mar.
       1916), 184-5.
       "Nicean" has no particular meaning.  Poe was very young
       when he wrote the poem and might have confused various
       myths.  Perhaps he meant "Phaecian."

CL491  PEMBERTON, J. M.  "Poe's 'To Helen': Functional Wordplay and
       a Possible Source," PN, III (Jun. 1970), 6-7.
       The Greek word for "Helen" also means "torch" or "fire-
       brand."  Poe was playing on this second meaning in making
       Helen "a magnetic personification of 'inspirational beauty'
       in one sense, and, in another...an apostrophized object
       which the speaker literally sees in a brilliant window-
       niche...." The double image explains Poe's revisions of
       the poem.

CL492  PITTMAN, DIANA.  "Key to the Mystery of Edgar Allan Poe: 'To
       Helen'," SLM, III (Nov. 1941), 499-501.
       Written not to Mrs. Stanard, but to the Greek ship
       *Hellas*, which was in the struggle against the Turks. Poe
       himself took part in that struggle! *See* CK237.

CL493  RENDELL, V.  "Poe: A Classical Reference," N&Q, IX, eleventh
       series (May 30, 1914), 427.
       Identifies "Nicean Barks" as Nicaea of Catullus, Poem
       46.

CL494  SCHWARTZ, ARTHUR.  "The Transport: A Matter of Time and
       Space," CEA Critic, XXXI (Dec. 1968), 14-15.
       The language of "To Helen" suggests a spacial and an
       emotional or spiritual journey.  "What seems to be taking
       place...is that the overt or visual level of the poem is
       giving us an in-time and in-space correlative of a
       completely internal here-and-now transcendence into sur-
       reality."

CL495  SNYDER, EDWARD D.  "Poe's Nicean Barks," CJ, XLVIII (Feb.
       1953), 159-69.
       The author discusses various interpretations of the
       classical image in the poem.

*CL: Interpretations of Individual Works*

CL496 TANNENBAUM, EARL. "Poe's 'Nicean Barks': 'Small Latins and Less Greek'," N&Q, CCIII, ns. 5 (Aug. 1958), 353-5.
A review of source studies of "Nicean Barks." Tannenbaum concludes that Poe was confused about history or simply liked the sound of the words.

CL497 WALKER, R. J. "Poe: A Classical Reference," N&Q, IX, eleventh series (Jun. 13, 1914), 472.
By "Nicean Barks" Poe meant the fleet built by Alexander the Great near his city of Nicaea.

CL498 WALKER, WARREN. "Poe's 'To Helen'," MLN, LXXII (Nov. 1957), 491-2.
The poet's love is not only as beautiful as the classical Helen. Her beauty "is an earthly manifestation of the immortal beauty of the soul; and the contemplation of her beauty has brought the poet 'home' spiritually." The problem is that in the Greek story Helen did not bring Ulysses home; she caused him to depart from Ithica.

CL499 WESTON, ARTHUR HAROLD. "The 'Nicean Barks' of Edgar Allan Poe," CJ, XXIX (Dec. 1933), 213-15.
A summary of interpretations of "Nicean Barks" and the suggestion that the lines are a misspelling of Catullus' "Nicaean."

*See also* A3, A49, CK214, CM18, CR38, CR47.


"The Token"

CL500 WOOD, FREDERICK T. "Source Wanted: 'The Token'," N&Q, CCV (Mar. 1960), 115.
Answer to query in N&Q, CCIV, 459.


"To One in Paradise"

CL501 BASLER, ROY P. "Byronism in Poe's 'To One in Paradise'," AL, IX (May 1937), 232-6.
Poe knew Byron's poems to Mary Chaworth, whom he considered the "incarnation of the ideal that haunted the fancy of the poet." Many of Poe's metaphors, especially those about ideal love, are Byronic.

CL502 MABBOTT, T. O. "Unrecorded Texts of Two of Poe's Poems," AN&Q, VIII (Aug. 1948), 67-8.
An early version of "To One in Paradise" appeared in the

*CL: Interpretations of Individual Works*

*Philadelphia Saturday Evening Post* (Jan. 9, 1841); and
"Lenore" appeared in the *New York Evening Mirror* (Nov. 28,
1844).

CL503  REDE, KENNETH.  "New Poe Manuscript," <u>AC</u>, III (Dec. 1926),
100-2.
    Reproduction of manuscripts of "The Coliseum" and "To
One in Paradise" with information regarding their early
publication.

*See also* B27, B52, CN4.


"To the River"

CL504  MABBOTT, T. O.  "Poe's 'To the River'," <u>Expl</u>, III, Q21 (Jun.
1945).
    Poe borrowed from Cowper's "The Stream, Addressed to a
Young Lady."

CL505  _____.  "'To the River'," <u>Expl,</u> III, Q21 (Apr. 1945).
    Query.


"Ulalume"

CL506  Anon.  "Poe's 'Ulalume'," <u>Expl</u>, I (Oct. 1942), 8.
    Brief note on Huxley's "The Vulgarity of Poe."

CL507  ADKINS, NELSON F.  "Poe's 'Ulaleme'," <u>N&Q</u>, CLXIV (Jan. 14,
1933), 30-1.
    Discusses the influence of Willis Gaylord Clark's "To
the Autumn Leaf" on "Ulalume."

CL508  BAILEY, J. O.  "The Geography of Poe's 'Dream-Land' and
'Ulalume'," <u>SP</u>, XLV (Jul. 1948), 512-23.
    The source of the geographical details in the two poems
is Mercator's "Nautical Chart of the World."

CL509  BASLER, ROY P.  "Poe's 'Ulalume'," <u>Expl</u>, II (May 1944), 49.
Reprinted in *Sex, Symbolism and Psychology*.  New Brunswick,
Rutgers University Press, 1948, 184-7.
    The psyche  tries to prevent the narrator from dis-
covering that his second love will lead to frustration, as
his first love did, by reminding him of his ideal first
love--safe because dead.  The narrator discovers finally
that "the self can find fulfillment only in death" and
that "absolute fulfillment means annihilation."

EDGAR ALLAN POE: AN ANNOTATED BIBLIOGRAPHY

*CL: Interpretations of Individual Works*

CL510  BLUMENFELD, J. P.  "Poe's 'Ulalume,' Line 43," N&Q, CXCVII
       (Mar. 29, 1952), 147.
            A source may be ll. 586-90 of Wordsworth's "Guilt and
       Sorrow," II, 586-90.

CL511  BROOKS, CLEANTH and ROBERT PENN WARREN.  "'Ulalume'," *Under-
       stand Poetry*.  Rev. Ed. New York: Henry Holt, 1950, 194-
       201.
            Regards the poem as immature, vague and confusing.

CL512  CARLSON, ERIC W.  "Poe's 'Ulalume'," Expl, XI (Jun. 1953), 56.
            Denies Brooks-Warren allegation that certain lines of
       the poem have no meaning.  Concludes that the narrator and
       Psyche finally understand that "Astarte, the illusory
       promise of a sensual escape from grief-haunted memory, had
       been a product of his own subconscious self-pity...." *See*
       CL511.

CL573  _____.  "Symbol and Sense in Poe's 'Ulalume'," AL, XXXV (Mar.
       1963), 22-37.
            Repudiates the Miller-Basler Freudian interpretation of
       the poem that "the discovery of the tomb represents death
       through or of the sexual instinct" and demonstrates instead
       that it symbolizes "the revived power (through felt loss)
       of ideal love."  The poem concludes with a "tragic self-
       knowledge [through the reality of grief] which re-establishes
       the unity of the moral-emotional self." *See* CL509 and CL523.

CL514  CONNOLLY, THOMAS.  "Poe's 'Ulalume'," Expl, XXII, item 4
       (Sept. 1963).
            Disagrees with Miller's assertation that the poem is
       disorderly.  Believes Poe is expressing a conflict between
       the submerged memory of the dead Ulalume, chaste and frigid
       even in life, and Astarte, a new and carnal love. *See*
       CL523.

CL515  DAUGHRITY, K. L.  "Source for a line of Poe's 'Ulalume'," N&Q,
       CLXI (Jul. 11, 1931), 27.
            N. P. Willis' "My Birth-Place," *New York Mirror* (Mar.
       28, 1828).

CL516  KIEHL, JAMES.  "Valley of Unrest: A Major Metaphor in the
       Poetry of Edgar Allan Poe," *Thoth,* V (Win. 1964), 42-52.
            Examines "The Valley of Unrest," "The Sleeper" and
       "Ulalume" for evidence of the scenes of the Valley of Un-
       rest, a metaphor of the fallen, mortal world.

245

*CL: Interpretations of Individual Works*

CL517  KIRBY, JOHN P.  "Poe's 'Ulalume'," <u>Expl</u>, I (Oct. 1942), 8.
Analysis of the rhythm.

CL518  LEARY, LEWIS.  "Poe's 'Ulalume'," <u>Expl</u>, VI, item 25 (Feb.1948).
The "misty mid regions" can be seen in a painting by
landscape artist Robert Walter Weir.

CL519  MABBOTT, T. O.  "The Astrological Symbolism of Poe's 'Ulalume'," <u>N&Q</u>, CLXI (Jul. 11, 1931), 26-7.
An unhappy situation in love (possibly a reference to
his romance with Mrs. Osgood) is symbolized in the fact
that "Astarte's bediamond crescent" comes "up through the
lair of the lion."  A source of the symbolism may be
Spenser.

CL520  _____.  "Poe's 'Ulalume'," <u>Expl</u>, I, item 25 (Feb. 1943).
The poem teaches that a new love cannot replace an old
one.  Poe's Dim Lake of Auber is Daniel Francois Esprit
Auber's "Le Lac des Fees."

CL521  _____.  "Poe's 'Ulalume'," <u>Expl</u>, VI, item 57 (Jun. 1948).
Agrees with Leary that Weir's painting is a source of
the scene in the poem. *See* CL518.

CL522  _____.  "Poe's 'Ulalume'," <u>N&Q</u>, CLXIV (Feb. 25, 1933), 143.
Three sources of the poem may be Willis Gaylord Clark's
"To the Autumn Leaf," Mrs. Elizabeth Oakes-Smith's "The
Summons Answered," and a poem by Mrs. R. S. Nichols.

CL523  MILLER, JAMES JR.  "'Ulalume' Resurrected," <u>PQ</u>, XXXIV (Apr.
1955), 197-205.
The key to the work is to view the protagonist as the
narrator--not as someone within the poem, but as someone
<u>writing</u> it.  The incoherence of "Ulalume" is actually a
reflection of the incoherence and torment of the narrator
as he discovers "his deep-set frustration... the full real-
ization of the inevitable link between sexual love and
death."  Ulalume is "Death itself, a personification of
turbulent sexual impulse combined with its inevitable
destruction."

CL524  MULQUEEN, JAMES E.  "The Meaning of Poe's 'Ulalume'," <u>ATQ</u>, I
(I Quarter 1969), 27-30.
Poe is using Astarte not in her traditional sense as a
fertility goddess but "as a symbol of a Life Principle
which has nothing to do with material reality, but which
represents rather a concept of divine non-material unity."

*CL: Interpretations of Individual Works*

In the poetic dialogue between a man and his soul, hope
for divine unity dies with the appearance of the tomb.

CL525 OMANS, GLEN A. "Poe's 'Ulalume': Drama of the Solipsistic
Self," *Papers on Poe: Essays in Honor of J. Ward Ostrom.*
Springfield, Ohio, 1972.
In many of Poe's stories, the "valid vision of supernal
beauty" gives way to terror when the narrator discovers
"the solipsistic nature of his vision."

CL526 PATTEE, FRED LEWIS. "Poe's 'Ulalume'," *Side-Lights on American Literature.* New York: Century Co., 1922, 327-42.
Poe wrote "Ulalume" at the end of the most difficult
period in his life, and the poem captures the terror of
his world, his sense of isolation, his confusion, momentary
hope and ultimate despair. It is the product of an abnormal mind which split into two parts that converse with
each other.

CL527 PITTMAN, DIANA. "Key to the Mystery of 'Ulalume'," SLM, III
(Aug. 1941), 371-8.
*See* CK237.

CL528 ROUTH, JAMES. "Notes on the Sources of Poe's Poetry: Coleridge, Keats, Shelley," MLN, XXIX (Mar. 1914), 72-5.
The meter in "Ulalume" echoes that in "Prometheus Unbound" (Act III); "Fairy Land" is a satire on "Kubla Khan";
possible sources of "Al Aaraaf" are "Kubla Khan," "Endymion," "Promtheus Unbound"; a source of "The Raven" is
Shelley's "The Cloud"; and "Lines Written Among the Euganean Hills" is a source of "Conqueror Worm," "Annabel Lee,"
and "Tamerlane."

*See also* A187, B236, CC112, CK260, CL484, CN4.


"The Unparalleled Adventure of One Hans Pfaall"

CL521 GRAVELY, WILLIAM H. JR. "A Few Words of Clarification on
'Hans Pfaal'," PN, V (Dec. 1972), 56.
Establishes that the story was composed between the end
of 1834 and Jan. 1835.

CL530 _____. "A Note on the Composition of 'Hans Pfaal'," PN, Jun.
1970), 2-4.
Takes issue with Bailey's analysis of Poe's sources
based on H. B. Latrobe's reminiscences.

*CL: Interpretations of Individual Works*

CL531  GREER, H. ALLEN.  "Poe's 'Hans Pfaall' and the Political
Scene," ESQ, LX (Fall 1970), 67-73.
Sees three levels of irony in the story.  Poe played to
a completely credulous audience, to an audience that would
see the story as a parody of "scientific" moon journeys,
and to an audience that would recognize it as "'a kind of
allegorical parody' of the life and times of Andrew
Jackson."

CL532  HOFFMAN, DANIEL.  "Send-ups," *London Magazine,* IX (Jan. 1970),
30-36.
Hoffman is reminded of "The Balloon Hoax" and "Hans
Pfaall" when he watches the space flights.

CL533  KETTERER, DAVID.  "Poe's Usage of the Hoax and the Unity of
"Hans Phaall'," *Criticism,* XIII (Fall 1971), 377-85.
Poe's use of hoax as a literary form is an outgrowth of
his idea that "man exists in a state of total deception."
Poe reveals in the grotesque Tales "the multiform, decep-
tive nature of the material world, deceptive because in a
Blakean sense, it is a fabricated product of the co-
ordinates of time, place, and self."

CL534  NICOLSON, MARJORIE H.  *Voyages to the Moon.* New York: Macmillan, 1948.
"Hans Pfaall" adds little to the tradition.

CL535  POSEY, MEREDITH N.  "Notes on Poe's 'Hans Pfaall'," MLN, XLV
(Dec. 1930), 501-7.
Three sources are cited: George Tucker's "A Voyage to
the Moon," AQR, (Mar. 1828); Rees' Cyclopedia; Sir John F.
W. Herschel's *A Treatise on Astronomy* (1834).

CL536  REISS, EDMUND.  "The Comic Setting of 'Hans Pfaall'," AL,
XXIX (Nov. 1957), 306-9.
The jocular structure of "Hans Pfaall" and the pun on
the Latin "follis" (meaning "windbag") suggest that the
story is comic and was probably an April Fools' joke.

CL537  WILKINSON, R. S.  "Poe's 'Hans Pfaall' Reconsidered," N&Q,
XIII (Sept. 1966), 333-7.
Poe's tale is "a subtle satire upon Tucker's *Voyage* in
particular, and previous 'moon-voyages' in general."

*See also* A48, A75, B151, CK363, CL332, CS17.

# Edgar Allan Poe: An Annotated Bibliography

*CL: Interpretations of Individual Works*

### "A Valentine"

CL538   ANON.   "Poe's Valentine," *Commonweal,* XV (Mar. 2, 1932), 481.

CL539   MABBOTT, T. O.   "Allusions to a Spanish Joke in Poe's 'A Valentine'," N&Q, CLXIX (Sept. 14, 1939), 189.
   An explanation of obscure lines (17-19) in Poe's "Valentine": Poe is punning on the name "Fernam Mendez Pinto," a Portuguese traveler of the 16th Century.

CL540   McLEAN, SIDNEY R.   "Poeana I.   A Valentine," Cpn, ns. I (Aut. 1935), 183-7.
   Concerning the date of a poem Poe wrote for Miss Louisa Oliver Hunter, with a biographical note on Miss Hunter.

### "The Valley of Unrest"

CL541   BASLER, R. P.   "Poe's 'The Valley of Unrest'," Expl, V, item 25 (Dec. 1946).   Reprinted in *Sex, Symbolism and Psychology.*   New Brunswick: Rutgers University Press, 1948, 197-201.
   The first part of the poem symbolizes the peaceful state of the psyche when emotion is expressed. In the second part, repression occurs, and the psyche fears the rediscovery of the repressed emotion.   "The final version of the poem has an almost purely psychic symbolism where the earlier versions convey a suggestion of traditional moralistic myth."

CL542   BLEDSOE, THOMAS F.   "On Poe's 'Valley of Unrest'," MLN, LXI (Feb. 1946), 91-2.
   "Nis" is a compound of the Latin "Dis" and "Nihil" and suggests the underworld, realms of shades and sorrow, and "the nothingness that follows tragic loss."

CL543   MABBOTT, T. O.   "Poe's 'The Valley of Unrest'," Expl, III Q19 (May 1945).
   Query.

*See also* CL516.

### "Von Kempelen and His Discovery"

CL544   HALL, THOMAS.   "Poe's Use of a Source: Davy's Chemical Researches and 'Von Kempelen and His Discovery'," PN, I (Oct. 1968), 28.

*CL: Interpretations of Individual Works*

Poe adapted a passage from *The Collected Works of Sir Humphrey Davy* to achieve verisimilitude.

CL545　POLLIN, BURTON.　"Poe's 'Von Kempelen and His Discovery':
Sources and Significance," *Etudes Anglaises,* XX (Jan.-Mar.
1967), 12-23.
Discusses Poe's concept of the "verisimilar," expecially
his use of the names of real people.

*See also* CK363, CT3.


"William Wilson"

CL546　GARGANO, JAMES W.　"Art and Irony in 'William Wilson'," ESQ,
LX (Fall 1970), 18-22.
"WW," like most of Poe's ironic tales, "expresses Poe's
view of the relation between man's inner, psychological
disorganization and his futility in the world at large."
Believing that he is seeking freedom from an external
enemy, Wilson is actually rushing toward destruction.

CL547　_____.　"'William Wilson': the Wildest Sublunary Visions,"
*Washington and Jefferson Literary Journal,* I (1967), 9-16.
The clear, mathematical structure of the tale demonstrates the protagonist's tragedy: his failure to realize
"the complexity and richness of his whole nature."

CL548　GREEN, GEORGE H.　"'William Wilson' and the Conscience of
Edgar Allan Poe," *Aberystwyth Studies,* XI (1929), 11-22.

CL549　MABBOTT, T. O.　"Numismatic References in Three American
Writers," *Numismatist,* XLVI (Nov. 1933), 688.
Concerning a reference in "WW" to "the exergues of
Carthaginian medals," an ancient coin.

CL550　ROTHWELL, K. S.　"Source for the Motto to Poe's 'William
Wilson'," MLN, LXXIV (Apr. 1959), 297.
The source is a passage from Chamberlayne's *Love's
Victory* (London, 1658).　Poe confused lines in this play
with a passage in Chamberlayne's *Pharonnida.*

CL551　THORNER, H. E. "Hawthorne, Poe and a Literary Ghost," NEQ, VII
(Mar. 1934), 146-54.
Traces the literary figure "Luis Enius" in the seven-
teenth-century and claims that he later became William
Wilson and General Howe.　Hawthorne and Poe borrowed the
idea from Irving's "An Unwritten Drama of Lord Byron."

# Edgar Allan Poe: An Annotated Bibliography

*CL: Interpretations of Individual Works*

CL552   WALSH, THOMAS F.   "The Other 'William Wilson'," <u>ATQ</u>, X (1971),
         17-25.
         Examines "WW" first in the light of the double's mythic
         associations with death and the diabolic and then in the
         light of the "science" of autoscopy.  Walsh disagrees with
         Rank, Guerard, Bonaparte and Rosenfield and invokes M.
         Lukianowicz's definition of autoscopy in an overcomplicated
         attempt to prove that the tale is not as simple as everyone
         has hitherto suspected.

*See also* B139, CC51, CL155, CO14, CS52.

*CM: Critical and Aesthetic Theories*

CM1   ABRAMS, M. H.   *The Mirror and the Lamp: Romantic Theory and
        the Citical Tradition*.   New York: W. W. Norton, 1958.
        Passing references to Poe's theory of the short poem.

CM2   ADKINS, NELSON.   "Chapter on American Cribbage: Poe and
        Plagiarism," <u>PBSA</u>, XLII (Oct. 3, 1948), 169-210.
        Detailed examination of Poe's attitude toward plagiar-
        ism and of specific charges he leveled against other
        writers.

CM3   ALBEE, JOHN.   "Poe and Aristotle," *Dial*, XXXIV (Mar. 16,1903),
        192.
        Brief discussion about Poe's attitude toward long
        poetry.

CM4   ANDERSON, DAVID D.   "A Comparison of the Poetic Theories of
        Emerson and Poe," <u>Person</u>, XLI (Aut. 1960), 471-83.
        The aesthetics of Poe and Emerson are antithetical.
        Emerson was interested in the connection between poetry
        and truth.  To him, the poet intuitively perceives the
        unity behind variety in nature. Poe, on the other hand,
        saw the poet as a man of reason who searches for a way
        to express Beauty and is not concerned with truth.

CM5   BAGLEY, C. L.   "Early American Views of Coleridge as a Poet,"
        *Research Studies of Washington State University*, XXXII
        (1964), 292-307.

CM6   BALDWIN, SUMMERFIELD.   "The Aesthetic Theory of Edgar Allan
        Poe," <u>SR</u>, XXVI (Apr. 1918), 210-21.
        Examines Poe's contribution to the development of Amer-
        ican criticism.  He invented the short story, understood

*CM: Critical and Aesthetic Theories*

the "artistic values of horror," and came close to recon-
ciling Aristotelians and Platonists in his theory that
imitation pleases because "by creating another reality it
helps us to escape the terrible fact of everyday existence."

CM7   BATE, WALTER J.   "Edgar Allan Poe," *Criticism: the Major
      Texts*. New York: Harcourt Brace, 1952.
         Discusses Poe as a Romantic.

CM8   BELDEN, HENRY M.   "Observation and Imagination in Coleridge
      and Poe, a Contrast," *Papers in Honor of Charles Frederick
      Johnson*. ed. by Odell Shepard and Arthur Adams. Hartford:
      Trinity College, 1928.
         Finds similarity in their imagery and differences in
      their social attitudes and ideas about nature.

CM9   BLAIR, WALTER.   "Poe's Conception of Incident and Tone in the
      Tale," <u>MP</u>, XLI (May 1944), 228-40.
         Poe knew that the psychology of the reader dictates how
      incidents should be selected and presented.  The artist
      selects the effects he wishes to produce and then chooses
      the appropriate incidents.  Tone is thus connected with
      incident and plot.

CM10  BRADDY, HALDEEN.   "Edgar Allan Poe's Last Bid for Fame,"
      *Studies in Medieval, Renaissance and American Literature*.
      Fort Worth: Texas Christian University Press, 1971, 134-43.
         Brief, familiar essay on Poe as critic.

CM11  BROOKS, VAN WYCK.   "Poe in the North," *The World of Washing-
      ton Irving*. New York: E. P. Dutton, 1944, 443-57.
         Essay on Poe's influence as a literary critic who
      sought to end puffing and to attack indiscriminate censure
      of American artists.  Brooks believes Poe was limited by a
      narrow vision and range and by erratic judgment.  Poe
      focused on aesthetics at a time when such an emphasis was
      essential to American art.

CM12  BURKE, KENNETH.   "'The Principle of Composition'," *Poetry*,
      XCIX (Oct. 1961), 46-53.
         Discusses the "essential rightness of Poe's concern with
      'the principle' of composition....He really did ask himself
      as a <u>critic</u> what principles he found (or thought he found)
      implicit in his act as poet....he thus formulated the
      aesthetic principles...which seemed to him the conceptual
      equivalents of the principles that had implicitly guided
      him in the writing of the poem."  Concludes that "regard-

*CM: Critical and Aesthetic Theories*

less of how any work arose...the critic should aim to formulate the principles of composition implicit in it."

CM13  CARGILL, OSCAR.  "The Laggard Art of Criticism," CE, VI (Feb.
1945), 245.
A few lines on Poe's inventiveness and provocativeness
as a critic.

CM14  CARY, RICHARD.  "Poe and the Literary Ladies," TSLL, IX
(Spr. 1967), 91-101.
Poe's criticism of female authors is unreliable because
he was prejudiced by his Southern chivalric attitudes.

CM15  CHINOL, ELIO.  "Poe's Essays on Poetry," SR, LXVIII (Sum.
1960), 390-7.
Chinol denies the link between Poe's theories of pure
poetry (poetry aesthetically atonomous and absolutely free
from concerns outside art) and his later definition of pure
poetry as a composition "entirely free from all logical
conceptual content yet [containing] an infinite range of
meanings invoked by the musical nucleus of the line."

CM16  CLARK, HARRY HAYDN.  "Changing Attitudes in Early American
Literary Criticism," *Development of American Literary
Criticism*. ed. by Floyd Stovall, Chapel Hill: University
of North Carolina Press, 1959, 15-75.
Poe crusaded against puffing and was one of the first
American critics interested in formulating a body of
aesthetics which would focus on the work itself, particu-
larly on its structure or "design."

CM17  CODY, SHERMAN.  "Poe as Critic," Put, V (Jan. 1909), 438-40.
Advice to readers to look at all of Poe's work, not
just at selections which prove Griswold's charges.

CM18  COLBY, ROBERT A.  "Poe's 'Philosophy of Composition'," UKCR,
XX (1954), 211-14.
"'To Helen' and 'The Philosophy of Composition' really
represent two facets of Poe's aesthetical theory--its
symbolization and its abstract philosophical statement."

CM19  COOKE, A. L.  "Edgar Allan Poe, Critic," *Cornhill Magazine*,
CL (Nov. 1934), 588-97.
General account of Poe's critical theories.

CM20  COX, J. L.  "Poe as Critic," EJ, XXI (Nov. 1932), 757-63.

CM21  DAMERON, J. LASLEY and LOUIS CHARLES STAGG.  *An Index to Poe's*

*CM: Critical and Aesthetic Theories*

*Critical Vocabulary.* Hartford: Transcendental Books, 1966. Reprinted in ESQ, XLVI (I Quarter 1967), 1-51.

CM22 _____. "Poe and *Blackwood*'s Alexander Smith on Truth and Poetry," MissQ, XXII (1969), 355-9.
Poe's position that truth is more suited for prose than poetry is similar to a theory in Alexander Smith's essay, "The Philosophy of Poetry," Bl (Dec. 1835).

CM23 DE MILLE, GEORGE E. "Poe," *Literary Criticism in America.* New York: Dial Press, 1931, 86-118.
Compares Poe with Lowell and discusses Poe's attempt to subject the emotions to rational analysis, his "hysterical admiration" of second-rate writers, his warfare against "literary idiocy," his insistence on formulating aesthetic laws. De Mille credits him with being the first American critic to formulate a system of literary criticism, to make the short story a respectable form, and to develop a theory of poetry.

CM24 _____. "Poe as Critic," AM, IV (Apr. 1925), 433-40.
Emphasizes Poe's recognition that drama is the most realistic genre and suggests that he anticipated the late nineteenth-century movement toward realism and naturalism.

CM25 FAGIN, N. BRYLLION. "Poe--Drama Critic," *Theatre Annual* (1946), 23-8.

CM26 FOERSTER, NORMAN. "Edgar Allan Poe," *American Criticism.* New York: Houghton Mifflin, 1928, 1-52.
Detailed analysis of Poe's critical theories which claims that Poe allowed poetry to depict morality but not to preach it. The idea of a moral and aesthetic fusion in art is in his aesthetic theory as it was in his life.

CM27 _____. "Quantity and Quality in the Aesthetics of Poe," SP, XX (Jul. 1923), 310-35.
Poe's concept of the quantity of pleasure is contained in his theories about the unity and beauty of art (elements in achieving intensity). His theory about quality relates to his belief that the lyric poem must lead the poet to a perception of ideal beauty. The idea is Shelleyan not Platonic.

CM28 FOGLE, RICHARD H. "Organic Form in American Criticism, 1840-1870," *The Development of American Literary Criticism.* ed. by Floyd Stovall, Chapel Hill: University of North Carolina Press, 1955.

*CM: Critical and Aesthetic Theories*

Poe was a critical transcendentalist who destroyed "the organic synthesis of art and life, of truth and beauty." He focused not on Beauty itself, which is a shadow, but on the effect of Beauty--the psychological response of the reader to it. He reduced Coleridge's theory of symbolism to a theory of suggestiveness "without reference to what is suggested," thus developing aesthetics of form without content.

CM29   FRUIT, JOHN PHELPS. "Rationale of the Short Story According to Poe," PL, XVI (Mar. 1905), 57-65.
Brief, uninformative discussion of Poe's theories of the short story.

CM30   GARMON, GERALD M. "Emerson's 'Moral Sentiment' and Poe's 'Poetic Sentiment': a Reconsideration," PSt, VI (Jun.1973), 19-21.
"...the opinions of Emerson and Poe on art and morality are not so antithetical as has been suggested."

CM31   GINGERICH, SOLOMON F. "The Conception of Beauty in the Works of Shelley, Keats, and Poe," UMPLL, VIII (1932), 169-94.
Poe's theory of Beauty was more limited than that of Keats and Shelley. Poe failed to distinguish between the feeling of the heart and the excitement of the soul, and he eliminated moral and natural Beauty from his definition.

CM32   HART, LORING E. "The Beginnings of Longfellow's Fame," NEQ, XXXVI (Mar. 1963), 63-76.
Notes Poe's attacks on Longfellow.

CM33   KELLY, GEORGE. "Poe's Theory of Beauty," AL, XXVII (Jan. 1956), 521-36.
Discusses Poe's theory of Beauty as the basis of his theories of poetry. Poe's essential hypothesis is the hypostasis of Beauty as a "transempirical and ideal entity ...whose essence is beyond the empirical knowledge of humanity." The poet strives to apprehend and communicate this essence in poetry. Poe's purpose was "to establish a distinct area of mind devoted solely to converting perceptions of the beautiful into responses of pleasure."

CM34   _____. "Poe's Theory of Unity," PQ, XXXVII (Jan. 1958), 34-44.
Discusses the development of Poe's unity of effect.

CM35   KERN, A. A. "Poe's Theory of Poetry," *Bulletin of Randolph Macon Woman's College*, XIX (1932).

*CM: Critical and Aesthetic Theories*

CM36   KRUTCH, JOSEPH WOOD.  "Poe's Idea of Beauty," *Nation,* CXXII
          (Mar. 17, 1926), 285-7.
              Poe's criticism is highly personal, and its purpose is
          "to support a predetermined taste....He creates for his
          work a different significance by inventing an aesthetic
          which assigns to them new values."

CM37   LASER, MARVIN.  "The Growth and Structure of Poe's Concept of
          Beauty," ELH, XV (Mar. 1948), 69-84.
              Laser discusses the influence of Coleridge, Shelley's
          "Defense," and phrenology on the development of Poe's
          critical philosophy.  Poe turned to phrenology to explain
          Coleridge's distinction between fancy and imagination and
          his concept of pleasure and beauty.

CM38   _____.  "Poe's Critical Theories--Sense or Nonsense?" ESQ,
          XXXI (II Quarter 1963), 20-3.
              General review of Poe's critical theories concludes with
          emphasis on their shortcomings.  "Given the narrowness of
          his views and his interests, Poe obviously does not estab-
          lish a critical method which is applicable to the bulk of
          literature written before or since his time, whatever the
          genre."

CM39   LENTRICCHIA, FRANK.  "Four Types of Nineteenth-Century
          Poetic." *Journal of Aesthetics and Art Criticism,* XXVI
          (1968), 351-66.
              Discusses the Poe-Baudelaire aesthetic.

CM40   MABBOTT, T. O.  "A Review of Lowell's Magazine," N&Q, CLXXVIII
          (Jun. 29, 1940), 457-8.
              Reprint of Poe's review of Lowell's *Pioneer.*

CM41   MARKS, EMERSON.  "Poe as Literary Theorist: a Reappraisal,"
          AL, XXXIII (Nov. 1961), 296-306.
              Poe's shortcomings are his blindness "to the aesthetic
          value of a complex whole that resides in a writer's control
          of a great mass of material," his "ultra-romantic limita-
          tions of taste," his indifference to comedy and satire, his
          emphasis on originality, and his repudiation of didacticism.
          Certain of his theories, however, are valid today: his
          "preference for the functional over the merely decorative
          image," his pioneering efforts with problems of moral and
          cognitive values in art, and his efforts to define the
          nature of the creative process.

CM42   MENANDER.  "The Aesthetic of Poe," TLS (Jun. 17, 1944), 291.
              General remarks on Poe's poetry.

*CM: Critical and Aesthetic Theories*

CM43 MONROE, HARRIET. "Poe and Longfellow," *Poetry*, XXIX (Feb. 1927), 266-74.
     Believes that Poe fought singlehandedly against the poor taste of the reading public and the literary circles of the day, particularly the New England group.

CM44 MOORE, CHARLES L. "Poe's Place as a Critic," *Dial*, XXXIV (Feb. 16, 1903), 111-2.
     Poe's poetic principles are fallacious. In limiting the length of a poem, he denied the value of poetry by Aeschylus, Dante, and Shakespeare.

CM45 MOSSOP, D. J. "Poe's Theory of Pure Poetry," DUJ, XVII (Mar. 1956), 60-7.
     Poe distinguished not only between the elevation of the soul and the quickening of passions, but also between "the bitter sweet excitement of the soul" and the excitement aroused by the theme of the poem. The former is the true poetic sentiment, aroused by the dispassionate emotion in the poem. This distinction is too fine to be valuable. Poe confuses "the simple indulgence in the pleasing, impassioned emotion with the value of the poem itself."

CM46 MULQUEEN, JAMES E. "The Poetics of Emerson and Poe," ESQ, LV, part I (II Quarter 1969), 5-11.
     A close comparison of Emerson and Poe which concludes that "both poetics have their roots in systems of ontology," both regard the imagination as the faculty which can perceive the ideal unity, both found "the source of poetry in intuitions of ontological truths."

CM47 PAYNE, L. W. "Poe and Emerson," *Texas Review*, VII (Oct. 1921), 54-69.

CM48 POLLIN, BURTON R. "Du Bartas and Victor Hugo in Poe's Criticism," MissQ, XXIII (1969-70), 46-55.
     On Poe's inaccurate analysis of Du Bartas.

CM49 PRESCOTT, F. C. "Poe's Definition of Poetry," *Nation*, LXXXVIII (Feb. 4, 1909), 110.
     Discusses similarities in the aesthetic theories of Poe and Griswold.

CM50 PRITCHARD, JOHN PAUL. "Edgar Allan Poe," *Criticism in America*. Norman: University of Oklahoma Press, 1956, 70-86.
     Believes that with Poe, literary criticism got underway in America. "If younger critics could have availed themselves of his practice in the light of Emerson's theorizing,

*CM: Critical and Aesthetic Theories*

American criticism might have developed both wider and
deeper insights at an early stage of its history."

CM51     ____. "Edgar Allan Poe," *Return to the Fountains*. Durham:
Duke University Press, 1942, 26-44.
Pritchard discusses the Horatian and Aristotelian ele-
ments in Poe's work, which Poe acquired through Coleridge,
Schlegel, and Goethe, and his general indebtedness to
classical theories of criticism.

CM52     ____. "Horace and Edgar Allan Poe," <u>CW</u>, XXVI, (Mar. 6, 1933),
129-33.
Pritchard traces Horatian ideas in Poe's work.

CM53     ____. *Literary Wise Men of Gotham: Criticism in New York,
1815-1860*. Louisiana State University Press, 1963.
Mention of Poe in connection with New York literary
developments.

CM54 REGAN, ROBERT. "Hawthorne's 'Plagiary': Poe's Duplicity,"
<u>NCF</u>, XXV (Dec. 1970), 281-98.
Poe's accusation of plagiarism in his review of Hawthorne's *Twice Told Tales* is a spoof.

CM55 RICHARDSON, CHARLES F. "Poe's Doctrine of Effect," <u>UCPMP</u>, XI
(1922), 179-86.
Somewhat confused essay questioning the need for an
artist to concern himself only with unity of effect, which
is not "a very high aim, though often harmless and legiti-
mate--even useful."

CM56 SAN JUAN, E. JR. "The Form of Experience in the Poems of
Edgar Allan Poe," <u>GaR</u>, XXI (Spr. 1967), 65-80.
Believes Poe's poetics involves a "philosophy of life,
a complete world outlook. The recurrent tendency to essen-
tialize and reduce sensory impressions and material data
into forms of beauty may...characterize Poe's basic poetic
impulse."

CM57 SCHOETTLE, ELMER. "A Musician's Commentary on Poe's 'The
Philosophy of Composition'," *Forum* (Houston), IV (1964),
14-15.

CM58 SCHWARTSTEIN, LEONARD. "Poe's Criticism of William W. Lord,"
<u>N&Q</u>, CC, ns. 2 (Jul. 1955), 312.

CM59 SIMPSON, LEWIS R. "Touching 'The Stylus': Poe's Vision of
Literary Order," *Studies in American Literature*. ed. by

Waldo McNeir and Leo B. Levy, Baton Rouge: Louisiana
State University Press, 1960, 33-48.
Discusses Poe's efforts to establish the *Stylus,* a
dream of imposing literary order on American letters.

CM60 SMITH, BERNARD. "The Quest of Beauty in Romance: Poe," *Forces
in American Criticism.* New York: Harcourt Brace, 1939,
185-202.
Poe was a product of the Romantic movement, from which
he drew his ideas about sensationalism, the value of the
pure imagination, and his self-absorption. He accepted
myths of the agrarian South, banished didacticism from
literature, and confused truth with moral preaching. His
primary value lies in his effort to focus on the pleasurable aspects of literature in an overly moral age.

CM61 SMITH, H. E. "Poe's Extension of His Theory of the Tale,"
MP, XVI (Aug. 1918), 195-203.
Smith discusses the application of Poe's theory of the
short story to the novel and the relation of the two forms.
Poe's theories were expounded earlier than is generally
believed: in his 1836 review of *Sketches by Boz* and in his
comments on Lady Dacre's Winifred in *Countess of Nithsdale.*
The source of his ideas is probably Black's translation
of August William Schlegel's *Lectures on Dramatic Art and
Literature.*

CM62 SNELL, GEORGE. "First of the New Critics," QRL, II (1945),
333-40.
Rather vague and general essay on Poe's contribution to
literary criticism. Poe was the first to develop principles of textual criticism and had great integrity as a
critic.

CM63 SNYDER, E. D. "Poe and Amy Lowell," MLN, XLIII (Mar. 1928),
152-3.
In "The Rationale of Verse" Poe anticipated Amy Lowell's
theory of polyphonic prose (placing rhymes at unusual and
unanticipated intervals).

CM64 STEIN, ROGER B. *John Ruskin and Aesthetic Thought in America
1840-1900.* Cambridge, Massachusetts: Harvard University
Press, 1967, 83-5.

CM65 STOVALL, FLOYD. *American Idealism.* Norman: University of
Oklahoma Press, 1943.
Brief discussion of similarities between Poe's and
Emerson's theories of beauty. Both saw "in the beauty of

*CM: Critical and Aesthetic Theories*

nature a means by which the mind is led to a conception of absolute beauty...." Poe stands with American writers who contributed to the American theory of idealism. Poe and Emerson agreed that man's soul can transcend limitations of nature, and both mistrusted human understanding.

CM66 _____."Introduction," *The Development of American Literary Criticism*. Chapel Hill: University of North Carolina Press, 1955.

Considers Poe a "bulwark against the fallacious opinion, persisting to this day in Europe, that an American writer is not strictly American unless he breaks completely with the European tradition and renounces both its methods and its standards."

CM67 VARNER, J. G. "Poe and Miss Barrett of Wimpole Street," *Four Arts*, II (Jan. and Feb. 1935), 4-5, 14-15.

Discussion of Poe's unfavorable review of *The Drama of Exile and Other Poems*, Miss Barrett's reaction to it, and her opinion of Poe's poetry.

CM68 WALCUTT, CHARLES C. "The Logic of Poe," CE, II (Feb. 1941), 438-44.

Poe confused the cause of Beauty with its effect, insisting that Beauty is first an essence (and therefore the cause of poetry) and then the effect of a poem.

CM69 WELLEK, RENE. *A History of Modern Criticism 1750-1950*. III, New Haven and London: Yale University Press, 1965.

Describes Poe's lack of originality and coherence, but attributes to him the distinction of having suggested "the main motifs of much later thought on poetry."

CM70 WILSON, EDMUND. "Poe as a Literary Critic," *Nation*, CLV (Oct. 31, 1942), 452-3.

Poe fought American literary egotism, British injustices to American literature, and the New England literary monopoly. He resembles Shaw and Eliot in his vigorous, bold, and incisive criticism and in his insistence on formulating general critical principles. He wrote the only first-rate classical prose of his period.

CM71 WILSON, JAMES SOUTHALL. "Poe's 'Philosophy of Composition'," NAR, CCXXIII (Dec.-Jan.-Feb. 1927), 675-84.

Wilson reconstructs Poe's critical theories and discusses Poe's desire "to create a definite psychological state upon the consciousness of his readers." He also

*CM: Critical and Aesthetic Theories*

suggests that Schlegel's *Lectures on Dramatic Art* was a
source of Poe's aesthetic.

CM72　WINTER, WILLIAM. "Longfellow," *Old Friends*. New York:
　　　　Moffat, Yord & Co., 1909.
　　　　　　Poe's criticisms of Longfellow were hostile and un-
　　　　just, but Poe was a madman.

*See also* B133, B157, B161, CJ31, CJ36, CJ38, CJ54, CK144, CK205,
　　　　CK207, CK262, CK314, CO4, CO25.


*CN: Metrics*


CN1　ALLEN, GAY WILSON. "Edgar Allan Poe," *American Prosody*, New
　　　　York: American Book Company, 1935, 56-89.
　　　　　　Allen discusses Poe's erroneous belief that English
　　　　verse is quantitative not accentual and analyzes the
　　　　prosody of his major poems.

CN2　ALLEN, JAMES L. JR. "Stanza Pattern in the Poetry of Poe,"
　　　　TSL, XII (1967), 111-120.
　　　　　　Poe's stanzaic irregularities are "intentional and
　　　　purposeful outgrowths of his prosodic theory."

CN3　BELGION, MONTGOMERY. "The Mystery of Poe's Poetry," EIC, I
　　　　(Jan. 1951), 51-66.
　　　　　　General discussion of Poe's prosody.

CN4　CAPUTI, ANTHONY. "The Refrain in Poe's Poetry," AL, XXV
　　　　(May 1953), 169-78.
　　　　　　Caputi analyzes the refrains in "To One in Paradise,"
　　　　"Bridal Ballad," "Eldorado," "The Raven," "Ulalume," and
　　　　"The Bells." In his theory of the refrain, Poe emphasized
　　　　monotone and identity and experimented by varying the
　　　　context of the refrain and by using it to produce great
　　　　emotional excitement. Caputi also discovers a discrepancy
　　　　between Poe's poetical conception and his poetry.

CN5　GHISELIN, BREWSTER. "Reading Spring Rhythms," *Poetry*, LXX
　　　　(May 1947), 86-93.
　　　　　　Gerard Manly Hopkins called the meter of "The Raven"
　　　　double-nochaic-depodic verse.

CN6　HEARN, LAFCADIO. "Poe's Verse," *Interpretations of Literature*,
　　　　II, New York: Dodd, Mead & Co., 1917, 150-66.
　　　　　　Discussion of Poe's use of language, repetitions, sound,

revival of old Saxon words, and an analysis of "The Bells," the most musical poem of the nineteenth century.

CN7   LENHART, CHARMENZ.   "Poe and Music," *Music Influence on American Poetry*.   University of Georgia Press, 1956, 125-61.
      Detailed discussion of Poe's interest in music and his recognition of the religious importance of music and of the relationship between music and man's soul.  Poe believed that music is superior to poetry because it is more indefinite.  Lenhart examines Poe's effort to imitate music metrically, to ally sound and sense, and to achieve certain musical effects through feminine and identical rhymes, alliteration, and tone.

CN8   PETTIGREW, RICHARD C.   "Poe's Rime," AL, IV (May 1932), 151-9.
      Poe's poetry was not technically perfect.  He had a very narrow range of technical inventiveness and often resorted to imperfect vowel identity, imperfect identity of final consonants, identical rhymes, coining proper names to rhyme, and repetitions.  "Measured...by his own critical standard, Poe is decidedly inconsistent in his resort to poetic license of several kinds."

CN9   SCHLICHTER, NORMAN C.   "The Rhythm of Poe," *Poetry*, XXVIII (1937), 269-73.
      Poe's rhythms capture the rhythms of life and eternity.

CN10  WERNER, W. L.   "Poe's Theories and Practice in Poetic Technique," AL, II (May 1930), 157-65.
      Discussion of Poe's use of sound, his inconsistencies, his identical and false rhymes, condemnation of irregular meter, objections to violations of natural diction and archaisms.  Poe failed to attain perfect rhyme and stanzaic symmetry.

*See also* CL229, CL488, CM63, CP10.


*CO: Readings and Sources*


CO1   Anon.   "A List of Books from Poe's Library," N&Q, CC, ns. II (May 1955), 222-23.

CO2   ALLEN, MOZELLE S.   "Poe's Debt to Voltaire," UTSE, XV (1935), 63-75.

CO:   *Readings and Sources*


CO3   ALTERTON, MARGARET.  "An Additional Source of Poe's Critical
Theory," *University of Iowa Humanistic Studies,* II (1926).

CO4   _____.  "Origins of Poe's Critical Theory," *University of Iowa
Humanistic Studies,* II (Apr. 15, 1925).
Studies the influence of British periodicals (especially
B1) on Poe's critical theories and discovers that Poe
derived several ideas from stories in B1: types of horror
for effective writing, the Life-in-Death theme, the association of the Galvanic battery with anatomical dissection,
and the association of beauty with disease.  Poe was also
influenced by Schlegel and by the legal profession, which
taught him principles of beauty and logic.

CO5   BAILEY, J. O.  "Poe's 'Stonehenge'," SP, XXXVIII (Oct. 1941),
645-51.
"Some Account of Stonehenge, the Giants Dance, a Ruin
in England" is from Rees' *Cyclopaedia,* Vol. XXXV.

CO6   BAKER, H. T.  "Poe and Hazlitt," *Nation,* LXXXVII (Oct. 8,
1908), 335.
Poe was probably familiar with Hazlitt's work, expecially with Hazlitt's exposure of Campbell's plagiarism.

CO7   BENTON, RICHARD P.  "Poe's Acquaintance with Chinese Literature," PN, II (Apr. 1969), 34.
"If he did not know much about Chinese literature, at
least he knew something...."

CO8   _____.  "The Works of N. P. Willis as a Catalyst of Poe's
Criticism," AL, XXXIX (Nov. 1968), 315-24.
Willis inspired some of Poe's best criticism and
prompted him to develop two basic critical principles.

CO9   CAMPBELL, KILLIS.  "Marginalia on Longfellow, Lowell and
Poe," MLN, XLII (Dec. 1927), 516-21.
Several notes on Poe's sources and Griswold's forgeries.
A source of "Bon-Bon" is *Pantagruel,* Bk 2.

CO10  _____.  "Poe's Indebtedness to Byron," *Nation,* LXXXVIII (Mar.
11, 1909), 248-9.
Poe's work reflects a Byronic mood and imitates Byron's
general method and style.  Poe borrowed themes and language
from "Manfred," "Childe Harold," and "The Giaour."

CO11  _____.  "Poe's Reading," UTSE, V (1925), 166-96.
A survey of the books and authors Poe knew.

# EDGAR ALLAN POE: AN ANNOTATED BIBLIOGRAPHY

*CO: Readings and Sources*

CO12 _____. "Poe's Reading: Addenda and Corrigenda," UTSE, VII (1927), 175-80.

CO13 CARTER, BOYD. "Poe's Debt to Charles Brockden Brown," PrS, XXVII (Sum. 1953), 190-6.

CO14 COBB, PALMER. "The Influence of E. A. T. Hoffmann on the Tales of Edgar Allan Poe," SP, III (1908), 1-104.
Cobb examines various estimates of Poe's indebtedness to German literature, the influence of German literature in America 1830-1850, and Poe's knowledge of German. He compares Hoffmann's "Elixiere des Teufels" with Poe's "WW"; "Magnetiseur" with "Ragged Mountains"; "Die Jesuterkirche in G" with "The Oval Portrait"; and "Doge und Dogaressa" with "Assignation." Poe was attracted to Hoffmann by Scott's article on the German writer in FQR.

CO15 DAMERON, J. LASLEY. "Poe and *Blackwood's* on the Art of Reviewing," ESQ, XXXI (II Quarter 1963), 29-31.
Describes an essay in Bl (Nov. 1824) that may have influenced Poe's ideas about the methods of reviewing in British periodical literature.

CO16 _____. "Poe and *Blackwood's* Thomas Doubleday on the Art of Poetry," ESQ, XLIX (Dec. 1968), 540-2.
Influence of Doubleday's essay "How Far is Poetry an Art" (*Blackwood's*, XI, Feb. 1822) on Poe's aesthetics.

CO17 _____. "Poe's Reading of British Periodicals," MissQ, XVIII (Win. 1964-65), 19-25.
Reexamines Poe's indebtedness to British periodicals and extends Alterton's study.

CO18 DAUGHRITY, K. L. "Notes: Poe and *Blackwood's*," AL, II (Nov. 1930), 289-92.
The author traces Poe's use of Bl.

CO19 GRUENER, G. "Notes on the Influence of E.T.A. Hoffmann upon Edgar Allan Poe," PMLA, XIX (Mar. 1904), 1-25.
Discovers sources of Poe's tales in Hoffmann's works: The idea for "Tales of the Folio Club" came from *Rahmenerzahlung*; the title, "Tales of the Grotesque and Arabesque" came from an article by Sir Walter Scott in FQR, and there are similarities between *Metzengerstein in Das Majorat* and

*CO: Readings and Sources*

"FHU." Both Poe and Hoffmann employed the rhetorical device of repeating a speaker's words after the interpolated "he said" or "I say."

CO20 _____. "Poe's Knowledge of German," MP, II (Jun. 1904), 125-40.
Tries to prove that Poe's German was fluent. *See* CO43.

CO21 HAVILAND, THOMAS. "How Well did Poe Know Milton?" PMLA, LXIX (Sept. 1954), 841-60.
Poe rejected Milton's ideas about the place of truth in poetry, but in other areas their aesthetics are similar. Milton was a touchstone for Poe, who was influenced by his grandeur, organ tones, and inversions of natural word order.

CO22 HOLMS, HARRIET R. "What Did Mill Mean to Poe?" *Mill Newsletter,* VI (1971), 20-1.
Suggests a study on Poe's interest in John Stuart Mill.

CO23 JACKSON, DAVID K. "Poe's Knowledge of Law during the *Messenger* Period," AL, X (Nov. 1938), 331-9.
Jackson denies three claims in Alterton's *The Origins of Poe's Critical Theory:* that Poe studied legal methods to make his work convincing; that he was the law student for whom William Wirt published advice in the SLM; and that he wrote certain articles that Alterton attributes to him. *See* CO4.

CO24 JORDAN, HOOVER H. "Poe's Debt to Thomas Moore," PMLA, LXIII (Jun. 1948), 753-57.

CO25 LUBELL, ALBERT J. "Poe and A. W. Schlegel," JEGP, LII (Jan. 1953), 1-12.
Discussion of the influence of Schlegel's *Lectures on Dramatic Art and Literature* on Poe's aesthetics, particularly on his ideas about unity, totality of interest, and Greek drama.

CO26 MABBOTT, T. O. "Evidence that Poe Knew Greek," N&Q, CLXXXV (Jul. 27, 1943), 39-40.

CO27 _____. "Poe's Word 'Porphyrogene'," N&Q, CLXXVII (Dec. 2, 1939), 403.
The word comes from Gibbons' description of Constantine

*CO:Readings and Sources*

Porphyrogenitus in *Decline and Fall of The Roman Empire* and means "rightly ruling and cultured."

CO28 _____. "Puckle and Poe," N&Q, CLXIV (Mar. 25, 1933), 205-6.
Concerning references to and borrowings from James Puckle, English character writer.

CO29 MAROVITZ, SANFORD. "Poe's Reception of C. W. Weber's Gothic Western, 'Jack Long: or the Shot in the Eye'," PSt, IV (Jun. 1971), 11-13.
Discusses the appeal of this story to Poe.

CO30 MATTHEWS, JOSEPH CHESLEY. "Did Poe Read Dante?" UTSE, XVIII (1938), 123-36.
Poe probably read the *Inferno*, but most of his quotations from Dante are second hand.

CO31 MORE, PAUL ELMER. "Origins of Poe and Hawthorne," Ind, LIV (Oct. 16, 1902), 2453-60. Reprinted in *Shelburne Essays*. First series, Boston and New York: Houghton Mifflin, 1904, 51-70.
The literature of Poe and Hawthorne is deeply rooted in American culture and contributed to the tradition of Wigglesworth, Edwards, Freneau, and Brown. They derived their Gothicism from the religious supernaturalism of the Puritans which persisted, long after the religious tradition had eroded, in the symbolism of the national literature. Their popularity depends upon their substitution of symbols of fear and terror for Christian mythology no longer believed. *See* CK93, CO46.

CO32 NEWLIN, PAUL A. "Scott's Influence on Poe's Grotesques," ATQ, II (II Quarterly 1969), 9-12.
Traces a connection between Scott's literary principles, defined in "On the Supernatural in Fictitious Compositions," and Poe's.

CO33 NORMAN, EMMA K. "Poe's Knowledge of Latin," AL, VI (Mar. 1934), 72-77.
Poe quoted twenty-three Latin authors, including Horace, Ovid, and Virgil.

CO34 PERRY, MARVIN B. JR. "Keats and Poe," *English Studies in Honor of James Southall Wilson*. Richmond: William Byrd Press, 1951, 45-52.
On Keat's influence.

*CO: Readings and Sources*

CO35 PHILIPS, EDITH. "The French of Edgar Allan Poe," AS, II (Mar.
1927), 270-4.
Poe only knew a few French phrases, which he employed
again and again for effect. *See* CK22.

CO36 POCHMANN, HENRY A. "Germanic Materials and Motifs in the
Short Story: Edgar Allan Poe," *German Culture in America.*
Madison: University of Wisconsin Press, 1957, 388-408.
On the influence of German literature and culture on
Poe.

CO37 POLLIN, BURTON R. "Poe and Godwin," NCF, XX (Dec. 1965),
237-53.
Investigates Godwin's considerable influence on Poe's
work, especially in his use of alienated heroes, morbid
psychology and suspense. Poe, however, ignored Godwin's
social criticism.

CO38 _____. *"Poe as Miserrimus--*From British Epitaph to American Epithet," RLV, XXX (Jul.-Aug. 1967), 347-61.
Discusses the influence of the novel *Miserrimus* by
Frederick Manselle Reynolds on Poe. This is the Reynolds
to whom Poe referred on his deathbed.

CO39 _____. "Poe's Use of D'Israeli's *Curiosities* to Belittle
Emerson," PN, III (Dec. 1970), 38.
Poe's style of denegrating Emerson in Gr (Dec. 1846) is
drawn from D'Israeli's *Curiosities of Literature.*

CO40 RENDALL, V. "Dumas and Poe," TLS (Nov. 28, 1929), 1001.
Poe's detective stories may have been influenced by
Voltaire's "Le Vicomte de Bragelonne" and "Zadig."

CO41 SANDLER, S. GERALD. "Poe's Indebtedness to Locke's *An Essay
Concerning Human Understanding*," BUSE, V (Sum. 1961), 107-
21.
Traces the influence of Lockian ideas on "Morella,"
"Colloquy", "Purloined Letter," and *Eureka.* In the first
story, Poe modifies Locke's principle of personal identity;
in the second, he considers the philosophical implications
of perception, duration and time; in the third, the limitations of mathematical reasoning; and in *Eureka*, Poe comments on the methods of ancient philosophers and on Locke's
definition of infinity.

CO42 SCHICK, JOSEPH S. "Poe and Jefferson," VMHB, LIV (Oct. 1946),
316-20.

*CO: Readings and Sources*

Jefferson influenced Poe's style and ideas about education.

CO43   SCHREIBER, CARL F. "Mr. Poe at His Conjurations Again," Cpn,
       I, part 2 (May 1930).
           Poe only knew three pages of German although he tried to
       convince people that he knew much more. *See* CO20.

CO44   SCHWARTZSTEIN, LEONARD. "Poe's Critism of William W. Lord,"
       N&Q, CC (Jul. 1955), 312.
           "In one instance, at least, Poe charged plagiarism as a
       pretext for displaying his pretended learning."

CO45   STOVALL, FLOYD. "Poe's debt to Coleridge," UTSE, X (Jul.
       1930), 70-127.
           A long and detailed discussion of the influence of
       Coleridge on Poe's theories of art and on his important
       stories.

CO46   WOODBRIDGE, BENJAMIN M. "Supernaturalism in Hawthorne and
       Poe," *Colorado College Publication*, II (Nov. 1911), 135-
       54.
           Repudiates More's idea that like Hawthorne, Poe inher-
       ited an affinity for the supernatural from the Puritans.
       In Poe's stories, the ethical motif is missing, and he con-
       centrates only on sensation. Poe has greater affinity with
       German Romantics. Like them he has a penchant for romantic
       irony or self-parody, for sensations, an over-developed
       self-consciousness. *See* CO30.

*See also* B34, B76, B85, B86, B226, CC49, CJ6, CJ57, CK31, CK65,
       CK180, CK188, CK235, CK252, CK298, CM21, CM37, CM51, CM60,
       CM61, CS52.

*CP: Religious Themes*

CP1   ANON. "Religion of Edgar Allan Poe," CO, LXIX (Sept. 1920),
      408-10.
          Brief discussion of essay by C. Alphonso Smith. *See*
      CP8.

CP2   BAILEY, ELMER J. *Religious Thought in the Greater American
      Poets*. Boston and Chicago: The Pilgrim Press, 1922, 32-
      47.
          Poe's religious beliefs were vague and superficial, and
      his ideas about death and immortality not consistent.
      Basically, his conception of God was theistic.

# EDGAR ALLAN POE: AN ANNOTATED BIBLIOGRAPHY

*CP:Religious Themes*

CP3 CAMPBELL, KILLIS. "Poe's Knowledge of the Bible," SP, XXVII
(Jul. 1930), 546-51.
Although Campbell agrees that Poe was interested in theology and had a mystical bent, he refutes W. M. Forrest's
claim that Poe knew the Bible intimately and was profoundly
influenced by it. *See* CP6.

CP4 CHAPMAN, EDWARD M. "The Masters of Fiction--I," *English Literature in Account with Religion, 1800-1900*. Boston and
New York: Houghton Mifflin, 1910, 260-67.
View of Poe's work as a "genuine religious apologetic."
We see in his work "the misery of a man who has lost his
faith, who has been taken from the realm of light and
reason and been subject to daemonic influences."

CP5 EDGE, H. T. "Edgar Allan Poe as Seer," *Theosophical Path*, XI
(1937), 246-55.
Many of Poe's ideas were theosophic: his belief that
unity broke into multiplicity, that there is an infinite
number of universes and that the consciousness relaxes but
is not obliterated in death.

CP6 FORREST, WILLIAM M. *Biblical Allusions in Poe*. New York:
MacMillan, 1928.
Forrest sees all of Poe's work as a spiritual and moral
exercise reflecting his fundamental Pantheism, Vedantism
and Yoginism. Poe's interest in contemporary occult science is evidence that he was a mystic to whom only visions
were real. Forrest performs a valuable service to Poe
scholarship by disproving the popular notion that Poe was
ignorant of or disinterested in religion, but he completely overstates his case.

CP7 HALLINE, ALLAN G. "Moral and Religious Concepts in Poe,"
*Bucknell University Studies*, II (Jan. 1951), 120-50.
Occupies middle ground between critics who overestimates
Poe's interest in religion and the Bible and those who consider him amoral. Considers Poe a deist, and eventually a
pantheist (in *Eureka*), who believed in immortality, never
denied traditional Christianity, and tried to impart a
spiritual significance to scientific theories. Also believes that Poe was concerned with ethical problems. *See*
CP6 and CP8.

CP8 SMITH, C. ALPHONSO. "Poe and the Bible," *Davidson College
Magazine*, XXXVI (1920), 1-4; also in *Biblical Review*
(1920).

## CP: Religious Themes

Tends to overemphasize the influence of the Bible on Poe's work. Considers him a fundamentalist.

CP9 STROMBERG, JEAN S. "The Relationship of Christian Concepts to Poe's 'Grotesque' Tales," *Gordon Review* (Wenham, Massachusetts) XI (1968), 144-58.
Discusses Poe's use of Christianity and his distortion of Christian theory to convey "his central theme of dehumanized man."

CP10 STRONG, AUGUSTUS H. "Edgar Allan Poe," *American Poets and Their Theology*. Philadelphia: Griffith and Rowland Press, 1916, 159-206.
In a rather disorganized essay which discusses Poe's biography and prosody as well as his theology, Strong decides that Poe only pretended to be an atheist, that behind his torment was fear of God.

CP11 WELLS, GABRIEL. "Poe as a Mystic," ABC, V (Feb. 1934), 54-5.
Brief and highly subjective discussion about mysticism in Poe.

*See also* CK335.

## CQ: Reputation

CQ1 ANON. "Poe's new Reputation," UKCR, XIV (Oct. 1943), 17-19.

CQ2 _____. "Some Twentieth-Century Estimates of Poe," *American Review of Reviews* (Feb. 1909), 225-8.

CQ3 ALLEN, GAY WILSON. "American Criticism of Poe since the Poe Centenary," unpublished, 1931.
Warns against confusing Poe's work with his life, a failure of most Poe critics.

CQ4 CAMPBELL, KILLIS. "Contemporary Opinion of Poe," PMLA, XXXVI (Jun. 1921), 142-66.
Campbell concludes that Poe was known chiefly as a critic and short story writer but was ignored as a poet until after the publication of "The Raven" in 1845.

CQ5 DAMERON, J. LASLEY. "Poe at Mid-Century: Anglo-American Criticism. 1928-1960," BSUF, VIII (Win. 1967), 36-44.
Poe became recognized as a major literary figure during this period.

*CQ: Reputation*

CQ6   FRENCH, JOHN C. *In His Own Country*. Baltimore: J. H. Furst
      Co., 1939.
      French discusses Poe's reputation in Baltimore and the
      role that city played in the development of Poe's repu-
      tation.

CQ7   GOHDES, CLARENCE. *American Literature in Nineteenth-Century
      England*. Columbia University Press, 1944.
      Occasional reference to Poe's popularity in England.

CQ8   HUBBELL, JAY B. "Edgar Allan Poe," *Who Are the Major American
      Writers?* North Carolina: Duke University Press, 1972,
      51-57.
      Brief essay on Poe's reputation.

CQ9   HUGHES, DAVID. "The Influence of Poe," FortnR, ns. 964 (Nov.
      1949), 342-3.
      On Poe's popularity in England.

CQ10  LEVINE, STUART. "Scholarly Strategy: The Poe Case," AQ, XVII
      (1965), 133-44.
      Discusses the failure of Poe criticism and scholarship,
      making the point that it has not been cumulative.

CQ11  MOORE, RAYBURN. "Prophetic Sounds and Loud: Allen, Stovall,
      Mabbott, and Other Recent Work on Poe," GaR, XXV (Win.
      1971), 481-88.

CQ12  OWLETT, F. C. *Bibliophile,* II (Jan. 1909), 231-4.
      Regarding Poe's poor reputation in America.

CQ13  QUINN, PATRICK. "Poe and Nineteenth Century Poetry," *Amer-
      ican Literary Scholarship*. Durham, North Carolina: Duke
      University Press, 1970, 1971.
      Reviews and evaluates Poe scholarship for 1968 and 1969.

CQ14  REIN, DAVID M. "The Appeal of Poe Today," ESQ, LX (Fall 1970),
      29-33.
      Superficial and rather old-fashioned discussion of Poe's
      popularity. His work "is not only more true to reality
      than most horror fiction, but it is also better con-
      structed."

CQ15  ROBBINS, J. ALBERT. "Nineteenth-Century Poetry," *American
      Literary Scholarship: an Annual*. Durham, North Carolina:
      Duke University Press, 1965, 1966, 1967, 1968, 1969.
      Reviews and evaluates Poe scholarship in each volume
      from 1963 to 1967.

# Edgar Allan Poe: An Annotated Bibliography

### CQ: Reputation

CQ16 _____. "The State of Poe Studies," PN, I (Apr. 1968), 1-2.
"It is frustrating to see such quantities of scholarship on Poe add up to so little."

CQ17 THOMPSON, G. R. "The Poe Case: Scholarship and 'Strategy',"
PN, I (Apr. 1968), 3.

CQ18 TRENT, WILLIAM P. "Poe's Rank as a Writer," *East and West,* I
(Aug. 1900), 305-13.
Pedantic essay on Poe's popularity in Europe and
America.

*See also* Sections A, B, and CC *passim* and B176, B230, B260, B264,
B265, CB11, CB35, CK165.


### CR: Influence

CR1 ANON. "The Underground Reputation of Ambrose Bierce," CurLit,
XLVII (Sept. 1909), 279-80.

CR2 APPEL, ALFRED JR. *Vladimir Nabokov: The Annotated Lolita.*
New York, 1970.
Points out more than twenty references to Edgar Allan
Poe in *Lolita.*

CR3 BRADLEY, SCULLEY. "Poe on the New York Stage in 1855," AL,
IX (Nov. 1937), 353-4.
*The Bankrupt,* by George Henry Boker, is indebted to Poe
for two devices: the cryptogram and the use of induction in
solving the crime.

CR4 BRASHER, THOMAS L. "A Whitman Parody of 'The Raven'?" PN, I
(Oct. 1968), 30.
The parody, which appeared in the *Brooklyn Daily Eagle,*
was probably written by Whitman.

CR5 CAMPBELL, FELICIA F. "A Princedom by the Sea," *Lock Haven
Review,* X (1968), 39-46.
Allusions to Poe in *Lolita.*

CR6 CHARI, V. K. "Poe and Whitman's Short-Poem Style," WWR, XIII
(Sept. 1967), 95-97.
Poe's possible influence on Whitman.

CR7 COLWELL, JAMES and GARY SPITZER. "'Bartelby' and 'The Raven':
Parallels of the Irrational," GaR, XXIII (Spr.1969),37-43.

*CR: Influence*

Comparison of the two works in terms of method,
structure, devices, mood and the theme of negation.


CR8   DAMERON, J. LASLEY.   "Symbolism in the Poetry of Poe and
      Stephen Crane," ESQ, LX (Fall 1970), 22-9.
         Discusses both poets' use of the bizarre, of paradoxes,
      of the unworldly, of landscape imagery to invoke despair
      and antipathy to the real world.


CR9   DAVISON, NED J.   "'The Raven' and 'Out of the Cradle End-
      lessly Rocking'," PN, I (Apr. 1968), 5.
         Discusses similarities in diction, symbol and episode.


CR10  DEFALCO, JOSEPH.   "Whitman's Changes in 'Out of the Cradle'
      and Poe's 'Raven'," WWR, XVI (1970), 22-7.
         Whitman revised certain lines to emphasize his optimism
      over Poe's pessimism.


CR11  DUBOIS, ARTHUR E.   "Poe and *Lolita*," CEA Critic, XXVI (Mar.
      1964), 7.
         Numerous references to Poe's work in *Lolita* are pointed
      out.


CR12  FABRE, MICHEL.   "Black Cat and White Cat: Richard Wright's
      Debt to Edgar Allan Poe," PSt, IV (Jun. 1971), 17-19.


CR13  HAVERSTICK, IOLA S.   "A Note on Poe and *Pym* in Melville's
      *Omoo*," PN, II (Apr. 1969), 37.
         Possible influence of NAGP on Melville.


CR14  HAYFORD, HARRISON.   "Poe in the Confidence Man," NCF, XIV
      (Dec. 1959), 207-19.
         The passenger who appears in the conversation between
      the confidence man (as cosmopolitan) and Mark Winsome
      is Edgar Allan Poe.


CR15  HILL, JOHN.   "Poe's 'The Fall of the House of Usher' and Frank
      Norris' Early Short Stories," HLQ, XXVI (Nov. 1962), 111-12.
         Discusses a parallel between "FHU" and Norris' "A Case
      for Lombroso" and "His Single Blessedness."

CR16  HINDUS, MILTON. "Whitman and Poe: a Note," WWN, III (1957), 5-6.
         Compares "The Raven" with "Out of the Cradle Endlessly
      Rocking," especially with regard to their treatment of
      death.

*CR: Influence*

CR17  HOWARTH, HERBERT.  "Laurence Durrell and Some Early Masters,"
      *Books Abroad,* XXXVII (Win. 1963), 5–11.
          Durrell is indebted to Poe for sensibility, rhythm and
      shock.

CR18  JACKSON, D. K. "An Estimate of the Influences of the *Southern
      Literary Messenger,*" SLM, (1939), 508–14.
          During Poe's editorship, the periodical set a high
      standard for itself and for rival publications.  "...no
      doubt his criticism had a beneficent influence on American
      authors and the reading public."

CR19  KENNEDY, J. GERALD.  "Jeffrey Aspern and Edgar Allan Poe: A
      Speculation," PSt, VI (Jun. 1973), 17–18.
          Poe may have been the prototype for Jeffrey Aspern.
      "The dead poet might thus be said to serve a symbolic
      purpose, in that Aspern, like Poe, represented that
      deplorable deficiency in American culture which led James
      to expatriation."

CR20  KRONEGGER, MARIA ELISABETH.  *James Joyce and Associated Image
      Makers.*  New Haven: College and University Press, 1968.
          Detailed analysis of the imagery of James Joyce,
      "Joyce's imagistic kinship to Edgar Allan Poe," and a
      comparison of Joyce and Poe to impressionists, post-
      impressionists and surrealists.

CR21  _____. "Joyce's Debt to Poe and the French Symbolists," RLC,
      XXXIX (1965), 243–54.
          Influence of Poe's principles of composition on the
      French Symbolists and Joyce.

CR22  _____. "The Theory and Unity of Effect in the Works of Edgar
      Allan Poe and James Joyce," RLC, XL (1966), 226–34.

CR23  LAUTER, PAUL.  "The Narrator of 'The Blessed Damozel'," MLN,
      LXXIII (May 1958), 344–8.
          Discussion of Poe's influence on Rossetti's poetry.

CR24  MABBOTT, T. O.  "Echoes of Poe in Rossetti's 'Beryl Song',"
      N&Q, CLXVI (Mar. 10, 1934), 171.

CR25  _____. "George H. Derby: A Debt to Poe," N&Q, CLXVI (Mar.
      1934), 171.
          Derby used the motto of "How to Write a Blackwood
      Article" as the motto for "Phoenixiana."

CR26  _____. "Joel Chandler Harris: a Debt to Poe," N&Q, CLXVI

*CR: Influence*

(Mar. 3, 1934), 151.
>Harris took the title of one of his stories from Poe's "One-Thousand-and-Second Tale of Scheherazade."

CR27 MARKS, A. H. "Two Rodericks and Two Worms: 'Egotism, or the Bosom Serpent' as Personal Satire," PMLA, LXXIV (Dec. 1959), 607-12.
>Two passages in Hawthorne's story refer to Poe, indicating that Hawthorne wrote the tale to "criticize through personal satire Poe's outlook on literature and life."

CR28 MARVIN, F. R. "Maupassant and Poe," *Fireside Papers,* Boston, 1915.

CR29 McALEER, JOHN J. "Poe and the Gothic Elements in *Moby Dick*," ESQ, XXVII (II Quarter 1962), 34.

CR30 MICHAEL, MARY KYLE. "Stevenson and Poe," *Exercise Exchange,* XIV (1966-67), 21.
>A comparison of Stevenson's essay "El Dorado" with Poe's poem "Eldorado."

CR31 MILLER, A. C. "The Influence of Edgar Allan Poe on Ambrose Bierce," AL, IV (May 1932), 130-50.
>Bierce borrowed Poe's critical theories, short stories, plot techniques, and treatment of the supernatural; but he usually modified what he borrowed and combined different themes from Poe with great effect.

CR32 PHILLIPS, ELIZABETH. "The Hocus-Pocus of *Lolita*," *Literature and Psychology,* X (Sum. 1960), 97-101.
>On Poe as inspiration for the novel. "...*Lolita* is a satire in an orthodox Freudian view of the life and writings of Edgar Allan Poe."

CR33 PRIOR, LINDA. "A Further Word on Richard Wright's Use of Poe in *Native Son*," PN, V (Dec. 1972), 52-3.
>Cites evidence of Poe's influence on Wright.

CR34 PROFFER, CARL R. *Keys to Lolita.* Bloomington: Indiana University Press, 1968, 34-45.
>On allusions to Poe in *Lolita.*

CR35 REILLY, JOHN E. "Poe in Pillory: an Early Version of a Satire by A. J. Duganne," PSt, VI (Jun. 1973), 9-12.
>Reprints the lines lampooning Poe.

CR36 RUBIN, LARRY. "An Echo of Poe in *Of Time and the River*," PN,

III (Dec. 1970), 38-9.
Questionable analysis of Poe's influence on Wolfe.

CR37 RUBIN, LOUIS. "Edgar Allan Poe: a Study in Heroism," *The Curious Death of the Novel*. Baton Rouge: Louisiana State University Press, 1967, 47-67.
Vague essay asserting that images in T. S. Eliot's *The Wasteland* are derived from "FHU."

CR38 RUNDEN, JOHN P. "Rossetti and a Poe Image," N&Q, CCIII ns. 5 (Jun. 1958), 257-8.
Similarity between "To Helen" and "The Portrait," 1847.

CR39 SCHERTING, JACK. "The Bottle and the Coffin: Further Speculations on Poe and *Moby Dick*," PN, I (Oct. 1968), 22.
Traces elements of "MSFB" in Melville's novel.

CR40 _____. "Poe's 'The Cask of Amontillado': a Source for Twain's 'The Man That Corrupted Hadleyburg'," *Mark Twain Journal*, XVI (Sum. 1972), 18-20.

CR41 SMITH, REED. "The History of the Detective Story," NCR, (Oct. 6, 1912), 3-10.
Brief remarks on Arthur Conan Doyle's debt to Poe.

CR42 SNELL, GEORGE. "Poe Redivivus," ArQ, I (Sum. 1945), 49-57.
A discussion of Poe's considerable influence on Ambrose Bierce and Lafcadio Hearn in matters of form, style, and aesthetic theory.

CR43 SPROUT, MONIQUE. "The Influence of Poe on Jules Verne," RLC, XLI (Jan.-Mar. 1967), 37-53.
Verne was indebted to Poe for method, incident and character.

CL44 STERN, SEYMOUR. "Griffith and Poe," *Films in Review*, II (Nov. 1951), 23-28.
Stern discusses Poe's influence on the film producer D. W. Griffith.

CR45 STEVENS, ARETTA J. "Faulkner and 'Helen'--a Further Note," PN, I (Oct. 1968), 31.
Discusses a Poe image in *The Hamlet*.

CR46 STONE, EDWARD. *A Certain Morbidness*. Carbondale: Southern Illinois University Press, 1969, 140-168.
Compares Poe and Faulkner and discusses the use of association and stream-of-consciousness in "Murders."

*CR: Influence*

CR47 STRONKS, JAMES. "A Poe Source for Faulkner? 'To Helen' and
'A Rose for Emily'," *PN*, I (Apr. 1968), 11.
Relieves that Faulkner derived descriptions of Emily
from Poe's poem.

CR48 THOMAS, J. D. "Composition of Wilde's *The Harlot House*," *MLN*,
LXV (Nov. 1950), 485-8.
Possible sources are "FHU" and "Masque."

CR49 TRAVIS, MILDRED. "The Idea of Poe in *Pierre*," *ESQ*, L (I Quarter 1968), 59-62.
Melville integrates and comments upon Poe's life and
critical theories in *Pierre*. "He seems to use Poe's life
and works as an objective correlative of the suffering
artist whom he both pities and satirizes and, further,
whose fate he fears." Pierre's tragic mistake, like Poe's,
was his belief that he could choose beauty and neglect
truth.

CR50 TUTTLETON, JAMES W. "The Presence of Poe in *This Side of
Paradise*," *ELN*, III (Jun. 1966), 284-9.
Suggests that the book is laced with allusions to Poe's
life, poetry and tales.

CR51 _____. "A Note on 'The Bell-Tower': Melville's 'Blackwood
Article'," *PSt*, VI (Jun. 1973), 28-9.
Similarities in these stories and others by Melville
"suggest that Poe's stories gave Melville direction and
detail for a critical (if wit-laden) comment on the craft
of writing."

CR52 WAGES, JACK D. "Isaac Asimov's Debt to Edgar Allan Poe," *PSt*,
VI (Jun. 1973), 29.

CR53 WOOD, CLEMENT. "The Influence of Lanier and Poe on Modern
Literature," *SLM*, I (Apr. 1939), 237-42.
Poe was the chief innovator of the short story, science
fiction, and detective fiction. He taught writers to speak
out, not to be hypocritical, and to use contemporary speech
patterns.

CR54 WOODWARD, ROBERT H. "Poe's Raven, Faulkner's Sparrow, and
Another Window," *PN*, II (Apr. 1969), 37-8.
A brief paragraph on the Quentin section of *The Sound
and the Fury* contains imagery which Faulkner found in
"The Raven."

*See also* CB25, CK71, CK94, CK105-6, CK135, CK163, CK188, CK208, CK258,
CK289, CK317, CL176, CL193, CL195, CL381, CM62, and section
CS *passim*.

*CS: Foreign Reception and Influence*

GENERAL

CS1 ANON. "Poe's Centenary," <u>BPLQ</u>, I (Oct. 1949), 151-5.
Brief review of Poe's reputation in Europe. His popularity there depends on his themes of fear, terror, love
and death--themes which appeal to the English taste for
the neo-Gothic.

CS2 BANDY, WILLIAM T. *The Influence and Reputation of Edgar
Allan Poe in Europe*. Lecture at the 37th Annual Commemo-
ration of the Edgar Allan Poe Society, Oct. 1959; the
Edgar Allan Poe Society of Baltimore, Inc., 1962.
Discusses Poe's influence in Europe, which began in
France in 1844 with the publication of a short story based
on "WW" and identifies G.B., the French adapter of Poe's
tales, as Gustave Brunet. Bandy also assesses Poe's
influence on Baudelaire (largely exaggerated), Mallarmé,
Valéry and Jules Verne and his reputation in Germany,
Russia and Spain. Although Russia is not far behind France
in admiration for Poe, his reputation there has been im-
peded by Soviet theories about social realism.

CS3 _____. *A Tentative Checklist of Translations of Poe's Works*.
Madison, Wisconsin, 1959.
Translations in French, Russian, German, Danish, Span-
ish, Swedish, Rumanian, Latin, Italian, Polish, Hungarian,
Greek, Norwegian, Czech. Only the French and Spanish
sections are complete.

CS4 GOHDES, CLARENCE. "The Reception of Some Nineteenth-Century
American Authors in Europe," *The American Writer and the
European Tradition*. Minneapolis: University of Minnesota
Press, 1950.
One paragraph discussion of Poe's extensive influence
on Parnassian, Symbolist and Surrealist literature in
Europe.

*See also* B4, CJ70.

CZECHOSLOVAKIA

CS5 BABLER, O. F. "Czech Translations of Poe's 'The Raven'," <u>N&Q</u>,
CXCII (May 31, 1947), 235.

FRANCE

CS6 ANON. "The Art Named Symbolist," *New York Times* (Nov.19,1893).
Brief note on Baudelaire's interest in Poe.

*CS: Foreign Reception and Influence*

CS7   \_\_\_\_\_. "Baudelaire and Poe," B1, CXCIII (Mar. 1913), 417-19.
      Brief comparison of the careers and writings of the two men.

CS8   ALEXANDER, JEAN. *Affidavits of Genius. Edgar Allan Poe and the French Critics: 1847-1924.* Port Washington, New York: Kennikat Press, 1971.
      Anthology of French criticism of Poe, including essays by Forgues, Baudelaire, Renaud, Mallarmé and Valéry, with detailed introduction on the Poe myth in France.

CS9   \_\_\_\_\_. "Poe's 'For Annie' and Mallarmé's 'Nuit d'Idumée'," MLN, LXXVII (Dec. 1962), 534-6.
      A discussion of Mallarmé's interpretation of Poe's poem.

CS10   ANICHKOV, E. "Baudelaire and Edgar Poe," *Contemporary World,* II (1909), 75-100.
      Poe's distinguishing feature is his cool analytical power, which enables him to emerge from a moment of hot passion a detached yankee.

CS11   BALAKIAN, ANNA. "Influence and Literary Fortune: The Equivocal Junction of Two Methods," *Yearbook of Comparative and General Literature,* No. 11 (1962), 24-31.
      Brief notes on Poe's influence on Baudelaire.

CS12   BANDY, W. T. "Baudelaire and Poe," *Texas Quarterly,* Supp. to I (1958), 28-35.
      Summary of Beaudelaire's interest in Poe.

CS13   \_\_\_\_\_. *Baudelaire and Poe: An Exhibition in Conjunction with the Inauguration of the Center for Baudelaire Studies* (Furman Hall, Vanderbilt University) Apr. 9-13, 1969.
      Catalogue of one hundred items in the Poe-Baudelaire collection at the Center for Baudelaire Studies.

CS14   \_\_\_\_\_. "An Imaginary Translation of Poe," RLC, XXXIII (1959), 87-90.
      Regarding an 1846 French translation of Poe.

CS15   \_\_\_\_\_. "A New Light on Baudelaire and Poe," YFS, no. 10 (Aut. 1952), 65-9.
      Baudelaire took information for his 1852 essay on Poe from two articles by J. M. Daniel in the SLM (Nov. 1849 and Mar. 1850).

CS16   \_\_\_\_\_. "Poe's Secret Translator: Amédée Pichot," MLN, LXXIX (Mar. 1964), 277-80.

*CS: Foreign Reception and Influence*

Translation of "The Gold Bug" into "Le Scarabée d'or" in 1844 by Amédée Pichot.

CS17 BAUDELAIRE, CHARLES. *BAUDELAIRE ON POE.* trans. and ed. by Lois and Francis E. Hyslop. Pennsylvania: Bald Eagle Press 1952.
Contains Baudelaire's three essays on Poe (1852, 1856, 1857), the Prefaces to "Mesmeric Revelation," "Berenice," "The Philosophy of Furniture," "The Raven," "Hans Pfaall," and a list of Poe's works translated by Baudelaire.

CS18 _____. "New Notes on Edgar Allan Poe," Preface to *Nouvelles histoires extraordinaires par Edgar Poe.* trans. by Lois and Francis Hyslop, 1857. Reprinted in CN16.
Poe was stifled by the "American atmosphere...a greedy world, hungry for material things." He saw through the lies of democracy. His central theme is perversity; he "imperturbably affirmed the natural wickedness of man."

CS19 BURCH, FRANCIS F. "Poe's French Centenary," *Month,* XVI (Dec. 1956), 330-3.
Brief description of Poe's immense influence on French literature since 1845.

CS20 CAMBIAIRE, C. P. "The Influence of Edgar Allan Poe in France," RR (Oct.-Dec. 1926), 319-37.
Camiaire reviews Poe's influence on the Parnassians, the symbolists, Decadents, Neo-Classicists, and the Vers-Librists, and specifically on Baudelaire, Rimbaud, Mallarmé, Verlaine, Hauptmann, Gautier, Maupassant, and Villiers de l'Isle-Adam.

CS21 DuBOS, CHARLES. "Poe and the French Mind," Ath, No. 4732 (Jan. 7, 14, 1921), 26-7, 54-5.
Attempts to explain what Poe had in common with the French. Both tended to reduce the spiritual to the physical, to replace originality with contrivances and to push an idea as far as it can go.

CS22 FORTIER, ALICE. "Poe in France," ABUV, II, third series (1909), 161-70.
Traces the appearance of Poe's stories in France from 1841 and discusses Poe's influence on Baudelaire, Gautier, de Maupassant, Mallarmé, and Rostand.

CS23 HASWELL, HENRY. "Baudelaire's Self-Portrait of Poe: 'Edgar Allan Poe: sa vie et ses ouvrages'," *Romance Notes,* X

*CS: Foreign Reception and Influence*

(1969), 253-61.
Baudelaire's image of Poe is discussed.

CS24 HYSLOP, LOIS and FRANCIS. "Introduction," *Baudelaire on Poe:
Critical Papers*. trans. and ed. by Lois and Francis E.
Hyslop, Jr. State College, Pennsylvania: Bald Eagle Press,
1952.
Baudelaire was attracted to Poe's love of the exotic,
to his morbid subjects and to his tragic life. He appre-
ciated Poe's desire to ban didacticism and utilitarianism
from poetry and his idea that perversity is a primitive
impulse of the human heart. Baudelaire believed that Poe
deliberately induced drunken stupors to write better and
to attain visions.

CS25 JONES, P. MANSELL. "Poe and Baudelaire: 'The Affinity',"
MLR, XL (Oct. 1945), 279-83.
Baudelaire responded to Poe's love of exotic, morbid
subjects, his tragic life, his idea that perversity is a
primitive impulse of the human heart, his desire to eliminate didactic poetry, his love of the beautiful, and his
deliberate attempt to invoke visions through drunken
stupors. Their affinity lies in their involvement with
"that type of spiritual polarity, that violent contrast of
moods, which he called 'Spleen et Idéal,' the pull of a
world of evil, hardship, deception, ennui exerted upon the
aspirations of the spirit...a sense of radical pathological
ambivalence."

CS26 _____. "Poe and Baudelaire and Mallarmé: a Problem of Literary
Judgement," MLR, XXXIX (Jul. 1944), 236-46.
Baudelaire responded to Poe very subjectively--ignoring
his lack of taste, technical crudities, sentimentality and
melodrama. He believed that Poe was in control of his art,
and he admired Poe's craftsmanship.

CS27 JONES, RHYS S. "The Influence of Poe on Paul Valéry Prior to
1900," CLS, XXI-XXII (1946), 10-15.

CS28 LOCKSPEISER, EDWARD. "Debussy and Edgar Allan Poe," *Listener*,
LXVIII (Oct. 18, 1962), 609-19.
"...together with the influence of Wagner the dream-like
symbolism in Poe's tales became the most vital stimulating
factor in Debussy's imagination."

CS29 _____. "Debussy's Dream House," *Opera News*, XXXIV (Mar. 21,
1970), 8-12.
Poe's influence on Debussy.

*CS: Foreign Reception and Influence*

CS30 MORRIS, G. D. "French Criticism of Poe," <u>SAQ</u>, XIV (Oct.1915), 324-9.
    Study of negative French criticism of Poe since 1853.

CS31 MOSS, SIDNEY P. "Poe as Probabilist in Forgues' Critique of the *Tales*," <u>ESQ</u>, LX (Fall 1970), 4-13.
    Reprint and analysis of Forgues' essay on Poe (<u>RDM</u>, Oct. 15, 1846).

CS32 NIESS, R. J. "Letter from Stéphane Mallarmé," <u>MLN</u>, XLV (May 1950), 339-41.
    Translation of letter from Mallarmé to Sarah Helen Whitman.

CS33 PAGE, CURTIS H. "Poe in France," *Nation,* LXXXVIII (Jan. 14, 1909), 32-4.
    Poe's popularity in France rests in his devotion to art for art's sake, in the perversity and grotesqueness of his work, and in his logic.

CS34 QUINN, PATRICK F. *Poe and France: The Last Twenty Years.* Baltimore: Edgar Allan Poe Society and the Enoch Pratt Free Library, 1970.
    On French criticism of Poe.

CS35 RHODES, S. A. "The Influence of Poe on Baudelaire," <u>RR</u>, XVIII (Oct. to Dec. 1925), 329-33.
    Poe had little influence on Baudelaire.

CS36 RICHARD, CLAUDE. "Poe's Studies in Europe: France," <u>PN</u>, II (Jan. 1969), 20-23.
    Review of French scholarship.

CS37 _____, JEAN-MARIE BONNET and PATRICK F. QUINN. "Raising the Wind: or the French Editions of the Works of Edgar Allan Poe," <u>PN</u>, I (Apr. 1968), 11-13.

CS38 ROSE, MARILYN G. "'Emmanuèle'--'Morella': Gide's Poe Affinities," <u>TSLL</u>, V (Spr. 1963), 127-37.
    Poe was the source of Gide's "principle characterizations and conventions of his early work."

CS39 ROSSELET, JEANNE. "Poe in France," *Poe in Foreign Languages and Tongues.* ed. by John Calvin French. Baltimore: Johns Hopkins Press, 1941.
    Rather general remarks on Poe's influence on Baudelaire, Mallarmé and Valéry.

# Edgar Allan Poe: An Annotated Bibliography

*CS: Foreign Reception and Influence*

CS40 SAMUEL, DOROTHY J. "Poe and Baudelaire, Parallels in Form
and Symbol," <u>CLAJ</u>, III (Dec. 1959), 88-105.
Relates similarities in their life and work.

CS41 SCHNEIDER, JOSEPH. "French Appreciation of Edgar Allan Poe,"
<u>CER</u>, XXV (Sept. 1927), 427-37.
In a comprehensive discussion of Poe's French reputation, Schneider concludes that French appreciation generally rests on his least admirable qualities. Schneider
believes that Etienne made the most valuable contribution
to Poe criticism in France.

CS42 SCHWARTZ, W. L. "The Influence of Edgar Allan Poe on Judith
Gautier," <u>MLN</u>, XLII (Mar. 1927), 171-3.
The influence came by way of Baudelaire's translation
of Poe.

CS43 STONIER, G. W. "Books in General," <u>NSN</u>, XXIV (Aug. 29,1942),
143.
If it had not been for Baudelaire, Poe would have been
forgotten.

CS44 TURQUET-MILNES, GLADYS R. *The Influence of Baudelaire in
France and England.* London: 1913, 63-72.

CS45 VALÉRY, PAUL. "On Poe's *Eureka*," trans. by Malcolm Cowley,
*Variety,* I (1927), 123-37. Reprinted in CJ16.
Discusses *Eureka* as "one of the rare modern examples
of a total explanation of the material and spiritual
universe, a <u>cosmogony</u>."

CS46 VIRTANEN, REINO. "Allusions to Poe's Poetic Theory in
Valéry's *Cahiers,*" *Poetic Theory/Poetic Practice.* ed. by
Robert Scholes. Iowa City: Midwest Modern Language Asso-
ciation, 1969.
Analysis of the influence of Poe's poetic theories on
Valéry.

CS47 _____. "Irradiations of *Eureka:* Valéry's Reflections on Poe's
Cosmology," <u>TSL</u>, VII (1962), 17-25.
Discusses Valéry's appreciation of *Eureka* in *Cahiers.*

CS48 WETHERILL, P. M. "Edgar Allan Poe and Madame Sabatier," <u>MLQ</u>,
XX (Dec. 1959), 334-59.
Concerning Poe's influence on Baudelaire's Sabatier
cycle.

*See also* B74, B229, B230, CJ18, CJ61, CK109, CK188, CR21.

# Edgar Allan Poe: An Annotated Bibliography

## CS: Foreign Reception and Influence

### GERMANY

CS49 ANON. "Poe, the Pathfiner, a German Poet's Worshipful Tribute," CO, LXII (Feb. 1917), 121-3.
Discussion of Hans Heinz Ewer's essay, which praises Poe as a forerunner of significant tendencies in modern literature.

CS50 BABLER, O. F. "German Translations of Poe's 'The Raven'," N&Q, CLXXIV (Jan. 1, 1938), 9-10.
Babler prints several German translations of "The Raven" to prove how difficult it is to translate this poem.

CS51 COBB, PALMER. "Edgar Allan Poe and Friedrich Spielhagen: Their Theory of the Short Story," MLN, XXV (Mar. 1910), 67-72.
According to Spielhagen, the criterion of excellence by which Poe measured all genres was their ability to excite by elevating the soul. In recognizing Poe's constructive genius, Spielhagen anticipated by several decades the most recent Poe critics. His theory of the short story is a restatement of Poe's theory of lyric poetry, and he is responsible for transmitting this doctrine to Germany.

CS52 _____. "Poe and Hoffmann," SAQ, VIII (Jan. 1909), 68-81.
Poe and Hoffmann "share a view of the world which eliminates the commonplace and glorifies the marvelous" and a belief in the reality of the supernatural. In addition, they both treat the theme of double existence, hypnotism, and metempsychosis. Cites similarities between "WW" and "Elixirs of the Devil," "Ragged Mountains" and "The Hypnotist."

CS53 EDMUNDS, A. J. "German Translations of Poe's 'The Raven'," N&Q, CLXXIV (Feb. 5, 1938), 106.
Concerning *Four American Poems,* translated into German by Charles Theodore Eben, 1864.

CS54 EDWARD, GEORG. "Poe in Germany," ABUV, II, third series (1909), 170-83.
Discusses German editions and translations of Poe's work and the first German study of Poe by Friedrich Spielhagen in 1860. Germany regards Poe as a modern author and the "most characteristic American poet," who understood American life, its criminal tendencies and the pathological side of American temperament. He was destroyed by Northern industrialism.

# Edgar Allan Poe: An Annotated Bibliography

*CS: Foreign Reception and Influence*

CS55  GROLIG, MORIZ. *Edgar Allan Poe: Bibliographie*. Minden: J. C. C. Bruns, hofbuchlandlung, 1907, 181-236.

CS56  HEWITT-THAYER, HARVEY. *American Literature as Viewed in Germany*. Chapel Hill: University of North Carolina Press, 1958.
    Brief notes rather than developed discussion.

CS57  LAST, R. W. "Eliot, Poe and Usinger," *Affinities: Essays in German and English Literature*. London: Wolff, 1971, 346-53.
    On Usinger's analysis of Poe.

CS58  MABBOTT, T. O. "German Translations of Poe's 'The Raven'," N&Q, CLXXIV (Jan. 29, 1838), 88.
    Brief notes on translations of Poe's work into Spanish and German.

CS59  MITCHELL, McBURNEY. "Poe and Spielhagen: Novelle and Short Story," MLN, XXIX (Feb. 1914), 36-41.
    Denies Palmer Cobb's theory that Spielhagen introduced Poe's theory of the short story to Germany. Spielhagen, who spoke disparagingly of most of Poe's stories, owed his ideas about the form more to Germany than to Poe.

CS60  PETERS, H. F. "Ernst Junger's Concern with Edgar Allan Poe," CL, X (Spr. 1958), 144-9.
    Junger was attracted to Poe's treatment of terror, self-analysis, and to his anticipation of "the mechanical horrors that have become reality in our time." Both writers were aware of man's capacity for self-destruction. Poe was a rationalist, Junger a mystic.

CS61  SCHAUMANN, HERBERT. "Poe in Germany," *Poe in Foreign Languages and Tongues*. ed. by John Calvin French. Baltimore: Johns Hopkins Press, 1941.
    Very general remarks on the similarities between Poe and such German writers as Hoffmann and Tieck.

CS62  TIMPE, EUGENE. *American Literature in Germany: 1861-1872*. Chapel Hill: University of North Carolina Press, 1964.
    German reception of American authors from Barlow to Howells.

## HUNGARY

CS63  KORPONY, BÉLA. "Edgar Allan Poe in Hungary." *Hungarian*

*CS: Foreign Reception and Influence*

*Studies in English* (Louis Kossuth University, Debrecen),
I (1963), 43-62.

CS64 RADÓ, GYÖRGY. "The works of Edgar Allan Poe in Hungary,"
*Babel,* XII (1966), 21-2.
Poe's popularity in Hungary.


INDIA

CS65 PAVNASKAR, SADANAND R. "Poe in India: A Bibliography, 1955-
1969," <u>PN</u>, V (Dec. 1972), 49-50.


JAPAN

CS66 KING, JAMES ROY. Essay in *Papers on Poe: Essays in Honor of
J. Ward Ostrom.* Springfield, Ohio, 1972.
Discusses Poe's influence on recent Japanese literature.


RUMANIA

CS67 ADERMAN, RALPH. "Poe in Rumania: A Bibliography," <u>PN</u>, III
(Jun. 1970), 19-20.


RUSSIA

CS68 ASTROV, VLADIMIR. "Dostoievsky on Edgar Allan Poe," <u>AL</u>, XIV
(Mar. 1942), 70-2.
Poe's psychological subtlety and fantastic realism are
characteristic of the Russian mind. In his essay on Poe,
Dostoievsky stresses the poet's "singular synthesis of un-
fettered imagination, keen psychological penetration, and
unparalleled mastery of artistic detail." He explains that
the fantastic elements in his tales are merely external and
that his power of detail is extraordinary. Hoffmann is a
greater poet because he "possesses an ideal of purity and
inherent human beauty"; his humor, malice, and realism are
in harmony with the desire for beauty. Poe's fantastical-
ness, on the other hand, is material, and his "imagination
betrays the true American."

CS69 BANDY, W. T. "Were the Russians the First to Translate Poe?"
<u>AL</u>, XXXI (Jan. 1960), 479-80.
The Russian claim is unfounded.

# EDGAR ALLAN POE: AN ANNOTATED BIBLIOGRAPHY

*CS: Foreign Reception and Influence*

CS70   BROWN, GLENORA W. and DENNING B. BROWN. *A Guide to Soviet Russian Translations of American Literature.* New York: King's Crown Press, 1954.
      Russian translations of Poe in the 1920's.

CS71   BRUSOV, VALERY. "Preface," *Edgar Poe: Full Collection of Poems.* Moscow-Leningrad, 1926.
      Defense of Poe against the new regime's suspicions about his mysticism. Brusov believes that Poe was a leader in experimental psychology.

CS72   DELANEY, JOAN. "Poe's 'The Gold Bug' in Russia: A Note on First Impressions," AL, XLII (Nov. 1970), 375-79.
      Poe was originally introduced in Russia as a children's author.

CS73   DOSTOEVSKI, FYDOR M. "Three Tales of Edgar Allan Poe," *Wremia,* trans. Vladimir Astrov, 1861. Reprinted in CJ16.
      Discusses Poe as "a strange though enormously talented writer" with a great imagination and gift for detail. Yet he is inferior to Hoffmann because his fantasies are "strangely 'material'....Even his most unbounded imagination betrays the true American."

CS74   GOGOL, JOHN M. "Two Russian Symbolists on Poe," PN, III (Dec. 1970), 36-7.
      Influence of Poe on Konstantin Balmont (1867-1943) and Aleksandr Blok (1880-1921).

CS75   GOHDES, CLARENCE and others, eds. *Russian Studies of American Literature: a Bibliography.* Chapel Hill: University of North Carolina Press, 1969, 145-50.

CS76   KEEFER, LUBOR. "Poe in Russia," *Poe in Foreign Languages and Tongues.* ed. by John Calvin French. Baltimore: Johns Hopkins Press, 1941.
      Discusses Poe's influence on Dostoevsky, Andrew, Mareshenhovsky, and others. The cult of Poe in Russia reached an apogee with the poet Konstantin Balmont. The nineteenth-century regarded him as a supreme master of literature, while the Stalin regime repudiated his "bourgeois philosophy" and mysticism. Keefer also surveys Russian criticism and translations of Poe.

CS77   KRASNOSELSKY, A. "To the Psychology of Indefinite Strivings," *Russian Wealth,* XI (1900), 27-55.

CS78   LIBMAN, VALENTINA. *Russian Studies of American Literature:*

*CS: Foreign Reception and Influence*

*a Bibliography.* ed. by Clarence Gohdes, trans. by Robert V. Allen. Chapel Hill: University of North Carolina Press, 1969, 3, 28, 145-150.

CS79 MAGIDOFF, ROBERT. "American Literature in Russia," SRL (Nov. 2, 1946).
Brief discussion of the inestimable influence of Poe's poetry in Russia and his more moderate but also significant influence on Russian prose writers, particularly Dostoevsky.

CS80 PURDY, S. B. "Poe and Dostoyevsky," SSK, IV (Win. 1967), 169-71.
Dostoevsky's *Uncle's Dream* was influenced by Poe's "The Man That Was Used Up." Poe also probably inspired Dostoevsky to develop the theme of perversity.

CS81 YARMOLINSKY, ABRAHAM. "The Russian View of American Literature," Bkm, XLIV (Sept. 1916), 44-8.
Brief discussion of Poe's popularity in Russia--the only American whom the Slavs have taken to heart, "with all his unearthliness and morbidity, his fantastic rationalism and superexcited aestheticism, with all his dreams and nightmares."

## SCANDINAVIA

CS82 ANDERSON, CARL L. *Poe in North Light.* Durham, North Carolina: Duke University Press, 1973.
The Scandinavian response to Poe's life and work. Especially important is Strindberg's knowledge of Poe.

CS83 _____. *Swedish Acceptance of American Literature.* Philadelphia: University of Pennsylvania Press, 1957.
Describes Poe as one of the "chief representatives of American literature" in Sweden before 1920.

CS84 BENSON, ADOLPH B. "Scandinavian References in the Works of Poe," JEPC, XL (Jan. 1941), 73-90.
Discusses Poe's knowledge of Scandinavians, references to Swedenborg in his work, and "The Natural History of Norway," by Reverend Erich Pontoppidan, a possible source of "Descent."

## SERBIAN AND CROATIAN LITERATURE

CS85 BASIC, SONJA. "Edgar Allan Poe in Serbian and Croatian

# Edgar Allan Poe: An Annotated Bibliography

Literature," *Studia Romanica et Anglica Zagrebiensia,*
nos. 21-22, 305-10.

## SPAIN AND SPANISH AMERICA

CS86  ENGLEKIRK, JOHN E.  "A Critical Study of Two Tales by Amando
      Nervo," NMQR, II (Feb. 1932), 53-65.
      Englekirk discusses the "Poesque" elements in the
      stories.

CS87  _____. *Edgar Allan Poe in Hispanic Literature.* New York:
      Instituto De las Españas en los Estados Unidos, 1934.
      Reissued New York: Russell and Russell, 1972.
      Treats Poe's direct influence in South America and his
      introduction into Spain by Baudelaire.

CS88  _____. "'The Raven' in Spanish America," *Spanish Review,* I
      (Nov. 1934), 52-6.
      Popularity and influence of the poem.

CS89  ERICKSON, MARTIN.  "Three Guatemalan Translators of Poe,"
      *Hispania,* XXV (1942), 73-8.
      The translators are Domingo Estrada, Guillermo F. Hall
      and Maria Cruz.

CS90  FERGUSON, JOHN de LANCEY.  "Edgar Allan Poe," *American Liter-*
      *ature in Spain.* New York: Columbia University Press, 1916,
      55-87.
      The author discusses Poe's reputation in Spain and
      claims that he never exerted any influence there, in spite
      of his popularity.

CS91  INGE, M. THOMAS.  "Migual de Unamuno's *Canciones* on American
      Literature," *Arlington Quarterly,* II (1969), 83-97.
      Poe's influence on Unamuno.

CS92  _____ and GLORIA DOWNING.  "Unamuno and Poe," PN, III (Dec.
      1970), 35-6.
      Reprints an essay on Unamuno (translated into English)
      called "Artistic Morality" (*La Nación,* Aug. 19, 1923).

CS93  JOHNSTON, MARJORIE.  "Ruben Darlo's Acquaintance with Poe,"
      *Hispania,* XVII (1934), 271-8.

CS94  KNOX, ROBERT.  "La Mariposa Negra and 'The Raven'," *Symposium,*
      XI (1957), 111-16.

# Edgar Allan Poe: An Annotated Bibliography

*CS: Foreign Reception and Influence*

Notes similarities between "The Raven" and Nicodemes Pastor Diaz's work.

CS95　LIMA, ROBERT.　"A Borges Poem on Poe," PSt, VI (Jun. 1973), 29-30.
Reprints the poem.

CS96　SALINAS, PEDRO.　"Poe in Spain and Spanish America," *Poe in Foreign Languages and Tongues*. ed. by John Calvin French. Baltimore: Johns Hopkins Press, 1941.
General remarks on the Spanish interest in Poe's stories and the South American interest in his poems.　Adds little to Englekirk's research.

CS97　WALSH, THOMAS.　"Julio Herrer y Reissig, A Disciple of Edgar Allan Poe," PL, XXXIII (Dec. 1922), 601-7.

CS98　WATSON, DON.　"Borges and Poe," *Virginia Weekly* (Mar. 18, 1968), 3.
Discusses Borges' lecture on Poe.

CS99　WOODBRIDGE, HENSLEY C.　"Poe in Spanish America: Addenda and Corrigenda," PN, IV (Dec. 1971), 46.

CS100　_____.　"Poe in Spanish America: a Bibliographical Supplement," PN, II (Jan. 1969), 18-19.

*See also* CS58.

*CT: Interest in Cryptography*

CT1　BANDY, W. T.　"Poe's Solution of the Frailey Land Office Cipher," PMLA, LXVIII (Dec. 1953), 1240-1.
Corrections of Wimsatt's solution of the cipher.

CT2　DREDD, FIRMIN.　"Poe and Secret Writing," Bkm, XXVIII (Jan. 1909), 450-1.
Unperceptive essay on Poe's interest in cryptography.

CT3　EVANS, HENRY RIDGLEY.　*Edgar Allan Poe and Baron Von Kemplen's Chess-Playing Automaton*.　Kenton, Ohio: International Brotherhood of Magicians, 1939.
Poe's keen, analytical mind solved the secret of the automaton in all but a few of its mechanical details.

CT4　FRIEDMAN, WILLIAM F.　"Edgar Allan Poe, Cryptographer," AL, VIII (Nov. 1936), 266-80. Also *Signal Corps Bulletin*, XCVII (Jul. to Sept. 1937), 41-53, (Oct. to Dec. 1937), 54-75.

# Edgar Allan Poe: An Annotated Bibliography

*CT: Interest in Cryptography*

In cryptography, Poe saw an opportunity to secure his
popular reputation. Actually, he was only a dabbler in
the science and solved very simple problems.

CT5 KERN, A. A. "News for Bibliophiles," *Nation*, XCVII (Oct. 23,
1913), 381-2.
 Discussion of Tolman's corrections of "The Gold Bug."
 *See* CK350.

CT6 WIMSATT, WILLIAM K. "What Poe Knew about Cryptography," PMLA,
LVIII (Sept. 1943), 754-79.
 General discussion of Poe's interest in cryptography and
conclusion that he solved only simple substitution-type
ciphers.

*See also* CD46.

*CU: Checklist of Dissertations*

CU1 ALBRIGHT, DANIEL. "An Account of the Discussion of Narrative
Technique from Poe up to James," University of Chicago,
1956.

CU2 ALEXANDER, JEAN AVON. "Affidavits of Genius, French Essays
on Poe, From Forgues to Valéry." University of Washington,
1960.

CU3 ALLEN, MOZELLE. "Poe's Debt to Gautier, to Pascal, and to
Voltaire," University of Texas, 1940.

CU4 ALTERTON, MARGARET. "The Origins of Poe's Critical Theory,"
University of Iowa, 1925.

CU5 ANDERSON, DON M. "Edgar Allan Poe's Influence on Baudelaire's
Style," University of Iowa, 1955.

CU6 ANGUS, EUGENE IRVING. "'How to Write a Blackwood Article':
Poe's Aesthetic Satire in *Tales of the Grotesque and
Arabesque*," University of Massachusetts, 1973.

CU7 ARNOLD, JOHN WESLEY. "The Poe Perplex: a Guide to the Tales,"
University of Massachusetts, 1967.

CU8 BASS, WILLIAM. "Edgar Allan Poe as a Critic of Southern
Writers and Literature," University of North Carolina,
1954.

# Edgar Allan Poe: An Annotated Bibliography

*CU: Checklist of Dissertations*

CU9    BIERLY, CHARLES EVERETT. *"Eureka* and the Drama of the Self:
       a Study of the Relation between Poe's Cosmology and his
       Fiction," University of Washington, 1957.

CU10   BROWN, HENRY MALVERN. "Characterization in the Prose Fiction
       of Edgar Allan Poe," University of North Carolina at Chapel
       Hill, 1971.

CU11   CAIN, HENRY EDWARD. "James Clarence Mangan and the Poe-Mangan
       Question," Catholic University of America, 1929.

CU12   CALCOTT, EMILY. "The Influences of I Disraeli," University of
       Virginia, 1931.

CU13   CAMBIAIRE, CELESTIN. "The Influence of Edgar Allan Poe in
       France," University of Iowa, 1927.

CU14   CASALE, O. A. "Edgar Allan Poe and Transcendentalism: Con-
       flict and Affinity," University of Michigan, 1965.

CU15   COBB, PALMER. "The Influence of E.T.A. Hoffmann on the Tales
       of Edgar Allan Poe," Columbia University, 1908.

CU16   CRONON, JOHN JOSEPH. "Poe and the Theory of the Short Story,"
       University of Michigan, 1970.

CU17   CULHANE, MARY J. "Thoreau, Melville, Poe and the Romantic
       Quest," University of Minnesota, 1945.

CU18   DAMERON, JOHN LASLEY. "Poe in the Twentieth Century: Poe's
       Literary Reputation, 1828-1960, and a Bibliography of Poe
       Criticism, 1942-1960," University of Tennessee, 1962.

CU19   DELANEY, JOAN. "Edgar Allan Poe's Tales in Russia: Legend
       and Literary Influence, 1847-1917," Harvard University,
       1966/7.

CU20   ENGLEKIRK, JOHN E. "Edgar Allan Poe in Hispanic Literature,"
       Columbia University, 1935.

CU21   ENSLEY, HELEN OLIVER. "The Ryhthm of Poe's Poetry," Uni-
       versity of Tennessee, 1970/71.

CU22   FISHER, BENJAMIN FRANKLIN. "Gothic Techniques in Poe's Short
       Stories," Duke University, 1969.

CU23   FOSTER, EDWARD. "A Study of Grim Humor in the Works of Poe,
       Melville, and Twain," Vanderbilt University, 1957.

# EDGAR ALLAN POE: AN ANNOTATED BIBLIOGRAPHY

*CU: Checklist of Dissertations*

CU24    FOX, HUGH B. "Poe and Cosmology: The God-Universe Relationship in a Romantic Context," University of Illinois, 1959.

CU25    FRANK, FREDERICK STILSON. "Perverse Pilgrimage: The Role of
the Gothic in the Works of Charles Brockden Brown, Edgar
Allan Poe, and Nathaniel Hawthorne," Rutgers University,
1968.

CU26    GAILLARD, DAWSON F. "A Study of Poe's Concern with Man's
Powers of Cognition," Tulane University, 1970/71.

CU27    GOTTSCHALK, HANS W. "The Imagery of Poe's Poems and Tales:
A Chronological Study," University of Iowa, 1949.

CU28    GRAVELY, WILLIAM H. JR. "The Early Political and Literary
Career of Thomas Dunn English," University of Virginia,
1954.

CU29    GRIFFITH, MALCOLM ANSTELL. "The Grotesque in American Fiction," Ohio State University, 1966.

CU30    HALLIBURTON, DAVID G. "The Grotesque in American Literature:
Poe, Hawthorne and Melville," University of California at
Riverside, 1967.

CU31    HAMMOND, ALEXANDER LANCE. "Edgar Allan Poe's 'Tales of the
Folio Club'," Northwestern University, 1970/71.

CU32    HART, ALDEN WADSWORTH. "The Poetry of Edgar Allan Poe," University of Oregon, 1972.

CU33    HECHT, HARVEY EDGAR. "The Use and Development of the Narrator
in the Short Fiction of Edgar Allan Poe," University of
Tennessee, 1972.

CU34    HESSER, FRANCIS M. "Representative Early American Satirists,"
University of Wisconsin, 1947.

CU35    HUDSON, RUTH. "Poe's Craftsmanship in the Short Stories,"
University of Virginia, 1934.

CU36    HUGHES, JAMES NICHOLS. "The Dialect of Death in Poe, Dickinson, Emerson, and Whitman," University of Pennsylvania,
1969.

CU37    HULL, WILLIAM D. "A Canon of the Critical Works of Poe
with a Study of Poe the Magazinist," University of Virginia, 1941.

# Edgar Allan Poe: An Annotated Bibliography

CU38    HUSSEY, JOHN PATRICK.   "Ascent and Return: The Redemptive
        Voyage of Poe's Hero," University of Florida, 1971.

CU39    HUTCHERSON, DUDLEY.   "One Hundred Years of Poe: A Study of
        Edgar Allan Poe in American and English Criticism, 1827-
        1927," University of Virginia, 1936.

CU40    HYNEMAN, ESTHER F.   "The Contemporaneous Reputation of Edgar
        Allan Poe with an Annotated Bibliography of Poe Criticism,
        1827-1967," Columbia University, 1968.

CU41    JACOBS, ROBERT.   "Poe's Heritage from Jefferson's Virginia,"
        Johns Hopkins University, 1953.

CU42    KELLY, GEORGE.   "The Aesthetic Theories of Edgar Allan Poe:
        An Analytical Study of his Literary Criticism," University
        of Iowa, 1953.

CU43    KELLY, THOMAS BYRNE.   "Poe's Gothic Masques," University of
        Connecticut, 1972.

CU44    KENNEDY, RALPH CLARENCE. "The Poems and Short Stories of
        Edgar Allan Poe: Their Composition, Publication and
        Reception," University of Arkansas, 1960.

CU45    KREMENLIEV, ELVA BAER.   "The Literary Uses of Astronomy in the
        Writings of Edgar Allan Poe," University of California at
        Los Angeles, 1965.

CU46    KUNHNELT, HARRO. "Edgar Allan Poe and Dante Gabriel Rossetti,"
        Innsbruck, 1948.

CU47    LAVERTY, CARROLL.   "Science and Pseudo-Science in the Writings
        of Edgar Allan Poe," Duke University, 1951.

CU48    LERNER, ARTHUR.   "Psychoanalytically Oriented Criticism of
        Three American Poets: Poe, Whitman and Aiken," University
        of Southern California, 1968.

CU49    LEVINE, STUART F.   "The Proper Spirit: A Study of the Prose
        Fiction of Edgar Allan Poe," 1948.

CU50    LIGON, JOHN.   "On Desperate Seas: A Study of Poe's Imagin-
        ative Journeys," University of Washington, 1961.

CU51    LUBELL, ALBERT.   "Edgar Allan Poe, Critic and Reviewer,"
        New York University, 1951.

*CU: Checklist of Dissertations*

CU52    MABBOTT, THOMAS O. "An Edition of Poe's *Politian*," Columbia University, 1923.

CU53    MEISTER, JOHN G. "The Descent of the Irrelative One: the Metaphysics and Cosmology of Edgar Allan Poe's *Eureka*," University of Pennsylvania.

CU54    MILLER, JOHN CARL. "Poe's English Biographer, John Henry Ingram," University of Virginia, 1954.

CU55    MONAHAN, DEEN W. "Edgar Allan Poe and the Theme of the Fall," Pennsylvania State University, 1968.

CU56    MOONEY, STEPHEN L. "Poe's Grand Design: a Study of Theme and Unity in the Tales," University of Tennessee, 1960.

CU57    MOSS, SIDNEY. "Poe's Literary Battles," University of Illinois, 1954.

CU58    NEWLIN, PAUL ARTHUR. "The Uncanny in the Supernatural Short Fiction of Poe, Hawthorne and Jones," University of California at Los Angeles, 1967.

CU59    NIRENBERG, MORTON. "The Critical Reputation of American Literature in German Periodicals, 1820-1850," Johns Hopkins University, 1967/68.

CU60    OELKE, KARL. "The Rude Daughter: Alchemy in Poe's Early Poetry," Columbia University, 1972.

CU61    OSOWSKI, JUDITH M. "Structure and Metastructure in the Universe of Edgar Allan Poe: an Approach to *Eureka*, Selected Tales, and *The Narrative of Arthur Gordon Pym*," Washington State University, 1972.

CU62    OSTROM, JOHN W. "A Critical Edition of the Letters of Edgar Allan Poe," University of Virginia, 1947.

CU63    PETERSON, DEWAYNE AUGUST. "Poe's Grotesque Humor," Duke University, 1962.

CU64    PHILLIPS, ELISABETH. "Edgar Allan Poe: the American Context," University of Pennsylvania, 1957.

CU65    PHILLIPS, ELIZA C. "The Literary Life of John Tomlin, Friend of Poe," University of Tennessee, 1954.

# EDGAR ALLAN POE: AN ANNOTATED BIBLIOGRAPHY

*CU: Checklist of Dissertations*

CU66    QUINN, PATRICK.  "The French Face of Edgar Allan Poe,"
        Columbia University, 1953.

CU67    REECE, JAMES B.  "Poe and the New York Literati," Duke
        University, 1954.

CU68    REILLY, JOHN EDWARD.  "Poe in Imaginative Literature,"
        University of Virginia, 1964/65.

CU69    REMLEY, BRENDA B.  "Edgar Allan Poe: Paradox and Ambivalence
        as a Narrative Technique," Indiana University, 1971.

CU70    SALZBERG, JOEL.  "The Grotesque as Moral Aesthetic: a Study
        of the Tales of Edgar Allan Poe," University of Oklahoma,
        1967.

CU71    SIEGEL, GERALD.  "The Poe-esque Tale in American Magazines,
        1830-1960," George Washington University, 1972.

CU72    SKAGGS, CALVIN LEE.  "Narrative Point of View in Edgar Allan
        Poe's Criticism and Fiction," Duke University, 1966.

CU73    ST. ARMAND, BARTON LEVI.  "In the American Manner: an Inquiry
        into the Aesthetics of Emily Dickinson and Edgar Allan
        Poe," Brown University, 1968.

CU74    STEWART, ROBERT.  "Textural Notes for the Tales of Edgar Allan
        Poe, Virginia. Ed. Vols. II to VI," University of Vir-
        ginia, 1901.

CU75    THOMPSON, G. R.  "Poe's Romantic Irony" a Study of the Gothic
        Tales in a Romantic Context," University of Southern
        California, 1967.

CU76    TOURTELLOT, FRANCES.  "Edgar Allan Poe on Style," University
        of Washington, 1940.

CU77    VARNADO, SEABORN.  "The Numinous in the Work of Edgar Allan
        Poe," Fordham University, 1964.

CU78    VAUGHAN, JOSEPH.  "Literary Opinions of Edgar Allan Poe,"
        University of Virginia, 1940.

CU79    WHIPPLE, WILLIAM.  "A Study of Edgar Allan Poe's Satiric
        Patterns," Northwestern University, 1951.

# Edgar Allan Poe: An Annotated Bibliography

*CU: Checklist of Dissertations*

CU80    WYSS, HAL H.  "Involuntary Evil in the Fiction of Brown,
        Cooper, Hawthorne, Poe and Melville," Ohio State
        University, 1971.

CU81    ZIPES, JACK DAVIS.  "Studies in the Romantic Hero in German
        and American Literature," Columbia University, 1965.

*Chronological Index*

(Italicized key numbers indicate a later reference to an article
originally published during the indicated year.)

| | |
|---|---|
| 1845 | A8, A14, A15, A19, A22, A31, A35, A42, A47, A58, A66, A83, A87, A92, A103, A104, A113, A115, A122-A125, A128, A129, A132, A133, A136, A149, A153, A157, A164, A173, A175, A192, *A195, A199* |
| 1846 | A43, A51, A60, A73, A85, A105-A109, A142, A150, A154, A174, A182, A186, *A195, A199* |
| 1847 | A6, A57, A90, A119, A140, *A195* |
| 1848 | A21, A23, A24, A36, A45, A89, A91, A110, A114, A148, A187 |
| 1849 | A1, A4, A5, A18, A25, A26, A28, A29, A38, A52, A59, A63-A65, A68, A69, A74, A93, A138, A144, A156, A165, A166, A179, A181, A188-A190 |
| 1850 | A17, A61, A62, A71, A72, A99, A111, A112, A116, A120, A121, A130, A135, A137, A139, A159, A168-A172, B196, *CC18* |
| 1851 | A172, B11, B35, B85, B111, B236, *B265* |
| 1852 | A135, B5, B16, B22, B35, B83, B126, B138, B227 |
| 1853 | B17, B24, B26, B27, B40, B52, B86, B226 |
| 1854 | B1, B13, B18, B28, B116, B124 |
| 1855 | B48, B116 |
| 1856 | A139, B50, B53, B61, B63, B64, B103, B122, B240 |
| 1857 | B7, B77, B95, B233, B234, B239, CS18 |
| 1858 | B15 |
| 1859 | A184 |
| 1860 | B90, B146, B175, B246, CC112 |
| 1861 | CS73 |
| 1862 | B112 |
| 1863 | B123 |
| 1864 | *B261* |
| 1865 | |
| 1866 | B250 |

| | |
|---|---|
| 1867 | B77, B114, B214, B218 |
| 1868 | B74, B162 |
| 1869 | B80, B93, B201 |
| 1870 | B155 |
| 1871 | B19 |
| 1872 | B129, B224 |
| 1873 | |
| 1874 | B71, B147, B148, B164 |
| 1875 | B30, B54, B81, B92, B96, B106, B145, B152, B159, B197, B198, B223, B230, B244, B247, B249, *CC11* |
| 1876 | B94, B120, B143, B144, B151, B156, B158, B167, B212, B243 |
| 1877 | B49, B78, B142, B188, B202 |
| 1878 | B58, B119, B139, B150, B158, B232 |
| 1879 | B133, B157 |
| 1880 | B2, B23, B36, B37, B65, B134, B168, B178, B222 |
| 1881 | B21, B42, B51, B100, B215, B219, B220 |
| 1882 | B4, B41, B46, B115, B118, B165, B187, B248 |
| 1883 | B20, B47, B149, B200 |
| 1884 | B31, B44, B56, B62, B184, B205, B258 |
| 1885 | B9, B12, B33, B39, B59, B88, B99, B128, B135, B140, B153, B182, B204, B221, B231, B253, CI1 |
| 1886 | B70, B141, B163, B166, B251, CA8 |
| 1887 | B110, B125, B172, B206 |
| 1888 | B206, B208 |
| 1889 | B104, B192, B203, B207, B216, B225, B238 |
| 1890 | B154, B195, B252 |
| 1891 | B67, B68, B91, B130, B131, B185 |

1892    B3, B25, B43, B98, B161, B195, B217, B248

1893    A16, B84, B121, B127, B189, B228, CS6

1894    B97, B213, B241, B242, B254-B257, CD50

1895    B32, B45, B55, B60, B79, B101, B136, B173, B176, B179, B190, B211, B235, CB2

1896    B10, B34, B105, B109, B174, B245

1897    B29, B73, B76, B137, B160, B183, B194, C17

1898    B6, B107, B169, B177, B193, B199, B229, CD14

1899    B8, B14, B38, B57, B66, B69, B72, B75, B87, B102, B108, B113, B117, B132, B170, B171, B180, B181, B186, B191, B209, B210, B237

1900    CC85, CH16, CK125, CK131, CK178, CK304, CK366, CL404, CQ18, CS77

1901    CA50, CC15, CC84, CC85, CC179, CC215, CE5, CH6, CI14, CI26, CJ39, CK2, CK35, CK161, CK224, CK256, CK337, CU74

1902    CA4, CC34, CC46, CC187, CD3, CE4, CG11, CH10, CK101, CK159, CK295, CO31

1903    CC49, CC59, CC68, CC76, CC89, CC153, CD7, CD38, CD49, CH8, CI28, CJ34, CK9, CK11, CK60, CK82, CK151, CK344, CL424, CM3, CM44

1904    CA62, CC81, CC94, CC146, CC204, CK20, CK56, CK92, CK194, CK220, CK350, CO19, CO20, CO31

1905    B253, CI21, CI32, CI33, CK87, CK147, CK353, CM29

1906    CC7, CC21, CC86, CC122, CJ43, CK166, CK288, CL38

1907    CC2, CC3, CC21, CC72, CC78, *CC147*, CE7, CG10, CG14, CI8, CI34, CJ48, CJ77, CK41, CK70, CK106, CK214, CK225, CL127, CL418, CS55

1908    CG2, CI30, CK216, CO6, CO14, CU15

1909    B82, B253, CA10, CA16, CB8, CC5, CC48, CC58, CC98, CC99, CC107, CC145, CC155, CC171, CC176, CC195, CC198, CC199, CC206, CD12, CD17, CG9, CI3, CI4, CI10, CI13, CI27, CI31, CJ71, CK4, CK31, CK51, CK79, CK98, CK103, CK134, CK160, CK170, CK185, CK213, CK246, CK274, CK291, CK309, CK312,

CK315, CK367, CL224, CM17, CM49, CM72, CO10, CQ2, CQ12, CR1, CS10, CS22, CS33, CS52, CS54, CT2

1910    CC188, CD11, CI18, CJ72, CK6, CK8, CK23, CK34, CK53, CK226, CK242, CK351, CL29, CL95, CL208, CL398, CL443, CP4, CS51,

1911    CA13, CE2, CJ26, CK59, CK104, CK323, CO46,

1912    CA14, CA32, CC28, CC29, CC32, CC131, CC159, CC208, CC209, CE3, CJ63, CK171, CK272, CK317, CK352, CL17, CR41

1913    CG5, CK28, CK63, CK217, CK260, CL48, CS7, CS44, CT5

1914    CA3, CK52, CL493, CL497, CL528, CS59

1915    CC132, CD10, CK46, CK315, CL1, CR28, CS30

1916    CA64, CC6, CC189, CC191, CC210, CF1–CF6, CF8, CG1, CG21, CH19, CH21, CI11, CI17, CK25, CK118, CL415, CL490, CP10, CS81, CS90,

1917    CA12, CC8, CC170, CE5, CI36, CJ28, CN6, CS49

1918    CA24, CA66, CK61, CK240, CK263, CL250, CL413, CM6, CM61

1919    CC31, CK135, CK247

1920    A157, CA33, CC158, CC218, CK135, CK223, CK270, CK384, CL130, CL449, CP1, CP8

1921    CA5, CC135, CD1, CJ20, CJ66, CJ70, CM47, CQ4, CS21,

1922    CC121, CC128, CD18, CK7, CK196, CK206, CK316, CL16, CL416, CL526, CM55, CP2, CS97,

1923    CC26, CC207, CG3, CI6, CK65, CK105, CK228, CK259, CK268, CM27, CU52

1924    CA43, CC36, CD47, CD48, CH5, CI12, CI19, CI24, CK21, CJ31, CK132, CL412,

1925    CC43, CC92, CC123, CC212, CD40, CE1, CG20, CG23, CI15, CI25, CK81, CK191, CK327, CK376, CM24, CO4, CO11, CS35, CU4

1926    CA15, CA38, CC69, CC156, CC169, CC172, CC201, CC213, CC216, CD39, CH7, CH13, CH18, CI9, CJ1, CJ41, CJ55, CK234, CK236, CK377, CL36, CL503, CM36, CO3, CS20, CS71

| | |
|---|---|
| 1927 | B259, CA58, CA65, CC71, CC183, CG12, CJ40, CK62, CK95, CK266, CK301, CK326, CK349, CK380, CK381, CL377, CL425, CM43, CM71, CO9, CO12, CO35, CS41, CS42, CS45, CU13 |
| 1928 | CC33, CC114, CD20, CG18, CJ32, CJ46, CJ49, CK86, CK248, CK271, CK296, CL27, CL174, CL548, CM8, CM26, CM26, CP6 |
| 1929 | CC1, CC12, CC57, CC116, CC124, CC167, CC217, CJ74, CK167, CK320, CL5, CL374, CL379, CO40, CU11 |
| 1930 | CA11, CA44, CB34, CC9, CC36, CC75, CD4, CJ56, CK80, CK139, CK168, CK169, CK254, CK375, CL136, CL141, CL234, CL357, CL444, CL474, CL535, CN10, CO18, CO43, CO45, CP3 |
| 1931 | CA23, CA44, CB12, CC24, CC30, CC83, CC147, CC193, CI2, CI29, CJ6, CJ27, CK33, CK43, CK66, CK102, CK220, CK298, CK333, CK335, CK378, CL10, CL485, CL515, CL519, CM23, CQ3, CU12 |
| 1932 | CA28, CA40, CB17, CC161, CH12, CJ14, CK37, CK100, CK180, CK204, CK309, CK328, CL19, CL25, CL40, CL205, CL230, CL411, CL538, CM20, CM31, CM35, CN8, CR31, CS86 |
| 1933 | CA27, CA31, CA37, CA56, CA60, CB18, CC17, CC77, CC100, CC154, CC163, CH2, CK21, CK44, CK49, CK142, CK267, CK301, CK355, CK356, CL59, CL116, CL142, CL300, CL349, CL356, CL375, CL378, CL390, CL442, CL499, CL507, CL522, CL549, CM52, CO28 |
| 1934 | CA25, CA47, CA59, CC93, CC103, CC194, CD13, CI5, CI16, CJ30, CJ58, CK58, CK77, CK188, CK192, CK218, CK369, CL33, CL78, CL84, CL100, CL131, CL220, CL386, CL387, CL399, CL442, CL446, CL478, CL551, CM19, CO33, CP11, CR24–CR26, CS87, CS88, CS93, CU35 |
| 1935 | B267, CA1, CA2, CA34, CA35, CC105, CC117, CC178, CC211, CD6, CD43, CD46, CI37, CJ42, CK14, CK365, CL2, CL91, CL458, CL540, CM67, CN1, CO2, CU20 |
| 1936 | CA61, CC97, CC101, CC104, CD2, CH4, CK37, CK64, CK99, CL101, CL235, CL316, CL400, CL402, CL406, CL434, CL486, CT4, CU39 |
| 1937 | CA22, CC23, CC74, CC108, CC119, CC130, CC162, CD19, CI23, CJ69, CK152, CK182, CK232, CK370, CK382, CL4, CL21, CL118, CL176, CL303, CL304, CL330, CL501, CN9, CP5, CR3, CT4 |
| 1938 | CA19, CC42, CD22, CK17, CK120, CK219, CK289, CK383, CL41, CL288, CL388, CL432, CO23, CO30, CS50, CS53, CS58 |
| 1939 | CA41, CC102, CC160, CC180–CC182, CG19, CH3, CI35, CK208, CK314, CL197, CL278, CL539, CM60, CO27, CQ6, CR18, CR53, CT3 |

1940 CB4, CC109, CC118, CC127, CC202, CD31, CH1, CL39, CL55, CL206, CM40, CU3, CU76, CU78

1941 CA49, CA55, CA67, CB3, CB7, CB21, CB29, CC50, CC65, CC96, CC129, CC137, CC192, CC214, CD28, CD35, CG22, CJ7, CJ47, CJ60, CK67, CK113, CK122, CK130, CK153, CK203, CK273, CL99, CL134, CL180, CL326, CL372, CL385, CL438, CL462, CL466, CL492, CL527, CM68, CO5, CS39, CS61. CS76. CS84, CS96, CU37

1942 B260, B264, B266, CA9, CA36, CA45, CC47, CC125, CD27, CD36, CH17, CJ10, CK258, CL23, CL42, CL44, CL145, CL223, CL267, CL328, CL331, CL332, CL373, CL410, CL506, CL517, CM51, CM70, CS43, CS68, CS89

1943 A198, CA21, CA29, CA48, CC11, CC20, CC22, CC40, CC61, CC115, CC152, CC175, CG6, CK141, CK200, CK257, CK364, CL28, CL45, CL152, CL227, CL283, CL311, CL340, CL419, CL420, CL475, CL483, CL489, CL520, CM65, CO26, CQ1, CT6

1944 CC51, CC80, CC120, CC173, CH20, CJ5, CK47, CK189, CK235, CL13, CL120, CL228, CL229, CL240, CL339, CL343, CL476, CL509, CM9, CM11, CM42, CQ7, CS26

1945 CA30, CC55, CC185, CK85, CK208, CK262, CL12, CL96, CL98, CL121, CL203, CL392, CL481, CL504, CL505, CL543, CM13, CM62, CR42, CS25, CU17

1946 B89, B265, CA17, CC126, CJ68, CK227, CK386, CL90, CL323, CL541, CL542, CM25, CO42, CS27, CS79

1947 CA42, CC87, CK287, CK300, CK318, CL105, CL393, CL461, CN5, CS5, CU34, CU62

1948 CB23, CC110, CC112, CC148, CD29, CK84, CK91, CK227, CK313, CL90, CL114, CL236, CL240, CL327, CL436, CL440, CL502, CL508, CL509, CL518, CL521, CL534, CL541, CM2, CM37, CO24, CU46, CU49

1949 A194, B246, CB15, CB16, CC44, CC73, CC90, CC111, CC186, CD9, CD42, CJ9, CJ29, CK3, CK5, CK10, CK36, CK39, CK50, CK83, CK109, CK265, CK341, CL30, CL80, CL129, CL146, CL175, CL199, CL289. CL391, CL441, CL477, CO9, CS1, CU27

1950 CC4, CC82, CI20, CK149, CK343, CL6, CL52, CL160, CL216, CL318, CL325, CL511, CR48, CS4, CS32,

1951 CA51, CC13, CD15, CK93, CK138, CK186, CK196, CK209, CK285, CK371, CK388, CL32, CL37, CL179, CL252, CL409, CL423, CN3, CO34, CP7, CR44, CU47, CU51, CU79

1952    CC35, CD34, CJ11, CJ19, CK13, CK27, CK114, CK140, CK173, CK210, CK319, CK340, CK377, CL62, CL189, CL190, CL355, CL510, CM7, CS15, CS17, CS24

1953    CB10, CC52-CC54, CC142, CC144, CC190, CJ45, CK108, CK115, CK340, CL104, CL107, CL154, CL170, CL204, CL207, CL279, CL281, CL293, CL459, CL495, CL512, CN4, CO13, CO25, CT1, CU41, CU42, CU66

1954    CB11, CC62, CC95, CK89, CK162, CL20, CL56, CL63, CL65, CL75, CL77, CL155, CL248, CL297, CL457, CM18, CO21, CS70, CU8, CU28, CU54, CU57, CU65, CU6̄7

1955    A193, CA20, CA52, CC174, CD25, CD44, CK179, CK221, CK233, CK341, CK387, CL3, CL47, CL523, CM28, CM58, CM66, CO1, CO44, CU5,

1956    CA39, CB19, CC10, CC60, CC133, CC141, CC200, CD45, CF7, CG15, CH15, CJ18, CK96, CK281, CK284, CK345, CK359, CL122, CL148, CL169, CL277, CL306, CM33, CM45, CM50, CN7, CS19, CU1

1957    CC140, CD33, CJ9, CJ23, CJ52, CJ61, CK97, CK119, CL15, CL161, CL181, CL187, CL276, CL366, CL498, CL536, CO36, CR16, CS83, CS94, CU9, CU23, CU64

1958    CC25, CC134, CC143, CK42, CK107, CK157, CK177, CK252, CK261, CK293, CK360, CK361, CL67, CL123, CL272, CL414, CL429, CL496, CM1, CM34, CR23, CR38, CS12, CS56, CS60, CU24

1959    CB1, CB14, CC37, CC106, CH14, CJ25, CJ78, CK19, CK40, CK116, CK148, CK190, CK338, CK341, CK358, CK372, CK374, CK379, CL153, CL156, CL164, CL183, CL367, CL369, CL484, CL550, CM16, CR14, CR27, CS3, CS14, CS40, CS48

1960    B263, CA63, CB20, CB24, CB30, CC151, CC165, CJ53, CJ65, CK68, CK110, CK112, CK123, CK156, CK176, CK202, CK215, CK282, CK286, CK311, CK385, CL31, CL35, CL54, CL86, CL135, CL177, CL192, CL193, CL233, CL237, CL344, CL482, CL500, CM4, CM15, CM59, CR32, CS69, CU2, CU44, CU56

1961    CC177, CC205, CD23, CJ13, CK71, CK144, CK175, CK181, CK245, CK269, CK297, CK322, CK363, CL66, CL85, CL88, CL119, CL151, CL159, CL184, CL222, CL261, CL264, CL447, CM12, CM41, CO41, CU50

1962    CC41, CJ8, CK15, CK76, CK244, CK247, CK294, CK303, CK373, CL166, CL241, CL245, CL262, CL285, CL302, CL353, CL370, CL394, CL452, CR15, CR29, CS2, CS9, CS11, CS28, CS47, CU18, CU63

1963    A199, CC14, CC63, CC136, CD16, CD24, CG4, CG16, CJ50, CJ59,
        CJ76, CK30, CK128, CK137, CK143, CK174, CK183, CK195, CK230,
        CK329, CK331, CL18, CL79, CL103, CL126, CL137, CL162, CL165,
        CL168, CL190, CL265, CL266, CL294, CL299, CL337, CL401,
        CL405, CL430, CL431, CL513, CL514, CM32, CM38, CM53, CO15,
        CR17, CS38, CS63

1964    B262, CB31, CJ22, CJ54, CK146, CK179, CK239, CK306, CK308,
        CK321, CK330, CL97, CL147, CL149, CL158, CL185, CL186, CL210,
        CL226, CL239, CL287, CL310, CL321, CL396, CL407, CL516, CM5,
        CM57, CO17, CR11, CS16, CS62, CU68, CU77

1965    B253, B262, CA7, CB5, CC66, CD21, CD41, CJ3, CJ36, CJ62,
        CJ67, CK48, CK54, CK126, CK155, CK163, CK212, CK229, CK231,
        CK278, CK283, CK332, CK362, CL34, CL87, CL115, CL139, CL150,
        CL163, CL167, CL263, CL286, CL314, CL333, CL336, CL453,
        CL469, CL471, CM69, CO37, CQ10, CQ15, CR21, CU14, CU45, CU81

1966    CB9, CG17, CH11, CJ16, CJ24, CK12, CK16, CK24, CK73, CK90,
        CK124, CK129, CK193, CK197, CK222, CK253, CK280, CK302, CL74,
        CL82, CL196, CL201, CL254, CL258, CL282, CL312, CL347, CL351,
        CL360, CL537, CM21, CQ15, CR22, CR30, CR50, CS64, CU19,
        CU29, CU72

1967    CA46, CB5, CC139, CD30, CE6, CJ64, CK32, CK94, CK127, CK184,
        CK237, CK238, CK251, CK299, CK339, CK361, CL64, CL69, CL76,
        CL81, CL93, CL117, CL124, CL138, CL238, CL256, CL257, CL259,
        CL268, CL280, CL309, CL319, CL352, CL361, CL363, CL545,
        CL547, CM14, CM21, CM56, CM64, CN2, CO38, CQ5, CQ15, CR6,
        CR37, CR43, CS80, CU7, CU30, CU58, CU59, CU70, CU75

1968    A195, CA53, CB27, CB28, CC18, CC27, CC91, CC113, CC164,
        CC184, CD5, CG7, C122, CK29, CK45, CK55, CK72, CK76, CK78,
        CK88, CK111, CK117, CK136, CK154, CK158, CK198, CK241, CK249,
        CK275, CK303, CK342, CK357, CL9, CL46, CL49, CL68, CL102,
        CL111, CL140, CL188, CL198, CL225, CL231, CL232, CL249,
        CL255, CL269-CL271, CL290-CL292, CL295, CL313, CL324,
        CL338, CL371, CL381, CL395, CL421, CL422, CL427, CL433, CL451,
        CL456, CL468, CL494, CL544, CM39, CO8, CO16, CP9, CQ15-CQ17,
        CR4, CR5, CR9, CR20, CR34, CR39, CR45, CR47, CR49, CS37,
        CS98, CU25, CU40, CU48, CU55, CU73

1969    CA54, CB6, CB22, CB25, CB32, CB33, CB35, CC64, CC67, CC88,
        CC138, CC157, CC168, CC203, CD32, CJ2, CJ12, CJ17, CJ38,
        CJ73, CJ79, CK38, CK164, CK172, CK211, CK276, CK277, CK279,
        CK290, CK307, CK334, CL11, CL22, CL43, CL72, CL109, CL110,
        CL132, CL144, CL182, CL202, CL214, CL221, CL284, CL308,
        CL320, CL348, CL362, CL365, CL380, CL382, CL403, CL435,
        CL437, CL439, CL455, CL463, CL464, CL470, CL524, CM22, CM46,
        CM48, CO7, CO32, CQ15, CR7, CR13, CR46, CR54, CS13, CS23,
        CS36, CS46, CS75, CS78, CS91, CS100, CU22, CU36, CU53

1970    A197, CB6, CB13, CB26, CC16, CC39, CG13, CJ4, CJ51, CJ57,
        CK18, CK22, CK26, CK75, CK201, CK205, CK207, CK255, CK264,
        CK310, CK324, CK346, CK348, CL7, CL24, CL60, CL71, CL73,
        CL112, CL113, CL125, CL143, CL195, CL200, CL212, CL213,
        CL215, CL217, CL219, CL242, CL243, CL247, CL273, CL301,
        CL315, CL334, CL341, CL342, CL345, CL358, CL417, CL445,
        CL448, CL454, CL465, CL467, CL479, CL488, CL491, CL530-
        CL532, CL546, CM54, CO39, CQ13, CQ14, CR2, CR8, CR10, CR36,
        CS36, CS29, CS31, CS34, CS67, CS72, CS74, CS92, CU16, CU21,
        CU26, CU31

1971    CA26, CA57, CB6, CB26, CC19, CC38, CC45, CC70, CC196, CD26,
        CG8, CJ15, CJ37, CK1, CK305, CK354, CK368, CL51, CL209,
        CL246, CL260, CL274, CL296, CL298, CL307, CL322, CL350,
        CL364, CL368, CL376, CL389, CL428, CL472, CL533, CL552, CM10,
        CO22, CO29, CQ11, CR12, CS8, CS57, CS99, CU10, CU38, CU69,
        CU80

1972    A196, B261, CA6, CA18, CC79, CC166, CC197, CD8, CH9, CJ35,
        CJ44, CJ75, CK57, CK69, CK74, CK133, CK145, CK150, CK165,
        CK199, CK250, CK292, CK325, CK336, CK347, CL26, CL53, CL57,
        CL58, CL61, CL70, CL83, CL89, CL92, CL94, CL133, CL157,
        CL171-CL173, CL178, CL191, CL194, CL218, CL251, CL305,
        CL317, CL329, CL346, CL354, CL359, CL383, CL397, CL408,
        CL426, CL450, CL460, CL525, CL529, CO8, CR33, CR40, CS65,
        CS66, CS87, CU32, CU33, CU43, CU60, CU61, CU71

1973    CC56, CC150, CD37, CJ33, CK121, CL8, CL14, CL50, CL106,
        CL108, CL244, CL253, CL275, CL335, CL473, CL480, CM30, CR19,
        CR35, CR51, CR52, CS82, CS95, CU6

Articles lacking dates:  A2, A7, A10, A67, A98, A134, A147, A176,
        CK187, CK243, CL128, CL211, CS85

*Author Index*

Anon.   A1-90, B1-64, CA1-6, CB1-3, CC1-13, CD1-9, CG1, CG2, CH1-5,
    CI1-13, CK1-9, CL51, CL396, CL506, CL538, CO1, CP1, CQ1, CQ2,
    CR1, CS1, CS6, CS7, CS49.
Abel, Darrel   CC14, CK10, CL47, CL146, CL279
Abernathy, Julian   CK11
Abrams, M.H.   CM1
Adams, John F.   CL397
Adams, Percy   CL373
Adams, Robert M.   CK12
Adams, R.P.   CK13
Adams, William H.D.   B65
Aderman, Ralph   CS67
Adkins, Nelson F.   CL446, CL507, CM2
Adler, Jacob H.   CL56
Albee, John   CM3
Albright, Daniel   CU1
Alderman, Edwin A.   CE1
Alexander, Jean   CS8, CS9, CU2
Alfriend, E.M.   CC15
Allabeck, Steven   CC16
Allan, Carlisle   CC17
Allen, Gay Wilson   CN1, CQ3
Allen, Hervey   CJ1, CL2
Allen, James L. Jr.   CN2
Allen, Michael   CJ2
Allen, Mozelle S.   CO2, CU3
Almy, Robert F.   CL330
Alterton, Margaret   CJ3, CK14, CL378, CO3, CO4, CU4
Amacher, Richard E.   CL88
Anderson, Carl L.   CS82, CS83
Anderson, David D.   CM4
Anderson, Don M.   CU5
Angier, Minna   B66
Angus, Eugene Irving   CU6
Anichov, E.   CS10
Appel, Alfred Jr.   CL57, CR2
Archibald, R.C.   CB4
Argus   B67

Arndt, Karl J.  CL386
Arnold, John  CL268
Arntson, Herbert E.  CC18
Askew, Melvin  CK15
A.S.P.  A91
Asselineau, Roger  CJ4
Astrov, Vladimir  CS68
Atherton, Gertrude  B68
Auden, W.H.  CK16
Auslander, Joseph  CK17
Austin, Henry  B69, B70

Babcock, Merten C.  CK18
Babler, O.F.  CS5, CS50
Bagley, C.L.  CM5
Bailey, Elmer J.  CP2
Bailey, J.O.  CK19, CL147, CL331, CL332, CL372, CL508, CO5
Bailey, M.E.  CG3
Baird, W.  B71
Baker, Christopher  CL89
Baker, Harry T.  CO6, CL398
Balakian, Anna  CS11
Baldwin, C.S.  CK20
Baldwin, Summerfield  CM6
Bales, Kent  CL58
Bandy, W.T.  CC19, CL7, CL104, CL310, CL393, CL447, CS2, CS3,
     CS12-16, CS69, CT1
Barcuse, B.  CK21
Barnes, Dora  CJ5
Barrows, A.C.  B72
Barzun, Jacques  CK22
Basic, Sonja  CS85
Baskett, Sam S.  CL123
Basler, Roy P.  CL90, CL114, CL240, CL241, CL436, CL501, CL509,
     CL541
Basore, John W.  CK23
Bass, William  CU8
Bate, Walter J.  CM7
Bates, Katherine Lee  B73
Baudelaire, Charles  CS16, CS17
Baum, Paull F.  CL477
Baxter, Nancy N.  CL464
Bayless, Joy  CC20, CL399
Baym, Nina  CK24
Beach, John  CL478
Beardsley, Aubrey Vincent  CH6, CH7
Beaver, Kate W.  CI14
Beebe, Maurice  CL148, CL149
Belden, Henry M.  CL91, CM8
Belgion, Montgomery  CN3
Bell, Landon  CJ6, CK25

Breen, E.J.  CK43
Brenner, Edgar  CA8
Brenner, Rica  CK44
Briggs, Charles F.  A92, A93, B78
Brigham, Clarence Saunders  CA9, CL25
Brinton, Christian  CH8
Broderick, John C.  CL239
Brooks, Cleanth  CK45, CL152, CL511
Brooks, Van Wyck  CK46, CK47, CM11
Brophy, Brigid  CK48
Brophy, Liam  CK49, CK50
Broussard, Louis  CJ12
Brown, Denning B.  CS70
Brown, Glenora W.  CS70
Brown, Henry Malvern  CU10
Brown, Wallace C.  CL13
Browne, Irving  B79
Browne, William H.  B80, B81
Brownell, William C.  CK51
Bruce, Phillip A.  CC29, CE2, CG5, CK52
Bruno, Guido  CI17
Brusov, Valery  CS71
Bryant, William Cullen  B82
Buchholz, Heinrich Ewald  CI18, CK53
Bullard, F. Lauriston  CC30
Buranelli, Vincent  CJ13, CK54
Burch, Francis F.  CL401, CS19
Burke, Kenneth  CM12
Burr, C. Chauncy  B83
Burroughs, John  B84
Burt, Donald C.  CK55
Burton, Richard  CK56
Burton, William E.  A94
Butterfield, R.W.  CK57

Cabell, James Branch  CK58
Cain, Henry Edward  CU11
Cairns, William B.  CK59, CL1
Calcott, Emily  CU12
Calvert, George M.  A95
Cambiaire, Celestin P.  CS20, CU13
Cambon, Glauco  CK60
Cameron, Kenneth  CL34-5
Campbell, Felicia F.  CR5
Campbell, Josie P.  CL334
Campbell, Killis  CA10-14, CC31-33, CD11, CD12, CF1, CJ14, CK61-65,
    CL59, CL224, CL443, CO9-12, CP3, CQ4
Canario, John W.  CL467
Canby, Henry Seidel  CK66
Candelarie, Cordella  CL335
Canny, James R.  CA29

Caputi, Anthony  CN4
Cargill, Oscar  CK67, CL402, CM13
Carley, C.V.  CL366
Carlson, Eric T.  CK68
Carlson, Eric W.  CJ15, CJ16, CK69, CL119, CL512, CL513
Carlton, W.N.C.  CA15
Carson, David L.  CL115
Carter, Boyd  CL459, CO13
Carter, H. Holland  CK70
Carter, John F.  CC34
Carter, Robert  A96
Cary, Richard  CK71, CL285, CM14
Casale, Ottavio M.  CK72, CU14
Cauthen, I.B. Jr.  CC35, CH9, CL6
Cecil, L. Moffitt  CK73, CK74, CL336, CL337
Chamberlain, Jacob Chester  CA16
Chamberlin, Joseph Edgar  CC36
Chandler, Alice  CK75
Chandler, J.R.  A97, A98
Chapman, Edward M.  CP4
Chapman, John Jay  CI19
Chari, V.K.  CR6
Charvat, William  CA17, CC37, CK76
Chase, Lewis  CD13, CF2-6, CJ17
Cherry, Fannye N.  CL474
Chesterton, G.K.  CK77
Chiari, Joseph  CJ18
Chinol, Elio  CM15
Chivers, Thomas Holly  A99, B85, B86, CJ19
Christopher, J.R.  CK78
Church, Henry W.  CL2
Church, Randolph  A193
Churchill, William  CK79
Clark, C.E.Frazer Jr.  CC38
Clark, David L.  CL379
Clark, George P.  CC39, CL60, CL61
Clark, Harry Haydn  CM16
Clark, Lewis Gaylord  A100-112
Claudel, Alice M.  CL437, CL92, CL479
Clough, Wilson O.  CK80, CL93
Cloyd, E.L.  CE3
Clutton-Brock, A.  CJ20
Coad, Oral  CK81, CL120
Cobb, Palmer  CO14, CS51-2, CU15
Coburn, Frederick Simpson  CH10
Coburn, Frederick W.  CC40
Cody, Sherwin  B87, CJ21, CK82, CM17
Cohen, B. Bernard  CC41
Cohen, Hennig  CL153
Cohen, J.M.  CK83
Cohen, Lucian A.  CC41

Colby, Robert A.   CM18
Cole, Samuel V.   B88
Colton, Cullen B.   CC42
Colton, George   A113
Colwell, James L.   CL403, CR7
Comstock, S.   CC43
Connely, Willard   CF7
Conner, Frederick W.   CL128, CL129
Connolly, Thomas   CL514
Cooke, Alice L.   B260, CM19
Cooke, John E.   B89
Cooke, Philip Pendleton   A114
Cooper, C.B.   CL36
Cooper, Lettice   CC44
Cooper, L.U.   CJ22
Courson, Della   CL404
Courtney, John F.   CC45
Covici, Pascal Jr.   CL338
Cowie, Alexander   CK84
Cowley, Malcolm   CK85, CK86
Cox, Elethea   CK87
Cox, James   CK88
Cox, J.L.   CM20
Coyle, William   B261
Craig, Hardin   CK14
Crane, Alexander T.   CC46
Crawford, Polly P.   CL230
Cronin, James   CL154
Cronon, John Joseph   CU16
Culhane, Mary J.   CU17
Culver, Francis B.   CC47
Cumston, Charles Greene MD   CC48
Cunliff, Marcus   CK89
Cunliffe, W. Gordon   CK146
Curti, Merle   CK90
Curtis, George   B90
Curtis, William O.   B91
Curwen, Henry   B92
Cutler, S.P.   B93

Dailey, Charlotte F.   CG9
Dalby, John Watson   B94
Daly, C.D.   CK91
Dameron, J. Lasley   CA18, CB9, CL405, CM21, CM22, CO15-17, CQ5,
     CR8, CU18
Damon, Samuel Foster   CC49
Dana, Charles A.   A115
Dandridge, Danske   CK92
Daniel, John M.   A116
Daniel, Robert   CK93
Danner, Richard   CK94

Darling, Ritchie  CL384
Darnall, F.M.  CK95
Daughrity, K.L.  CL116, CL515, CO18
D'Avanzo, Mario L.  CL480
Davidson, Edward  CJ23, CK96
Davidson, Frank  CL48
Davidson, Gustav  CL225
Davidson, I.W.  B95
Davis, David B.  CK97
Davis, H.C.  CC50
Davis, Harriet E.  CJ24
Davis, Jack L.  CL242, CL243
Davis, Jeff  CL155
Davis, June  CL242, CL243
Davis, Malcolm  CK98
Davis, Richard Beale  B262, CC51, CL156
Davison, Ned J.  CR9
DeCasseres, Benjamin  CL130
Dedmond, Francis B.  CB10, CB11, CC52-54, CI20, CL37, CL62, CL63
Defalco, Joseph  CL435, CR10
Defoe, M.  CC55
DeGrazia, Emilio  CC56
DeLa Mare, Walter  CK99
Delaney, Joan  CS72, CU19
DeMille, George E.  CM23, CM24
De Ternant, Andrew  CC57
Dickinson, Thomas H.  CK100
Didier, Eugene L.  B96-100, CC58, CC59, CK101
Dietz, Frieda Meredith  CG6
Dimmock, Thomas  B101
Dinamov, S.  CK102
Diskin, Patrick  CL312
Dixon, Jeanne  CL19
Doherty, Edward  CA19
Dolson, E.C.  CL38
Dorset, Gerald  CJ25
Dostoevsky, Fydor M.  CS73
Douglas, Norman  CK103
Douglas-Lithgow, R.A.  CJ26, CK104
Dow, Dorothy  CJ27
Dow, J.E.  A117, A118
Dowdey, Clifford  CC60
Dowell, Richard W.  CL368
Dowling, Albert W.  CH11
Downing, Gloria  CS92
Doxey, William S.  CL64
Doyle, Sir Arthur Conan  CK105, CK106
Dredd, Firmin  CT2
Driskell, Daniel  CL94
DuBois, Arthur E.  CL39, CR11
Dubos, Charles  CS21

Dudley, Fred A.  CL40
Duffy, Charles  CC61
Dugdale, Jennie B.  B102
Dunlop, G.B.  CL339
Durham, F.M.  CL481
Durick, Jeremiah  CK107
DuSolle, John S.  A119
Duyckinck, Everet A.  A120, A121, B103
Dwight, John S.  A122
Dyson, Arthur Thomas  CI21

Eaton, Vincent L.  CA120
Eaves, T.C.Duncan  CC62
Edge, H.T.  CP5
Edgerton, Kathleen  CC63
Edmunds, A.J.  CS53
Edward, Georg  CS54
Ehrlich, Heyward  CC64
Eliot, T.S.  CK108-110
Elkins, W.R.  CK111
Ellis, T.H.  B104
Elwell, T.E.  CA21, CL340
Empric, Julienne H.  CC14
Englekirk, John E.  CA22, CA23, CS86-88, CU20
English, Thomas Dunn  A123-125, B105
Engstrom, Alfred G.  CL20, CL272
Ensley, Helen Oliver  CU21
Erickson, Martin  CS89
Evans, Henry Ridgley  CT3
Evans, Mary Garrettson  CB12, CC65
Evans, Oliver  CK112
Ewers, Hanns Heinz  CJ28
Exman, Eugene  CC66

Fabre, Michel  CR12
Fagin, N. Bryllion  CJ29, CK114, CM25
Fairfield, Frances  B106
Falco, Nicholas  CC67
Falk, Doris  CL26, CL144
Feidelson, Charles Jr.  CK115
Felheim, Marvin  CL65
Ferguson, J. Delancey  CH12, CS90
Fiedler, Leslie A.  CK116, CK117
Field, Eugene  B107, CD14
Fisher, Benjamin Franklin IV  CL244, CL298, CU22
Fisher, Mary  B108
Fitch, George Hamlin  CK118
Fitzgerald, Bishop Oscar P.  CC68
Flanagan, Thomas  CK119
Flesher, Helen G.  B109
Fletcher, J.B.  B110

Fletcher, John Gould  CK120
Flory, Wendy S.  CK121
Flower, Newman  CC69, CH13
F.M.D.  CK113
Foerster, Norman  CM26, CM27
Fogle, Richard H.  CM28
Folsom, Merrill  CI22
Foote, Dorothy N.  CL66
Forbes, E.A.  CE4
Forclaz, Roger  CL49
Forrest, William M.  CP6
Forster, John  A126
Forsythe, Robert S.  CL406
Fortier, Alice  CS22
Fossum, Richard H.  CL67
Foster, Edward  CU23
Fowler, Lorenzo  B111, B112
Fox, Hugh B.  CU24
Foxe, Dr. Arthur N.  CK122
Fraiberg, Louis  CK123
Frank, Frederick Stilson  CU25
Franklin, H. Bruce  CK124
Frasconi, Antonio  CH14
Frayne, Anthony  CJ30
Freehafer, John  CL68
Freeman, Fred B. Jr.  CC70, CG7, CG8
Freeman, John  CC71
French, John C.  CA24, CQ6
French, Joseph Lewis  CC72-74
French, Warren G.  B263
Friedman, William F.  CT4
Friesner, Donald Neil  CL226
Frost, Prof.  A127
Fruit, John Phelps  B113, CK125, CM29
Frushell, Richard C.  CL53
Fuller, Margaret  A128, A129
Fussell, Edwin  CK126, CL407

Gaillard, Dawson F.  CU26
Gale, Robert L.  CB13
Galloway, David  CK127
Gargano, James W.  CK128, CL54, CL69, CL245, CL468, CL482, CL546,
    CL547
Garmon, Gerald M.  CL157, CM30
Garnett, R.S.  CC75
Garrett, Walter  CL246
Garrison, Joseph M. Jr.  CK129, CL247
Gary, Lorena M.  CK130
Gates, Lewis  CK131
Gates, William B.  CL387
Gerber, Gerald E.  CL8, CL9, CL212, CL213, CL286

Ghiselin, Brewster  CN5
Gibson, Thomas W.  B114
Gilbert, Frank  B115
Gilder, J.L.  CC76
Gilfillan, George  B116
Gill, William F.  B117-120
Gimbel, Richard  CB14
Gingerich, Solomon F.  CM31
Glassheim, Eliot  CL365
Gogol, John M.  CS74
Gohdes, Clarence  CQ7, CS4, CS75
Gold, Joseph  CL158
Goldberg, Isaac  CJ31, CK132
Goldhurst, William  CK133, CL70, CL202
Gonzales, Joseph F.  CL287
Goodwin, K.L.  CL159
Goodwin, Katharine C.  CC77
Gordon, Caroline  CL160
Gordon, John D.  CB15
Gosse, Edmond  B121, CJ32, CK134, CK135
Gostwick, J.W.  B122
Gottschalk, Hans W.  CU27
Goudiss, Charles MD  CC78
Gove-Nichols, Mary  B123, CC147
Graham, George R.  A130, B124
Granger, Byrd Howell  CL408
Grant, Vernon W.  CK136
Gravely, William H. Jr.  CC79, CC80, CL203, CL409, CL529, CL530,
    CU28
Graves, Charles M.  CC81
Gray, John W.  CK137
Greeley, Horace  A131-133
Green, A.W.  CK138
Green, Andrew  CL410
Green, George H.  CL411, CL548
Greenlaw, Edward  CK139
Greer, H. Allen  CL531
Greer, Louise  CK140
Gregory, Horace  CK141
Grey, James  CK142
Griffin, William Elliot  CL412
Griffith, Clark  CK143-145, CL248
Griffith, Malcolm Anstell  CU29
Griggs, Earl Leslie  CL374
Griswold, Hatty  B125
Griswold, Rufus White  A134
Griswold, Rufus Wilmot  A135-140, B126
Grolig, Moriz  CS55
Gross, Seymour L.  CL15, CL369
Grubb, Gerald  CC82
Gruener, G.  CO19, CO20

Guilds, John C. Jr.  CL161, CL306
Gwathmey, Edward M.  CC83


Hagemann, E.R.  CD15
Hagopian, John V.  CK146
Haight, D.C.  CI23
Hale, Edward Everett Jr.  B127, CK147
Hale, Sarah Joseph A.  A141
Halfey, James  CK148, CL162
Halio, Jay L.  CL249
Hall, Carroll  CA25
Hall, Thomas  CL544
Halliburton, David G.  CJ33, CU30
Halline, Allan G.  CP7
Halsey, Francis Whiting  CC84
Hamilton, Clayton  CL250
Hamilton, Robert  CK149
Hammond, Alexander L.  CK150, CL22, CU31
Hancock, A.E.  CK151
Haraszti, Zoltan  CB16
Harbert, Earl N.  CD16
Harkey, Joseph H.  CL71
Harrington, H.F.  B128
Harris, Kathryn Montgomery  CL72
Harrison, James A.  CC85, CC86, CD17, CG9, CJ34
Hart, Alden Wadsworth  CU32
Hart, John S.  B129
Hart, Loring  CM32
Hart, Richard H.  CB29
Hartley, Lodwick  CL163
Harwell, Richard B.  CC87
Hassell, J. Woodrow Jr.  CL204
Haswell, Henry  CS23
Hatvary, George Egon  CA26, CL282, CL313, CL321
Havelock, E.A.  CL483
Haverstick, Iola S.  CL360, CR13
Haviland, Thomas  CO21
Hawkins, John  CL314
Hawthorne, Julian  B130, B131
Haycraft, Howard  CK152, CK153, CL394
Hayford, Harrison  CR14
Hayter, Alethea  CK154
Hearn, Lafcadio  CN6
Heartman, Charles F.  CA27-29, CB17, CB18
Hecht, Harvey Edgar  CU33
Heintzelman, Arthur W.  CH15
Helfers, M.C.  CC88
Helms, Randel  CL341
Hemstreet, Charles  CC89
Hennings, F.J.  CL73
Hertz, Robert M.  CK115

Hervey, John L.   B132
Hervey, Thomas K.   A142
Hess, Jeffrey A. CL112
Hesser, Francis M.   CU34
Hewitt, John Hill   A143, CC90
Hewitt-Thayer, Harvey  CS56
H.H.J.   CL95
Higginson, Thomas Wentworth   B133-135
Hill, Archibald A.   CL164
Hill, John S.   CC91, CL165, CL166, CR15
Hindin, Michael  CL455
Hindus, Milton  CR16
Hinz, Evelyn J.   CL342
Hirsch, David H.   CL117, CL380, CL381
Hirst, Henry B.   A144-146
Hoagland, Clayton  CL131
Hoffman, Daniel  CJ35, CL251, CL532, CO22
Hoffman, Michael J.   CL167
Hofrichter, Laura  CK156
Hogrefe, Pearl  CC92
Hogue, L.Lynn  CL200
Holden, E.   A147
Holman, Harriet R.   CL132, CL133, CL315
Holms, Harriet R.   CO22
Holsapple, C.K.   CL205, CL288
Holt, Palmer C.   CL302, CL484
Honig, Edwin  CK157
Hoole, William S.   CC93
Hopkins, E.A.   A148
Hopkins, Fred M.   B136
Hough, Graham  CK158
Hough, Robert L.   CJ36
Houk, Annelle S.   CL211
Howard, Frances  CH16
Howard, William L.   CC94
Howarth, Herbert  CR17
Howarth, William L.   CJ37
Howe, M.A.DeWolfe   B137, CK159
Howells, William Dean  CK160, CK161
Hubbell, Jay B.   CA30, CB19, CC95, CC96, CK162-165, CQ8
Hubner, Charles  CK166
Hudson, Ruth Leigh  CL118, CL252, CU35
Hughes, David  CK167, CQ9
Hughes, James Nichols  CU36
Hull, William D.   CU37
Hungerford, Edward  CK168
Hunt, J.   A149
Hunt, Leigh  B138
Hunter, Rex  CI24
Hunter, W.B.   CL440
Hunter, William E.   B139

Keiley, Jarvis  CJ40
Kelly, George  CM33, CM34, CU42
Kelly, Thomas Byrne  CU43
Kendall, Lyle  CL168
Kennedy, J. Gerald  CR19
Kennedy, John Pendleton  A151
Kennedy, Ralph Clarence  CU44
Kent, Charles W.  CE5, CI26
Kent, Mariner J.  B163
Kerlin, R.T.  CL415
Kern, A.A.  CM35, CT5
Kettell, Samuel  A152
Ketterer, David  CL533
Kiehl, James  CL516
Kierly, Robert  CK184
Kilburn, P.E.  CL143
Kimball, William J.  CL389
Kime, Wayne R.  CL231, CL232
King, Clement  CL416
King, James Roy  CS66
King, Lucille  CL444
Kirby, John P.  CL517
Kirkley, Donald  CL390
Knapp, George L.  CK185
Knight, Grant  CK186
Knowlton, Edgar C.  CL376
Knox, Robert  CS94
K.N.V.  CL227
Kogan, Bernard  CC109
Korponay, Béla  CS63
Koster, Donald  CL253
Kramer, Aaron  CK187
Krappe, E.S.  CL55
Krasnoselsky, A.  CS77
Kremenliev, Elva Baer  CU45
Kreymborg, Alfred  CK188
Kronegger, Maria Elisabeth  CR20-22
Krutch, Joseph Wood  CC110, CJ41, CK189-191, CM36
Kummer, George  CL486
Kunhnelt, Harro  CU46
Kurtz, Leonard  CK192

Labree, Lawrence  A153, A154
Lafleur, L.J.  CL134
Laguardia, David  CL345
Lamb, M.J.  B164
Lamson, A.  A155
Lang, Andrew  B165, B166
Lanier, Emilio  CK193
Laser, Marvin  CM37, CM38
Last, R.W.  CS57

Lathrop, G.P.   B167
Latimore, George D.   CK194
Lauber, John   CL254
Laughlin, Clara E.   CG11
Lauter, Paul   CR23
Lauvriere, Emile   CJ42
Laverty, Carroll D.   CC111, CC112, CK195, CL206, CU47
Law, Robert A.   CL16
Lawrence, D.H.   CK196
Lawson, Lewis   CK197, CK198
Lea, Henry C.   B168
Lea, Robert   CK200
Leary, Lewis   CC113, CK199, CL518
Lebel, Robert   CK200
Lee, Grace F.   CL346
Lee, Helen   CH347
Lees, Daniel E.   CL417
Legler, H.E.   CL418
Leigh, Oliver   CJ43
Lemmon, Leonard   B130
Lenhart, Charmenz   CN7
Lentricchia, Frank   CM39
Lerner, Arthur   CK201, CU48
Leroy, A.   B228
Levin, Harry   CK202
Levine, Richard A.   CL348
Levine, Stuart   CJ44, CL233, CQ10, CU49
Lewis, C.L.   CK203
Lewisohn, Ludwig   CK204
Libman, Valentina   CS78
Liebman, Sheldon W.   CK205
Ligon, John   CU50
Lima, Robert   CS95
Lind, Robert   CK206
Lind, Sidney   CL461
Lindsay, Philip   CJ45
Lipscomb, Herbert   CL487
Livingston, Luther S.   B169
Lloyd, John Arthur Thomas   CA35, CC114, CJ46
Loberger, Gordon J.   CL465
Locard, Edmond   CJ47
Lockspeiser, Edward   CS28, CS29
Lograsso, A.H.   CC115
Lombard, Charles   CK207
Longfellow, Henry Wadsworth   A156
Lord, John B.   CL488
Lovecraft, Howard   CL208
Lowell, James Russell   A157
Lubbers, Klaus   CL255
Lubbell, Albert J.   CO25, CU51
Lucas, Frank L.   CK209

Lundquist, James  CL382
Lynch, James  CK210
Lynen, John F.  CK211
Lyons, Nathan  CK212


Mabbott, T.O.  A194, B265, B266, CA36-49, CB21, CC116-120, CD18-22,
    CK320, CL3, CL10, CL23, CL28, CL41, CL42, CL74, CL98, CL121,
    CL145, CL169, CL170, CL207, CL228, CL237, CL267, CL280, CL303,
    CL377, CL391, CL392, CL419, CL420, CL441, CL449, CL475, CL489,
    CL502, CL504, CL505, CL519-522, CL539, CL543, CL549, CM40,
    CO26-28, CR24-26, CS58, CU52
Mabie, Hamilton W.  B170, B171, CK213, CK214
McAleer, John J.  CR29
McCabe, Lida R.  CI28
McCarthy, Kevin M.  CL421
McClary, Ben Harris  CL214
McCorison, Marcus A.  CD23
MacCracken, Henry Noble  CI27
McCusker, Honor  CC129
MacDonald, Dwight  CK219
McDowell, Tremaine  CC130, CK232
McElderry, B.R.Jr.  CB23, CK233
McElrath, Joseph R. Jr.  CL215
McKeithan, D.M.  CL349
MacKintosh, Emily  B172
McLean, Frank  CK234
McLean, Sidney R.  CL540
McLuhan, H.M.  CK235
McNeal, Thomas H.  CL216
McVicker, Cecil Don  CL422
Macy, John A.  CC121, CJ48, CK216, CK217
Maddison, Carol Hopkins  CL135
Magidoff, Robert  CS79
Manly, Louise  B173
Marble, A.R.  CC122
Marchand, Ernest  CK218
Markham, Edwin  CK219, CK220
Marks, A.H.  CR27
Marks, Emerson  CM41
Marks, Jeannette Augustus  CC123
Marovitz, Sanford  CO29
Marrs, Robert L.  CB22, CL171
Marsh, John L.  CL172
Marshall, Thomas P.  CK221
Martin, E.J.  CC124
Martin, Terrence  CK22
Martindale, Colin  CL173
Martuza, Athar  CL383
Marvin, F.R.  CR28
Mason, Leo  CC125-127
Matherly, Enid P.  CK223

Morris, George P.   A158
Morrison, Claudia C.   CK249, CL256
Morrison, Robert   CL236
Morrisey, W.P.   CC137
Morse, James H.   B184
Morton, Maxwell   CJ49
Moskowitz, Sam   CB25
Moss, Sidney   A195, CC138-143, CJ50, CJ51, CK250, CL351, CL35,
     CS31, CU57
Mossop, D.J.   CM45
Moyne, Ernest John   CC144
Muchnick, Helen   CK251
Mulqueen, James E.   CL524, CM46
Murch, A.E.   CK252
Murphy, Christine   CL106
Murphy, George D.   CK253

Nakamura, Junichi   CJ52
Nash, Dr. Herbert   CC145
Neal, John   A159-161, CD27
Neale, Walter G.   CL304
Nelson, Charles A.   CI30
Nelson, Louise A.   CK254
Nelson, William   B185
Nethery, Wallace   CK255
Nevi, Charles N.   CL76
Nevins, G.S.   CL199
Newcomer, A.G.   B186, CA50, CC146, CK256
Newlin, Paul Arthur   CO32, CU58
Newmann, J.H.   CK257
Nichol, John   B187
Nichols, Mary Gove   B123, CC147
Nicolson, Marjorie H.   CL534
Niess, R.J.   CS32
Nirenberg, Morton   CU59
Nisbet, Ada   CA51, CA52
Noah, Major Mordecai M.   A162
Nobel, James A.   B188
Nolan, J. Bennett   CC148
Nordstedt, George   CL425
Norman, Emma K.   CO33
Norman, H.L.   CL176
Norris, W.B.   CL29
Norwood, G.   CK258

Ober, Warren   CJ53
Oberholtzer, Ellis P.   CC149
O'Brien, Edward J.H.   CK259
O'Connor, Roger   CL24
O'Donnell, Charles   CL353
Oelke, Karl   CC150, CU60

Olivero, Frederico  CK260
Olney, Clark  CK261
Olson, Bruce  CL177
Olybrius  CK262
Omans, Glen A.  CL525
Onderdonk, James L.  B189, B190
O'Neill, E.H.  CL283
Orvell, Miles D.  CL426
Osborne, William  CC151
Osgoode, Joseph  CK263
Osowski, Judy  CB26, CK264, CU61
Ostrom, John Ward  CC152, CD28-36, CU62
O'Sullivan, Vincent  B191
Otis, J.F.  A163
Ousby, Ian V.K.  CL317
Outis  A164
Owlett, G.C.  CQ12

Page, Curtis H.  CS33
Page, Thomas Nelson  B192
Painter, Franklin V.N.  CC153
Pancoast, Henry S.  B193
Parkes, Henry  CK265
Parks, Edd Winfield  CJ54
Parrington, Vernon L.  CK266
Parry, Albert  CK267
Partridge, Henry Norton  CC154
Pattee, Fred Lewis  CK268, CL526
Patterson, E.H.N.  A165, A166
Patterson, John  B194
Paul, Howard  B195
Paul, Raymond  CL322
Paulding, James Kirke  A167
Pavnaskar, Sadanand  CS65
Payne, L.W.  CM47
Pearce, Donald  CL77
Pearce, Roy Harvey  CK269
Peck, G.W.  A168, B196
Peden, William  CL354
Pemberton, J.M.  CL491
Pendennis  CI32
Perry, Bliss  CK270
Perry, Marvin B. Jr.  CO34
Perry, Wilbur  CK271
Peters, H.F.  CS60
Peterson, Dwayne  CU63
Pettigrew, Marie M.  CL4
Pettigrew, Richard C.  CL4, CN8
Philips, Edith  CO35
Philips, Mary Elizabeth  CJ55
Phillips, Eliza C.  CU65

Phillips, Elizabeth  CR32, CU64
Phillips, H. Wells  CL178
Phillips, William  CL179
Pickett, LaSalle Corbell  CK272
Pittman, Diana  CK237, CL99, CL180, CL438, CL462, CL492, CL527
Pochmann, Henry A.  CL181, CO36
Poe, Elisabeth Ellicott  CC155, CJ56
Poe, William Henry Leonard  CC156
Pole, James  CL78
Pollard, Percival  CK274
Pollin, Burton R.   A196, A197, CA53, CA54, CB27, CB28, CC157,
     CD37, CJ57, CK275-278, CL110, CL125, CL182, CL217, CL218,
     CL273, CL274, CL290-292, CL296, CL307, CL329, CL445, CL451,
     CL453, CL469, CL545, CM48, CO37-39
Pope-Hennessey, Una  CC157, CJ58
Porges, Irwin  CJ59
Porte, Joel  CK279
Posey, Meredith  CL535
Poulet, Georges  CK280, CK281
Pound, Louise  CL100, CL101
Powell, Thomas  A169
Praz, Mario  CK282
Prescott, F.C.  CM49
Prior, Linda  CR33
Pritchard, John Paul  CM50-53
Proffer, Carl R.  CR34
Pruette, Lorine  CC158, CK283
Pugh, Griffith  CK284
Purdy, S.B.  CS80·
Purves, James  B197, B198
Putnam, George P.  CC159

Quarles, Diana  CA55
Quiller-Couch, Arthur T.  B199
Quinn, Arthur Hobson  CB29, CC160, CJ60, CK285
Quinn, Patrick F.  CJ61, CK286, CL137, CL355, CQ13, CS34, CU66

Radó, György  CS64
Rago, Henry  CK287
Ramakrishna, D.  CL138, CL257, CL258
Ramsey, Paul J.  CL183
Randall, David A.  CB30, CB31
Randall, John H.  CL79
Ranking, B.M.  B200
Rans, Geoffrey  CJ62
Ransome, Arthur A.  CJ63, CK288
Rascoe, Burton  CK289
Rasor, C.L.  CL180
Rayan, Krishna  CK290
Rea, Joy  CL81, CL82, CL259
Rede, Kenneth  CA56, CB17, CG12, CL356, CL503

Rede, Willys  CC161
Redman, Catherine  CC162
Reece, James B.  CA57, CG13, CL293, CU67
Reed, Kenneth T.  CL260
Reed, Myrtle  CG14
Regan, Robert  CJ64, CM54
Reid, Captain Mayne  B201, CC163
Reid, Whitelaw  CK291
Reilly, John E.  CK292, CL470, CR35, CU68
Rein, David M.  CG15, CJ65, CK293, CK294, CL222, CQ14
Reiss, Edmund  CL536
Remley, Brenda B.  CU69
Rendell, V.  CL493, CO40
Rhea, R.L.  CL357
Rhodes, S.A.  CS35
Rice, Sara S.  B202
Richard, Claude  CC164, CL11, CL111, CL308, CL427, CS36, CS37
Richards, Irving  CA58
Richardson, Charles F.  B203, CK295, CM55
Richmond, Lee J.  CL305
Ridgely, J.V.  CL358-360
Riding, Laura  CK296
Ripley, George  A171
Robbins, J. Albert  CB32, CC165, CC166, CG16, CQ15, CQ16
Roberts, W.  CC167
Robertson, John Wooster, MD  B204, CB33, CJ66
Robinson, E. Arthur  CL184, CL471, CL472
Roche, A. John  CL275
Rocks, James E.  CL83
Rogers, David  CJ67
Roman, Robert C.  CK297
Roppolo, Joseph  CL294
Rose, Marilyn G.  CL102, CL185, CS38
Rosenfeld, Alvin H.  CC168, CG17, CL238
Rosenthal, Lewis  B205
Rothwell, K.S.  CL550
Rourke, Constance  CK298
Rousselet, Jeanne  CS39
Routh, James  CL528
Rubin, Joseph J.  CL385, CR37
Rubin, Larry  CR36
Rubin, Louis D. Jr.  CK299, CR37
Runden, John P.  CR38
Ryan, John K.  CK300
Ryan, Sylvester  CL318

Saintsbury, George  CK301
Sale, Marian M.  CK302
Salinas, Pedro  CS96
Salt, H.S.  B206
Salzberg, Joel  CL454, CU70

```
Sizer, Nelson  B211
Skaggs, Calvin Lee  CU72
Slaight, B.H.  CC179
Slicer, Thomas R.  CK312
Sloan, Daivd E.  CL50
Smart, Charles A.  CK313
Smiles, Samuel  B212
Smith  CD39
Smith, Bernard  CK314, CM60
Smith, Charles Alphonso  B213, CJ70, CK315-317, CP8
Smith, E. Oakes  B214
Smith, G. Barnett  B215
Smith, G.P.  CL300
Smith, H.  CG18
Smith, H.E.  CM61
Smith, Herbert F.  CL188
Smith, Julia  CG19
Smith, Reed  CR41
Smithline, Arnold  CL139
Smyth, Albert  B216, B217
Smyth, Ellison A.  CL208
Snell, George  CK318, CM62, CR42
Snodgrass, Dr. J.E.  A176-178, B218, B219
Snow, Edward R.  CL85
Snow, Sinclair  CL126
Snyder, Edward D.  CK319, CL495, CM63
Solomont, Susan  CL384
Somerville, J.A.  CC180
Spannuth, Jacob E.  CK320
Sparks, Archibald  CB34
Spaulding, K.A.  CL189
Spencer, Benjamin  CK321
Spencer, Edward  B220
Spiller, Robert E.  CK322
Spitzer, Gary  CL403
Spitzer, Leo  CL190
Spivey, Herman E.  CC181
Sprout, Monique  CR43
Stagg, Charles  CM21
St. Armand, Barton Levi  CL191, CL209, CU73
Stanard, Mary M.  CD40, CJ71, CK323
Starke, Aubrey  CC182
Starrett, Vincent  A198, CC183
Stauffer, Donald Barlow  CK324, CK325, CL263, CL309
Stebbing, W.  CK326
Stedman, Edmund Clarence  B221, B222, CI33, CI34
Steele, Charles W.  CL86
Stein, Allen F.  CL428
Stein, Roger B.  CM64
Stein, William Bysshe  CL192
Stern, Madeleine B.  CC184
```

Stern, Philip Van Doren   CC185, CC186
Stern, Seymour   CR44
Stevens, Aretta J.   CR45
Stevenson, Robert Louis   B223, CK327
Stewart, Charles D.   CL429
Steward, Robert Armistead   CJ72, CU74
Stockett, Letitia   CK328
Stockton, Eric W.   CL103, CL210
Stoddard, Richard Henry   B224-227, CC187
Stone, Edward   CK329, CK330, CL193, CR46
Stonier, G.W.   CS43
Stovall, Floyd   CD41, CE6, CG20, CJ73, CK331-333, CL5, CM65, CM66,
     CO45
Strandberg, Victor   CK334
Strickland, Sir Walter   CK335
Stromberg, Jean S.   CP9
Strong, Augustus H.   CP10
Stronks, James   CR47
Stroupe, John H.   CL363
Stuart, Esme   B228
Swanson, Donald R.   CL264
Sweeney, Gerard M.   CL108
Swigg, Richard   CK336
Swiggett, G.L.   B229, CK337
Swinburne, Algernon Charles   B230, CC188
Symons, Arthur   CC189


Tabb, John B.   B231
Taft, Kendall   CL297
Talley, Susan Archer   A179, B232, CC204, CJ77
Talley-Weiss, Susan Archer (*see* Talley, Susan Archer)
Tanasoca, Donald   CC190, CK338
Tannenbaum, Earl   CL496
Tannenbaum, Libby   CH20
Tanselle, G.Thomas   A199, CB35, CL370, CL430, CL431
Tarbox, Raymond   CK339
Tasistro, Louis F.   A180
Tate, Allen   CK340-343, CL160
Taylor, Archer   CL476
Taylor, Bayard   CA59
Taylor, N.   CK344
Taylor, Walter F.   CL220
Taylor, William Fuller   CK345
Thomas, J.D.   CR48
Thomas, M.   B233
Thompson, Gary R.   CK346-348, CL43, CL194, CL271, CL301, CL371,
     CL439, CL463, CQ17, CU75
Thompson, John Reuben   A181, B234, B235, CJ74
Thorner, H.E.   CL551
Thorp, Willard   CD42
Ticknor, Caroline   CC191, CG21

Timpe, Eugene   CS62
Tinker, Chauncey   CK349
Tinnon, J.A.   B236
Todd, William B.   CC192
Tolman, Albert H.   B237, CK350
Tourtellot, Frances   CU76
Towne, Charles H.   CC193
Townsend-Warner, Sylvia   CC194
Travis, Mildred   CR49
Traylor, M.G.   CI35
Trent, William P.   CC195, CK351-353, CQ18
Trieber, J. Marshall   CK354
Triplett, E.B.   CL432
Tuerk, Richard   CC196
Tupper, Martin Farquar   A182
Turnbull, Mrs. L.   CI36
Turner, Arlin   CC197, CL44, CL45, CL234, CL235
Turquet-Milnes, Gladys R.   CS44
Tuttleton, James W.   CR50, CR51
Tyler, Alice M.   CC198, CE7
Tynan, Daniel   CL364
Tytell, John   CL195


Valéry, Paul   CS45
VanCleef, Augustus   B238
Vanderbilt, Kermit   CL295
Van Doren, Carl   CK355
Van Nostrand, A.D.   CL140
Varnado, S.L.   CL395, CL433, CU77
Varner, Cornelia   CK356
Varner, John Greer   CA60, CA61, CD43, CL458, CM67
Vaughan, Joseph   CU78
Veler, Richard   CJ75
Victor, O.J.   B239
Vierra, Clifford C.   CL367
Vincent, H.P.   CG22
Virtanen, Reino   CS46, CS47


Wagenknecht, Edward   CJ76
Wages, Jack D.   CR52
Waggoner, Hyatt H.   CK357
Walcutt, Charles   CM68
Walker, I.M.   CL196
Walker, R.J.   CL497
Walker, Warren   CL498
Wallace, Alfred Russell   CA63, CL141
Wallace, Horace Burney   B240
Waller, W.F.   B241
Walsh, John   CL324
Walsh, Thomas   CS97
Walsh, Thomas F.   CL552

Warfel, Harry  CK358, CL197
Warren, Robert Penn  CL152, CL511
Wasserstrom, William  CK359
Waterman, Arthur E.  CL87
Watkins, Mildred Cabell  B242
Watkins, Walter Kendall  CC199
Watson, Don  CS98
Watts, Charles H.  CD44, CD45, CC200
Watts, Theodore  B243
Webb, Howard W. Jr.  CA63, CK360
Weber, John-Paul  CK361
Wegelin, Oscar  CC201, CC202
Weidman, Bette S.  CC203
Weiss, Miriam  CK362
Weiss, Susan Archer (*see* Talley, Susan Archer)
Weissbuch, Ted N.  CK363
Wellek, Rene  CM69
Wells, Gabriel  CP11
Wells, Henry  CK364
Wells, Ross  CK365
Wells, Samuel R.  B244
Wendell, Barrett  CK366, CK367
Werner, W.L.  CL229, CN10
Wertz, Linda  CK368
Wertz, S.K.  CK368
West, Muriel  CL265, CL266
Weston, Arthur Harold  CL499
Wetherill, P.M.  CS48
Wetzel, George  CL281
Wheeler, Paul Mowbray  B267
Whibley, Charles  B245
Whipple, William  CL276, CL277, CL457, CU79
White, William  CC205
Whiteside, Mary Brent  CK369
Whiting, Mary B.  CC206
Whitman, Sarah Helen  B246, B247, CG23
Whitman, Walt  B248, B249
Whitt, Celia  CL21
Whitty, James H.  CA64-66, CC207-11, CD46, CF8, CH21, CI37,
    CK370, CL434
Wigfall, Green A.  CK371
Wiener, Philip  CL142
Wilbur, Richard  CK372-374, CL319
Wilcox, Earl J.  CL198
Wilkinson, Ronald S.  CL31, CL537
Williams, Paul O.  CL46
Williams, Stanley T.  CC212
Williams, Valentine  CK375
Williams, William Carlos  CK376
Willis, Eola  CC213
Willis, Nathaniel Parker  A185-192

Wilmer, Lambert A.   A183, B250, CC214
Wilson, Edmund   CK377, CM70
Wilson, James Grant   B251, CC215
Wilson, James Southall   CC126, CD47, CD48, CH18, CK378-380, CM71
Wilson, Vylla Poe   CJ56
Wilt, Napier   CK381
Wimsatt, W.K.JR.   CL32, CL278, CL325, CL326, CT6
Winter, William   CM72
Winters, Ivor   CK382
Winwar, Frances   CJ78
W.M.G.   B252
Wood, Clement   CK383, CR53
Wood, Frederick T.   CL500
Woodberry, George Edward   B353-358, CD49, CD50, CK384
Woodbridge, Benjamin   CO46
Woodbridge, Hensley C.   CS99, CS100
Woodson, Thomas   CJ79
Woodward, Robert H.   CR54
Worthen, Samuel C.   CL327, CL328
Wroth, Lawrence C.   CC217
Wyld, Lionel D.   CK385
Wylie, Clarence P.   CK386
Wyllie, John Cook   CA67
Wyss, Hal H.   CU80

Yarmolinsky, Abraham   CS81
Yeats, William Butler   CK387
Yewdale, Merton   CC218
Yonce, Margaret   CL109
Young, Philip   CK388

Zipes, Jack Davis   CU81